The
North :
Bus Han

C000215074

British Bus Publishing

Body codes used in the Bus Handbook series:

Type:
A	Articulated vehicle
B	Bus, either single-deck or double-deck
BC	Express - high-back seating in a bus body
C	Coach
M	Minibus with design capacity of 16 seats or less
N	Low-floor bus (*Niederflur*), either single-deck or double-deck
O	Open-top bus (CO = convertible - PO = Partial open-top)

Seating capacity is then shown. For double-decks the upper deck quantity is followed by the lower deck.

Door position:-
C	Centre entrance/exit
D	Dual doorway.
F	Front entrance/exit
R	Rear entrance/exit (no distinction between doored and open)
T	Three or more access points

Equipment:-
L	Lift for wheelchair	TV	Training Vehicle.
M	Mail compartment	RV	Used as tow bus or Engineers vehicle.
T	Toilet	w	Vehicle is withdrawn from service.

e.g. - B32/28F is a double-deck bus with thirty-two seats upstairs, twenty-eight down and a front entrance/exit.
N43D is a low-floor bus with two doorways.

Re-registrations:-
Where a vehicle has gained new index marks the details are listed at the end of each fleet showing the current mark, followed in sequence by those previously carried starting with the original mark.

Other books in the series:
The Scottish Bus Handbook
The Ireland & Islands Bus Handbook
The Yorkshire Bus Handbook
The Lancashire, Cumbria and Manchester Bus Handbook
The Merseyside and Cheshire Bus Handbook
The North and West Midlands Bus Handbook
The East Midlands Bus Handbook
The South Midlands Bus Handbook
The North and West Wales Bus Handbook
The South Wales Bus Handbook
The Chilterns and West Anglia Bus Handbook
The East Anglia Bus Handbook
The South East Bus Handbook
The South West Bus Handbook
The South Central Bus Handbook

Annual books are produced for the major groups:
The 1999 Stagecoach Bus Handbook
The 1999 FirstBus Bus Handbook
The 1999 Arriva Bus Handbook

Associated series:
The Hong Kong Bus Handbook
The Leyland Lynx Handbook
The Model Bus Handbook
The Postbus Handbook
The Toy & Model Bus Handbook - Volume 1 - Early Diecasts
The Fire Brigade Handbook (fleet list of each local authority fire brigade)
The Fire Brigade Handbook - Special Appliances Volume 1
The Fire Brigade Handbook - Special Appliances Volume 2
The Police Range Rover Handbook

Earlier editions for some titles are still available. A catalogue is available from the publisher.

Contents

The North East Bus Handbook

The North East Bus Handbook is part of the Bus Handbook series that details the fleets of stage carriage and express coach operators. Where space allows other significant operators in the areas covered are also included. These handbooks are published by *British Bus Publishing* The current list is shown on page 2. This edition covers the counties and unitary authorities on the former counties of Cleveland, Durham, Northumberland and Tyne & Wear.

Quality photographs for inclusion in the series are welcome, for which a fee is payable. Please contact the publisher for details further details. Details of changes to the fleet information which would enhance the accuracy of that shown are also welcome.

More information on the Bus Handbook series is available from:

British Bus Publishing,
The Vyne,
16 St Margaret's Drive
Wellington
Telford,
Shropshire TF1 3PH

Series Editor: Bill Potter

Principal Editors for *The North East Bus Handbook:*
David Donati

Acknowledgements:
We are grateful to Keith Grimes, Ian Hope, Mark Jameson, Steve Sanderson, Terry Wightman, the PSV Circle and the operating companies for their assistance in the compilation of this book.

The front cover photo is by Tony Wilson; frontispiece by David Longbottom

Contents correct to August 1999

3rd Edition
ISBN 1 897990 45 6
Published by *British Bus Publishing Ltd*
The Vyne, 16 St Margaret's Drive, Wellington, Telford, TF1 3PH
© British Bus Publishing Ltd, May 1999
E-mail A2GWP@AOL.COM
internet: http://www.britishbuspublishing.co.uk

© British Bus Publishing, August 1999

A LINE COACHES

LB & DC Annis, Aline House, Davidson Street, Felling, Gateshead, NE10 9NY

XRW519S	Bedford YMT	Plaxton Supreme III	C53F	1978	Hall, Wallsend, 1980
APT116W	Leyland National 2 NL116AL11/1R		B49F	1980	Arriva Durham County, 1998
APT117W	Leyland National 2 NL116AL11/1R		B49F	1980	Arriva Durham County, 1998
OIL4572	Bedford YNT	Plaxton Supreme V	C53F	1982	Rhodes, Wawne, 1996
OIL4568	Leyland National 2 NL116AHLXB/1R		B49F	1983	Northumbria, 1998
B207GNL	Ford Transit 190	Alexander AM	B16F	1985	Calvary, Washington, 1995
OIL4571	Bedford YNV Venturer	Plaxton Paramount 3200 III	C52FT	1987	Ganal, Shotts, 1996
TJI6298	MCW MetroRider MF150/15	MCW	B25F	1987	Second City Travel, Birmingham, 1997
JUI2067	Hestair-Duple 425 SDA1512	Duple 425	C57F	1991	Hargreaves, Hebden Bridge, 1998
CUI20	DAF MB230LTF615	Van Hool Alizée	C51FT	1993	Welsh, Upton, 1998

Previous Registrations:

CUI20	K551RJX	OIL4572	XVC12X, CEC147, AAC966X
JUI2067	J980MNR	TJI6298	E805UDT
OIL4568	A129FDC	XRW519S	XRW519S, CUI20
OIL4571	D439BCJ, A1KRT, D785USA		

Livery: White and red

Depot: Green Lane Industrial Estate, Pelaw

Pictured working the Mecca Bingo contract Leyland National OIL4568 is a national 2 that was new to United before it was divided in preparation for the sale of the National Bus Company. This example went with the new Northumbria fleet before joining A Line in 1998. *David Longbottom*

ALTONA

AC, G & M Hunter, Unit K4 Skillian Business Centre, Green Lane, Felling
Gateshead, NE10 0QH

VUL159S	Volvo B58-56	Plaxton Supeme III	C51C	1978	Glenton Tours, 1986
LHS744V	Ailsa B55-10	Alexander AV	B44/35F	1979	Weardale Motors, Stanhope, 1998
577TVO	Ford R1114	Wadham Stringer Vanguard	BC29F	1987	HMB Travel, Gateshead, 1998
HUI3584	LAG G355Z	LAG Panoramic	C28FT	1987	Ocean Storage, Hackbridge, 1992
E991JLF	Mercedes-Benz 811D	Robin Hood	BC16F	1988	Wings, Hayes, 1990
E350NOK	Renault-Dodge G13	Wadham Stringer Vanguard	BC..F	1988	MoD, 1998 (?)
HUI3912	Hestair-Duple SDA1512	Duple 425	C53FT	1988	
G178SMW	Volkswagen Transporter	Advance Vehicle Bodies	M8	1990	Selwyns, Runcorn, 1995
K717GBF	Mercedes-Benz 811D	Autobus Classique	C29F	1990	
K725GWR	Volvo B10M-61	Plaxton Excalibur	C41FT	1992	Dodsworth, Boroughbridge, 1996
L63YJF	Volvo B6-9.9m	Caetano Algarve II	C35F	1993	Ralphs, Langley, 1995
N103EMB	Mercedes-Benz 814L	Buscraft Buffalo	C35F	1996	
R510SCH	Iveco EuroMidi CC80.E18	Indcar Maxim	C29F	1998	

Previous registrations:

577TVO	OHV199Y	HUI3584	D390XCD, MIW8345, D390XCD
E991LLF	E490JLK, WET880	HUI3912	E306FCU

Livery: White and black

Buscraft Buffalo bodywork is illustrated in this picture of Altona's N108EMB. The vehicle is based on a forward control Mercedes-Benz chassis, allowing a front entrance to be built ahead of the front axle. The vehicle is seen arriving at Wembley Stadium for one of the end of season play-offs. *Keith Grimes*

AMBERLINE

D Boyd, Earsdon Road, West Monkseaton, Whitley Bay, Tyne & Wear, NE25 9SX

1	C973UEF	Ford Transit 190	Ford	M14	1986	private owner, 1994
2	D580EWS	Freight Rover Sherpa	Dormobile	B16F	1986	Badgerline, 1990
3	G276TST	Leyland-DAF 400	Dormobile	B18F	1989	Magicbus, Perth, 1990
4	C511DYM	Iveco Daily 49.10	Robin Hood City Nippy	B21F	1985	London Buses, 1991
5w	E629AMA	Iveco Daily 49.10	Carlyle Dailybus 2	B21F	1988	Trent, 1993
6w	D747ERV	Iveco Daily 49.10	Robin Hood City Nippy	B25F	1987	Robin Hood, Rudyard, 1994
7	D751GBP	Iveco Daily 49.10	Robin Hood City Nippy	BC25F	1987	Waylands, Beccles, 1994
8	F80JNL	Freight Rover Sherpa	Freight Rover	M14	1989	Cousins, Belmont, 1994
9	E734WEC	Iveco Daily 49.10	Carlyle Dailybus 2	B21F	1987	OK Travel, 1995
11	G151UAS	Freight Rover Sherpa	Dormobile	B20F	1989	Grierson, Fishburn, 1995
12	F809BOE	Freight Rover Sherpa	Freight Rover	M14	1989	Walker, Redcar, 1996
14	G796UBB	Ford Transit VE6	Phoenix	B25F	1990	Go-Ahead (OK), 1996
15	F42XVP	Mercedes-Benz 811D	Optare StarRider	B26F	1988	London Central, 1998
16	D626MDB	MCW MetroRider MF151/3	MCW	B23F	1987	Titlesure, Bedlington, 1999

Previous Registrations:
E734WEC   E961SVP

Livery: Orange and red

Amberline operate a fleet of minibuses, the largest being a 26-seat StarRider. Pictured in Newcastle is Iveco Daily E734WEC, which has the Carlyle Dailybus 2 body style. A similar body was built liberally on the Sherpa when it was known as the Citybus 2. *Terry Wightman*

ARRIVA NORTH EAST

ARRIVA serving Northumbria - ARRIVA serving the North East

Arriva North East Ltd, Arriva House, Admiral Way, Sunderland, SR3 3XP

131	K131FKW	Bova FHD12.290	Bova Futura	C44FT	1992	
132	K132FKW	Bova FHD12.290	Bova Futura	C44FT	1992	
133	L33NMS	Bova FHD12.340	Bova Futura	C44FT	1993	
135	J20NMS	Bova FHD12.290	Bova Futura	C44FT	1992	
136	WSV570	Bova FHD12.340	Bova Futura	C44FT	1994	
137	WSV571	Bova FHD12.340	Bova Futura	C44FT	1994	
138	WSV572	Bova FHD12.340	Bova Futura	C44FT	1994	
139	WLT859	Bova FHD12.290	Bova Futura	C46FT	1993	
140	M122UUB	Bova FHD12.340	Bova Futura	C46FT	1994	
191	NGR685P	Bristol LH6L	Eastern Coach Works	B43F	1976	United, 1986
193	LPT701T	Bristol LH6L	Eastern Coach Works	B43F	1979	United, 1986
194	LPT707T	Bristol LH6L	Eastern Coach Works	B43F	1979	United, 1986
195	MUP712T	Bristol LH6L	Eastern Coach Works	B43F	1979	United, 1986
196	AFB593V	Bristol LH6L	Eastern Coach Works	B43F	1980	United, 1986
202	XSV689	Leyland Tiger TRCTL11/3RH	Duple 320	C53F	1986	Kentish Bus, 1997
203	WSV565	Leyland Leopard PSU3E/4RT	Duple 320(1987)	C55F	1977	United, 1986
205	WSV567	Leyland Leopard PSU3E/4RT	Duple 320(1987)	C55F	1977	United, 1986
214	XSV691	Leyland Tiger TRCTL11/3ARZA	Plaxton Paramount 3200 III	C53F	1988	Maidstone & District, 1998
215	YSU870	Leyland Tiger TRCTL11/3ARZ	Plaxton Paramount 3500 III	C53F	1988	Maidstone & District, 1998
216	YSU871	Leyland Tiger TRCTL11/3ARZ	Plaxton Paramount 3500 III	C53F	1988	Maidstone & District, 1998
217	F188HKK	Leyland Tiger TRCL10/3ARZA	Duple 340	C53F	1989	Maidstone & District, 1998
218	F189HKK	Leyland Tiger TRCL10/3ARZA	Duple 340	C53F	1989	Maidstone & District, 1998
219	TSU636	Leyland Tiger TRCTL11/3R	Duple Laser	C53F	1983	Maidstone & District, 1997
220	869SVX	Leyland Tiger TRCTL11/3R	Duple Laser	C53F	1983	Maidstone & District, 1997
221	YOT607	Leyland Tiger TRCTL11/3R	Duple Laser	C53F	1983	Maidstone & District, 1997
222	VAY879	Leyland Tiger TRCTL11/3R	Duple Laser	C53F	1983	Maidstone & District, 1997
239	SND296X	Leyland Leopard PSU5D/4R	Plaxton Supreme V	C53F	1981	Kentish Bus, 1991
242	B262KPF	Leyland Tiger TRCTL11/2RH	Plaxton Paramount 3200 IIE	C51F	1985	Kentish Bus, 1992
243	B265KPF	Leyland Tiger TRCTL11/2RH	Plaxton Paramount 3200 IIE	C51F	1985	Kentish Bus, 1992
244	B273KPF	Leyland Tiger TRCTL11/2RH	Plaxton Paramount 3200 IIE	C51F	1985	Kentish Bus, 1992
245	B279KPF	Leyland Tiger TRCTL11/3RH	Plaxton Paramount 3200 IIE	C51F	1985	Kentish Bus, 1992
246	B276KPF	Leyland Tiger TRCTL11/3RH	Plaxton Paramount 3200 IIE	C51F	1985	Kentish Bus, 1992
247	B277KPF	Leyland Tiger TRCTL11/3RH	Plaxton Paramount 3200 IIE	C51F	1985	Kentish Bus, 1992
248	B284KPF	Leyland Tiger TRCTL11/3RH	Plaxton Paramount 3200 IIE	C53F	1985	The Shires, 1996
249	YSU896	Leyland Tiger TRCTL11/2R	Plaxton Paramount 3200 E	C53F	1984	Maidstone & District, 1998
250	EDZ215	Leyland Tiger TRCTL11/2R	Plaxton Paramount 3200 E	C53F	1983	Hunters, 1994

Arriva continues to expand the number of vehicles in corporate livery. Two Duple 340-bodied Leyland Tigers joined the North East fleet in 1998 from Maidstone. Shown here is 218, F189HKK.
David Longbottom

251-267 — DAF SB220LC550 — Optare Delta — BC48F* — 1989-90 — *252/4/6/8 are B48F

251	G251SRG	255	G255UVK	258	G258UVK	261	H261CFT	264	H264CFT
252	G252SRG	256	G256UVK	259	H259CFT	262	H262CFT	266	H266CFT
253	G253SRG	257	G257UVK	260	H598CNL	263	H263CFT	267	H267CFT
254	G254SRG								

268	F701ECC	DAF SB220LC550	Optare Delta	BC48F	1989	Crosville Cymru, 1997
269	F702ECC	DAF SB220LC550	Optare Delta	BC48F	1989	Crosville Cymru, 1997

271-280 — Scania L113CRL — East Lancashire European — NC45F — 1996

271	P271VRG	273	P273VRG	275	P275VRG	277	P277VRG	279	P279VRG
272	P272VRG	274	P274VRG	276	P276VRG	278	P278VRG	280	P814VTY

281-290 — Scania L113CRL — East Lancashire European — NC45F — 1995

281	N281NCN	283	N283NCN	285	N285NCN	287	N287NCN	289	N289NCN
282	N282NCN	284	N284NCN	286	N286NCN	288	N288NCN	290	N290NCN

291	R291KRG	DAF DE33WSSB3000	Plaxton Prima	C51F	1997	
292	R292KRG	DAF DE33WSSB3000	Plaxton Prima	C51F	1997	
293	R293KRG	DAF DE33WSSB3000	Plaxton Prima	C51F	1997	
294	R294KRG	DAF DE33WSSB3000	Plaxton Prima	C51F	1997	

301	C263XEF	Leyland Olympian ONLXB/1R	Eastern Coach Works	BC42/30F	1986	United, 1986
302	C264XEF	Leyland Olympian ONLXB/1R	Eastern Coach Works	BC42/30F	1986	United, 1986

303-312 — Leyland Olympian ONCL10/2RZ Alexander RH — BC43/33F — 1988

303	F303JTY	305	F305JTY	307	F307JTY	309	F309JTY	311	F311JTY
304	F304JTY	306	F306JTY	308	F308JTY	310	F310JTY	312	F312JTY

313	C616ANW	Leyland Olympian ONLXB/1R(TL11)	Eastern Coach Works	BC42/30F	1985	West Riding, 1993
314	C617ANW	Leyland Olympian ONLXB/1R(TL11)	Eastern Coach Works	BC42/30F	1985	West Riding, 1993
315	C613ANW	Leyland Olympian ONLXB/1R(TL11)	Eastern Coach Works	BC42/30F	1985	West Riding, 1993
316	C614ANW	Leyland Olympian ONLXB/1R(TL11)	Eastern Coach Works	BC42/30F	1985	West Riding, 1993
317	EEH901Y	Leyland Olympian ONLXB/1R	Eastern Coach Works	BC41/32F	1983	Kentish Bus, 1990
318	EEH908Y	Leyland Olympian ONLXB/1R	Eastern Coach Works	BC41/32F	1983	Kentish Bus, 1990
319	SPY205X	Leyland Olympian ONLXB/1R	Eastern Coach Works	BC41/32F	1982	United, 1986
320	SPY210X	Leyland Olympian ONLXB/1R	Eastern Coach Works	BC41/32F	1982	United, 1986
321	WDC212Y	Leyland Olympian ONLXB/1R	Eastern Coach Works	BC41/32F	1982	United, 1986
322	SPY204X	Leyland Olympian ONLXB/1R	Eastern Coach Works	BC41/32F	1982	United, 1986

370-377 — Volvo Olympian YN2RC18Z4 — Northern Counties Palatine II — BC45/27F — 1994

370	M370FTY	372	M372FTY	374	M374FTY	376	M376FTY	377	M377FTY
371	M371FTY	373	M373FTY	375	M375FTY				

381-393 — Scania N113DRB — East Lancashire Cityzen — BC43/31F — 1996

381	N381OTY	384	N384OTY	387	N387OTY	390	N390OTY	392	N392OTY
382	N382OTY	385	N385OTY	388	N388OTY	391	N391OTY	393	N393OTY
383	N383OTY	386	N386OTY	389	N389OTY				

401-405 — Leyland Olympian ONLXB/1R — Eastern Coach Works — B44/32F — 1982 — United, 1986

401	SPY201X	402	SPY202X	403	SPY203X	404	WDC211Y	405	WDC213Y

406	C259UAJ	Leyland Olympian ONLXB/1R	Eastern Coach Works	B45/32F	1985	United, 1986
407	C260UAJ	Leyland Olympian ONLXB/1R	Eastern Coach Works	B45/32F	1985	United, 1986
408	C261UAJ	Leyland Olympian ONLXB/1R	Eastern Coach Works	B45/32F	1985	United, 1986
409	C262UAJ	Leyland Olympian ONLXB/1R	Eastern Coach Works	B45/32F	1985	United, 1986

410-420 — Volvo Olympian — Northern Counties Palatine II — B43/29F — 1997

410	P410CCU	413	P413CCU	415	P415CCU	417	P417CCU	419	P419CCU
411	P411CCU	414	P414CCU	416	P416CCU	418	P418CCU	420	P420CCU
412	P412CCU								

The fleets of Northumbria and United - divided in preparation for their sale by National Bus - were again placed under a single management in the spring of 1999. Purchasing policies of the two operations had varied. Supplied new to Northumbria, and seen in that livery, is Scania 383, N383OTY which has an East Lancashire Cityzen body.

421-429		Volvo Olympian YN2RV16Z4		East Lancashire		B44/30F	1994	Arriva Southern Counties (C&NS) 1998	
421	M685HPF	**423**	M687HPF	**425**	M689HPF	**427**	M691HPF	**429**	M693HPF
422	M686HPF	**424**	M688HPF	**426**	M690HPF	**428**	M692HPF		

504	OCU809R	Leyland Fleetline FE30AGR		Alexander AL		B44/29F	1977	Busways, 1994	
505	OCU810R	Leyland Fleetline FE30AGR		Alexander AL		B44/29F	1977	Busways, 1994	
506	OCU812R	Leyland Fleetline FE30AGR		Alexander AL		B44/29F	1977	Busways, 1994	
527	BPT919S	Bristol VRT/SL3/6LXB		Eastern Coach Works		B43/31F	1977	United, 1986	

536-553		Bristol VRT/SL3/6LXB		Eastern Coach Works		B43/31F	1978-79 United, 1986		
536	CPT734S	**540**	CPT738S	**543**	DUP745S	**546**	DUP753S	**548**	HUP758T
538	CPT736S	**541**	CPT739S	**544**w	DUP747S	**547**	HUP757T	**553**	OBR769T

558-572		Bristol VRT/SL3/6LXB		Eastern Coach Works		B43/31F	1980	United, 1986	
562	SGR783V	**558**	SGR777V	**563**	SGR784V	**570**	SGR795V	**572**	SGR797V

576-584		Bristol VRT/SL3/6LXB		Eastern Coach Works		B43/31F	1980	United, 1986	
576	XPT802V	**580**	APT810W	**581**w	APT811W	**583**	APT816W	**584**w	APT817W

Opposite, top:- **Vehicles allocated to the Arriva North East's two operating licences are identified by the area shown under the name. Former Northumbria vehicles still carry that name while United vehicles carry North East. Pictured heading for Newcastle is Northern Counties-bodied Volvo Olympian 370, M370FTY.**
Malcolm King
Opposite, bottom:- **The number of Bristol VRs continues to diminish. One of the oldest remaining is 536, CPT734S, seen at Holy Island.** *Tony Wilson*

The North East Bus Handbook

The 1997 double-deck requirement of Northumbria was met by the supply of eleven Volvo Olympians. Following from the 1994 intake they carry the Palatine 2 bodywork from Northern Counties. In the two years since these were built the product from this facility has totally changed, low floor Presidents are now assembled there while the name of the bodybuilder has changed to Plaxton. *Richard Godfrey*

| 590 | PAJ827X | Bristol VRT/SL3/6LXB | Eastern Coach Works | B43/31F | 1981 | |
| 591 | PAJ829X | Bristol VRT/SL3/6LXB | Eastern Coach Works | B43/31F | 1981 | |

592-597		Daimler Fleetline CRG6LXB	Northern Counties	B43/32F	1976-77 GM Buses, 1987	
592	PRJ486R	**594**	PRJ489R	**595**	PRJ490R	**596** PRJ492R	**597** PRJ494R
593	PRJ488R					

| 598 | OBN505R | Leyland Fleetline FE30AGR | Northern Counties | B43/34F | 1977 | GM Buses, 1987 |
| 599 | PTD639S | Leyland Fleetline FE30AGR | Northern Counties | B43/34F | 1977 | GM Buses, 1987 |

601-607		MCW Metrobus DR101/14	MCW	H43/28D	1981-82 London North, 1998; * 601 is DR101/12
601	BYX210V	**603** KYV643X	**605** KYV698X	**606** KYV730X	**607** KYV790X
602	KYO624X	**604** KYV646X			

| 798 | L532EHD | DAF SB220LC550 | Ikarus CitiBus | B48F | 1994 | North Western (Starline), 1997 |
| 799 | L533EHD | DAF SB220LC550 | Ikarus CitiBus | B48F | 1994 | North Western (Starline), 1997 |

801-827		MCW MetroRider MF150/27*	MCW	BC25F* 1987 *801/3-6 are MF150/21
				*804 is B23F; 813/5 are B21F

801	E801BTN	**810**	E810BTN	**815**	E815BTN	**820**	E820BTN	**825**	E825BTN
803	E803BTN	**812**	E812BTN	**817**	E817BTN	**823**	E823BTN	**826**	E826BTN
804	E804BTN	**813**	E813BTN	**818**	E818BTN	**824**w	E824BTN	**827**	E827BTN
806	E806BTN	**814**	E814BTN	**819**	E819BTN				

| 828 | E676DCU | MCW MetroRider MF150/63 | MCW | BC21F | 1987 | Rochester & Marshall, 1994 |

Hexham is home to nine minibuses, seven full-size single-decks and nine double-deck buses. Optare MetroRiders now form the allocation though here Mercedes-Benz 965, G174YRE was seen on town services.
Tony Wilson

820-845

		MCW MetroRider MF150/27		MCW		BC25F*	1987	*845 is B23F	
829	E829BTN	832	E832BTN	836	E836BTN	841	E841BTN	845	E845BTN
831	E831BTN	833	E833BTN	840	E840BTN	844	E844BTN		

846	H840UUA	Optare MetroRider	Optare MR09	B25F	1990	Lancaster, 1993	
847	J363BNW	Optare MetroRider	Optare MR09	B23F	1991	Lancaster, 1993	
850	J366BNW	Optare MetroRider	Optare MR03	B29F	1992	Lancaster, 1993	

851-858

		Optare MetroRider		Optare MR07		BC28F*	1992-93	*855-8 are BC29F	
851	K851RBB	853	K853RBB	855	L855WRG	857	L857WRG	858	L858WRG
852	K852RBB	854	K854RBB	856	L856WRG				

859-871

		Optare MetroRider		Optare MR17		BC29F	1995		
859	M859KCU	862	M862KCU	865	M865KCU	868	M868KCU	870	M870KCU
860	M860KCU	863	M863KCU	866	M866KCU	869	M869KCU	871	M871KCU
861	M861KCU	864	M864KCU	867	M867KCU				

872-876

		Optare MetroRider		Optare MR17		B31F	1995		
872	M872LBB	873	M873LBB	874	M874LBB	875	M875LBB	876	M876LBB

877-896

		Optare MetroRider		Optare MR17		B31F	1996		
877	N877RTN	881	N881RTN	885	N885RTN	889	N889RTN	893	P893XCU
878	N878RTN	882	N882RTN	886	N886RTN	890	N890RTN	894	P894XCU
879	N879RTN	883	N883RTN	887	N887RTN	891	N891RTN	895	P895XCU
880	N880RTN	884	N884RTN	888	N192RVK	892	P892XCU	896	P896XCU

897-901   Optare MetroRider   Optare   B31F   1997

897	P56XTN	898	P57XTN	899	P58XTN	900	P59XTN	901	P61XTN

902-923   Optare MetroRider MR15   Optare   B31F   1997-98

902	P902DRG	907	R907JNL	912	R912JNL	916	R916JNL	920	R920JNL
903	P903DRG	908	R908JNL	913	R913JNL	917	R917JNL	921	R921JNL
904	P904DRG	909	R909JNL	914	R914JNL	918	R918JNL	922	R922JNL
905	P905JNL	910	R910JNL	915	R915JNL	919	R919JNL	923	R923JNL
906	P906JNL	911	R251JNL						

924	H886CCU	Optare MetroRider MR03	Optare	B25F	1991	Arriva Southern Counties (KT), 1999
925	H889CCU	Optare MetroRider MR03	Optare	B25F	1991	Arriva Southern Counties (KT), 1999
926	H890CCU	Optare MetroRider MR03	Optare	B25F	1991	Arriva Southern Counties (KT), 1999
965	G174YRE	Mercedes-Benz 811D	Carlyle	B33F	1990	Stevensons, 1994
966	G175DRF	Mercedes-Benz 811D	LHE Commuter	B33F	1990	Stevensons, 1994
969	H129CDB	Mercedes-Benz 811D	LHE Commuter	B31F	1990	Arriva North West, 1999
970	H130CDB	Mercedes-Benz 811D	LHE Commuter	B31F	1990	Arriva North West, 1999

1234	H278LEF	Leyland Tiger TRCL10/3ARZA	Alexander Q	B55F	1990	
1235	H279LEF	Leyland Tiger TRCL10/3ARZA	Alexander Q	B55F	1990	

1306-1315   Leyland Tiger TRCTL11/2RP   Plaxton Paramount 3200 III   C53F*   1987   *1312 is C47F

1306	E266KEF	1310	E270KEF	1312	E272KEF	1313	E273KEF	1315	E275KEF
1308	E268KEF	1311	E271KEF						

1331w	C38CWT	Leyland Tiger TRCTL11/2RH	Plaxton Paramount 3200 IIE	C53F	1986	West Riding, 1992
1334w	A119EPA	Leyland Tiger TRCTL11/2R	Plaxton Paramount 3200 E	C53F	1983	London & Country, 1992
1343	C43CWT	Leyland Tiger TRCTL11/2RH	Plaxton Paramount 3200 IIE	C53F	1986	West Riding, 1993
1344	C34CWT	Leyland Tiger TRCTL11/2RH	Plaxton Paramount 3200 IIE	C49F	1986	West Riding, 1993
1345	C35CWT	Leyland Tiger TRCTL11/2RH	Plaxton Paramount 3200 IIE	C53F	1986	West Riding, 1993
1346	C41CWT	Leyland Tiger TRCTL11/2RH	Plaxton Paramount 3200 IIE	C49F	1986	West Riding, 1993
1403	C133HJN	Leyland Tiger TRCTL11/3RH	Plaxton Paramount 3200 IIE	C53F	1986	Eastern National, 1989
1404	B112GRR	Leyland Tiger TRCTL11/3RH	Plaxton Paramount 3200 II	C51F	1985	Trent, 1991
1405	B113GRR	Leyland Tiger TRCTL11/3RH	Plaxton Paramount 3200 II	C51F	1985	Trent, 1991
1406	A949KAJ	Leyland Tiger TRCTL11/3R	Plaxton Paramount 3200 E	C57F	1983	Vanguard, Bedworth, 1991
1410	B110GRR	Leyland Tiger TRCTL11/3R	Plaxton Paramount 3200 II	C51F	1985	Trent, 1991
1415	B111GRR	Leyland Tiger TRCTL11/3RH	Plaxton Paramount 3200 II	C51F	1985	Trent, 1991
1416	B114GRR	Leyland Tiger TRCTL11/3RH	Plaxton Paramount 3200 II	C51F	1985	Trent, 1991
1417	B115GRR	Leyland Tiger TRCTL11/3RH	Plaxton Paramount 3200 II	C51F	1985	Trent, 1991
1431	YLX281	Leyland Tiger TRCTL11/3R	Duple Laser	C50F	1983	Maidstone & District, 1997
1432	445YMU	Leyland Tiger TRCTL11/3R	Duple Laser	C50F	1983	Maidstone & District, 1997
1434	648WHK	Leyland Tiger TRCTL11/3R	Duple Laser	C53F	1983	Maidstone & District, 1997

1501	J661UHN	MAN 11.190 HOCLR	Optare Vecta	B42F	1991	
1502	J620UHN	MAN 11.190 HOCLR	Optare Vecta	B42F	1991	

1503-1543   MAN 11.190 HOCLR   Optare Vecta   B42F   1993   *1509-13 are BC42F

1503	K503BHN	1512	K512BHN	1520	L520FHN	1528	L528FHN	1536	L536FHN
1504	K504BHN	1513	K513BHN	1521	L521FHN	1529	L529FHN	1537	L537FHN
1505	K505BHN	1514	K514BHN	1522	L522FHN	1530	L530FHN	1538	L538FHN
1506	K506BHN	1515	K515BHN	1523	L523FHN	1531	L531FHN	1539	L539FHN
1507	K507BHN	1516	K516BHN	1524	L524FHN	1532	L532FHN	1540	L540FHN
1508	K508BHN	1517	K517BHN	1525	L525FHN	1533	L533FHN	1541	L541FHN
1509	K509BHN	1518	K518BHN	1526	L526FHN	1534	L534FHN	1542	L542FHN
1510	K510BHN	1519	L519FHN	1527	L527FHN	1535	L535FHN	1543	L543FHN
1511	K511BHN								

United purchased 51 of the MAN 11.190 midibus chassis between 1991 and 1994. The product was distributed by Optare who placed their Vecta body on the type. Now in corporate livery is 1502, J620UHN, one of the original pair. During 1998-99 Arriva have been concentrating certain chassis types into some fleets. North East have gained Vectas from Arriva Cymru and Arriva Midlands North where each fleet contained only small numbers of the type. *Phillip Stephenson*

1544-1551   MAN 11.190 HOCLR   Optare Vecta   B42F   1993-94

1544	L544GHN	1546	L546GHN	1548	L548GHN	1550	L550GHN	1551	L551GHN
1545	L545GHN	1547	L547GHN	1549	L549GHN		

1552	M501AJC	MAN 11.190 HOCLR	Optare Vecta	B42F	1995	Arriva Cymru, 1998
1553	M502AJC	MAN 11.190 HOCLR	Optare Vecta	B42F	1995	Arriva Cymru, 1999
1554	M503AJC	MAN 11.190 HOCLR	Optare Vecta	B42F	1995	Arriva Cymru, 1999
1555	M504AJC	MAN 11.190 HOCLR	Optare Vecta	B42F	1995	Arriva Cymru, 1999
1556	K140RYS	MAN 11.190 HOCLR	Optare Vecta	BC37F	1993	Arriva Midlands North, 1999
1557	UOI772	MAN 11.190 HOCLR	Optare Vecta	BC37F	1993	Arriva Midlands North, 1999
1558	L102MEH	MAN 11.190 HOCLR	Optare Vecta	B42F	1994	Arriva Midlands North, 1999

1601-1643   Dennis Dart SLF   Plaxton Pointer 2   N39F   1997-98

1601	R601MHN	1610	S610KHN	1619	S619KHN	1628	S628KHN	1636	S636KHN
1602	R602MHN	1611	S611KHN	1620	S620KHN	1629	S629KHN	1637	S637KHN
1603	R603MHN	1612	S612KHN	1621	S621KHN	1630	S630KHN	1638	S638KHN
1604	R604MHN	1613	S613KHN	1622	S622KHN	1631	S631KHN	1639	S639KHN
1605	R605MHN	1614	S614KHN	1623	S623KHN	1632	S632KHN	1640	S640KHN
1606	R606MHN	1615	S615KHN	1624	S624KHN	1633	S633KHN	1641	S641KHN
1607	R607MHN	1616	S616KHN	1625	S625KHN	1634	S634KHN	1642	S642KHN
1608	S608KHN	1617	S617KHN	1626	S626KHN	1635	S635KHN	1643	S643KHN
1609	S609KHN	1618	S618KHN	1627	S627KHN		

1701	T	Dennis Dart SLF	Plaxton Pointer MPD	N29F	1999
1702	T	Dennis Dart SLF	Plaxton Pointer MPD	N29F	1999

2448	D648CVN	Mercedes-Benz L608D	Reeve Burgess	B20F	1986	
2451	D651CVN	Mercedes-Benz L608D	Reeve Burgess	B20F	1986	
2453	D653CVN	Mercedes-Benz L608D	Reeve Burgess	B20F	1986	
2466	D466EAJ	Mercedes-Benz L608D	Reeve Burgess	B20F	1987	
2473	D473EAJ	Mercedes-Benz L608D	Reeve Burgess	B20F	1987	
2479	D479EAJ	Mercedes-Benz L608D	Reeve Burgess	B20F	1987	

2601-2605   Optare MetroRider MR33   Optare   B25F   1994

2601	L601FHN	2602	L602FHN	2603	L603FHN	2604	L604FHN	2605	L605FHN

2606-2645   Optare MetroRider MR35   Optare   B25F   1996-97

2606	P606FHN	2614	P614FHN	2622	P622FHN	2630	P630FHN	2638	P638FHN
2607	P607FHN	2615	P615FHN	2623	P623FHN	2631	P631FHN	2639	P639FHN
2608	P608FHN	2616	P616FHN	2624	P624FHN	2632	P632FHN	2640	P640FHN
2609	P609FHN	2617	P617FHN	2625	P625FHN	2633	P633FHN	2641	P641FHN
2610	P610FHN	2618	P618FHN	2626	P626FHN	2634	P634FHN	2642	P642FHN
2611	P611FHN	2619	P619FHN	2627	P627FHN	2635	P635FHN	2643	P643FHN
2612	P612FHN	2620	P620FHN	2628	P628FHN	2636	P636FHN	2644	P644FHN
2613	P613FHN	2621	P621FHN	2629	P629FHN	2637	P637FHN	2645	P645FHN

2701-2725   Optare MetroRider MR15   Optare   B31F   1997-98

2701	R701MHN	2706	R706MHN	2711	R711MHN	2716	R716MHN	2721	R721MHN
2702	R702MHN	2707	R707MHN	2712	R712MHN	2717	R717MHN	2722	R722MHN
2703	R703MHN	2708	R708MHN	2713	R713MHN	2718	R718MHN	2723	R723MHN
2704	R704MHN	2709	R709MHN	2714	R714MHN	2719	R719MHN	2724	R724MHN
2705	R705MHN	2710	R710MHN	2715	R715MHN	2720	R720MHN	2725	R725MHN

3001-3025   Mercedes-Benz 0405   Optare Prisma   B49F   1995

3001	M301SAJ	3006	N806XHN	3011	N511XVN	3016	N516XVN	3021	N521XVN
3002	M302SAJ	3007	N807XHN	3012	N512XVN	3017	N517XVN	3022	N522XVN
3003	M303SAJ	3008	N808XHN	3013	N513XVN	3018	N518XVN	3023	N523XVN
3004	M304SAJ	3009	N809XHN	3014	N514XVN	3019	N519XVN	3024	N524XVN
3005	M305SAJ	3010	N810XHN	3015	N515XVN	3020	N520XVN	3025	N525XVN

3026	L100SBS	Mercedes-Benz 0405	Wright Cityranger	B51F	1993	Arriva Midlands North, 1999

3130-3142   Leyland National 2 NL116HLXCT/1R*   B49F   1983-84   *3134 has a 6HLXB engine

3130	A130FDC	3134	A134FDC	3136	A136FDC	3138	A138FDC	3142	A142FDC
3131	A131FDC	3135	A135FDC	3137	A137FDC	3140	A140FDC		

3143	RHG882X	Leyland National 2 NL116AL11/1R (6HLXCT)	B52F	1982	
3147	ARN895Y	Leyland National 2 NL116AHLXB/1R	B52F	1983	Shearings, 1991
3148	ARN896Y	Leyland National 2 NL116AHLXB/1R	B52F	1983	Shearings, 1991
3149w	ARN897Y	Leyland National 2 NL116AHLXB/1R	B52F	1983	Shearings, 1991
3150	ARN898Y	Leyland National 2 NL116AHLXB/1R	B52F	1983	Shearings, 1991
3152	A542PCW	Leyland National 2 NL116AHLXCT/1R	B49F	1984	Blackpool, 1991
3153	A543PCW	Leyland National 2 NL116AHLXCT/1R	B49F	1984	Blackpool, 1991
3505	SIB6705	Leyland 10351B/1R (6HLXB) East Lancs Greenway(1992)	B41F	1978	Kentish Bus, 1998
3506	SIB6706	Leyland NL106AL11/1R(6HLXB) East Lancs Greenway(1992)	B41F	1981	Kentish Bus, 1998
3508	SIB6708	Leyland NL106AL11/1R(6HLXB) East Lancs Greenway(1992)	B41F	1982	Kentish Bus, 1998

Opposite,top:- **The Optare MetroRider has been the principal competitor to Mercedes-Benz minibuses for the UK market, this integral vehicle being much acclaimed for reliability. 1997 saw the arrival of a batch of larger MR15 models from which 2711, R711MHN is seen in Darlington.** *Terry Wightman*
Opposite, bottom:- **Mercedes-Benz have been trying to enter the UK market for some years through the provision of a chassied version of the O405 citybus for bodying by UK builders. The type has been completed by Alexander, Wright and Optare. Twenty five with Optare Prisma bodywork arrived with United in 1995 and have since been joined by the sole examples latterly with Stevensons. From the 25, 3014, N514XVN is seen heading for Lingdale while still in the livery of Tees.** *Phillip Stephenson.*

3509	SIB1279	Leyland 10351B/1R	East Lancs Greenway(1992)	B41F	1979	Kentish Bus, 1998	
3510	SIB1280	Leyland 10351B/1R	East Lancs Greenway(1992)	B41F	1979	Kentish Bus, 1998	
3511	SIB1281	Leyland 10351B/1R	East Lancs Greenway(1992)	B41F	1979	Kentish Bus, 1998	
3512	SIB1282	Leyland 10351B/1R	East Lancs Greenway(1992)	B41F	1978	Kentish Bus, 1998	
3513	SIB1283	Leyland 10351B/1R	East Lancs Greenway(1992)	B41F	1979	Kentish Bus, 1998	
3514	SIB1284	Leyland 10351B/1R	East Lancs Greenway(1992)	B41F	1978	Kentish Bus, 1998	
3515	SIB1285	Leyland 10351B/1R	East Lancs Greenway(1992)	B41F	1979	Kentish Bus, 1998	
3516	SIB1286	Leyland 10351B/1R	East Lancs Greenway(1992)	B41F	1979	Kentish Bus, 1998	
3517	SIB1287	Leyland 10351B/1R	East Lancs Greenway(1992)	B41F	1979	Kentish Bus, 1998	
3518	SIB1288	Leyland 10351B/1R	East Lancs Greenway(1992)	B41F	1979	Kentish Bus, 1998	
3519	PDZ6261	Leyland 1035A1/1R	East Lancs Greenway(1994)	B41F	1977	Kentish Bus, 1998	
3520	PDZ6262	Leyland 1035A1/1R	East Lancs Greenway(1994)	B41F	1977	Kentish Bus, 1998	
3521	SIB6715	Leyland 1051/1R/0402(6HLXB)	East Lancs Greenway(1993)	B41F	1973	Kentish Bus, 1998	
3522	SIB6716	Leyland 1051/1R/0402(6HLXB)	East Lancs Greenway(1993)	B41F	1974	Kentish Bus, 1998	
3523	SIB6710	Leyland NL106L11/1R	East Lancs Greenway(1992)	B41F	1981	Arriva Southern Counties (K&S), 1998	
3524	SIB6712	Leyland 10351A/1R	East Lancs Greenway(1992)	B41F	1979	Arriva Southern Counties (K&S), 1998	
3744	WAO399Y	Leyland National 2 NL116HLXB/1R		B52F	1983	Shearings, 1991	
3745	WAO395Y	Leyland National 2 NL116HLXB/1R		B52F	1983	Shearings, 1991	
3747	WRA224Y	Leyland National 2 NL116AHLXB/1R		B52F	1983	Trent, 1991	
3748	WRA225Y	Leyland National 2 NL116AHLXB/1R		B52F	1983	Trent, 1991	
3749	RRA219X	Leyland National 2 NL116AHLXB/1R		B52F	1981	Trent, 1991	
3751	DOC31V	Leyland National 2 NL116L11/1R		B50F	1980	West Midlands Travel, 1995	
3756	VBG89V	Leyland National 2 NL116L11/2R(6HLXB)		B49F	1980	Arriva North West, 1999	
3758	CCY819V	Leyland National 2 NL116L11/1R(6HLXB)		BC49F	1980	Yorkshire Bus (WR), 1997	
3759	HED204V	Leyland National 2 NL116AL11/1R(6HLXB)		B49F	1980	Yorkshire Bus (WR), 1997	
3760	HED205V	Leyland National 2 NL116AL11/1R(6HLXB)		B49F	1980	Yorkshire Bus (WR), 1997	
3761	VBG93V	Leyland National 2 NL116AL11/1R(6HLXB)		B49F	1980	Yorkshire Bus (WR), 1997	
3762	XWA72X	Leyland National 2 NL116L11/1R(6HLXB)		B49F	1982	Yorkshire Bus (WR), 1997	
3763	XWA73X	Leyland National 2 NL116L11/1R(6HLXB)		B49F	1982	Yorkshire Bus (WR), 1997	
3764	XWA74X	Leyland National 2 NL116L11/1R(6HLXB)		B49F	1982	Yorkshire Bus (WR), 1997	
3765	XWA75X	Leyland National 2 NL116L11/1R(6HLXB)		B49F	1982	Yorkshire Bus (WR), 1997	
3766	EWT206Y	Leyland National 2 NL116HLXB/1R		B49F	1982	Yorkshire Bus (WR), 1997	
3767	EWT208Y	Leyland National 2 NL116HLXB/1R		B49F	1983	Yorkshire Bus (WR), 1997	
3768	EWT210Y	Leyland National 2 NL116HLXB/1R		B49F	1983	Yorkshire Bus (WR), 1997	
3769	BPR48Y	Leyland National 2 NL116HLXB/1R		B49F	1983	Yorkshire Bus (WR), 1997	
3770	BPR49Y	Leyland National 2 NL116HLXB/1R		B49F	1983	Yorkshire Bus (WR), 1997	
3771	NTU11Y	Leyland National 2 NL116HLXB/2R		B52F	1983	Arriva North West (BL), 1999	
3772	NTU12Y	Leyland National 2 NL116HLXB/2R		B52F	1983	Arriva North West, 1999	
3773	NTU13Y	Leyland National 2 NL116HLXB/2R		B52F	1983	Arriva North West, 1999	

4001-4005

	DAF SB220LC550		Optare Delta		B51F	1990		
4001	G209HCP	4002	G210HCP	4003	G211HCP	4004	G212HCP	4005	G214HCP

4006	J866UPY	DAF SB200LC550	Optare Delta	B49F	1992
4007	J867UPY	DAF SB200LC550	Optare Delta	B49F	1992

4008-4022

	DAF SB220LC550		Optare Delta		B49F		1993	
4008	K408BHN	4011	K411BHN	4014	K414BHN	4017	K417BHN	4020	L420FHN
4009	K409BHN	4012	K412BHN	4015	K415BHN	4018	L418FHN	4021	L421FHN
4010	K410BHN	4013	K413BHN	4016	K416BHN	4019	L419FHN	4022	L422FHN

4023-4058

	DAF DE02GSSB220		Plaxton Prestige		N45F		1998	
4023	R423RPY	4031	R431RPY	4038	R438RPY	4045	S345KHN	4052	S352KHN
4024	R424RPY	4032	R432RPY	4039	R439RPY	4046	S346KHN	4053	S353KHN
4025	R425RPY	4033	R433RPY	4040	R440RPY	4047	S347KHN	4054	S354KHN
4026	R426RPY	4034	R434RPY	4041	S341KHN	4048	S348KHN	4055	S355KHN
4027	R427RPY	4035	R435RPY	4042	S342KHN	4049	S349KHN	4056	S356KHN
4028	R428RPY	4036	R436RPY	4043	S343KHN	4050	S350KHN	4057	S357KHN
4029	R429RPY	4037	R437RPY	4044	S344KHN	4051	S351KHN	4058	S358KHN
4030	R430RPY								

4059	R701KCU	DAF DE02SB220GS	Northern Counties Paladin	B39F	1997

4060-4073

	DAF DE02GSSB220		Plaxton Prestige		N41F		1998	
4060	S702KFT	4063	S705KFT	4066	S708KFT	4069	S711KFT	4072	S714KRG
4061	S703KFT	4064	S706KFT	4067	S709KFT	4070	S712KRG	4073	S715KRG
4062	S704KFT	4065	S707KFT	4068	S710KFT	4071	S713KRG		

The Optare Delta was introduced by United Bus - a consortium including the Leeds bodybuilder, DAF and two Dutch coachworks - at the turn of the decade. The model has now ceased as no low-floor version of the body has been announced. United had acquired over twenty, with a similar number at Northumbria, including 268, F701ECC, one of two from Crosville Cymru. *David Longbottom*

4074-4079

DAF DE02GSSB220 — Plaxton Prestige — N41F — 1999

4074	T74AUA	4075	T75AUA	4076	T76AUA	4078	T78AUA	4079	T79AUA

5001-5005

Leyland Lynx LX2R11C15Z4S — Leyland Lynx — B49F — 1990

5001	G508EAJ	5002	G509EAJ	5003	G510EAJ	5004	G511EAJ	5005	G512EAJ

5006-5018

Leyland Lynx LX2R11C15Z4S — Leyland Lynx 2 — B49F — 1991

5006	H31PAJ	5009	H253PAJ	5012	J652UHN	5016	J656UHN	5018	J658UHN
5007	H32PAJ	5011	J651UHN	5013	J653UHN	5017	J657UHN		

7202-7238

Leyland Olympian ONLXB/1R — Eastern Coach Works — B45/32F* 1982-84 7202-4/10 ex West Riding, 1993
*7233/4 are BC42/28F; 7206/14 are B44/32F

7202	XWY477X	7208	SPY208X	7217	WDC217Y	7227	AEF227Y	7235	A235GHN
7203	XWY478X	7210	CWR505Y	7218	WDC218Y	7228	AEF228Y	7236	A236GHN
7204	XWY479X	7214	WDC214Y	7223	AEF223Y	7233	A233GHN	7237	A237GHN
7206	SPY206X	7215	WDC215Y	7225	AEF225Y	7234	A234GHN	7238	A238GHN
7207	SPY207X	7216	WDC216Y	7226	AEF226Y				

7239	A563KWY	Leyland Olympian ONLXB/1R	Eastern Coach Works	BC42/28F	1983	West Riding, 1994

7240-7247

Leyland Olympian ONLXB/1R — Eastern Coach Works — B45/32F 1984-85 KentishBus , 1998
7245-7 Arriva Southern Counties(KT), 1998

7240	A240GHN	7242	A242GHN	7244	A244GHN	7246	B246NVN	7247	B247NVN
7241	A241GHN	7243	A243GHN	7245w	B245NVN				

One of five Leyland Olympians with high-back seating is 7265, C265XEF, seen leaving Darlington on an express working to Crook. *Terry Wightman*

7250	B45NDX	Leyland Olympian ONLXB/1RV	East Lancashire	B40/33F	1985	Stevensons, 1993	
7251	B251NVN	Leyland Olympian ONLXB/1R	Eastern Coach Works	B45/32F	1985		
7252	B252PHN	Leyland Olympian ONLXB/1R	Eastern Coach Works	B45/32F	1985		
7253	B253PHN	Leyland Olympian ONLXB/1R	Eastern Coach Works	B45/32F	1985		
7255	B255RAJ	Leyland Olympian ONLXB/1R	Eastern Coach Works	B45/32F	1985		
7256	B256RAJ	Leyland Olympian ONLXB/1R	Eastern Coach Works	B45/32F	1985		
7258	B598SWX	Leyland Olympian ONLXB/1R	Eastern Coach Works	BC40/31F	1984	West Riding, 1994	
7263	E963PME	Leyland Olympian ONLXB/1R	Optare	B47/29F	1988	London Cityrama, 1992	
7265w	C265XEF	Leyland Olympian ONLXB/1R	Eastern Coach Works	BC42/30F	1986		
7266	C266XEF	Leyland Olympian ONLXB/1R	Eastern Coach Works	BC42/30F	1986		
7267	C267XEF	Leyland Olympian ONLXB/1R	Eastern Coach Works	BC42/30F	1986		
7268	C268XEF	Leyland Olympian ONLXB/1R	Eastern Coach Works	BC42/30F	1986		

7271-7275

Leyland Olympian ON2R50C13Z4 Alexander RH B45/29F 1993

7271	L271FVN	7272	L272FVN	7273	L273FVN	7274	L274FVN	7275	L275FVN

7276	G21HHG	Leyland Olympian ONCL10/1RZ Leyland	B47/31F	1989	Atlas Bus, 1994

7279-7285

Leyland Olympian ONCL10/1R Northern Counties B43/32F 1989 Atlas Bus, 1994

7279	G756UYT	7280	G757UYT	7281w	G758UYT	7284	G761UYT	7285	G762UYT

7286-7294

Leyland Olympian ONLXB/1R Roe B47/29F 1982-83 Metrobus, Orpington, 1997

7286	UWW13X	7288	CUB60Y	7290	CUB63Y	7292	CUB66Y	7294	CUB69Y
7287	UWW14X	7289	CUB61Y	7291	CUB64Y	7293	CUB68Y		

Ancilliary Vehicles:-

192	VDV125S	Bristol LH6L	Eastern Coach Works	TV	1978	Moor-Dale, 1994
9990	GSU347	Leyland National 11351/1R		B49F	1975	Midland Red North, 1987
9991	UBR110V	Leyland National 2 NL116L11/1R		B49F	1981	United, 1986
9992	WSV569	Leyland National 2 NL116AL11/1R		B49F	1980	United, 1986
9993	LPT703T	Bristol LH6L	Eastern Coach Works	B43F	1983	
9995	UGR698R	Bristol VRT/SL3/6LXB	Eastern Coach Works	B43/31F	1976	

Previous Registrations:

445YMU	A177MKE	SIB6707	JCK850W
648WHK	A185MKE	SIB6708	LFR874X
681CXM	A178MKE	SIB6710	DBV844W
869SVX	A179MKE	SIB6712	BYW425V
A949KAJ	A672OKX, 7694VC	SIB6715	TPD176M
EDZ215	RMO203Y	SIB6716	UPE196M
GSU347	GOL399N	TSU636	A183MKE
J20NMS	J849MCN	VAY879	A182MKE
LHO992Y	AEF992Y, TBC658	WLT859	K121HWF
NMS700	G418WFP	WSV565	ABR865S
PDZ6261	UPB310S	WSV567	ABR867S
PDZ6262	UPB313S	WSV569	RDC736X
SIB1279	BPL484T	WSV570	E692JUT
SIB1280	EPD541V	WSV571	C160UHN, NMS700
SIB1281	BPL489T	WSV572	B337WFJ
SIB1282	YPL439T	XSV689	C256SPC
SIB1283	BPL479T	XSV691	E91OJT
SIB1284	YPL445T	YLX281	A176MKE
SIB1285	BPL480T	YOT607	A180MKE
SIB1286	BPL482T	YSU870	E186XKO
SIB1287	BPL483T	YSU871	E187XKO
SIB1288	EPD522V	YSU896	A135EPA
SIB6705	YPF762T		
SIB6706	LFR855X		

Allocations:-

Alnwick (Lisburn Street) - Northumbria

Tiger	219	220	222	242	243	244	248	249
	250							
MetroRider	859	890	891					
Bristol LH	193							
DAF/Delta	251	252	255					
Bristol VR	536	546	547	558				
Olympian	302	313	315	317				

Ashington (Lintonville Terrace) - Northumbria

MetroRider	813	815	846	847	850	852	853	877
	878	893	894	895	896	897	898	899
	908	909	910	911				
Leopard	203							
Tiger	1432							
DAF/Delta	253	254	257	258	263	264	266	267
	268	269						
DAF/Ikarus	798	799						
Bristol VR	530	562	565	570	572			
Olympian	308	309	310	311	421	422	424	

Berwick (Tweedmouth Industrial Park) - Northumbria

MetroRider	803	805	806	810	818	819	823	832
	836							
Bristol LH	191	196						
Leopard	221	239						
Tiger	202	245						
Olympian	304	316	318					

Bishop Auckland (Morland Street) - Durham County- The Eden

Outstations - Crook and Fishburn

Mercedes-Benz	2451	2466						
MetroRider	2613	2614	2642	2643	2644	2645	2709	2710
Tiger	1342	1343	1344	1345	1346	1404♣	1410	1415♣
MAN Vecta	1515	1526	1527	1528	1529	1546	1547	1548
	1549	1552						
Dart	1615	1616	1617	1618	1619	1620	1621	1622
	1623	1624	1626	1627	1628	1629	1630	1631
	1632	1633	1634	1635				
Lynx	5003	5004	5005	5006	5007	5008	5009	5010
	5011	5012	5013	5014	5015	5016	5017	5018
Olympian	7214	7240	7241	7242	7243	7244		

Blyth (Bridge Street) - Northumbria

MetroRider	812	820	825	826	829	831	833	840
	841	844	845	851	854	855	856	857
	858	860	866	867	868	869	870	871
	881	882	883	884	901	902	903	
Scania L	275	276	277	278	279	280	281	282
	283	285	286	287	288	289	290	
Olympian	301	314	319	320	321	322	401	402
	403	425	426	427	428	429		
Scania N	381	382	383	384	385	386	387	388
	389	390	391	392	393			

Darlington (Feethams) - Durham County

Outstation - Barnard Castle

MetroRider	2610	2629	2630	2631	2640	2641	2701	2702
	2703	2704	2705	2706	2707	2708	2711	2712
	2713	2714	2715	2716	2717	2718	2719	2720
	2721	2722	2723	2724				
Tiger	1234	1235						
MAN/Vecta	1518							
Dart	1601	1602	1603	1604	1605	1606	1607	1608
	1610	1611	1612	1613	1614			
Greenway	3505	3506	3507	3508				
DAF/Prestige	4055	4056	4057	4058				
Olympian	7215	7216	7246	7247	7266	7271	7272	

Durham (Waddington Steet) - Durham County

Mercedes-Benz	2453	2479						
MetroRider	2615	2616	2617	2618	2619	2620	2621	2622
	2623	2624	2625					
National	3130	3131	3134	3135	3136	3137	3138	3140
	3142	3143	3147	3148	3150	3152	3153	3773
	3774							
DAF/Delta	4016	4017	4018	4019	4020	4021	4022	
Olympian	7207	7218	7227	7228	7250	7251	7252	7253
	7255	7256	7273	7274	7275			

Hexham (Burn Lane)- Northumbria

MetroRider	803	804	814	828	879	880	900	922
	923							
Tiger	247	250						
DAF/Prima	291	292	293	294	295			
DAF/Prestige	4074	4075	4076	4077	4078			
Bristol VR	527	553						
Olympian	371	372	373	374	375	376	377	

Loftus (Whitby Road) - Tees & District - The Eden

Outstation at Whitby

MetroRider	2635	2636	2637	2638	2639			
National	3512	3519	3521	3524	3744	3745	3747	3748
	3749	3756	3758	3759	3760			
Tiger	1232	1311	1312	1314	1315	1431♣	1432♣	1433♣
	1434♣							
MAN/Vecta	1509	1510	1511	1512	1513	1534	1535	
DAF/Prestige	4050	4051	4052	4053	4054			

Morpeth (Park Lane) - Northumbria

MetroRider	816	872	873	874	875	876	885	886
	889	892	904	905	906	907	912	913
	914							
Tiger	202	214	215	215	216	217	218	
Bristol LH	193	194	195					
DAF/Delta	256	259	260					
Bristol VR	538	548	563	576				
Olympian	305	306	307					

Newcastle (Jesmond Road) - Northumbria - National Express

MetroRider	861	862	863	864	865	887	888	915
	916	917	918	919	920	921		
Bova	131X	132X	133X	135X	136X	137X	138X	
	139X	140X						
DAF/Delta	251	252	254	255	256	258	261	262
Scania L	271	272	273	274	281	282	283	284
DAF/Paladin	4059							
DAF/Prestige	4060	4061	4062	4063	4064	4065	4066	4067
	4068	4069	4070	4071	4072	4073		
Bristol VR	540	541	543	580	590	591		
Fleetline	504	505	506	592	593	594	595	596
	597	598	599					
Metrobus	601	605						
Olympian	303	312	370	403	404	405	406	407
	408	409	410	411	412	413	414	415
	416	417	418	419	420			

Peterlee (Davey Drive) - Durham County

MetroRider	2626	2627	2628					
Dart	1636	1643						
National	3514	3520	3761	3762	3763	3764	3765	3766
	3767	3768	3769	3770				
Tiger	1301	1302	1328	1333	1401	1402	1403	1412
Olympian	7263	7286	7287	7288	7289	7290	7291	7292
	7293	7295						

Pictured at Redcar resplendent in corporate livery is Mercedes-Benz O405 3026, L100SBS. Built in 1993, the vehicle has bodywork by Wright. The low floor version of the bus, the O405N the N standing for Niederflur is now being sold in the UK, the vehicles being fitted out at Mercedes' Barnsley premises.
Terry Wightman

Redcar (Railway Terrace) - Tees & District - The Eden

Tiger	1327	1405♣	1416♣	1417♣				
MAN/Vecta	1553							
National	3513	3518	3522					
MB/Prisma	3003	3004	3005	3006	3007	3008	3009	3010
	3011	3012	3013	3014	3015	3016	3017	3018
	3019	3020	3021	3022	3023	3024	3025	
Olympian	202	203	204	206	210	223	235	236
	237	238	256	258	279	280	281	282
	283	284	285	7206				

Richmond (Station Yard) - Durham County

MetroRider	2602	2603	2604	2605	2609	2632	2633	2634
Tiger	1306	1307	1308	1309	1310	1406		
MAN/Vecta	1530	1531	1532	1533	1551			
Olympian	7267	7268						

Stockton (Boathouse Lane) - Teeside

MetroRider	2606	2607	2608	2611	2612	2725		
Mercedes-Benz	2448							
National	3510	3511	3515	3516	3517	3523		
Tiger	1342	1343	1346					
MAN/Vecta	1501	1502	1503	1504	1505	1506	1507	1508
	1516	1517	1519	1520	1521	1522	1523	1524
	1525	1540	1541	1542	1543	1544	1545	
DAF/Delta	4001	4002	4003	4004	4005	4006	4007	4008
	4009	4010	4011	4012	4013	4014	4015	
DAF/Prestige	4023	4024	4025	4026	4027	4028	4029	4030
	4031	4032	4033	4034	4035	4036	4037	4038
	4039	4040	4041	4042	4043	4044	4045	4046
	4047	4048	4049					

Photographed while heading for Bishop Auckland is Dennis Dart 1630, S630KHN. The bodywork is by North East-based Plaxtons who produce single-deck buses and coach from their assembly plant in Scarborough. *Terry Wightman*

Stokesley (North Road) - Tees & District

Tiger	1327							
MAN/Vecta	1536	1537	1538	1539	1550	1551		
MB/Prisma	3001	3002						
Olympian	7225	7226	7233	7234	7239	7276	7277	7278
	7284							

Withdrawn and unallocated:-

MetroRider	824						
Mercedes-Benz	965	966	2473				
National	3149						
Leopard	205						
MAN/Vecta	1514	1516	1517				
Tiger	246	1313	1331	1334	1344		
Bristol VR	544	581	583	584			
Metrobuses	602	603	604	606	607		
Olympian	7203	7208	7217	7245	7258	7265	7294

BM TRAVEL

B Metcalfe, 3 Dunelm Court, Sedgefield, Stockton-on-Tees, TS21 2JS

MPL123W	Leyland Leopard PSU3E/4R	Duple Dominant IV Express	C49F	1981	Tetley, Leeds, 1998
G965WNR	Leyland Swift ST2R44C97A4	Reeve Burgess Harrier	B39F	1989	Gardiners, Spennymoor, 1997
M582JBC	Toyota Coaster HZB50R	Caetano Optimo III	C21F	1995	Ramsay, Elsrickle, 1997
M137FYJ	Mercedes-Benz 811D	Autobus Classique	C29F	1995	Airport Connection, Crawley, 1998
M271FNS	Mercedes-Benz 410D	Deansgate	M16	1995	
N589GBW	Dennis Javelin 12SDA2146	Caetano Algarve II	C49FT	1996	Dawson Rentals, 1998
N571GBW	Dennis Javelin 12SDA2155	UVG Unistar	C57F	1996	
P175ANR	Dennis Javelin 12SDA2155	Caetano Algarve II	C57F	1996	Supreme, Hadleigh, 1999
P593HHF	Mercedes-Benz 611D	?	C24F	1997	
P533UGA	Mercedes-Benz 814D	Mellor	BC33F	1997	
T576KGB	Mercedes-Benz Vario O814D	Mellor	BC33F	1999	

Livery: White

Depot: OK Service Station, Chilton

The latest arrival with BM Travel is also the latest product from Mercedes-Benz, the Vario. Badged for the 614 rating, this example joined the fleet in 1999. The vehicle is seen outside its home base in Clifton.
Terry Wightman

J C BELL & SONS

JC, J & R Bell, 1A Castlereagh Street, New Silksworth,
Sunderland, SR3 1HJ

RML109Y	Volvo B10M-61	Plaxton Viewmaster IV	C51F	1982	Pettigrew, Mauchline, 1988
B427PJF	Ford Transit 190	Robin Hood	B16F	1985	Snowdon, Easington Colliery, 1993
E127KYW	MCW MetroRider MF150/38	MCW	B25F	1987	Stagecoach Busways, 1996
E317BRM	MCW MetroRider MF150/36	MCW	BC25F	1988	Stagecoach Busways, 1997
JIL7905	Volvo B10M-60	Plaxton Paramount 3500 III	C49F	1990	Laidler, Wooller, 1997
G626EEM	Iveco Daily 49.10	Mellor	B16FL	1990	Pygall, Easington Colliery, 1998
J292SMO	Renault Master T35D	Atlas	M11	1991	
J295SMO	Renault Master T35D	Atlas	M11	1991	

Previous Registrations:

B427PJF	B402WTC	JIL7905	G503EFX, A3EXC, G370GJT

Livery: Cream, blue and orange; or orange and yellow.

Depot: Strangford Road, Seaham.

J C Bell & Sons operate Plaxton Viewmaster RML109Y seen here at Middleton-on-Teesdale while accompanying the Murton Colliery Band to the annual brass band concert. *J C Walton*

BELL BROS

NS, RJ & EW Bell, Coach House, 2 Drake Street, Spennymoor, County Durham, DL16 7UB

BHK209X	Leyland Tiger TRCTL11/2R	Duple Dominant II Express	C51F	1982	Southend, 1990
EBW101Y	Leyland Tiger TRCTL11/3R	Duple Dominant IV Express	C44FT	1983	Thames Transit, 1992
A132REO	Leyland Tiger TRCTL11/2R	Duple Laser Express	C53F	1984	Percival, Barrow-in-Furness, 1986
B425CMC	Leyland Tiger TRCTL11/3RZ	Duple Caribbean 2	C53F	1985	Daisy, Broughton, 1987
C807FMC	Leyland Tiger TRCTL11/3RZ	Plaxton Paramount 3200 II	C53F	1986	Frames Rickards, Brentford, 1990
F27RKX	Leyland Tiger TRCL10/3ARZA	Van Hool Alizée H	C49FT	1988	Luton & District, 1994
F722KGK	MAN 16.290 HOCLR	Jonckheere Deauville	C51FT	1989	Time, Thornton Heath, 1996
G702BEF	Volvo B10M-60	Van Hool Alizée H	C51FT	1989	Gardiners, Spennymoor, 1997

Previous Registrations:

F27RKX	F336SMD, SIB8528	F722KGK	F115YNV, NMC735	G702BEF
				G702BEF, UFE712

Livery: Blue and cream

Depot: Coulson Street, Spennymoor

Bell Bros also use the trading name Bonnie Heather and C807FMC is seen with both names displayed while on a trip to Keswick in Cumbria. The coach is the only Plaxton-bodied vehicle in the fleet and came from Frames-Rickards, the London-based coach operator and holder of the Royal Warrant for coach services.
J C Walton

The North East Bus Handbook

BOB SMITH TRAVEL

Bob Smith Travel Ltd, Kingsway, Langley Park, Durham DH7 9TB

Reg	Chassis	Body	Seating	Year	Notes
MWW564P	Leyland Leopard PSU3C/4R	Plaxton Supreme III Express	B49F	1976	On Target Training, 1993
OEW274R	Leyland Leopard PSU3C/4R	Plaxton Supreme III Express	C53F	1976	David Grasby, Oxhill, 1989
NPK236R	Leyland National 10351A/1R (Volvo)		B41F	1976	Volvo demonstrator, 1996
WGW579S	Leyland Leopard PSU5B/4R	Plaxton Supreme III	C53F	1978	Dodsworth, Boroughbridge, 1992
FRX869T	Leyland Leopard PSU5C/4R	Plaxton Supreme III	C53F	1979	Rennie, Dunfermline, 1990
AKU166T	Leyland National 10351B/1R (Volvo)		B44F	1979	Volvo demonstrator, 1996
BVP796V	Leyland Leopard PSU3E/4R	Willowbrook Warrior(1990)	B47F	1980	SUT, 1990
LCU434X	Leyland Leopard PSU5C/4R	Duple Dominant IV	C57F	1981	
AOD650Y	Leyland Tiger TRCTL11/3R	Plaxton Supreme V	C57F	1982	Dodsworth, Boroughbridge, 1992
RIW2830	Van Hool T815	Van Hool Acron	C48FT	1983	Solent, New Milton, 1996
A16BST	Leyland Tiger TRCTL11/3R	Van Hool Alizée	C53F	1984	Eddie Brown, Helperby, 1994
B997JTN	Leyland Tiger TRCTL11/3R	Duple Laser 2	C57F	1985	
A13BST	Scania K112CRB	Van Hool Alizée	C53F	1987	
B8BST	Volvo B10M-61	Plaxton Paramount 3500 III	C44FT	1988	
G148SUS	Mercedes-Benz 609D	Scott	BC24F	1990	
G97SKR	Iveco Daily 49.10	Phoenix	B23F	1990	Stagecoach South (EK), 1997
B9BST	Volvo B10M-60	Plaxton Expressliner	C46FT	1991	Dorset Travel Services, 1998
J485OHA	Iveco Daily 49.10	Carlyle Dailybus 2	B23F	1992	Robson, Thornaby, 1994
M267HTN	Ford Transit VE6	Ford	M14	1995	private owner, 1996
P2BST	Mercedes-Benz 711D	Dormobile Routemaker	BC24F	1996	

Previous Registrations:

A13BST	D424SKY	B9BST	H349MLJ	P2BST	P484TGA
A16BST	A162MNE	FRX869T	YYJ302T, 406DCD	RIW2830	DJF389Y, 5505ML
B8BST	E924UUB				

Named vehicles: A16BST *Lady Gail*; B997JTN *Lady Pamela*; A13BST *Lady Sarah*; BVP796V *Warrior*; B9BST *Lady Isabella*; RIW2830 *Lady Sheila*; NPK236R *Wor Alex*; AKU166T *Wor Bobby.*,

Livery: White and blue

Bob Smith Travel fleet is represented here by Iveco minibus J485OHA. The vehicle is seen arriving at Durham. This 23-seater joined the fleet in 1994 and has a Carlyle Dailybus 2 body. *Tony Wilson*

CARIS COACHES

GM Caris, 184 Saltwell Road, Gateshead, NE8 4XH

DNK412T	Ford R1014	Duple Dominant II Express	C35F	1979	D C Travel, Newcastle, 1998
HAZ7657	Leyland Tiger TRCTL11/3R	Duple Caribbean	C49FT	1983	Leeways, Rowlands Gill, 1997
A750UYL	Leyland Cub CU335	Wadham Stringer Vanguard	BC14FL	1984	D C Travel, Newcastle, 1998
B203GNL	Ford Transit 190	Alexander AM	B16F	1985	Girl Scouts, Sunniside, 1997
B240WTM	Ford Transit 160	Ford	M14	1985	Caris Taxis, Gateshead,1992
OIL4178	Mercedes-Benz L407D	Steedrive	BC20F	1986	South Tyneside DC, 1995
F409SVW	Ford Transit VE6	Ford	M14	1989	private owner, 1995
K940UBB	Leyland-DAF 400	Onyx	M16	1993	
N831NCU	LDV 400	LDV	M16	1995	Collinsdale, Low Fell, 1998
P130HBG	Mercedes-Benz 711D	Onyx	BC25F	1996	

Previous Registrations:

HAZ7657	A668YJR, LCN36, A668YJR	OIL4178	C93PRG

Livery: White, red, orange and yellow

Caris Coaches operate two Onyx-bodied minibuses, the later P130HBG is based on a Mercedes-Benz 711 chassis. Onyx are a growing minibus company who construct the vehicles in England. *Terry Wightman*

CLASSIC

Classic - Highstyle - Primrose - Moor-Dale - Hylton Castle

Classic Coaches (Continental) Ltd; Classic Buses (Stanley) Ltd; R&M Bisset Ltd,

Classic House, Morrison Rd, Annfield Plain, Stanley, DH9 7RX

Classic

GPC730N	Leyland National 11351/1R (Volvo)		B49F	1974	Reading Buses, 1996
TPE171S	Leyland National 11351A/1R (Volvo)		B49F	1977	Reading Buses, 1996
TOF695S	Leyland National 11351A/1R (Volvo)		B49F	1978	Midland, 1995
956CCE	Volvo B10M-61	Van Hool Alizée H	C49FT	1986	Scarlet Band, West Cornforth, 1993
527LPF	Volvo B10M-61	Van Hool Alizée H	C51FT	1987	Go-Ahead, 1998
CAZ6831	Volvo B10M-61	Plaxton Paramount 3500 III	C48FT	1987	Go-Ahead, 1998
G93ERP	Mercedes-Benz 709D	Dormobile Routemaker	B29F	1989	Derwent Coaches, Swalwell, 1998
387FYM	Leyland Tiger TRCTL10/3ARZM	Plaxton Paramount 3500 III	C49FT	1989	Go-Ahead, 1998
325CCE	Volvo B10M-60	Van Hool Alizée H	C49FT	1989	Durham City Coaches, 1995
WOJ802	DAF SB3000DKVF601	Van Hool Alizée H	C49FT	1989	Go-Ahead, 1998
UGD735	DAF SB3000DKVF601	Van Hool Alizée H	C49FT	1989	Go-Ahead, 1998
JSK346	Volvo B10M-60	Plaxton Paramount 3500 III	C53F	1990	Go-Ahead, 1998
TVE804	DAF SB3000DKVF601	Van Hool Alizée H	C49FT	1991	Go-Ahead, 1998
J988TVU	Mercedes-Benz 709D	Plaxton Beaver	B23F	1992	Derwent Coaches, Swalwell, 1998
593CCE	Volvo B10M-60	Plaxton Expressliner	C46FT	1992	First Western National, 1998
656CCE	Volvo B10M-60	Plaxton Expressliner	C46FT	1992	First Western National, 1998
K945OEM	Mercedes-Benz 811D	Marshall C16	B27F	1993	MTL (North), 1998
K947OEM	Mercedes-Benz 811D	Marshall C16	B27F	1993	MTL (North), 1998
K948OEM	Mercedes-Benz 811D	Marshall C16	B27F	1993	MTL (North), 1998
685XHY	DAF SB3000DKVF601	Van Hool Alizée H	C49FT	1993	Go-Ahead, 1998
L656ADS	Volvo B10M-60	Van Hool Alizée H	C53F	1993	Park's of Hamilton,1995

A rainy day in London's Trafalgar Square sees M40CLA working a British Coach Holidays' excursion. It is one of three Caetano Algarve-bodied Volvo B10Ms in the Classic fleet. Classic expanded its coach operations with the purchase of the High-style coach business from Go-Ahead.
Colin Lloyd

Classic Coaches is part of the new Status Bus and Coach Group which also includes Border Buses and Viscount Central in the north west; Bakers of Biddulph in the north Midlands; MK Metro in Buckinghamshire and Cambridgeshire with Tellings-Golden Miller and The Londoners in the south east. Operations in the north east are shown here. Pictured in Hylton Castle livery is Van Hool Alizée HIL6461. *Keith Grimes*

M1CLA	Volvo B10M-62	Caetano Algarve II 3.5m	C53F	1994
M10CLA	Dennis Dart 9.8SDL3040	Plaxton Pointer	B40F	1994
M30CLA	Volvo B10M-62	Caetano Algarve II 3.5m	C53F	1995
M40CLA	Volvo B10M-62	Caetano Algarve II 3.5m	C53F	1995
N3CLA	Volvo B10M-62	Van Hool Alizée H	C49FT	1996
P3CLA	Volvo B10M-62	Plaxton Premiere 350	C51FT	1997
P6CLA	Volvo B10M-62	Plaxton Premiere 350	C49FT	1997
P7CLA	Volvo B10M-62	Plaxton Premiere 350	C49FT	1997
P9CLA	Volvo B10M-62	Plaxton Premiere 350	C51FT	1997
R183TKU	Volvo B10M-62	Plaxton Premiere 350	C49FT	1998
R6CLA	Volvo B10M-62	Plaxton Excalibur	C49FT	1998
R7CLA	Volvo B10M-62	Plaxton Excalibur	C49FT	1998
R8CLA	Volvo B10M-62	Plaxton Premiere 350	C49FT	1998
R9CLA	Volvo B10M-62	Plaxton Premiere 350	C49FT	1998
S5CLA	Volvo B10M-62	Plaxton Premiere 350	C49FT	1999
S6CLA	Volvo B10M-62	Plaxton Premiere 350	C49FT	1999
T1CLA	Volvo B10M-62	Plaxton Premiere 350	C51FT	1999
T2CLA	Volvo B10M-62	Plaxton Premiere 350	C51FT	1999

Opposite:- **Volvo coaches dominate the Classic group's fleet. Illustrated are two different body makes. The upper picture shows Jonckheere Deauville 45 K919UBB in Primrose livery while the lower picture is Classic's P9CLA liveried for Skibound. K919UBB was pictured at Newgate, Barnard Castle while the Plaxton coach is seen in London.** *J C Walton/Colin Lloyd*

Moor-Dale have been a keen user of Bova Futura coaches, though only two now remain. Shown here is recently withdrawn N50MDC. *Terry Wightman*

UWW512X	MCW Metrobus DR101/15	Alexander RH	B43/32F	1982	Midland (Stevensons), 1998
EKA156Y	MCW Metrobus DR102/29	Alexander RH	B45/33F	1982	Bluebird, Middleton, 1998
DEM759Y	MCW Metrobus DR102/29	Alexander RH	B45/33F	1982	MTL (Merseybus), 1997
DEM762Y	MCW Metrobus DR102/29	Alexander RH	B45/33F	1982	MTL (Merseybus), 1997
ACM770X	MCW Metrobus DR104/9	Alexander RH	B45/31F	1982	MTL (Merseybus), 1996

Hylton Castle Coaches

TJI1683	Volvo B10M-61	Plaxton Supreme VI	C53FT	1982	Wickson, Walsall Wood, 1997
FDZ8195	Volvo B10M-61	Van Hool Alizée H	C53F	1984	Catch-a-Bus, East Boldon, 1997
FDZ1635	Volvo B10M-61	Van Hool Alizée H	C53F	1984	Catch-a-Bus, East Boldon, 1997
HIL6462	Volvo B10M-61	Van Hool Alizée H	C49FT	1984	Catch-a-Bus, East Boldon, 1997
HIL6461	Volvo B10M-61	Van Hool Alizée H	C53F	1985	Catch-a-Bus, East Boldon, 1997
F166XCS	Mercedes-Benz 609D	Scott	C24F	1989	Catch-a-Bus, East Boldon, 1997
F810OCN	Mercedes-Benz 609D	Reeve Burgess Beaver	B20F	1989	Catch-a-Bus, East Boldon, 1997
M63WEB	Volvo B10M-62	Plaxton Premiere 320	C53F	1995	Kenzie, Shepreth, 1998

Opposite, top:- **Classic Highstyle livery is applied to JSK346, a Plaxton Paramount 3500, built on a Volvo B10M chassis.** *David Longbottom*

Opposite, bottom:- **Classic took their Plaxton Excalibur R7CLA to the 1998 Brighton Coach Rally. The vehicle is seen in a livery that uses an effecive split between the two shades of red applied.** *Keith Grimes collection*

Primrose

PIL2165	Leyland Tiger TRCTL11/3RH	Duple Laser 2	C53FT	1985	
PIL2166	Leyland Tiger TRCTL11/3RH	Duple Laser 2	C53FT	1985	
PIL2167	Leyland Tiger TRCTL11/3RH	Duple 340	C49F	1986	Crosville Wales, 1988
PIL2169	Leyland Tiger TRCTL11/3RH	Duple 340	C49F	1986	Crosville Wales, 1988
PIL2164	Leyland Tiger TRCTL11/3ARZA	Duple 340	C53FT	1989	
PIL2168	Leyland Tiger TRCTL11/3ARZA	Duple 340	C49F	1991	
PIL2163	Volvo B10M-60	Van Hool Alizée H	C53F	1991	
PIL2160	Volvo B10M-62	Van Hool Alizée HE	C53F	1995	Park's of Hamilton, 1998
PIL2161	Volvo B10M-60	Jonckheere Deauville 45	C51FT	1993	Sinclair, Greenhead, 1998
PIL2162	Volvo B10M-60	Jonckheere Deauville 45	C51FT	1993	
PIL2170	Volvo B10M-62	Jonckheere Deauville 45	C51FT	1995	

Moor-Dale

01w	HKR11	Bova FHD12.290	Bova Futura	C49FT	1990	Northumbria, 1994
02	N2MDC	Bova FHD12.340	Bova Futura	C49FT	1995	
04	N4MDC	Bova FHD12.340	Bova Futura	C49FT	1995	
06w	NIL8887	Bova FHD12.290	Bova Futura	C49FT	1988	Northumbria, 1994
07	NIL4867	Bova FHD12.280	Bova Futura	C49FT	1984	Go-Ahead (OK), 1997
09	NIL2190	Bova FHD12.280	Bova Futura	C49FT	1985	Go-Ahead (OK), 1997
17	JVJ529	Volvo B10M-61	Plaxton Paramount 3500 III	C49FT	1987	
22	P22MDC	Volvo B10M-62	Berkhof Axial 50	C49FT	1997	
31	IIL9167	Volvo B10M-60	Plaxton Paramount 3500 III	C49FT	1989	
33	GSU346	Volvo B10M-60	Berkhof Excellence 2000	C49FT	1991	
34	GSU348	Volvo B10M-60	Berkhof Excellence 2000	C49FT	1993	
35	OSU895	Volvo B10M-62	Berkhof Excellence 2000	C47FT	1994	
50	N50MDC	Bova FHD12.340	Bova Futura	C34FT	1996	
87	TPN102S	Bristol VRT/SL3/6LXB	Eastern Coach Works	CO43/27D	1978	Northumbria, 1994

Previous Registrations

325CCE	F657JJR	NIL2190	B876HWP, HYY3, B113MNP, LSK807, B113MNP
387FYM	G349RTA, 425BYK, 961KVK	NIL4867	3TRB, RJU130Y, A504KFP, 685XHY, A504KFP
527LPF	D29BEW	NIL8887	E693JUT, GSU346, E693JUT
593CCE	J244LGL	OSU895	L385YCN
656CCE	J245LGL	PIL2160	LSK500, M826HNS
685XHY	K805BHN	PIL2161	L3KMS
956CCE	VDM175	PIL2162	K919UBB
CAZ6831	D814SGB, WHA325, D855FRF	PIL2163	H912EFT
FDZ1635	A173MNE	PIL2164	G141NPT
FDZ8195	A174MNE	PIL2165	B251JNL
GSU346	H383DBB	PIL2166	B252JNL
GSU348	K384RJR	PIL2167	C74KLG, XFM225
HIL6461	B488UNB	PIL2170	M416KCU
HIL6462	YMV352Y	TJI1683	UCX429X
HKR11	G119HVK, WSV513, NSM100	TVE804	J804TAJ
IIL9167	F381NVK	UGD735	F803UEF, 373FGB
J988TVU	J58MHF, J7SLT	VDM175	From new
JSK346	G61RGG	WOJ802	F802UEF
JVJ529	D269XRG		

Livery: Red, maroon and gold (Classic); primrose yellow and red (Primrose); white, red and yellow (Hylton Castle); gun-metal, red and yellow (Highstyle) and turquoise, red and navy (Moor-Dale)

COCHRANE'S

I&M Cochrane, Whitehouse Farm, Shotton Colliery, Durham, DH6 2NG

RRR517R	Bedford YMT	Plaxton Supreme III Express	C53F	1976	Watson, Blyth, 1987
1230HN	Bedford YMT	Plaxton Supreme IV	C53F	1979	Brown, Bedford, 1997
IAZ3924	Volvo B58-61	Plaxton Supreme IV	C57F	1979	Mullany, Watford, 1996
OAY294	DAF MB2000DKFL600	Plaxton Paramount 3200	C49FT	1983	EDT Travel, Hull, 1997
E500KEF	Volvo B10M-61	Caetano Algarve	C49FT	1987	Classic, Annfield Plain, 1998

Previous registrations:

1230HN	YAN815T	IAZ3924	GGD669T
E500KEF	E500KEF, 593CCE	OAY294	ANA443Y

Livery: White, red and yellow

The Caetano Algarve body was imported into Britain through agents Salvador Caetano UK Ltd of Heather in Leicestershire. Pictured on a visit to Wembley is Cochrane's Volvo E500KEF. A total of 311 Algarve 1s and 391 Algarve IIs have been supplied to the UK market, mostly on Volvo chassis, with DAF, Dennis and Bedford also featuring. *Colin Lloyd*

COMPASS ROYSTON

Compass Royston Travel Group Ltd, Bowesfield Lane, Stockton-on-Tees, TS18 3EG

Reg	Chassis	Body	Type	Year	History
LDC70P	Daimler Fleetline CRL6-30	Northern Counties	B43/31F	1975	Cleveland Transit, 1993
MOU746R	Bristol VRT/SL3/6LXB	Eastern Coach Works	B43/27D	1976	Nottingham, 1994
TMA326R	Bristol VRT/SL3/501	Eastern Coach Works	B43/31F	1976	PMT, 1991
WWY119S	Bristol VRT/SL3/6LXB	Eastern Coach Works	B43/31F	1977	Abbott, Stockton, 1992
TWN935S	Bristol VRT/SL3/501	Eastern Coach Works	B43/31F	1978	East Midland, 1993
HSD85V	Leyland Fleetline FE30AGR	Alexander AD	B44/31F	1980	Clydeside, 1995
HHN555V	Ford R1014	Plaxton Supreme IV	C45F	1980	Atkinson, Ingleby Arncliffe, 1993
322XTJ	Leyland Leopard PSU3E/4R	Duple Dominant II	C50F	1980	East Yorkshire Travel, 1995
EHE241V	Leyland Leopard PSU3E/4R	Duple Dominant II	C50F	1980	East Yorkshire Travel, 1995
BUH235V	Bristol VRT/SL3/501	Eastern Coach Works	B43/31F	1980	Red & White, 1993
GTX752W	Bristol VRT/SL3/501	Eastern Coach Works	B43/31F	1980	Red & White, 1993
MJI4693	Ford R1114	Plaxton Supreme IV	C53F	1981	Pridgeon, Charlton Kings, 1989
LIW4291	Volvo B10M-61	Duple Goldliner	C53F	1982	Lewis, Greenwich, 1997
PBZ8343	Volvo B10M-61	Plaxton Supreme V	C57F	1983	Atkinson, Ingleby Arncliffe, 199
HIL9271	Volvo B10M-61	Plaxton Paramount 3200	C53F	1983	Essex Coachways, Bow, 1997
1624WY	Volvo B10M-61	Plaxton Paramount 3500 III	C51F	1983	Darlington, 1995
4695WY	Volvo B10M-61	Plaxton Paramount 3500 III	C49F	1983	Darlington, 1995
TAZ4059	Volvo B10M-61	Plaxton Paramount 3200 II	C53F	1985	National Holidays, 1997
C223PTY	Mercedes-Benz L608D	Reeve Burgess	BC19F	1986	Go-Ahead (Northen), 1998
C401VVN	Mercedes-Benz L608D	Reeve Burgess	BC19F	1986	North East Bus (United), 1998
C429VVN	Mercedes-Benz L608D	Reeve Burgess	BC19F	1986	North East Bus (United), 1998
MIW9046	Volvo B10M-60	Plaxton Paramount 3500 III	C53F	1990	Dodsworth, Boroughbridge, 1994
LIL9814	Volvo B10M-60	Van Hool Alizée	C53F	1990	Wilson, Carnwath, 1996
LIL9815	Volvo B10M-60	Plaxton Paramount 3500 III	C50F	1990	Wallace Arnold, 1994
LIL9816	Volvo B10M-60	Plaxton Paramount 3500 III	C51F	1990	Wallace Arnold, 1994
MJI6254	Volvo B10M-60	Plaxton Premiére 350	C50F	1992	Wallace Arnold, 1995
M886WAK	Volvo B10M-62	Plaxton Premiére 350	C49FT	1995	
M992HHS	Volvo B10M-62	Jonckheere Deauville 45	C53F	1995	Park's of Hamilton, 1996
M993HHS	Volvo B10M-62	Jonckheere Deauville 45	C53F	1995	Park's of Hamilton, 1996
N32AAJ	Volvo B10M-62	Plaxton Premiére 320	C57F	1996	
P820GAJ	Volvo B10M-62	Jonckheere Mistral 50	C51FT	1997	
P821GAJ	Volvo B10M-62	Jonckheere Mistral 50	C51FT	1997	
P790GHN	Volvo B10M-62	Jonckheere Mistral 50	C51FT	1997	
R167SEF	Volvo B10M-62	Plaxton Premiére 350	C49FT	1997	
R168SEF	Volvo B10M-62	Plaxton Premiére 350	C49FT	1997	
R762OVN	Volvo B10M-62	Plaxton Premiére 350	C49FT	1998	
R763OVN	Volvo B10M-62	Plaxton Premiére 350	C49FT	1998	
R511WDC	Volvo B10M-62	Plaxton Premiére 350	C49FT	1998	
R512WDC	Volvo B10M-62	Plaxton Premiére 350	C49FT	1998	
S1MFC	Volvo B10M-62	Plaxton Premiére 350	C49FT	1998	
S121OEF	Volvo B10M-62	Plaxton Premiére 350	C49FT	1999	
S122OEF	Volvo B10M-62	Plaxton Premiére 350	C49FT	1999	
S13ORO	Volvo B10M-62	Plaxton Premiére 350	C49FT	1999	
T811JHN	Volvo B10M-62	Berkhof Axial 50	C49FT	1999	

Previous Registrations:

322XTJ	EHE238V	LIL9815	G522LWU	MJI4693	UDD266X
1624WY	FUA382Y	LIL9816	G523LWU	MJI6254	J709CWT
4295WY	FUA384Y	LIW4291	FHS748X	PBZ8343	AAJ674Y, GAZ4618
HIL9271	FUA390Y, 999BWC, UJN215Y	MIW9046	G719NWY	TAZ4059	B930MLN, B931MLN, 834EYD, B931MLN
LIL9814	G340HSC				

Livery: White and red; white and orange (National Holidays) LIL9814/5; white and blue (Leger Travel) R763OVN

Opposite:- **Compass Royston is based at Stockton and operate tours and day excursions from the area. In addition school duties require double-deck buses which will also be used for some local service work in 1999. Pictured at Whitby** *(above)* **is Jonckheere Mistral P820GAJ wearing the traditional livery, while the new livery is displayed on Plaxton Premiére 350, R511WDC seen in Trafalgar Square. The company currently operate two football team coaches, S1MFC for Middlesborough FC and S13ORO for Scarborough FC.**
Tony Wilson/Colin Lloyd

CROSSROADS

J Field, Leafield, Elm Crescent, Kimblesworth, Chester-le-Street, DH2 3QJ

LUG85P	Leyland Atlantean AN68A/1R	Roe		B43/33F	1975	Yorkshire Rider, 1994
LUG91P	Leyland Atlantean AN68A/1R	Roe		B43/33F	1975	Bell, Spennymoor, 1994
LUG106P	Leyland Atlantean AN68A/1R	Roe		B43/33F	1975	Yorkshire Rider, 1994
LUG112P	Leyland Atlantean AN68A/1R	Roe		B43/33F	1975	Yorkshire Rider, 1994
UPT101V	Leyland Leopard PSU3B/3R	Plaxton Paramount 3200			19	Mary in Dales, 1999
KPJ247W	Leyland Atlantean AN68/1R	Roe		B43/33F	1980	County, 1997
KPJ252W	Leyland Atlantean AN68/1R	Roe		B43/33F	1980	County, 1997
LUK10P	Volvo B58-61	Duple Dominant IV		C53F	1982	Priory, North Sheilds, 1998
A789UYL	Leyland Cub CU335	Wadham Stringer Vanguard		B24FL	1984	Greencroft Coaches, 1997
C200SLN	Leyland Cub CU335	Wadham Stringer Vanguard		BC22FL	1986	M Track, Crayford, 1997
D314PDM	Iveco Daily 49.10	Robin Hood City Nippy		B12FL	1986	M Track, Crayford, 1997
J781LNL	DAF 400	DAF		M16	1992	

Previous registrations:
LUK10P   TND116X, LIB6350, ONL707X

Livery: Red and white

Seen in Durham, Crossroads only Volvo LUK10P is a B58 with Duple Dominant IV bodywork, which was delivered new to Shearings. Much of the work undertaken by Crossroads revolves around school duties for which six Leyland Atlanteans are owned. *Terry Wightman*

D C TRAVEL

Starcalibre Ltd, North Bank Garage, Turner Street, Amble, Northumerland, NE65 0DH

YGR191R	Leyland Leopard PSU3E/4R	Plaxton Supreme III	C53F	1976	
MBC545V	Leyland Leopard PSU3E/4R	Duple Dominant II	C53F	1979	
JUI3085	Leyland Royal Tiger B50	Plaxton Paramount 3500	C49FT	1984	
TJI6572	Bova FLD12.250	Bova Futura	C53F	1984	Thomas, Portchester, 1998
IIL6235	Volvo B10M-61	Caetano Algarve	C49FT	1986	Diamond-Glantawe, Morriston, 1998
AIW6466	Hestair Duple SDA1510	Duple 425	C55FT	1987	
LBZ4329	Hestair Duple SDA1510	Duple 425	C54FT	1988	

Previous registrations:

AIW6466	E452CGM	MBC545V	EHE236V, RJI5722
IIL6235	C685KDS	TJI6572	125EJU, 5048PP, A901KRT, A7YEY, A84RUM
JUI3085	A325XHE, TJI6572	YGR191R	OWV280R, AIW6466
LBZ4329	E125LAD		

Named vehicles: MBC545V *Lady Claire*; AIW6466 *Lady Louise*; LBZ4239 *Lady Charlotte*; JUI3085 *Lady Jessica..*

Livery: Purple and yellow

Whitby is the setting for this picture of DC Travel's IIL6235, a Volvo B10M with Caetano Algarve bodywork. This operator has recently relocated in Amble and recent sales have eliminated the remaining light-weight chassis. *Tony Wilson*

DELTA

Delta - Cleveland Coaches

Delta Coaches Ltd, Blue House, Point Road, Stockton-on-Tees, TS18 2PJ

IIL2271	Bristol RELL6G	Eastern Coach Works	B53F	1971	Excelsior, Telford, 1988
AHT212J	Bristol RELL6L	Eastern Coach Works	B50F	1971	Bexhill Bus, 1994
IIL1839	Bristol RELL6G	Eastern Coach Works	B53F	1972	North Devon, 1986
HHW916L	Bristol RELL6G	Eastern Coach Works	B50F	1972	Bexhill Bus, 1994
VRN86R	Leyland Leopard PSU3D/4R	Duple Dominant I	C47F	1977	Hart, Stockton, 1995
PVB803S	Leyland Leopard PSU3E/4R	Duple Dominant II Express	C49F	1978	Thorpe, Horbury, 1991
BPY402T	Leyland Leopard PSU3E/4R	Plaxton Supreme IV Express	C53F	1979	Stagecoach Transit (C), 1995
CVN400T	Bedford YLQ/S	Duple Dominant II	C35F	1979	Stagecoach Transit (C), 1995
HPY426V	Leyland Leopard PSU3F/4R	Plaxton Supreme IV Express	C53F	1980	Stagecoach Transit (C), 1995
OHN427X	Leyland Leopard PSU3F/4R	Plaxton Supreme IV Express	C53F	1981	Stagecoach Transit (C), 1995
OHN428X	Leyland Leopard PSU3F/4R	Plaxton Supreme IV Express	C53F	1981	Stagecoach Transit (C), 1995
OHN429X	Leyland Leopard PSU3F/4R	Plaxton Supreme IV Express	C53F	1981	Stagecoach Transit (C), 1995
HRG920W	Leyland Tiger TRCTL11/3R	Duple Dominant	C55F	1981	Hart, Stockton, 1995
MTN874X	Leyland Tiger TRCTL11/3R	Duple Dominant	C55F	1982	Hart, Stockton, 1995
NDW139X	Leyland Tiger TRCTL11/2R	Plaxton Supreme V Express	C53F	1982	Gordon's, Rotherham, 1998
HIL6581	Volvo B10M-61	Jonckheere Jubilee P50	C49FT	1982	Jason, St Mary Cray, 1992
FIL8694	Leyland Tiger TRCTL11/3R	Padane ZX	C47FT	1982	Crescent, North Walsham, 1992
FSV578	Leyland Tiger TRCTL11/3R	Duple	C51F	1983	Hart, Stockton, 1995
A851UYM	Leyland Royal Tiger RT	Plaxton Paramount 3500	C53F	1984	Farrow, Melton Mowbray, 1992
HIL6408	Volvo B10M-61	Jonckheere Jubilee	C49FT	1986	Cantabrica, St Albans, 1993
D468YTN	Mercedes-Benz L608D	Reeve Burgess	C19F	1986	Bedlington & District, 1994
E811UHF	Mercedes-Benz 811D	Coachcraft	BC24F	1987	Neal & Patterson, Chippenham, 1993
OIB3512	Leyland Royal Tiger RTC	Roe Doyen	C53F	1987	Stagecoach Transit (C), 1995
PJI4986	Volvo B10M-61	Van Hool Alizée	C49FT	1988	Stagecoach Transit (C), 1995
85ROD	Volvo B10M-61	Plaxton Paramount 3500 III	C53FT	1988	Dodsworth, Boroughbridge, 1993
HIL6755	Volvo B10M-61	Duple 320	C53F	1988	Oriel, Enstone, 1990
H201XKH	Leyland Swift ST2R44C97T5	Reeve Burgess Harrier	C37F	1990	Stagecoach Transit (C), 1995
K5URE	Scania K113TRB	Van Hool Alizée SH	C48FT	1993	Allison's Coaches, Dunfermline, 1999
L404LHE	Scania K113CRB	Van Hool Alizée HE	C53F	1994	
USU907	Volvo B10M-62	Jonckheere Deauville	C53F	1994	
P630FTV	Volvo B10M-62	Jonckheere Mistral 50	C53FT	1997	
S25VVK	Volvo B10M-62	Plaxton ###	C53FT	1998	

Previous Registrations:

85ROD	E711TYG, HIL6755	HIL6755	F231OFP
A851UYM	A851UYM, HIL6587	IIL1839	TWX198L
D468YTN	D839UCU, 813VPU, D36YTN, KSU462	IIL2271	BVF668J
FIL8694	XPP289X	OIB3512	D455GHN
FSV578	FWH24Y	PJI4986	E304OPR, XEL608, E402SEL, XEL24, E455SEL, XEL24, E647SEL
HIL6408	C27GKX, 450CCH	USU907	M659GJF
HIL6581	ENV828X, 674SHY, ORL374X		

Livery: Red (buses); white, red and blue (Delta); white, yellow and orange (Cleveland coaches)

Opposite:- **Delta acquired the coaching operation of Stagecoach Transit during 1997 and continue to use the Cleveland Coaches name with a yellow and orange livery as illustrated in the upper picture which shows Plaxton-bodied HPY426V. The Delta name is carried by the majority of the fleet and this comprises a mainly white scheme as illustrated by Leyland Royal Tiger HIL6587, formerly A851UYM before re-registration. This rear engined chassis carries a Plaxton body, while one of the integral Doyen bodies is also operated by the company. Delta's buses carry a red livery.** *David Longbottom/JC Walton*

DODDS of ASHINGTON

J & M Dodds, 85 Seventh Row, Ashington, Northumberland, NE63 8HX

OAT603V	Volvo B58-61	Plaxton Supreme IV	C50F	1980	East Yorkshire Travel, 1995
D833KWT	Freight Rover Sherpa	Dormobile	BC16F	1987	Hennings, Thornley, 1994
E146KYW	MCW MetroRider MF150/38	MCW	B25F	1987	Stagecoach Busways, 1997
E979CCN	DAF MB230DKFL600	Plaxton Paramount 3200 III	C53F	1987	Rowells, Low Prudhoe, 1998
F132SMT	Mercedes-Benz 609D	Reeve Burgess Beaver	C23F	1989	Staines, Brentwood, 1994
LIL8970	Volvo B10M-60	Plaxton Paramount 3500 III	C49FT	1989	Premier Travel Services, 1995
LIL8971	Volvo B10M-61	Van Hool Alizée H	C51F	1989	MacPhail, Newarthill, 1995

Previous Registrations:

LIL8970	F325DCL		LIL8971	G879ODS	OAT603V	TNP9V, 787EYC

Livery: White

Depot: North Seaton Industrial Estate, Ashington

Dodds of Ashington is the name used by a small operation based in this Northumbrian town. Until recently local services were provided by the MetroRider, though this is now mostly used on school contract work.
David Longbottom

DURHAM CITY COACHES

Durham City Coaches Ltd, New Road Garage, Brandon Lane,
Brandon, Co Durham DH7 1PL

MRJ101W	Leyland Leopard PSU5D/5R	Plaxton Supreme IV	C49F	1981	Hall, Robin Hoods Bay, 1996
JSV487	Volvo B10M-61	Duple Caribbean	C55F	1982	Classic, Annfield Plain, 1998
MJI4735	Volvo B10M-61	Plaxton Paramount 3200 II	C57F	1985	Galloway, Harthill, 1996
L752YGE	Volvo B10M-62	Jonckheere Deauville 45	C53F	1994	Stonehouse Coaches, 1997
L7MJD	Volvo B10M-60	Jonckheere Deauville 45	C53F	1994	Wallace Arnold, 1998
N898NNR	Volvo B10M-62	Jonckheere Deauville 45	C53F	1995	Lochs and Glens, 1999
N2DCC	Volvo B10M-62	Jonckheere Deauville 45	C49FT	1996	
P7DCC	Volvo B10M-62	Jonckheere Mistral 50	C49FT	1997	
R7DCC	Volvo B10M-62	Jonckheere Mistral 50	C49FT	1998	
T7DCC	Volvo B10M-62	Jonckheere Mistral 50	C49FT	1999	

Previous Registrations:

JSV467	RBB359Y	L7MJD	L943NWW	MJI4735	B998YKJ

Livery: Black, red and gold

Durham City Coaches use a black-based livery as shown in this picture of N2DCC. A high proportion of the fleet comprises Jonckhere products and, with the latest arrivals, there are now three Mistral. N2DCC was the last only Deauville model purchased new. *Terry Wightman*

DURHAM TRAVEL

Durham Travel Services Ltd, Byron House, Seaham Grange, Co Durham SR7 0PW

8	N8DTS	Scania K113TRB	Irizar Century 12.37	C49FT	1996	
9	N9DTS	Scania K113TRB	Irizar Century 12.37	C49FT	1996	
10	R10DTS	Scania K113CRB	Irizar Century 12.35	C49FT	1998	
11	R11DTS	Scania K113CRB	Irizar Century 12.35	C49FT	1998	
12	T12DTS	Scania K124IB6	Irizar Century 12.37	C51FT	1999	
15	J15DTS	Scania K113CRB	Van Hool Alizée	C49FT	1992	
19	M131HVR	Scania K113CRB	Van Hool Alizée	C44FT	1995	
22	N22DTS	Volvo B10M-66SE	Plaxton Expressliner 2	C44FT	1995	
23	N23DTS	Volvo B10M-66SE	Plaxton Expressliner 2	C44FT	1996	
24	P24WNL	Volvo B10M-66SE	Plaxton Expressliner 2	C44FT	1996	
25	P25WNL	Volvo B10M-66SE	Plaxton Expressliner 2	C44FT	1996	
26	S26DTS	Scania K124IB4	Van Hool Alizée II	C44FT	1999	
27	S27DTS	Scania K124IB4	Van Hool Alizée II	C44FT	1999	
28	L28ABB	Scania K113CRB	Van Hool Alizée	C44FT	1994	
34	M34HJR	Scania K113CRB	Van Hool Alizée	C44FT	1995	
36	M36HJR	Scania K113CRB	Van Hool Alizée	C49FT	1995	
37	M37HJR	Scania K113CRB	Van Hool Alizée	C49FT	1995	
38	M38HJR	Scania K113CRB	Van Hool Alizée	C49FT	1995	
39	M39HJR	Scania K113CRB	Van Hool Alizée	C49FT	1995	
56	P56XNL	Volvo B10M-66SE	Plaxton Expressliner 2	C44FT	1996	
57	P57XNL	Volvo B10M-66SE	Plaxton Expressliner 2	C44FT	1996	
58	P58XNL	Volvo B10M-66SE	Plaxton Expressliner 2	C44FT	1996	
59	P59XNL	Volvo B10M-66SE	Plaxton Expressliner 2	C44FT	1996	

Tyne & Wear Care Bus

206	N306NBB	Renault Master T35D	Oughtred & Harrison	M11	1995	Go-Coastline, 1997
207	N307NBB	Renault Master T35D	Oughtred & Harrison	M11	1995	Bell & Lewis, 1997
208	N308NBB	Renault Master T35D	Oughtred & Harrison	M11	1995	Go-Coastline, 1997
231	M31FJR	Renault Master T35D	Atlas	M11	1994	Go-Coastline, 1997
232	M32FJR	Renault Master T35D	Atlas	M11	1994	Bell & Lewis, 1997
246	M246KBB	Renault Master T35D	Oughtred & Harrison	M11	1995	Go-Coastline, 1997
247	M247KBB	Renault Master T35D	Oughtred & Harrison	M11	1995	Bell & Lewis, 1997
248	M248KBB	Renault Master T35D	Oughtred & Harrison	M11	1995	Bell & Lewis, 1997
249	M249KBB	Renault Master T35D	Oughtred & Harrison	M11	1995	Go-Coastline, 1997
251	M251KBB	Renault Master T35D	Oughtred & Harrison	M11	1995	Bell & Lewis, 1997
252	M252KBB	Renault Master T35D	Oughtred & Harrison	M11	1995	Go-Coastline, 1997
253	M253KBB	Renault Master T35D	Oughtred & Harrison	M11	1995	Go-Coastline, 1997
254	M254KBB	Renault Master T35D	Oughtred & Harrison	M11	1995	Go-Coastline, 1997
255	M255KBB	Renault Master T35D	Oughtred & Harrison	M11	1995	Go-Coastline, 1997
256	M256MRD	Renault Master T35D	Atlas	M11	1991	Go-Coastline, 1997
269	M869KFT	Renault Master T35D	Oughtred & Harrison	M11	1995	Go-Coastline, 1997
270	M870KFT	Renault Master T35D	Oughtred & Harrison	M11	1995	Bell & Lewis, 1997
271	M871KFT	Renault Master T35D	Oughtred & Harrison	M11	1995	Go-Coastline, 1997
282	N152NTY	Renault Master T35D	Oughtred & Harrison	M11	1995	Go-Coastline, 1997
283	N153NTY	Renault Master T35D	Oughtred & Harrison	M11	1995	Bell & Lewis, 1997
284	N154NTY	Renault Master T35D	Oughtred & Harrison	M11	1995	Go-Coastline, 1997
293	J293SMO	Renault Master T35D	Atlas	M11	1991	Go-Coastline, 1997
294	J294SMO	Renault Master T35D	Atlas	M11	1991	Bell & Lewis, 1997
296	J296SMO	Renault Master T35D	Atlas	M11	1991	Bell & Lewis, 1997
297	J297SMO	Renault Master T35D	Atlas	M11	1991	Go-Coastline, 1997
298	J298SMO	Renault Master T35D	Atlas	M11	1991	Go-Coastline, 1997
299	J299SMO	Renault Master T35D	Atlas	M11	1991	Go-Coastline, 1997
	S448OCU	Renault Master T35D	Atlas	M11	1999	
	R433MHC	Renault Master T35D	Atlas	M11	1998	

Previous registrations

871R	RJI5755		BYW435V	YXI3751	NEO832R

Liveries: Green and cream (6/7, 15/9); Green and white (Care buses)

*Opposite:-***Durham Travel provide many National Express services in addition to running the Tyne & Wear Care service. The upper picture shows 56, P56XNL, while in its own striking livery is Scania 11, R11TDS, one of five Irizar Century coaches currently operated.** *Colin Lloyd/Terry Wightman*

ERB SERVICES

E Brown, Hannington Place, Byker Bridge, Newcastle-upon-Tyne, NE6 1JT

A2	R667GCU	Mercedes-Benz 312D	Minibus Options	M16	1997	
	N717STY	Mercedes-Benz 412D	Minibus Options	M15	1996	
	B674CJW	Ford Transit 160	Dewey	M14L	1985	Lowdon, Sunnyside, 1996
	H898VWA	Ford Transit VE6	Dormobile	M14L	1991	Smith SD, Rotherham, 1997
B1	D884WTY	Mercedes-Benz 609D	Devon Conversions	BC18FL	1987	Jumbulance Project, Newcastle, 1991
B2	E857ETY	Mercedes-Benz 609D	Reeve Burgess Beaver	BC24F	1988	
B3	F108MVK	Mercedes-Benz 609D	Reeve Burgess Beaver	BC23F	1989	
C1	T284BNL	Mercedes-Benz Vario O810	Autobus Classique Nouvelle 2	C33F	1999	
C2	G665OVO	Mercedes-Benz 814D	Reeve Burgess Beaver	BC33F	1990	Ace, Mansfield, 1992
C4	N507NVK	Mercedes-Benz 814D	Plaxton Beaver	BC33F	1995	
C5	K961RMW	Mercedes-Benz 811D	Plaxton Beaver	BC33F	1992	Andy Jones, Tetbury, 1995
	K894CSG	Mercedes-Benz 814D	Plaxton Beaver	BC33F	1992	Kelty Minicoaches, 1999
	H856NOC	Iveco Daily 49.10	Carlyle Dailybus 2	B21F	1991	Carlyle demonstrator, 1992
	TBI4569	Leyland Swift ST2R44C97T5	Elme Orion	BC33FL	1991	Jumbulance, Newcastle, 1997

Previous registrations:

K961RMW	K30ARJ		TIB4569	H210XHG

Livery: Maroon and cream

The Plaxton Beaver has been produced with many variations, the more common being the bus version with express doors and one aimed for the private hire market with a single leaf door. Pictured here is ERB's K961RMW which contains thirty-three seats and is one of five similar vehicles currently in use. Plaxton acquired the Reeve Burgess business and later moved from Chesterfield to Anston near Sheffield, in 1991, continuing to build the product but under the Plaxton name. *David Longbottom*

ESCORT

T Wilson, 2 Rennie Road, Skippers Lane Industrial Estate, Middlesborough, TS6 6PX

HIL3078	DAF MB200DKVL600	Jonckheere Jubilee	C49FT	1986	Watsons, Guisborough, 1995
4439TW	Volvo B10M-61	Caetano Algarve	C53F	1985	Daish, Shanklin, 1996
WFU469V	Leyland Fleetline FE30AGR	Roe	B45/29D	1980	Myall & Walsh, Hyde, 1996
CAY213Y	Bova EL28/581	Bova Europa	C53FT	1983	Hurdiss, Worcester, 1997
VWG360Y	DAF MB200DKTL600	Plaxton Paramount 3200	C57F	1983	Continental, Middlesbrough, 1998

Previous Registrations:

4439TW	B723MBC, HHC794	CAY213Y	CAY213Y, UCJ402

HIL3078	C362SVV

Livery: White

Escort's fleet includes Jonckheere Jubilee coach HIL3078 which is seen near its base. Jonckheere build coaches at a unit in Roeselare in Belgium, the Jubilee being the first model to be imported into the UK in significant numbers having replaced the Bermuda in 1982. *David Longbottom*

FAIRLEY'S

R Fairley, 28 Hawthorn Road, Spennymoor, County Durham, DL16 7EN

802KRO	Volvo B58-61	Duple Dominant IV	C54F	1981	Cousins, Belmont, 1995
EKA157Y	MCW Metrobus DR102/29	Alexander RH	B45/33F	1982	MTL (Merseybus), 1996
BBV774Y	Bedford YNT	Plaxton Paramount 3200	C53F	1983	Hodson, Gisburn, 1997
4796EL	Volvo B10M-61	Van Hool Astral	C47/11FT	1984	Ellerby, Wolsingham, 1990
C617XVU	Freight Rover Sherpa	Mellor	M12	1986	GEC Marconi, Edinburgh, 1997
C631PAU	DAF MB200DKFL615	Plaxton Paramount 3200 II	C53F	1986	B&M Coaches, Sedgefield, 1998
E767HJF	Toyota Coaster HB31R	Caetano Optimo	C21F	1988	Martin, Normanton, 1997
G816NCA	Mercedes-Benz 814D	North West Coach Sales	BC26F	1989	Buckle, Heath Charnock, 1996
M784VJO	Dennis Javelin 12SDA2148	Caetano Algarve II	C49FT	1995	B&M, Coaches, Sedgefield, 1996
N990AEF	Mercedes-Benz 814L	Buscraft Impala	C31F	1996	Earl, Stockton, 1998

Previous Registrations:

802KRO	TSU300W	4796EL	A904JEF	BBV774Y	BBV774Y, HAZ2958

Livery: White and purple

Depot: Unit 13, Tudhoe Industrial Estate, Tudhoe

During Spring 1999 several of the Football League clubs from the north east paid visits to Wembley for Divisional play-offs. For each visit there was a cavalcade of coaches. Fairley's Volvo 802KRO was pictured making its arrival. This vehicle is now the oldest coach in the fleet. *Colin Lloyd*

FIRST CHOICE TRAVEL

HT Cooper, Strawberry Farm, Gilesgate Moor, Durham, DH1 2RQ

EAV810V	Volvo B58-56	Duple Dominant II Express	C53F	1980	Scandle, Prudhoe, 1997
USU643	Volvo B58-61	Duple Dominant IV	C53F	1981	Austin Earlston, 1998
OIL8657	Volvo B10M-61	Jonckheere Jubilee	C50FT	1983	Dover, Hetton, 1999
D139VRP	Mercedes-Benz L608D	Robin Hood	B20F	1986	Mk Metro, 1998
EYD2T	Volvo B10M-61	Duple 340	C46FT	1987	East Yorkshire Travel, 1997
KAZ4551	Volvo B10M-60	Van Hool Alizée	C53F	1989	Wilson, Carnwath, 1998
PIL9326	Volvo B10M-60	Van Hool Alizée	C53F	1989	?, 1998
G116ERF	Mercedes-Benz 609D		B25F	1989	?, 1999

Previous registrations:

EYD2T	D33OKH	PIL9376	F953WSF, SV2923, F953WSF
KAZ4551	F953WSF, SV2923	USU643	ASM377W
OIL8657	A312XHE, 163PPB, A425XOS, LIB9415, A926MSH		

Livery: White or silver with red, green and orange.

Van Hool Alizée KAZ4551 from First Choice Travel is seen in Sunderland while operating a private hire. The vehicle is one of two Van Hool coaches in the fleet which is based in Durham. The company have ceased to undertake local services and the Leyland Nationals were sold earlier in 1999. School contract and continental tours now provide work for the fleet. *Terry Wightman*

GALAXY TRAVEL

M Briggs, 29 Fernwood, Redcar, Cleveland, TS10 4NF

KDW330P	Leyland National 11351/1R		B49F	1976	Provincial, 1997
LFM527T	Bedford YMT	Plaxton Supreme III Express	C53F	1979	Hart, Stockton, 1993
89HBC	Leyland Leopard PSU5D/5R	Plaxton Supreme IV	C49F	1980	Stagecoach Transit, 1998
WSV517	Volvo B58-61	Duple Dominent III	C57F	1981	Henning, Thornley, 1995
A966KAJ	Mercedes-Benz L608D	Plaxton Mini Supreme	C25F	1984	Luckett, Fareham, 1990
MIL4397	Bova FHD12.280	Bova Futura	C49FT	1984	Renton, Edinburgh, 1996
MIL9302	Bova FHD12.250	Bova Futura	C49F	1984	J&C Newton Aycliffe, 1992
B674EVW	Bedford VAS5	Plaxton Supreme IV	C29F	1985	Roberts Coaches, Maerdy, 1998

Previous Registrations

89HBC	CTD133V	MIL4397	A658EMY, HIL5689, A678FRC
A966KAJ	A600OHD, WSV520	WSV517	HSP593W, 4585SC, XGB63W
B674EVW	B95PLU, FHV504		

Depot: Limerick Road, Redcar.

GARDINERS

Gardiner Bros Ltd, Coulson Street, Spennymoor, Co Durham, DL16 7RS

KHT116P	Leyland National 11351/1R		B52F	1976	Badgerline, 1994
E814BMJ	MCW MetroRider MF150/35	MCW	B25F	1987	Smith, Ashington, 1997
WBB962	Volvo B10M-61	Plaxton P'mount 3200(1990)	C57F	1987	Wilson, Carnwath, 1989
WDO759	Volvo B10M-60	Van Hool Alizée	C55F	1989	
UFE712	Volvo B10M-60	Plaxton Paramount 3500 III	C49FT	1991	Park's of Hamilton
H684YGO	Optare MetroRider MR03	Optare	B26F	1991	Epsom Buses, 1999
H685YGO	Optare MetroRider MR03	Optare	B26F	1991	Epsom Buses, 1999
L5GAR	Volvo B10M-60	Jonckheere Deauville 45	C53FT	1997	Dunn Line, Nottingham, 1999

Previous Registrations:

L5GAR	M731KJU	WBB962	D960HMS
UFE712	H945DRJ	WDO759	F830XAJ

Livery: White, orange and brown.

KHT116P is the sole Leyland National remaining on Durham local services operated by Gardiners. It is supported by three MetroRiders. *Terry Wightman*

Gardiners' L5GAR index mark adorns the latest arrival in the fleet, a Jonckheere bodied Volvo. The vehicle is seen in Sunderland and following its arrival all the large coaches are now Volvo products. *Terry Wightman*

GARNETTS

L Garnett, Unit E1 Romanway Industrial Estate, Tindale Crescent,
Co Durham, DL14 9AW

NEL113P	Leyland Leopard PSU3C/4R	Plaxton Supreme III Express	C49F	1976	Highway, Portsmouth, 1993
LJA621P	Leyland Atlantean AN68A/1R	Northern Counties	B43/32F	1976	Maidstone & District, 1997
MVK515R	Leyland Atlantean AN68A/2R	Alexander AL	B48/33F	1976	Northumbria, 1997
RUS311R	Leyland Atlantean AN68A/1R	Alexander AL	B45/31F	1976	Fairley's, Tudhoe, 1997
SRJ746R	Leyland Atlantean AN68A/1R	Northern Counties	B43/32F	1977	Maidstone & District, 1997
RCU835S	Leyland Fleetline FE30AGR	Alexander AL	B44/27F	1977	Bainbridge, Clifton, 1997
VFT190T	Leyland Atlantean AN68/2R	MCW	B49/37F	1979	Go-Ahead Northern (T), 1992
XPG196T	Leyland Atlantean AN68A/1R	Roe	B43/30F	1979	Kentish Bus, 1997
YNL213V	Leyland Atlantean AN68A/2R	MCW	B49/37F	1979	Go-Ahead Northern, 1991
KBH845V	Leyland Leopard PSU3E/4R	Plaxton Supreme IV	C53F	1979	OK Travel, 1997
SPT964V	Leyland Leopard PSU3E/4R	Plaxton Supreme IV Express	C53F	1980	OK Travel, 1997
CUL139V	Leyland Titan TNLXB2RRSp	Park Royal	B44/24D	1980	Allison's Dunfermline, 1999
EPH222V	Leyland Atlantean AN68A/1R	Roe	B43/30F	1980	Maidstone & District, 1997
EPH231V	Leyland Atlantean AN68A/1R	Roe	B43/30F	1980	Kentish Bus, 1997
KPJ265W	Leyland Atlantean AN68B/1R	Roe	B43/30F	1981	Arriva Southern Counties (KT), 1998
KYW372X	Leyland Titan TNLXB2RR	Leyland	B44/26F	1981	Allison's Dunfermline, 1999
A886SYE	Leyland Titan TNLXB2RR	Leyland	B44/26D	1983	London Central, 1998
RIL3998	Volvo B10M-61	Jonckheere Jubilee P599	C49F	19##	###, 1999
NTK611	Leyland Tiger TRCTL11/3R	Duple Laser	C53F	1983	Arriva Southern Counties (NE), 1998
HIL5835	Volvo B10M-62	Caetano Algarve II	C53F	1995	Don Smith, Murton, 1998
M712MRU	Volvo B10M-62	Plaxton Excalibur	C49FT	1995	Excelsior, Bournemouth, 1999

Livery: White, red and yellow

Previous registrations:

HIL5835	M574JBC		NTK611	A181MKE
M712MRU	A4EXC		RIL3998	?

While the mainstay of Garnetts' operation is school contract work, excursions are also undertaken. Pictured while performing a Wembley run is Leyland Leopard NEL113P. Visible in the picture is the doorway arrangement fitted to the express version which, from the mid 1970s to mid 1980s, allowed the vehicle to qualify for a bus grant towards its inital cost.
Keith Grimes

GEORGE BELL

G Bell, 13 Pottery Road, Sunderland, SR5 2BT

F911YWY	Mercedes-Benz 811D	Optare StarRider	B26F	1988	London Central, 1998
G222KWE	Mercedes-Benz 811D	Reeve Burgess Beaver	B26F	1989	City Line (Oxford), 1998
G621XLO	Mercedes-Benz 811D	Reeve Burgess Beaver	B29F	1989	City Line (Oxford), 1998
H11JYM	Mercedes-Benz 709D	Reeve Burgess Beaver	B25F	1990	Halton Mini Coaches, 1997
H104HDV	Mercedes-Benz 811D	Carlyle	B27F	1991	Thames Transit, 1998
H154UUA	Optare MetroRider MR03	Optare	B26F	1991	Stagecoach Selkent, 1998
L17LJE	Volvo B10M-60	Plaxton Premiere	C F	1994	?, 1999
M609WFS	Mercedes-Benz 709D	Alexander Sprint	B29F	1995	ALine, Felling, 1997

Previous Registrations:

H11JYM   H907SHL

Livery: White and blue (coaches), white (buses)

Depot: Pallion Quay, Pallion, Sunderland.

Recent fleet changes have seen the withdrawal of several minibuses including the Renault-Dodge S56 models which were a common sight in Sunderland. Pictured on Sunderland services is one of the Mercedes-Benz. *Terry Wightman*

GO NORTH EAST

Go-Northern - Go-Wear Buses - Go-Coastline - Go-Gateshead

Go-Ahead Group plc, 117 Queen Street, Bensham, Gateshead, NE8 2UA

333-346	Optare MetroRider MR03			Optare			B26F*	1991	*333/59/4-are B25F
333	J933JJR	336	J936JJR	339	J939JJR	342	J942JJR	345	J945JJR
334	J934JJR	337	J937JJR	340	J940JJR	343	J943JJR	346	J946JJR
335	J935JJR	338	J938JJR	341	J941JJR	344	J944JJR		

351-367	Optare MetroRider MR03			Optare			B26F*	1993	*367 is B35F
351	K351SCN	355	K355SCN	359	K359SCN	362	K362SCN	365	K365SCN
352	K352SCN	356	K356SCN	360	K360SCN	363	K363SCN	366	K366SCN
353	K353SCN	357	K357SCN	361	K361SCN	364	K364SCN	367	K367SCN
354	K354SCN	358	K358SCN						

372	L972WTY	Optare MetroRider MR05	Optare	B25F	1993
373	L973WTY	Optare MetroRider MR05	Optare	B25F	1993
374	L974WTY	Optare MetroRider MR05	Optare	B25F	1993
375	L975WTY	Optare MetroRider MR05	Optare	B25F	1993

376-402	Optare MetroRider MR13			Optare			B26F*	1993-94	*376-88/93-402 are B25F
376	L376YFT	382	L382YFT	388	L388YFT	393	M933FTN	398	M938FTN
377	L377YFT	383	L383YFT	389	L389AVK	394	M934FTN	399	M939FTN
378	L378YFT	384	L384YFT	390	L390AVK	395	M935FTN	400	M940FTN
379	L379YFT	385	L385YFT	391	L391AVK	396	M936FTN	401	L471YVK
380	L380YFT	386	L386YFT	392	L392AVK	397	M937FTN	402	L472YVK
381	L381YFT	387	L387YFT						

403-407	Optare MetroRider MR17			Optare			B25F*	1994	*403 is B31F
403	M3GYP	404	M504HNL	405	M505HNL	406	M506HNL	407	M507HNL

409-413	Optare MetroRider MR17			Optare			B26F	1995	
409	N409NTN	410	N410NTN	411	N411NTN	412	N412NTN	413	N413NTN

414-429	Optare MetroRider MR17			Optare			B25F	1996	
414	P414VRG	418	P418VRG	421	P421VRG	424	P424VRG	427	P427VRG
415	P415VRG	419	P419VRG	422	P422VRG	425	P425VRG	428	P428VRG
416	P416VRG	420	P420VRG	423	P423VRG	426	P426VRG	429	P429VRG
417	P417VRG								

431	E751VJO	MCW MetroRider MF150/26	MCW	B25F	1987	Oxford Citybus, 1998
434	E754VJO	MCW MetroRider MF150/26	MCW	B25F	1987	Oxford Citybus, 1998
438	E758XWL	MCW MetroRider MF150/51	MCW	B25F	1987	Oxford Citybus, 1998
439	E759XWL	MCW MetroRider MF150/51	MCW	B25F	1987	Oxford Citybus, 1998
445	F502ANY	MCW MetroRider MF150/109	MCW	B23F	1989	Oxford Citybus, 1998

448-469	Optare M850			Optare Solo			N25F	1998	
448	S248KNL	453	S253KNL	458	T458BCN	462	T462BCN	466	T466BCN
449	S249KNL	454	S254KNL	459	T459BCN	463	T463BCN	467	T467BCN
450	S250KNL	455	S255KNL	460	T460BCN	464	T464BCN	468	T468BCN
451	S251KNL	456	T456BCN	461	T461BCN	465	T465BCN	469	T469BCN
452	S252KNL	457	T457BCN						

Opposite:- **Go-Ahead has grown significantly from its northeast base now owning Brighton & Hove Bus and Coach Company, London Central Bus Company, London General Transport Services and Oxford Bus Company with its High Wycombe unit. In addition, Go-Ahead run two rail franchise companies. Pictured in the new livery are 340, J940JJR, an Optare MetroRider and double-deck Metrobus 3628, A628BCN.**
Tony Wilson

| 3489 | DVK489W | MCW Metrobus DR101/11 | MCW | | | B46/30F | 1980 | | |
| 3491 | DVK491W | MCW Metrobus DR101/11 | MCW | | | B46/30F | 1980 | | |

3501-3510

MCW Metrobus DR102/37* — MCW — B46/31F — 1983 — *3506-10 are DR132/1

3501	UTN501Y	3503	UTN503Y	3505	UTN505Y	3507	UTN507Y	3509	UTN509Y
3502	UTN502Y	3504	UTN504Y	3506	UTN506Y	3508	UTN508Y	3510	UTN510Y

3511-3519

MCW Metrobus DR101/12 — MCW — B43/29F 1980 — London General, 1998
*3511 is DR101/8, 3512/3 are DR101/9

3511	WYW55T	3513	BYX153V	3516	BYX218V	3518	BYX250V	3519	BYX268V
3512	BYX141V	3515	BYX217V	3517	BYX247V					

3520	C520LJR	Leyland Olympian ONCL10/1RV	Eastern Coach Works	BC45/27F	1985	
3521	C521LJR	Leyland Olympian ONCL10/1RV	Eastern Coach Works	BC45/27F	1985	
3522	C522LJR	Leyland Olympian ONCL10/1RV	Eastern Coach Works	BC45/27F	1985	
3523	C523LJR	Leyland Olympian ONCL10/1RV	Eastern Coach Works	BC45/27F	1985	
3527	EJR127W	Leyland Atlantean AN68A/2R	Alexander AL	BC45/33F	1981	Tyne & Wear PTE, 1981
3530	EJR130W	Leyland Atlantean AN68A/2R	Alexander AL	BC45/33F	1981	Tyne & Wear PTE, 1981
3534	GYE381W	MCW Metrobus DR101/12 *	MCW	B43/29F	1980	London General, 1997
3538	MBR438T	Leyland Atlantean AN68A/1R	Eastern Coach Works	B43/23F	1979	
3539	MBR439T	Leyland Atlantean AN68A/1R	Eastern Coach Works	B43/31F	1979	
3540	MBR440T	Leyland Atlantean AN68A/1R	Eastern Coach Works	B43/23F	1979	
3558	MBR458T	Leyland Atlantean AN68A/1R	Eastern Coach Works	B43/31F	1979	

3572-3617

Leyland Olympian ONLXB/1R — Eastern Coach Works — B45/32F — 1981-83

3572	JTY372X	3582	JTY382X	3592	JTY392X	3601	JTY401X	3610	JTY370X
3573	JTY373X	3584	JTY384X	3593	JTY393X	3602	JTY402X	3611	JTY371X
3574	JTY374X	3585	JTY385X	3594	JTY394X	3603	JTY403X	3612	SJR612Y
3575	JTY375X	3586	JTY386X	3595	JTY395X	3605	JTY405X	3613	SJR613Y
3577	JTY377X	3587	JTY387X	3597	JTY397X	3606	JTY406X	3614	SJR614Y
3578	JTY378X	3588	JTY388X	3598	JTY398X	3607	JTY407X	3615	SJR615Y
3579	JTY379X	3589	JTY389X	3599	JTY399X	3608	JTY408X	3616	SJR616Y
3580	JTY380X	3590	JTY390X	3600	JTY400X	3609	JTY409X	3617	SJR617Y
3581	JTY381X	3591	JTY391X						

3618-3648

MCW Metrobus DR102/43 — MCW — B46/31F — 1984

3618	A618BCN	3624	A624BCN	3631	A631BCN	3636	A636BCN	3642	A642BCN
3619	A619BCN	3625	A625BCN	3632	A632BCN	3637	A637BCN	3645	A645BCN
3620	A620BCN	3627	A627BCN	3633	A633BCN	3639	A639BCN	3646	A646BCN
3621	A621BCN	3628	A628BCN	3634	A634BCN	3640	A640BCN	3647	A647BCN
3622	A622BCN	3629	A629BCN	3635	A635BCN	3641	A641BCN	3648	A648BCN
3623	A623BCN	3630	A630BCN						

3649-3674

Leyland Olympian ONCL10/1RV* — Eastern Coach Works — B45/32F*1985 — *3652/67/8 are BC40/30F
*3674 has a Gardner 5LXCT engine; 3663 is B43/32F; 3669-71 are B45/32F

3649	C649LJR	3655	C655LJR	3660	C660LJR	3665	C665LJR	3670	C670LJR
3650	C650LJR	3656	C656LJR	3661	C661LJR	3666	C666LJR	3671	C671LJR
3651	C651LJR	3657	C657LJR	3662	C662LJR	3667	C667LJR	3672	C672LJR
3652	C652LJR	3658	C658LJR	3663	C663LJR	3668	C668LJR	3673	C673LJR
3653	C653LJR	3659	C659LJR	3664	C664LJR	3669	C669LJR	3674	C674LJR
3654	C654LJR								

3675-3679

Leyland Olympian ONCL10/1RZ — Alexander RH — B45/29F — 1989

3675	G675TCN	3676	G676TCN	3677	G677TCN	3678	G678TCN	3679	G679TCN

3680	BYX236V	MCW Metrobus DR101/12	MCW	B43/29F	1980	London General, 1998
3682	TSD611S	Leyland Atlantean AN68A/1R	Alexander AL	B45/33F	1977	OK Travel, 1995
3699	VFT199T	Leyland Atlantean AN68/2R	MCW	B49/37F	1979	OK Travel, 1995

Eastern Coach Works provided the bodywork on early Leyland Olympians delivered to the company while they were part of the National Bus Company. One of those fitted with high-back seating for use on the longer routes is 3671, C671LJR which is seen arriving in Newcastle on service 308. *Malcolm King*

3734-3748

Leyland Olympian ONLC10/1RV Eastern Coach Works B45/32F 1985

3734	B734GCN	3737	B737GCN	3740	B740GCN	3743	B743GCN	3746	B746GCN
3735	B735GCN	3738	B738GCN	3741	B741GCN	3744	B744GCN	3747	B747GCN
3736	B736GCN	3739	B739GCN	3742	B742GCN	3745	B745GCN	3748	B748GCN

3750-3778

MCW Metrobus DR102/55 MCW B46/31F* 1986 *3756 is BC43/29F

3750	C750OCN	3755	C755OCN	3760	C760OCN	3765	C765OCN	3771	C771OCN
3751	C751OCN	3756	C756OCN	3761	C761OCN	3766	C766OCN	3775	C775OCN
3752	C752OCN	3757	C757OCN	3762	C762OCN	3767	C767OCN	3776	C776OCN
3753	C753OCN	3758	C758OCN	3763	C763OCN	3768	C768OCN	3777	C777OCN
3754	C754OCN	3759	C759OCN	3764	C764OCN	3769	C769OCN	3778	C778OCN

3781-3789

MCW Metrobus DR102/58 MCW BC43/29F 1986

3781	C781OCN	3783	C783OCN	3785	C785OCN	3787	C787OCN	3789	C789OCN
3782	C782OCN	3784	C784OCN	3786	C786OCN	3788	C788OCN		

3793	AVK152V	Leyland Atlantean AN68A/2R	Alexander AL	B49/37F	1980	OK Travel, 1995
3794	AVK155V	Leyland Atlantean AN68A/2R	Alexander AL	B49/37F	1980	OK Travel, 1995
3795	AVK165V	Leyland Atlantean AN68A/2R	Alexander AL	B49/37F	1980	OK Travel, 1995
3796	AVK175V	Leyland Atlantean AN68A/2R	Alexander AL	B49/37F	1980	OK Travel, 1995
3806	F106UEF	Leyland Olympian ONCL10/2R	Northern Counties Palatine	B47/35F	1989	OK Travel, 1995
3807	F107UEF	Leyland Olympian ONCL10/2R	Northern Counties Palatine	B47/35F	1989	OK Travel, 1995
3808	K108YVN	Leyland Olympian ON2R56C16Z4	Northern Counties Palatine	B47/35F	1992	OK Travel, 1995
3809	K109YVN	Leyland Olympian ON2R56C16Z4	Northern Counties Palatine	B47/35F	1992	OK Travel, 1995
3810	K110YVN	Leyland Olympian ON2R56C16Z4	Northern Counties Palatine	B47/35F	1992	OK Travel, 1995

3811-3833 — Volvo Olympian — Northern Counties Palatine II — B47/30F — 1998

3811	S811FVK	3816	S816FVK	3821	S821OFT	3826	S826OFT	3830	S830OFT
3812	S812FVK	3817	S817FVK	3822	S822OFT	3827	S827OFT	3831	S831OFT
3813	S813FVK	3818	S818OFT	3823	S823OFT	3828	S828OFT	3832	S832OFT
3814	S814FVK	3819	S819OFT	3824	S824OFT	3829	S829OFT	3833	S833OFT
3815	S815FVK	3820	S820OFT	3825	S825OFT				

4660-4685 — Leyland National 2 NL116L11/1R — B49F* — 1980 — *4675 is B45F

4660	UPT660V	4665	UPT665V	4670	UPT670V	4675	UPT675V	4680	UPT680V
4661	UPT661V	4666	UPT666V	4671	UPT671V	4676	UPT676V	4681	UPT681V
4662	UPT662V	4667	UPT667V	4672	UPT672V	4677	UPT677V	4683	UPT683V
4663	UPT663V	4668	UPT668V	4673	UPT673V	4678	UPT678V	4684	UPT684V
4664	UPT664V	4669	UPT669V	4674	UPT674V	4679	UPT679V	4685	UPT685V

4686-4714 — Leyland National 2 NL116L11/1R — B49F* — 1980-81 — *4698/700/14 are B45F

4686	BGR686W	4695	FTN695W	4701	FTN701W	4706	FTN706W	4711	FTN711W
4687	BGR687W	4697	FTN697W	4702	FTN702W	4707	FTN707W	4712	FTN712W
4688	BGR688W	4698	FTN698W	4703	FTN703W	4708	FTN708W	4713	FTN713W
4691	WPT691V	4699	FTN699W	4704	FTN704W	4709	FTN709W	4714	FTN714W
4694	FTN694W	4700	FTN700W	4705	FTN705W	4710	FTN710W		

4715-4721 — Leyland National 2 NL116AHLXB/1R — B49F* — 1983 — *4717 is BC49F

4715	TJR715Y	4717	TJR717Y	4719	TJR719Y	4720	TJR720Y	4721	TJR721Y
4716	TJR716Y	4718	TJR718Y						

4722-4733 — Leyland Lynx LX1126LXCTZR1R* Leyland — B47F — 1989
*4728/33 are type LX116TL11ZR1S; 4729-32 are LX1126LXCTZR1S; 4733 fitted with Cummins engine

4722	F722LRG	4725	F725LRG	4728	F728LRG	4730	F730LRG	4732	F732LRG
4723	F723LRG	4726	F726LRG	4729	F729LRG	4731	F731LRG	4733	F733LRG
4724	F724LRG	4727	F727LRG						

4734-4747 — DAF SB220LC550 — Optare Delta — B49F — 1989

4734	G734RTY	4737	G737RTY	4740	G740RTY	4743	G743RTY	4746	G746RTY
4735	G735RTY	4738	G7348TY	4741	G741RTY	4744	G744RTY	4747	G747RTY
4736	G736RTY	4739	G7349TY	4742	G742RTY	4745	G745RTY		

4749	E107DJR	Volvo B10M-61	Duple 300	B55F	1987	Gypsy Queen, Langley Park, 1989

4750-4754 — DAF SB220LC550 — Optare Delta — B49F — 1990

4750	G755UCU	4751	G751UCU	4752	G752UCU	4753	G753UCU	4754	G754UCU

4756-4761 — DAF SB220LC550 — Optare Delta — B49F — 1993

4756	K756SBB	4758	K758SBB	4759	K759SBB	4760	K760SBB	4761	K761SBB
4757	K757SBB								

4768	J110SPB	Dennis Lance 11SDA3101	Alexander PS	B50F	1992	Dennis demonstrator, 1993

4769-4773 — Dennis Lance 11SDA3201 — Wright Pathfinder 320 — B40F — 1994

4769	L469YVK	4770	M470FJR	4771	M471FJR	4772	M472FJR	4773	M473FJR

4774	L141YTY	Dennis Lance 11SDA3112	Plaxton Verde	B49F	1994

4775-4788 — Dennis Lance 11SDA3113 — Optare Sigma — B47F — 1994

4775	L475CFT	4778	L478CFT	4781	L481CFT	4784	L484CFT	4787	L487CFT
4776	L476CFT	4779	L479CFT	4782	L482CFT	4785	L485CFT	4788	L488CFT
4777	L477CFT	4780	L470YVK	4783	L483CFT	4786	L486CFT		

4789-4793 — DAF SB220LC550 — Optare Delta — B49F — 1995

4789	M489HCU	4790	M490HCU	4791	M491HCU	4792	M492HCU	4793	M493HCU

Go-Ahead North East operate fourteen Leyland Lynx, a model with twelve supplied in 1989 before the company moved onto the Optare Delta. Two further examples arrived from Redby in 1998 and for a while carried non-year marks. Recently, one of the pair, 4857 has regained its original mark D340LSD as seen during August in the new Park Lane Transport Interchange in Gateshead. *Bill Potter*

4801-4807

DAF SB220LC550   Optare Delta   B51F   1992   OK Travel, 1995

4801	J201VHN	4803	J203VHN	4805	J205VHN	4807	J207VHN	4808	J208VHN
4802	J202VHN	4804	J204VHN	4806	J206VHN				

4808-4812

Volvo B10B-58   Alexander Strider   B51F   1994   OK Travel, 1995

4808	L208KEF	4809	L209KEF	4810	L210KEF	4811	L211KEF	4812	L212KEF

4813	N813WGR	Volvo B10B	Plaxton Verde	B51F	1996	
4814	N814WGR	Volvo B10B	Plaxton Verde	B51F	1996	
4815	N815WGR	Volvo B10B	Plaxton Verde	B51F	1996	
4816	N816WGR	Volvo B10B	Plaxton Verde	B51F	1996	
4817	F259GWJ	Leyland Lynx LX112L10ZR1R	Leyland Lynx	B51F	1989	Redby Travel, 1998
4818	H51NDU	Leyland Lynx LX2R11C15Z4S	Leyland Lynx 2	B49F	1991	Redby Travel, 1998
4819	J43GGB	Leyland Lynx LX2R11C15Z4S	Leyland Lynx 2	B49F	1991	Redby Travel, 1998

4820-4825

DAF SB220G5SB   Northern Counties Paladin   N42F   1997

4820	P320AFT	4822	P322AFT	4823	P323AFT	4824	P324AFT	4825	P325AFT
4821	P321AFT								

4837-4855

Volvo B10BLE   Wright Renown   N44F   1998

4837	R837PRG	4841	R841PRG	4845	R845PRG	4849	R849PRG	4853	R853PRG
4838	R838PRG	4842	R842PRG	4846	R846PRG	4850	R856PRG	4854	R854PRG
4839	R839PRG	4843	R843PRG	4847	R847PRG	4851	R851PRG	4855	R855PRG
4840	340GUP	4844	R844PRG	4848	R848PRG	4852	R852PRG		

4856	KAZ2752	Leyland Lynx LX5636LXCTFR1	Leyland Lynx	B47F	1986	Redby, Sunderland, 1998
4857	D340LSD	Leyland Lynx LX5636LXCTFR1	Leyland Lynx	B47F	1986	Redby, Sunderland, 1998

Optare offered their bodywork on Dennis Lance chassis in 1992 and this model, known as the Sigma has much in common with the Delta. It was supplied to Go-Ahead in 1994 along with other bodybuilders products also on the Dennis Lance. Fourteen Sigma buses are in the current fleet and are illustrated by 4785, L485CFT which is seen with Go-Gateshead titles. *Phillip Stephenson*

4862-4895			DAF DE02GSSB220		Plaxton Prestige		N41F*		1998-99 *4890-5 are N41F
4862	S862ONL	4865	S865ONL	4868	S868ONL	4890	S890ONL	4893	S893ONL
4863	S863ONL	4866	S866ONL	4869	S869ONL	4891	S891ONL	4894	S894ONL
4864	S864ONL	4867	S867ONL	4870	S870ONL	4892	S892ONL	4895	S895ONL

5131	D903EAJ	DAF MB230DKFL615	Duple 320	C57F	1987	OK Travel, 1995
5134	E906MDC	DAF MB230LB615	Duple 320	C57F	1988	OK Travel, 1995
5136	425BVK	DAF MB230LB615	Duple 320	C57F	1988	OK Travel, 1995
5137	E909MDC	DAF MB230LB615	Duple 320	C53F	1988	OK Travel, 1995

7041	961KVK	Volvo B10M-60	Plaxton Expressliner	C49FT	1990
7052	K2VOY	Volvo B10M-60	Plaxton Expressliner II	C46FT	1993
7053	K3VOY	Volvo B10M-60	Plaxton Expressliner II	C46FT	1993
7058	JCN822	Volvo B10M-60	Plaxton Expressliner II	C46FT	1995
7059	FCU190	Volvo B10M-60	Plaxton Expressliner II	C46FT	1995
7060	CU6860	Volvo B10M-62	Plaxton Expressliner II	C46FT	1996
7061	CU7661	Volvo B10M-62	Plaxton Expressliner II	C46FT	1996
7062	GSK962	Volvo B10M-62	Plaxton Expressliner II	C44FT	1997
7074	YSU874	Volvo B10M-62	Plaxton Expressliner II	C44FT	1997
7075	YSU875	Volvo B10M-62	Plaxton Expressliner II	C44FT	1997
7076	YSU876	Volvo B10M-62	Plaxton Expressliner II	C44FT	1997
7077	S977ABR	Volvo B10M-62	Plaxton Expressliner II	C44FT	1998
7078	S978ABR	Volvo B10M-62	Plaxton Expressliner II	C44FT	1998
7079	S979ABR	Volvo B10M-62	Plaxton Expressliner II	C44FT	1998

The early bodywork for the Dennis Dart from Wright of Ballymena, known as the Handy Bus, had a rather square appearance, the subsequent Wright styling being exceptionally well received. Seen heading for Stanley with Go-Northern titles is 8048, J948MFT. *Malcolm King*

8000	H802OPT	Dennis Dart 9.8SDL3004	Carlyle Dartline	B40F	1991		

8001-8040   Dennis Dart 9.8SDL3017   Wright Handy-bus   B40F   1991

8001	J601KCU	8009	J609KCU	8017	J617KCU	8025	J625KCU	8033	J633KCU
8002	J602KCU	8010	J610KCU	8018	J618KCU	8026	J626KCU	8034	J634KCU
8003	J603KCU	8011	J611KCU	8019	J619KCU	8027	J627KCU	8035	J635KCU
8004	J604KCU	8012	J612KCU	8020	J620KCU	8028	J628KCU	8036	J636KCU
8005	J605KCU	8013	J613KCU	8021	J621KCU	8029	J629KCU	8037	J637KCU
8006	J606KCU	8014	J614KCU	8022	J622KCU	8030	J630KCU	8038	J638KCU
8007	J607KCU	8015	J615KCU	8023	J623KCU	8031	J631KCU	8039	J639KCU
8008	J608KCU	8016	J616KCU	8024	J624KCU	8032	J632KCU	8040	J640KCU

8041-8065   Dennis Dart 9.8SDL3017   Wright Handy-bus   B40F   1992

8041	J941MFT	8046	J946MFT	8051	J951MFT	8056	K856PCN	8061	K861PCN
8042	J942MFT	8047	J947MFT	8052	J952MFT	8057	K857PCN	8062	K862PCN
8043	J943MFT	8048	J948MFT	8053	J953MFT	8058	K858PCN	8063	K863PCN
8044	J944MFT	8049	J949MFT	8054	J954MFT	8059	K859PCN	8064	K864PCN
8045	J945MFT	8050	J950MFT	8055	J955MFT	8060	K860PCN	8065	K865PCN

8066-8089   Dennis Dart 9.8SDL3017   Wright Handy-bus   B40F   1993

8066	K366RTY	8071	K371RTY	8076	K376RTY	8081	K381RTY	8086	K986SCU
8067	K367RTY	8072	K372RTY	8077	K377RTY	8082	K382RTY	8087	K987SCU
8068	K368RTY	8073	K373RTY	8078	K378RTY	8083	K383RTY	8088	K988SCU
8069	K369RTY	8074	K374RTY	8079	K379RTY	8084	K984SCU	8089	K989SCU
8070	K370RTY	8075	K375RTY	8080	K380RTY	8085	K985SCU		

8090	M890GBB	Dennis Dart 9.8SDL3040	Plaxton Pointer	B40F	1994
8091	M891GBB	Dennis Dart 9.8SDL3040	Plaxton Pointer	B40F	1994
8092	M892GBB	Dennis Dart 9.8SDL3040	Plaxton Pointer	B40F	1994

1997 saw the arrival of the first integral Optare Excel buses for Go-Ahead and this has been followed by a second batch of the longer L1150 model. One of these, 8147, R247OCU, is seen in Tynemouth. *Tony Wilson*

8093-8109

			Dennis Dart 9.8SDL3040		Marshall C 37		B40F	1994		
8093	M803GFT	8097	M807GFT	8101	M811GFT	8104	M814GFT	8107	M817GFT
8094	M804GFT	8098	M808GFT	8102	M812GFT	8105	M815GFT	8108	M818GFT
8095	M805GFT	8099	M809GFT	8103	M813GFT	8106	M816GFT	8109	M819GFT
8096	M806GFT	8100	M810GFT						

8110-8115

			Dennis Dart 9.8SDL3040		Plaxton Pointer		B40F	1994		
8110	M810HCU	8112	M812HCU	8113	M813HCU	8114	M814HCU	8115	M815HCU
8111	M811HCU								

8116	L315XBB	Dennis Dart 9.8SDL3017	Plaxton Pointer	B40F	1993	Diamond, Stanley, 1995

8117-8124

			Dennis Dart 9.8SDL3054		Marshall C 37		B40F	1995		
8117	N117WBR	8119	N119WBR	8121	N121WBR	8123	N123WBR	8124	N124WBR
8118	N118WBR	8120	N120WBR	8122	N122WBR				

8125-8132

			Optare L 1050		Optare Excel		N38F	1997		
8125	P925ACU	8127	P927ACU	8129	P929ACU	8131	P931ACU	8132	P932ACU
8126	P926ACU	8128	P928ACU	8130	P930ACU				

Opposite, top:- **Latterly used as a Dennis demonstrator, Lance 4768 is seen at Gosforth in Low Fell coaches livery. The vehicle has an Alexander PS bodywork.** *Tony Wilson*
Opposite, bottom:- **Delivered during the winter of 1998-99 was a batch of DAF low floor SB220 buses, and these have been allocated to Chester-le-Street depot. Pictured on lay-over at Durham bus station is 4867, S867ONL. The bodywork is Plaxton Prestige, a design which shows some influence from the Northern Counties bus facility now re-named Plaxton.** *Bill Potter*

8133-8147 — Optare L 1150 — Optare Excel — N41F — 1998

8133 R833NRG	8136 R836NRG	8139 R839NRG	8142 R242OCU	8145 R245OCU
8134 R834NRG	8137 R837NRG	8140 R340NTY	8143 R243OCU	8146 R246OCU
8135 R835NRG	8138 R838NRG	8141 R841NRG	8144 R244OCU	8147 R247OCU

8148-8157 — Optare L 1150 — Optare Excel — N41F — 1998

8148 S148OCU	8150 S150OCU	8152 S152OCU	8154 S154OCU	8156 S156OCU
8149 S149OCU	8151 S151OCU	8153 S153OCU	8155 S35NRG	8157 S157OCU

8158-8175 — Dennis Dart SLF — Plaxton Pointer SPD — N41F — 1999

8158 S358ONL	8162 S362ONL	8166 S366ONL	8170 S370ONL	8173 S373ONL
8159 S359ONL	8163 S363ONL	8167 S367ONL	8171 S371ONL	8174 S374ONL
8160 S360ONL	8164 S364ONL	8168 S368ONL	8172 S372ONL	8175 S375ONL
8161 S361ONL	8165 S365ONL	8169 S369ONL		

8176-8185 — Optare L1150 — Optare Excel — N41F — 1999

8176 T876RBR	8178 T878RBR	8180 T880RBR	8182 T882RBR	8184 T884RBR
8177 T877RBR	8179 T879RBR	8181 T881RBR	8183 T883RBR	8185 T885RBR

8401-8412 — Volvo B6-9.9M — Plaxton Pointer — B40F — 1993 — OK Travel, 1995

8401 L401FVN	8404 L404FVN	8407 L407GDC	8409 L409GPY	8411 L411GPY
8402 L402FVN	8405 L405GDC	8408 L408GDC	8410 L410GPY	8412 L412GPY
8403 L403FVN	8406 L406GDC			

8413-8433 — Volvo B6-9.9M — Alexander Dash — B40F — 1994-95 OK Travel, 1995

8413 L413KEF	8418 M418PVN	8422 M422PVN	8426 M426RDC	8430 M430RDC
8414 L414KEF	8419 M419PVN	8423 M423PVN	8427 M427RDC	8431 M431RDC
8415 L415KEF	8420 M420PVN	8424 M424PVN	8428 M428RDC	8432 M432RDC
8416 L416KEF	8421 M421PVN	8425 M425PVN	8429 M429RDC	8433 M433RDC
8417 L417KEF				

8434	N670VUP	Volvo B6-9.9M	Alexander Dash	B40F	1995	Redby, Sunderland, 1998
8435	N671VUP	Volvo B6-9.9M	Alexander Dash	B40F	1995	Redby, Sunderland, 1998

Ancilliary vehicles

446	F503ANY	MCW MetroRider MF150/109	MCW	B27F	1989	Oxford Citybus, 1998
447	F504ANY	MCW MetroRider MF150/109	MCW	B27F	1989	Oxford Citybus, 1998
4634	KBR634T	Leyland National 11351A/1R		DP23DL	1978	
5102	C102PCN	Leyland Tiger TRCTL11/3RH	Plaxton Paramount 3200 II	TV	1986	
5103	C103PCN	Leyland Tiger TRCTL11/3RH	Plaxton Paramount 3200 II	TV	1986	
5104	C104PCN	Leyland Tiger TRCTL11/3RH	Plaxton Paramount 3200 II	TV	1986	
5118	A718ABB	Leyland Tiger TRCTL11/2R	Plaxton Paramount 3200 E	C44FT	1984	
5128	C682JGR	Leyland Tiger TRCTL11/3R	Plaxton Paramount 3200 IIE	C46FT	1985	
5140	G702AEF	DAF MB230LB615	Duple 320	C53F	1989	Ex OK Travel, 1995
9914	D914URG	Bedford YMT	Plaxton Derwent II	B55F	1987	Low Fell Coaches, 1992
9961	PGR961T	Leyland Leopard PSU3E/4R	Plaxton Supreme IV Express	C53F	1979	Ex OK Travel, 1995
9962	SPT962V	Leyland Leopard PSU3E/4R	Plaxton Supreme IV Express	C53F	1980	Ex OK Travel, 1995
9963	SPT963V	Leyland Leopard PSU3E/4R	Plaxton Supreme IV Express	C53F	1980	Ex OK Travel, 1995

Previous Registrations:

340GUP	From new	FCU190	M59LBB
425BVK	G349RTA	GSK962	JSK346
961KVK	H141CVK	JCN822	M58LBB
CU6860	N760RCU	KAZ2752	D330LSD
CU7661	N761RCU	YSU874	From new
D340LSD	D340SLD, KAZ2753	YSU875	From new
E909MDC	E909MDC, YSU882	YSU876	From new
EDS508B	RCN699		

Depots and allocations:

Bishop Auckland (North Bondgate) - Go Northern

MetroRider	376	393	403	406	407	427	
Volvo B6	8405	8410	8412	8418	8419	8420	8421	8422
	8426	8427	8428	8429	8430	8431	8432
Volvo B10M	4749						
DAF/Delta	4802						
DAF/Duple	5131	5134	5136	5137			
Atlantean	3539	3558	3682	3699			
	3793	3794	3795	3796			
Metrobus	3489	3491	3511	3513	3752		
Olympian	3574	3584	3588	3806	3807	3808	3809	3810

Chester-le-Street (Picktree Lane) - Go Northern

MetroRider	335	336	337	339	421	422	423	424
Dart	8027	8036	8047	8052	8054	8055	8119	8120
	8121	8122	8123	8124			
Excel	8157	8176	8177	8178	8179	8181	8182	8183
	8184	8185					
National	4662	4666	4667	4669	4687	4688	4694	4695
	4705	4717	4720	4721			
DAF/Prestige	4862	4862	4864	4865	4866	4867	4868	4869
	4870	4890	4891	4892	4893	4894	4895
Volvo/Expressliner	7041	7052	7053	7058	7059	7060	7061	7062
	7074	7075	7076	7077	7078	7079	
Volvo B10B	4848	4849	4850	4851	4852	4853	4854	4855
Metrobus	3503	3504	3506	3507	3508	3509	
	3510	3512	3621	3623	3624	3625	3632	3647
	3680	3757	3758	3759	3785		
Olympian	3661	3667	3668	3669	3670	3671	

The MetroCentre in Gateshead is one of the handful of very large shopping centres in England, and its bus station throngs with passengers and vehicles. Special livery for the shuttle service between the town and the shopping complex is worn by 4823, P323AFT, a Northern Counties bodied DAF SB220. *Tony Wilson*

Gateshead (Sunderland Road) - Go Gateshead

MetroRider	340	384	407					
Dart	8074	8075	8079	8158	8159	8160	8161	8162
	8163	8164	8165	8166	8167	8168	8169	8170
	8171	8172	8173	8174	8175			
Volvo B6	8401	8402	8403	8404	8406	8407	8408	8409
	8411	8412	8413	8414	8415	8416	8417	8423
	8424	8425	8433	8434	8435			
National	4663	4672	4674	4700	4713	4715	4718	
Volvo B10B	4810	4811	4812					
DAF/Delta	4750	4751	4752	4753	4754	4756	4757	4758
	4759	4760	4761	4789	4790	4791	4792	4793
DAF/Palatine	4820	4821	4822	4823	4824	4825		
Lance	4768	4774	4775	4776	4777	4778	4779	4780
	4781	4782	4783	4784	4785	4786	4787	4788
Javelin	4767							
Metrobus	3618	3627	3629	3630	3633	3634		
	3635	3640	3645					
	3646	3648	3750	3751	3753	3754		
	3760	3761	3762	3763	3764	3765	3766	3769
	3771	3778						

South Shields (Mile End Road) - Go Coastliner

Dart	8001	8002	8003	8004	8005	8006	8007	8008
	8009	8010	8011	8012	8090	8091	8092	8110
	8111	8112	8113	8114	8115	8116		
Excel	8148	8149	8150	8151	8152	8153	8154	8155
	8156							
National	4676							
Olympian	3811	3812	3813	3814	3815	3816	3817	3818
	3819	3820	3821	3822	3823	3824	3825	3826
	3827	3828	3829	3830	3831	3832	3833	

Stanley (Chester Road) - Go Northern

MetroRider	414	415	416	417	418	419	420	428
Dart	8028	8029	8030	8031	8032	8033	8034	8035
	8037	8038	8039	8040	8041	8042	8043	8044
	8045	8046	8048	8049	8050	8051		
Excel	8180							
National	4660	4661	4664	4665	4668	4670	4671	4691
	4702	4703	4719					
DAF/Delta	4734	4735	4736	4737	4738	4739	4740	4741
	4742	4743	4744	4745	4746	4747		
Metrobus	3502	3505	3515	3517	3534	3620	3628	3636
	3637	3641	3775					
Olympian	3520	3521	3522	3523	3586	3599	3610	3617
	3660	3662	3666					

Sunderland (Deptford) - Go Wear Buses

MetroRider	333	338	341	343	344	367	372	373
	374	375	377	378	379	380	381	382
	383	386	387	388	394	399	400	401
	402	429	431	445				
Dart	8019	8021	8024	8025	8053	8056	8057	8058
	8059	8061	8062	8063	8064	8065	8066	8080
	8081	8082	8093	8094	8095	8096	8097	8098
	8099	8100	8101	8102	8103	8104	8105	8107
	8108	8109	8117					
Excel	8133	8134	8135	8136	8137	8138	8139	
	8140	8141						
National	4673	4675	4677	4678	4679	4680	4681	4683
	4684	4685	4686	4688	4697	4698	4699	4701
	4704	4709	4710	4711	4712	4714	4716	

More than fifty Leyland Nationals remain in the fleet though the majority of these have been extensivley refurbished with the fitting of low-level heating and Volvo engine units. The majority are with Go-Wear Buses and Go-Northern, whose 4700, FTN700W, is seen at Durham. *Tony Wilson*

Lynx	4722	4723	4724	4725	4726	4727	4728	4729
	4730	4731	4732	4733	4817	4818	4819	4856
	4857							
DAF/Delta	4801	4803	4804	4805	4805	4807		
Metrobus	3501	3516	3518	3619	3622	3755	3756	3767
	3768	3776	3777	3781	3782	3783	3784	3786
	3787	3789						
Olympian	3591							

Wallsend (Hadrian Road) - Go Coastline

MetroRider	334	345	389	390	391	392	409	410
	411	412	413					
Dart	8013	8014	8015	8016	8017	8022	8023	8026
	8060	8067	8068	8069	8084	8085	8086	8087
	8088	8089						
Excel	8125	8126	8127	8128	8129	8130	8131	8132
	8142	8143	8144	8145	8146	8147		
Lance	4769	4770	4771	4772	4773			
Atlantean	3527	3530	3538	3540				
Olympian	3572	3573	3575	3577	3578	3579	3580	3581
	3585	3587	3590	3592	3593	3598	3600	3601
	3602	3603	3605	3606	3607	3608	3609	3612
	3614	3653	3658	3674	3743	3744	3745	3746
	3747	3748						

Go-Northern's Chester-le-Street depot provide several vehicles for National Express duties. Pictured while leaving the north-east for Plymouth is 7075, YSU875, a Plaxton Expressliner 2 in Rapide livery.
Phillip Stephenson

Washington (Industrial Road) - Go Wear Buses

MetroRider	342	385	395	396	397	398	425	426
	434	438	439					
Solo	448	449	450	451	452	453	454	455
Dart	8106	8118						
National	4706	4707	4708					
Volvo B10B	4837	4838	4839	4840	4841	4842	4843	4844
	4845	4846	4847					
Olympian	3582	3595	3597	3611	3613	3615	3616	3651
	3652	3657	3659	3663	3665			
Metrobus	3631							

Winlaton (Cromwell Place) - Go Gateshead

MetroRider	346	351	352	353	354	355	356	357
	358	359	360	361	362	363	364	365
	366	404	405					
Dart	8000	8018	8020	8070	8071	8072	8073	8076
	8077	8078	8083					
Volvo B10B	4809	4810	4813	4814	4815	4816		
Olympian	3650	3654	3655	3656	3664	3672	3673	3675
	3676	3677	3678	3679	3734	3735	3736	3737
	3738	3739	3740	3741	3742			

Unallocated

Metrobus	3639	3642	3788
Olympian	3589		

GRIERSON

D & C J Grierson, Sedgefield Road Garage, Fishburn, Stockton-on-Tees, TS21 4DD

847LAA	Volvo B58-56	Plaxton Panorama Elite III Exp	C53F	1974	Hills, Stibb Cross, 1990
RCU826S	Leyland Fleetline FE30AGR	Alexander AL	B44/30F	1977	Stagecoach Busways, 1997
RCU828S	Leyland Fleetline FE30AGR	Alexander AL	B44/30F	1977	Stagecoach Busways, 1997
ARF149S	Volvo B58-61	Plaxton Supreme III	C53F	1978	Baker, Biddulph, 1991
CWG761V	Leyland Atlantean AN68A/1R	Roe	B43/29D	1979	Duff, Sutton-on-the-Forest, 1998
SBB85Y	Mercedes-Benz L508D	Reeve Burgess	BC19F	1982	National Blood Transfusion ,1992
VXI5357	Volvo B10M-61	Duple Dominant IV	C53F	1983	Buffalo, Flitwick, 1995
LIB377	Volvo B10M-61	Jonckheere Jubilee P90	C32/9FT	1983	A-one, Heywood, 1991
RJI4566	Volvo B10M-61	Plaxton Paramount 3200	C57F	1983	Lochview Coaches, Gourock, 1994
LIB854	Volvo B10M-61	Plaxton Paramount 3500	C53FT	1984	Stonehouse, Brotton, 1988
LIB574	Volvo B10M-53	Van Hool Astral	C50/12FT	1985	London Pullman, Basildon, 1993
LIB449	Volvo B10M-53	Jonckheere Jubilee P95	C52/13FT	1986	
D701TLG	Mercedes-Benz 609D	PMT	BC19F	1987	Swinden, Grenoside, 1995
LIB987	Volvo B10M-61	Plaxton Paramount 3200 III	C53F	1989	McMenemy, Ardrossan, 1998
F710COA	Volvo B10M-53	Plaxton Paramount 4000 III	C55/12DT	1989	Ayres, Dalkeith, 1996
GVL323	Volvo B10M-61	Plaxton Paramount 3500 III	C51FT	1990	Gordon, Kirkbride, 1991
H424DVM	Mercedes-Benz 609D	Made-to-Measure	C24F	1990	Varteg Motors, Garndiffaith, 1991
J684THN	DAF SBR3000DKZ570	Plaxton Paramount 4000 III	C55/19CT	1991	Abbott's, Leeming, 1997
M667GJF	Volvo B10M-62	Plaxton Premiere 350	C49FT	1994	Dunn Line, Nottingham, 1996

Previous Registrations:

847LAA	PUT313M, 138ASV	LIB854	A620UGD
ARF149S	XEH2S, 5658RU	LIB987	F678LGG
GVL323	F30UHP, 9840RU, F528VVC	RJI4566	7076LJ
LIB377	F538GHH, G930MAO	VXI5357	ENF575Y
LIB449	C415LRP		
LIB574	B416CGG		

Livery: Blue and red

The blue and red livery employed by Grierson is seen on Plaxton Supreme SLH7W, seen in Sunderland just prior to its withdrawal from service.
Terry Wightman

HENNINGS

D Henning, 20 Hartlepool Street South, Thornley, Durham, DH6 3BG

MRB804P	Bristol VRT/SL3/6LX	Eastern Coach Works	B43/34F	1975	Abbott's of Leeming, 1998
OCU817R	Leyland Fleetline FE30AGR	Alexander AL	B44/30F	1977	Stagecoach Busways, 1996
RCU837S	Leyland Fleetline FE30AGR	Alexander AL	B44/27F	1977	Stagecoach Busways, 1999
SVJ600S	Bedford VAS5	Plaxton Supreme III	C29F	1977	Castell Coaches, Trethomas, 1995
YUM517S	Bristol VRT/SL3/6LXB	Eastern Coach Works	B43/31F	1978	Abbott's of Leeming, 1999
MVT425V	Bedford SB5	Duple Dominant	C41F	1980	Stonehouse Coaches, 1999
KJR281X	Mercedes-Benz L508D	Reeve Burgess	BC19F	1981	Frank, Hartlepool, 1998
C47DHT	Dennis Domino SDA1202	Optare	B33F	1985	Stark, Bridge of Weir, 1995
D923VCN	Freight Rover Sherpa	Dormobile	BC16F	1986	Northumbria, 1995
D926VCN	Freight Rover Sherpa	Dormobile	BC16F	1986	Northumbria, 1997
D838KWT	Freight Rover Sherpa	Dormobile	BC16F	1987	West Riding, 1990
D754LRJ	Bedford VAS5	Plaxton Paramount 3200 II	C23FL	1987	Archer, Poulton-le-Fylde, 1999
w E133RAX	Freight Rover Sherpa	Carlyle Citybus 2	B20F	1987	Davies, Plean, 1995
E752VJO	MCW MetroRider MF150/26	MCW	B25F	1987	Go-Ahead (Go-Sunderland), 1999
E756VJO	MCW MetroRider MF150/26	MCW	B25F	1987	Hodgson, Barnard Castle, 1999
E855BRM	MCW MetroRider MF150/35	MCW	B25F	1988	Robson, Thornaby, 1998
F521NBR	Leyland Tiger TRCTL11/3ARZ	Plaxton Paramount 3500 III	C49FT	1989	
F130CEA	Mercedes-Benz L307D	Premier	M12	1989	Wheeler, Catshill, 1997
w H802SKY	Mercedes-Benz 709D	Reeve Burgess Beaver	B25F	1989	Northumbria, 1997

Previous Registrations:
F521NBR   F33LCU, CU7661

Livery: Cream

Depot: Low Road, Wheatley Hill

HENRY COOPER

L & G Greaves, Lane End Garage, Annitsford, Tyne & Wear NE23 7DB

JUP115T	Leyland Leopard PSU5C/4R	Plaxton Supreme III	C51F	1979	Gardiner, Spennymoor, 1998
TBR527V	Leyland Leopard PSU3E/4R	Duple Dominant	B55F	1979	United, 1993
JFT412X	Bedford YMQ	Duple Dominant III	C45F	1981	
C131HJN	Leyland Tiger TRCTL11/3RH	Plaxton Paramount 3200 IIE	C57F	1986	Arriva North East (DC), 1999
ESU110	Volvo B10M-61	Plaxton Paramount 3500 II	C49FT	1986	
671MBB	Volvo B10M-61	Plaxton Paramount 3500 III	C49FT	1988	
OBR297	Volvo B10M-61	Plaxton Paramount 3500 III	C51FT	1989	
526VVK	Volvo B10M-60	Plaxton Excalibur	C49F	1993	
EX180	Volvo B12T	Plaxton Excalibur	C51FT	1997	

Special event vehicle

PT2053	Daimler CK	Robson	B20F	1923	private owner, 1996

Previous Registrations:

526VVK	L352MKU	ESU110	C417OTN	OBR297	From new
671MBB	E967ECN	EX180	P397CCU		

Livery: Brown and cream

Opposite, top:- **Darlington town centre is the location of this picture of Hennings' E133RAX, a Freight Rover Sherpa with Carlyle Citybus 2 bodywork. The vehicle joined the fleet in 1995 and was new to Red & White in 1987 as part of the large conversion to minibuses that occured at the time.** *Terry Wightman*
Opposite, bottom:- **Two Plaxton Excalibur coaches carry Henry Cooper's colours. Photographed in Sunderland, 526VVK was operating on contract to David Urquhart Travel when seen, The Excalibur is the executive coach built by Plaxton though since 1998 the model has been available in a more standard specification as an alternative model.** *Terry Wightman*

HUNTER'S

Hunter Bros (Tantobie) Ltd, The Garage, 19 Johnson Terrace, Tantobie,
Stanley, Co Durham DH9 9TG

VWY845L	Bedford YRQ	Plaxton Panorama Elite III	C45F	1973	Baddeley, Holmfirth, 1976
RUP906M	Bedford YRT	Duple Dominant	C53F	1974	
JUP189T	Bedford YMT	Duple Dominant	B55F	1978	
WPT445V	Bedford YMT	Duple Dominant II	C53F	1980	
GVK820W	Bedford YMQ	Duple Dominant	B47F	1980	
PNM695W	Bedford YMQ-S	Duple Dominant II	C35F	1981	Tourmaster, Loughborough, 1984
NDW137X	Leyland Tiger TRCTL11/2R	Plaxton Supreme V Express	C53F	1982	Hill's, Tredegar, 1986
B634HBR	Bedford YNT	Duple Laser 2	C53F	1985	Hammell, Stanley, 1995
D341APG	Mercedes-Benz 609D	Reeve Burgess	B20F	1987	Taylor, Frimley, 1990
F901JBB	Mercedes-Benz 609D	Reeve Burgess Beaver	BC25F	1988	Lowdon Sunniside, 1995

Livery: White and black

The Bedford coach chassis remains favoured by many of those operators who loyally generated regular purchases while the chassis was available. Still looking smart is Hunters WPT455V which is fitted with Duple Dominant II bodywork. Unlike many of this design, the central aluminium trim still gleams.
David Longbottom

J & C

JH A N & D Jones, Belmont House, Groat Drive, Newton Aycliffe, DL5 6HY

DIB8484	Dennis Javelin 8.5SDL1915	Duple 320	C35F	1989	Mackie, Alloa, 1996
71XVO	Toyota Coaster HDB30R	Caetano Optimo II	C18F	1991	Capital, West Drayton, 1997
	Setra S210H	Setra	C35F	1993	Redwing, London, 1997
K171OCT	Mercedes-Benz 711D	Autobus Classique	C25F	1993	
L296TPW	Peugeot-Talbot Express	Crystals	M14	1994	
XCO182	Bova FHD12.280	Bova Futura	C49FT	1984	Maxfield, Aughton, 1998
N903SBB	Mercedes-Benz 412D	Minibus Options	M15	1996	Hillary, Prudhoe,1999
P77NEV	Bova FHD12.340	Bova Futura	C39FT	1997	
N8NEV	Bova FHD12.340	Bova Futura	C40FT	1998	
N9NEV	Bova FHD12.340	Bova Futura	C40FT	1998	

Previous Registrations:

71XVO	C151OAU, 8111PJ, C135VUJ	P77NEV	P744YUG
DIB8484	YBL526, F476WSC	XCO182	A665EMY, HIL7964

Livery: White; white (Siesta Club Class) N8/9NEV

Now one of the oldest coaches in the J&C fleet is DIB8484, an 8.5 metre Dennis Javelin with Duple 320 bodywork. The vehicle keeps company with short-length Setra S210, while the four Bova Futura coaches offer trips to the continent. *Bill Potter*

JIM HUGHES

J Hughes, Wear Street, Low Southwick, Sunderland, SR5 2BH

OSF877M	Bedford YRT	Plaxton Panorama Elite III	C53F	1974	Porteous, Hull, 1982
RFR883T	Bedford YMT	Plaxton Supreme IV	C46F	1979	Mercer, Longridge, 1984
AOA615A	Bedford YMT	Plaxton Supreme IV	C53F	1980	Brown, Meadowfield, 1997
PJI2408	Volvo B58-56	Plaxton Supreme IV	C53F	1980	Swaffham Coachways, 1989
OTP392	Volvo B10M-61	Van Hool Alizée	C49FT	1983	Loyne, Pelaw, 1991
PJI2407	Bedford YNT	Plaxton Paramount 3200 II	C53F	1985	Tate, Penshaw, 1991
OTP940	Volvo B10M-61	Van Hool Alizée	C49FT	1987	Cooper, Annisford, 1995
WSU486	Mercedes-Benz 609D	Reeve Burgess	C19F	1987	Bluebird Buses, 1996
E250WYS	Freight Rover Sherpa	Wright Jenkins	M16	1988	Main, Sunderland, 1989

Previous registrations:

AOR615A	XPT568V	PJI2407	C791RJU
OTP392	MHS664Y	PJI2408	LUA256V
OTP940	D540MVR	WSU486	From new

Livery: Grey, red and white

Strange wigs and jerseys signify that Jim Hughes' OTP392 was heading for Wembley when this picture was taken. The Van Hool Alizée is the square T8 design and one of a pair operated in the Jim Hughes fleet.
Keith Grimes

KINGS

K E King, Ferry Road, Middlesbrough, TS2 1PL

RXG810H	Ford R192	Plaxton Panorama Elite	C45F	1970	Rennison, Stockton, 1973
7204DD	Ford R1114	Plaxton Supreme III	C49F	1978	Crabbe, Stockton, 1996
BAJ707T	Ford R1114	Duple Dominant II	C53F	1979	
3376DD	Ford R1114	Duple Dominant II	C53F	1979	
MHN131W	Leyland National 2 NL116L11/1R		B49F	1981	Northumbria, 1997
WSV547	Scania K112CRS	Jonckheere Jubilee P50	C51FT	1983	Frost, Laxton, 1998
WSV548	Setra S228DT	Setra Imperial	C54/20CT	1984	
WSV549	Setra S228DT	Setra Imperial	C54/20CT	1984	
9506DD	Setra S215HD	Setra Tornado	C49FT	1986	Stirk, Standrop, 1991
4995DD	Scania K112CRB	Van Hool Alizée	C49FT	1986	Safford, Little Gramsden, 1990
3542DD	Volvo B10M-61	Van Hool Alizée H	C48FT	1988	Epsom Coaches, 1996
7061DD	Volvo B10M-61	Van Hool Alizée H	C48FT	1988	Epsom Coaches, 1996

Previous registrations:

3376DD	GHN79V	BAJ707T	BAJ707T, 3542DD
3542DD	E513YGC	RXG810H	RXG810H, 7061DD
4995DD	D112MKX	WSV547	DLX35Y
7061DD	E514YGC	WSV548	A964HVN
7204DD	UUX366S	WSV549	A965HVN
9506DD	D767NKY, D768NKY		

Livery: Cream, orange and brown

Pictured passing through Whitby is Setra Tornado 9506DD of Kings. The Tornado was a specific model of the Setra range and was built in Spain unlike the others which were built in the south German town of Nue Ulm. Kings' fleet also contains two of the double-deck Setra coach which is known as the Imperial. The final 200 series vehicles were built during 1998, with current production being a large range of vehicle in the 300 series. *Tony Wilson*

KINGSLEY'S

D Kingsley, Unit G Penshaw Way, Burtley, Co Durham, DH3 2SA

	620PDV	Volvo B58-61	Plaxton Viewmaster III	C50F	1977	Lyles, Batley, 1999
	B687JVK	Renault-Dodge G13	Wadham Stringer Vanguard	BC39F	1985	MoD, 1995 (-?-)
	MVS380	MAN SR280	MAN	C	1985	?, 1999
206w	TRN476V	Leyland Atlantean AN68A/1R	Eastern Coach Works	B45/31F	1981	Stagecoach Ribble, 1998
207	JKW286W	Leyland Atlantean AN68A/1R	Alexander AL	B45/32F	1981	Stagecoach Ribble, 1998
208	BPT917S	Bristol VRT/SL3/6XLB	Eastern Coach Works	B43/31F	1977	Northumbria, 1998
210	JWF493V	MCW Metrobus DR102/13	MCW	B46/30F	1980	Arriva Fox County, 1998
211	JWF494V	MCW Metrobus DR102/13	MCW	B46/30F	1980	Arriva Fox County, 1998
212	JHE160W	MCW Metrobus DR104/6	MCW	B46/31F	1981	Arriva Fox County, 1998
213	JHE193W	MCW Metrobus DR104/6	MCW	B46/31F	1981	Arriva Fox County, 1998
214	JHE167W	MCW Metrobus DR104/6	MCW	B46/31F	1981	Arriva Fox County, 1998
215	JHE145W	MCW Metrobus DR104/6	MCW	B46/31F	1981	Arriva Fox County, 1998
216	JHE189W	MCW Metrobus DR104/6	MCW	B46/31F	1981	Arriva Fox County, 1998
217	JHE192W	MCW Metrobus DR104/6	MCW	B46/31F	1981	Arriva Fox County, 1998
218	JHE179W	MCW Metrobus DR104/6	MCW	B46/31F	1981	Arriva Fox County, 1998

Previous Registrations:

620PDV	TGD974R	UMM852Y	HHC367Y, NFX667
MVS380	700CPO		

Livery: Blue and white (double-decks); white and red (coaches)

Kingsley's operate local services around Sunderland, though most of the double-deck buses are used on schools. While the majority are Metrobuses, four are Leyland Atlanteans, including 206, TRN476V, with Eastern Coach Works body, which was sold while the book was being prepared. *David Longbottom*

LEE'S OF DURHAM

C & J Lee, Mill Road Garage, Mill Road, Durham, DH7 8HE

EDF274T	Leyland Leopard PSU5C/4R	Plaxton Supreme IV	C57F	1979	Jones, Market Drayton, 1996
DIL6718	Volvo B10M-61	Duple Dominant IV	C53F	1982	Stanley Mackay, Edinburgh, 1991
HDZ9106	Volvo B10M-61	Duple Dominant IV	C57F	1983	Hunter, Garston, 1994
FIL8538	Volvo B10M-61	Plaxton Paramount 3500	C53FT	1984	Carryder, Catchgate, 1992
RJI4797	Leyland Tiger TRCTL11/3RZ	Plaxton Paramount 3500 II	C49FT	1984	Bond Bros, Willington, 1998
720HKH	MercedesBenz 811D	Whittaker Europa	BC23F	1988	Cooper, East Herrington, 1995
891HUM	Volvo B10M-60	Van Hool Alizée	C49FT	1989	Classic, Annfield Plain, 1996
N505CVW	DAF DE33WSSB3000	Van Hool Alizée	C49FT	1995	Harris, Grays, 1998
L5GAR	Volvo B10M-62	Jonckheere Deauville 45	C53FT	1994	Gardiner, Spennymoor, 1996
T88LEE	Bova FHD12.340	Bova Futura	C39FT	1999	

Previous registrations

720HKH	F424SPY		HDZ9106	ENF554Y
891HUM	F640CJL, WEE584, F578RTL, 656CCE		J116NJJ	A5EXL
DIL6718	MSF645X		RJI4797	B108NPY
FIL8538	A846UGB, 7921AT, A492WYS, LAW467W		RJI7003	?

Livery: Silver and metalic green

The Duple Dominant was in production when Volvo commenced production of their mid-engined chassis, the B10M. Some fifteen years later the chassis is still one of the more common to be found on coach duties in Britain. It is now being replaced by the B7 model which has already entered production. *Colin Lloyd*

LEVEN VALLEY

P W Thompson, 55 Marwood Drive, Great Ayton, Middlesbrough, TS9 6PD

E86MHG	Renault-Dodge S56	Northern Counties	B25F	1988	Preston Bus, 1998
L923UGA	Mercedes-Benz 709D	Dormobile Routemaker	B29F	1993	
M677JFP	Mercedes-Benz 709D	Alexander Sprint	B29F	1995	
N595WND	Mercedes-Benz 709D	Alexander Sprint	B27F	1995	Apply, Connisholme, 1998
N458RNR	Mercedes-Benz 711D	Leicester Carriage Builders	BC29F	1996	
P766BJU	Mercedes-Benz 709D	Leicester Carriage Builders	BC29F	1996	
P776BJU	Mercedes-Benz 709D	Leicester Carriage Builders	BC29F	1997	
P788BJU	Mercedes-Benz 709D	Midland Coach Concepts	B29F	1997	
T552UOX	Mercedes-Benz O814	Guy Franks	B27F	1999	

Named vehicles: P788BJU *St Michael II;* L923UGA *St Columba,* M677JFP *St Bede;* P776BJU *Endeavour;* P766BJU *St Hilda;* E86MHG *Discovery;* N458RNR *Sir William Wallace;* N595WND *St Cuthburt;* T552UOX *Astrea II.*

Livery: Yellow

Depot: Tilbury Road, Middlesbrough

Names, which are displayed near the entrance, are carried on all Leven Valley vehicles. Pictured here is *Sir William Wallace*, N458RNR, one of three Mercedes-Benz minibuses with Leicester Carriage Builders bodywork. *Phillip Stephenson*

The North East Bus Handbook

MICHAEL FRANKS

J Franks, 7 Attlee Crescent, Haswell, Durham, DH6 2EN

FWA476V	Leyland National 2 NL106L11/1R		B44F	1980	K-Line, Leeds, 1996
LUA328V	Leyland National 2 NL106L11/1R		B41F	1980	Delta, Kirkby-in-Ashfield, 1996
NDC238W	Leyland Leopard PSU3E/4R	Plaxton Supreme IV Express	C49F	1980	Arriva NE (Northumbria), 1998
NDC504W	Leyland Leopard PSU3F/4R	Plaxton Supreme IV Express	C49F	1980	Arriva NE (Northumbria), 1998
UWY87X	Leyland Leopard PSU3G/4R	Eastern Coach Works B51	B51F	1982	Balfour Beattie, 1998
HDZ5401	Renault S75	Wright T5303 Citybus	B28F	1980	First CentreWest (BeeLine), 1999
HDZ5402	Renault S75	Wright T5303 Citybus	B28F	1980	First CentreWest (BeeLine), 1999
HDZ5404	Renault S75	Wright T5303 Citybus	B28F	1980	First CentreWest (BeeLine), 1999
HDZ5410	Renault S75	Wright T5303 Citybus	B28F	1980	First CentreWest (BeeLine), 1999
HDZ5414	Renault S75	Wright T5303 Citybus	B28F	1980	First CentreWest (BeeLine), 1999
C52DHT	Dennis Domino SDA1202	Optare	B33F	1985	E Jones & Son, Rhosllanerchrugog, '95

Livery: Yellow, blue and orange

Depot: Don Smith coach depot, Murton

The latest arrivals with Michael Franks are Renault S75 minibuses displaced from First CentreWest. Pictured while still in Bee Line colours with the additional vinyls added for service 153, is HDZ5414. As we go to press five of the type have been reported. *Bill Potter*

MILL

L E Curnow, Hobson Service Station, Burnopfield, Newcastle-upon-Tyne, NE16 6ED

JIL2075	DAF MB200DKTL600	Van Hool Alizée	C48FT	1984	Taylor, Dinnington, 1996
C327OFL	Ford Transit 190	Dormobile	B16F	1986	North East Bus (United), 1996
MIL1062	Bova FHD12.280	Bova Futura	C49FT	1989	Colin's. Shepshed, 1995
P801AWR	Bova FHD12.340	Bova Futura	C49FT	1997	
T2LEC	Bova FHD12.340	Bova Futura	C49FT	1999	

Previous Registrations:

JIL2075	A542HRY, NIB6694, A802WSU	MIL1062	B312VWG, 827APT, 3253VU

Livery: White and blue

NORTH RIDER

E C Ward and W Wooldridge, Unit 3 Whitley Road, Newcastle upon Tyne, NE12 9SR

17	N117TCN	Iveco TurboDaily 59.10	Mellor	B27F	1996	
21	G576YTR	Iveco Daily 49.10	Phoenix	B25F	1996	Western Buses, 1996
22	L893YCN	Ford Transit VE6	Dormobile	B16F	1993	Go-Ahead (OK), 1996
23	L321BOD	Iveco TurboDaily 59.12	Mellor	B26D	1993	Thames Transit, 1996
25	J401KTY	Iveco Daily 49.10	Mellor	B23F	1992	NBTS, Newcastle, 1996
26	P126YTN	Iveco TurboDaily 59.12	Mellor	B27F	1997	
28	H702YUV	Iveco Daily 49.10	Reeve Burgess Beaver	B20F	1990	Oare's of Holywell, 1997
29	L881YVK	Dennis Dart 9.8SDL3035	Plaxton Pointer	B40F	1994	Catch-a-Bus, East Boldon, 1997
30	K30GGY	Iveco Daily 49.10	Marshall C29	B21F	1993	Waylands, Beccles, 1997
32	MIW1239	Leyland National 2 NL116L11/2R		B50F	1980	Stagecoach Transit, 1998
33	YRN818V	Leyland National 2 NL106L11/1R		B44F	1980	Blue Triangle, Rainham, 1998
34	K174CAV	Iveco TurboDaily 59.12	Marshall C31	B25F	1993	Stagecoach Cambus (V), 1998
35	K175CAV	Iveco TurboDaily 59.12	Marshall C31	B25F	1992	Stagecoach Cambus (V), 1998
36	K176CAV	Iveco TurboDaily 59.12	Marshall C31	B25F	1992	Stagecoach Cambus (V), 1998
37	K177CAV	Iveco TurboDaily 59.12	Marshall C31	B25F	1992	Stagecoach Cambus (V), 1998
38	EPD540V	Leyland National 10351B/1R		B41F	1979	Serene Travel, Bedlington, 1998
39	YSX932W	Leyland National 2 NL106AL11/1R		B44F	1981	Stagecoach Red & White, 1998
40	210WVK	DAF SB2300DHS585	Jonckheere Jubilee P50	C53F	1984	Eagre, Gainsborough, 1999
101	TYJ5S	Leyland Atlantean AN68A/1R	East Lancashire	B43/31F	1978	Brighton & Hove, 1998

Ancilliary vehicle

	VDV106S	Bristol LH6L	Eastern Coach Works	TV	1978	NE Bus(Teeside), 1998

Previous Registrations:

210WVK	A133TFL. 7126RE	IIL4597	G211LGK		MIW1239	KAJ214W

Livery: Green and white (buses); white, yellow and red (coaches)

Mill's Bova Futura MIL1062 is seen during a break at Thurrock services on the M25. Many of the coaches used by Mill come from The Netherlands - where Bova coaches are built, including a Dutch-built DAF that has Van Hool Alizée coachwork. *David Heath*

North Rider operate three Leyland National 2s including 32, MIW1239 shown here. This vehicle was new as a dual-doored vehicle to Hartlepool Transport before that operation became part of Cleveland Transit. *Phillip Stephenson*

NORTHUMBRIA COACHES

A & B G Smith, Old Area Workshops, Ellington Road, Ashington, NE63 8TS

IUI9031	Leyland Tiger TRCTL11/2R	Plaxton Paramount 3200 E	C53F	1983	Gardiners, Spennymoor, 1998
IUI2831	Bova FHD12.280	Bova Futura	C49FT	1985	Barnes, Bedlington, 1997
E615FRN	MCW MetroRider MF150/42	MCW	B25F	1987	HMB Services, Gateshead, 1997
IUI8062	Mercedes-Benz 609D	North West Coach Sales	BC24F	1990	Barnes, Bedlington, 1997
H668AGD	Mercedes-Benz 408D	Whittaker Europa	M15	1991	Barnes, Bedlington, 1997
IUI8123	Mercedes-Benz 609D	Made-to-Measure	BC24F	1991	Barnes, Bedlington, 1997
PIL7834	Volvo B10M-60	Caetano Algarve II 3.5m	C49FT	1993	Dorset Travel, 1998
PIL7835	Volvo B10M-60	Caetano Algarve II 3.5m	C49FT	1993	Dorset Travel, 1998
M152KJF	Toyota Coaster HZB50R	Caetano Optimo II	C21F	1994	Scan Coaches, London, 1999
N716FLN	Mercedes-Benz 814D	Cacciamali Ibis	C26F	1995	MTL (London), 1997
N717FLN	Mercedes-Benz 814D	Cacciamali Ibis	C26F	1995	MTL (London), 1997
R189LBC	Volvo B10M-62	Caetano Algarve II 3.5m	C49FT	1997	Smith, Peterlee, 1997

Previous registrations:

IUI2831	C151OAU, 8111PJ, C135VUY, 71XVO				
IUI8062	G532DKF	IUI8123	H615CGG	PIL7834	K594VBC
IUI8063	H910XGA	IUI9031	RMO201Y	PIL7835	K595VBC

Livery: White

Northumbria Coaches' N716FLN is a Mercedes-Benz 814 with Cacciamali Ibis bodywork. As can be seen, this coachbuilt minibus has replaced the traditional Mercedes cowl with a coach-built front. The model is built in Mariano in Italy where Cacciamali specialise on shorter passenger vehicles, mostly on Iveco chassis and this example was one of the first to be imported into the UK. *Colin Lloyd*

PRIORY

Priory Motor Coach Co Ltd, 59 Church Way, North Shields,Tyne & Wear, NE29 0AD

67	LIB6350	Bedford YNV Venturer	Plaxton Paramount 3200 II	C53F	1986	Rush, Newcastle, 1992
71	DJV830Y	Bedford YNT	Duple Dominant IV	C53F	1982	Wilby, Hildal, 1985
73	LIB6349	Bedford YNT	Plaxton Paramount 3200 II	C53F	1984	Greybird, Swalwell, 1992
74	WVV831S	Bedford YMT	Duple Dominant II	C53F	1978	Keebur & Watts, Leicester, 1983
79	YRG172V	Bedford YLQ	Plaxton Supreme IV	C45F	1979	
80	YRG173V	Bedford YLQ	Plaxton Supreme IV	C45F	1979	
82	YRG174V	Bedford YLQ	Plaxton Supreme IV	C45F	1979	
83	EBB156W	Bedford YMT	Plaxton Supreme IV	C53F	1980	

Previous Registrations:

LIB6349	PCN25		LIB6350	C341PVK

Livery: Two-tone green.

Depot: Northumberland Street, North Sheilds

Priory operate an all-Bedford coach fleet. One of two examples with Plaxton Paramount 3200 II body is LIB6349, pictured at Lindisfarne on the Northumbrian coast. This is based on the turbo-charged successor to the YMT model - the YNT. Since the company were no longer able to purchase new Bedfords, second hand vehicles have been acquired during the early 1990s. *J C Walton*

REDBY

Redby Travel Ltd, Strattons Garage Hendon Road, Hendon, Sunderland, SR2 8NT
J Stratton, Hendon Road, Hendon, Sunderland, SR2 8NT

SCK697P	Leyland National 11351A/1R		B49F	1976	Ribble, 1993
3418WY	Volvo B10M-61	Plaxton Paramount 3500	C49F	1983	Darlington, 1994
B717MDC	Volvo B10M-61	Duple Laser 2	C51FT	1984	Cochranes, Shotton, 1985
KAZ2751	Leyland Lynx LX112TL11FR1	Leyland Lynx	B52F	1986	Coombs, Weston-super-Mare, 1997
54FS	Volvo B10M-61	Jonckheere Jubilee P50	C49FT	1986	Cantabrica, Watford, 1993
523SC	Volvo B10M-60	Van Hool Alizée	C53F	1990	Smith, Murton, 1992
H83MOV	Dennis Dart 8.5SDL3003	Carlyle Dartline	B28F	1990	London United, 1999
H85MOV	Dennis Dart 8.5SDL3003	Carlyle Dartline	B28F	1990	London United, 1999
J45GGB	Leyland Lynx LX2R11C15Z4S	Leyland Lynx 2	B51F	1992	Tellings-Golden Miller, 1993
L83CNY	Volvo B6-8.5m	Marshall C33	BC32F	1993	Bebb, Llantwit Fardre, 1996
L84CNY	Volvo B6-8.5m	Marshall C33	BC32F	1993	Bebb, Llantwit Fardre, 1996
L608WWK	Volvo B6-9m	Plaxton Pointer	B40F	1994	Nefyn Coaches, 1999
M387KVR	Dennis Dart 9.8SDL3054	Northern Counties Paladin	B40F	1995	Bath Bus Company, 1999
M597SSB	Dennis Dart 9.8SDL3031	Plaxton Pointer	B29F	1995	Bryans, Denny, 1998
M833ECS	Volvo B10M-60	Jonckheere Deauville 45	C51F	1995	Parks of Hamilton, 1999
M111BUS	Volvo B10M-60	Jonckheere Deauville 45	C49FT	1995	
N21PCU	Volvo B10B-58	Alexander Strider	B51F	1995	
N811NHS	Volvo B10M-62	Jonckheere Deauville 45	C53F	1996	Park's of Hamilton, 1997
N120RJF	Volvo B10M-62	Jonckheere Deauville 45	C49FT	1996	Don Smith, Murton, 1998
P844KOT	Dennis Dart SLF	UVG Urbanstar	B39F	1996	UVG demonstrator, 1997

Previous Registrations:

54FS	C26GKX, 898CCH	3418WY	FUA383Y
523SC	G853UVK	B717MDC	B717MDC, 1922FS
M833ECS	M740KJU, LNN590	KAZ2951	D573LSJ

Livery: White, fawn and green

Allocations:-

Stagecoach franchise routes 14, 141, 139 &140

Lynx	J45GGB	KAZ2751
Volvo B6	L84CNY	
Dart	M597SSB	

Redby services - Remainder

Opposite top:- **Redby operate local bus services in Sunderland and a modern coach fleet which takes vehicles to many parts of Britain and Continental Europe. Pictured in Park Lane, London is Jonckheere bodied Volvo N120RJF, which joined the fleet in 1998.** Colin Lloyd
Opposite bottom:- **Redby is one of only a handful of operators to operate buses in a franchise agreement with Stagecoach. Currently five buses carry Stagecoach colours including Leyland Lynx KAZ2751, which was new to the AA Motor Services fleet in Ayr.** Terry Wightman

ROBSON

G J Robson, 20 Dishforth Close, Thornaby, Stockton-on-Tees, Cleveland, TS17 9PH

OSJ614R	Leyland Leopard PSU3C/3R	Alexander AY	B53F	1976	Clydeside Scottish, 1988
CBO29V	Leyland National 11351A/1R		B49F	1979	National Welsh, 1990
PEX611W	Leyland National 2 NL116L11/1R		B49F	1980	Delta, Kirkby-in-Ashfield, 1997
B363LOY	Leyland National 2 NL116TL11/3R		B49F	1984	British Airways, 1993
L27LSG	Mercedes-Benz 709D	Alexander Sprint	B25F	1993	
L89NSF	Mercedes-Benz 709D	Alexander Sprint	B25F	1994	

Livery: Brown and cream

Depot: Master Road, Thornaby

ST GEORGE TRAVEL

St George Travel Ltd, 9 Cedar Terrace, Harraton, Washington, Tyne & Wear, NE38 9BE

GPX587X	Mercedes-Benz L508D	Robin Hood	DP19F	1981	Transcity, Sidcup, 1992
G327LDT	Mercedes-Benz 609D	Whittaker	DP19F	1989	
H193BCU	Mercedes-Benz 709D	Reeve Burgess	B25F	1990	St Mary's Hospital, ##, 1995
M789WCM	Mercedes-Benz 709D	North West Coach Sales	B20F	1994	West Coast Motors, 1999
N590WND	Mercedes-Benz 709D	Alexander Sprint	B27F	1996	Dart Buses, Paisley, 1999
N592WND	Mercedes-Benz 709D	Alexander Sprint	B27F	1996	Thompson, South Bank, 1999

Livery: White

Depot: Philadelphia Centre, Houghton-le-Spring.

Opposite:- **Two vehicles from the Robson fleet are seen in Stockton at a spot often occupied by bus photographers. The upper picture shows Leyland National CBO29V which was new to Taff Ely while the lower picture shows L89NSF a Mercedes-Benz 709 that was new to the company.** *Phillip Stephenson*

ROTHBURY MOTORS

Rothbury Motors Ltd, Town Foot, Blenkinsop, Welfare Garage, West Cornforth, DL17 9LA

No 1	LAW127F	Bedford VAM70	Duple Viceroy	C45F	1969	Morgan, Great Bedwyn, 1980
No 2	WIB2042	Dennis Dorchester SDA810	Plaxton Paramount 3500 II	C51F	1985	Western Scottish, 1996
No 3	NIW7053	Ford R1114	Duple Dominant II	C53F	1979	Childs, Kiveton Park, 1992
No 4	NIW7054	Ford R1114	Plaxton Supreme IV	C53F	1979	McVay, Edinburgh, 1992
No 5	NIW7055	Ford R1114	Duple Dominant II	C53F	1980	Garratt, Leicester, 1990
No 6	SJI8096	Ford R1114	Plaxton Supreme IV Express	C53F	1979	Moffatt & Williamson, Gauldry, 1994
No 7	WIB5507	Mercedes-Benz L608D	Reeve Burgess	BC19F	1984	Keir, Glass, 1995
No 9	F514LCN	Ford Transit VE6	Rothbury Motors	M14	1989	Rush & Tomkins, Newcastle, 1990
No 11	PVV657	Mercedes-Benz L608D	Reeve Burgess	BC25F	1983	Hilton, Newton-le-Willows, 1996
	DRU238L	Ford R226	Plaxton Panorama Elite III	C53F	1973	Wansbeck, Wanderers JB, 1997
	B358GCU	Freight-Rover Sherpa	Freight-Rover	M8	1985	Redheugh Boys Club, 1998
	HFM964T	Ford R1114	Plaxton Supreme IV	C53F	1979	Metcalf, Sedbergh, 1999
	OEC963V	Ford R1114	Duple Dominant II	C53F	1979	Metcalf, Sedbergh, 1999
	TPX884	Leyland Tiger TRCTL11/3RH	Plaxton Paramount 3500 II	C49F	1985	National Holidays, 1998
	H183ACN	Ford Transit VE6	Ford	M8	1991	private owner, 1998
	VJI9916	Mercedes-Benz L608D	Reeve Burgess	BC19F	1984	Coastal Country, Whitby, 1996
	VJI9917	Ford R1114	?,			
	PIL9718	Dennis Dorchester SDA810	Plaxton Paramount 3500 II	C55F	1985	Nichols, Carlton, 1998

Previous registrations:

NIW7053	BTB694T		TPX884	B371VBA
NIW7054	CFX311T, 633UML, NFS852T		VJI9916	A349FAO
NIW7055	LFK65V		VJI9917	AWB818T
PIL9718	B404OSB, FSU661, B984EGG, YTY867		WIB2042	B204CGA, YSV735, B855OSB
PVV657	A450CRM		WIB5507	A691CSE
SJI8096	JGE514T			

Livery: White and two-tone blue

No. 2 in the Rothbury Motors fleet is a Dennis Dorchester with Plaxton Paramount 3500 bodywork. As with many coaches currently operated in Britain the vehicle carries one of the non-year index marks that originate in Northern Ireland, in this case WIB2042. The number of Plaxton bodied Dennis Dorchesters produced was forty three, with 34 including this example, being delivered new to the Scottish Bus Group. *David Longbottom*

SCARLET BAND COACHES

A Blenkinsop, Welfare Garage, West Cornforth, Ferryhill, Co Durham DL17 9LA

SCS333M	Leyland Leopard PSU3/3R	Alexander AY	BC53F	1974	Northern Scottish, 1988
PRA10R	Leyland Leopard PSU3C/4R	Alexander AT	BC49F	1976	Citibus, Middleton, 1994
PRA13R	Leyland Leopard PSU3C/4R	Alexander AT	BC53F	1976	Taylor, Morley, 1992
ESF228S	Leyland Leopard PSU3E/4R	Alexander AT	BC49F	1978	Reynolds, Waford, 1995
ESF229S	Leyland Leopard PSU3E/4R	Alexander AT	BC49F	1978	Reynolds, Waford, 1995
ESF230S	Leyland Leopard PSU3E/4R	Alexander AT	BC49F	1978	Reynolds, Waford, 1995
GMS279S	Leyland Leopard PSU3E/4R	Alexander AYS	B53F	1978	Go-Ahead (OK), 1998
OAT536V	Leyland Leopard PSU3E/4R	Plaxton Supreme IV Exp	C49F	1979	Lee, Langley Moor, 1997
258NOG	Van Hool T815	Van Hool Acron	C49FT	1983	
E905GCU	Renault-Dodge S56	Alexander AM	B25F	1988	Go-Ahead (Northern), 1997
E730CNM	MCW MetroRider MF150/72	MCW	B25F	1988	Welwyn-Hatfield Line, 1994
E976DGS	MCW MetroRider MF150/72	MCW	B25F	1988	Welwyn-Hatfield Line, 1994
F241TBC	Volvo B10M-60	Van Hool Alizée	C51FT	1989	
J200EOS	EOS E180Z	EOS 200	C53FT	1992	
R562KHA	Bova FHD12.340	Bova Futura	C49FT	1997	
T67JBA	Dennis Dart SLF	Plaxton Pointer MPD	N29F	1999	
T68JBA	Dennis Dart SLF	Plaxton Pointer MPD	N29F	1999	
T69JBA	Dennis Dart SLF	Plaxton Pointer MPD	N29F	1999	

Previous Registrations:

258NOG	From new	E976DGS	E482CNM	OAT536V	JKH194V, WLT694

Livery: Red, cream and maroon

Scarlet Band ceased operating their long established Bowburn to Ferryhill Station service in January 1999. Their latest arrivals are three low-floor Mini Pointer Darts for use on the Ferryhill to Sunderland and Sunderland & Ferryhill to Billingham services. Pictured arriving at the city's new bus station is the first of the trio, T67JBA. *Bill Potter*

SIESTA

Siesta International Holidays Ltd, 156 -158 Linthorpe Road, Middlesbrough, Cleveland TS1 3RB

G194JHD	Ford Transit VE6	Ford	M8	1990	
H150LVN	Ford Transit VE6	Ford	M8	1991	
H984LEF	DAF SBR3000DKZ570	Plaxton Paramount 4000 III	C55/19CT	1990	
J69GCX	DAF SBR3000DKZ570	Plaxton Paramount 4000 III	C55/19CT	1991	
J324HVV	EOS E180Z	EOS 200	C53FT	1991	
J517MNA	Ford Transit VE6	Deansgate	M14	1992	
M9SCC	Scania K113TRA	Berkhof Excellence 2000HD	C47/17FT	1995	
M10SCC	Scania K113TRA	Berkhof Excellence 2000HD	C47/17FT	1995	
N7SCC	Scania K113TRA	Berkhof Excellence 3000HD	C45/17FT	1996	
N8SCC	Scania K113TRA	Berkhof Excellence 3000HD	C45/17FT	1996	
P5SCC	Scania K113TRA	Berkhof Excellence 3000HD	C45/17FT	1996	
P6SCC	Scania K113TRA	Berkhof Excellence 2000HD	C45/17FT	1996	
R4SCC	Scania K124IB4	Berkhof Axial 50	C40FT	1998	
R14SCC	Scania K124IB4	Berkhof Axial 50	C40FT	1998	
R909ULA	Volvo B10M-62	Berkhof Axial 50	C49FT	1998	Limebourne, Battersea, 1999

Livery: White, red and yellow

Siesta's M9SCC was the first of seven Scania K113 tri-axle coaches for this fleet. The type is fitted with Berkhof Excellence 2000HD coachwork and are principally used on the long journeys to Spain and other European destinations. The vehicle is seen nearer home in London with one of the Plaxton Paramount 4000-bodied DAF coaches behind. *Colin Lloyd*

SNAITHS

H J Snaith, 31 Brierly Gardens, Otterburn, Newcastle-upon-Tyne, NE19 1HB

w	WFU708V	Ford R1114	Plaxton Supreme IV	C53F	1980	Zebra Holidays, Leeds, 1984
	UBC644X	Ford R1114	Plaxton Supreme V	C51F	1982	Allenways, Birmingham, 1985
	ANA446Y	DAF MB200DKFL600	Plaxton Paramount 3200	C51F	1983	Shearings, 1989
	A700USU	DAF MB200DKFL600	Plaxton Paramount 3200	C53F	1984	Southern, Barrhead, 1991
	C350DND	Volvo B10M-61	Plaxton Paramount 3200 II	C53F	1986	Shearings, 1993
	GJI8778	Volvo B10M-61	Plaxton Paramount 3200 II	C53F	1986	Gath, Thornhill Lees, 1995
	D24SAO	Renault-Dodge S56	Reeve Burgess	B23F	1986	Hampshire Bus, 1991
	D25SAO	Renault-Dodge S56	Reeve Burgess	B23F	1986	Hampshire Bus, 1991
	D108XPG	Freight Rover Sherpa	Dormobile	B16F	1986	Redby, Sunderland, 1995
	D944VCN	Freight Rover Sherpa	Dormobile	B16F	1986	Northumbria, 1995
	D216GLJ	Freight Rover Sherpa	Dormobile	B16F	1987	Graham, Gilsland, 1995
	D253HFX	Volvo B10M-61	Plaxton Paramount 3200 III	C53F	1987	Woodstones, Kidderminster, 1994
	D259HFX	Volvo B10M-61	Plaxton Paramount 3200 III	C53F	1987	Woodstones, Kidderminster, 1994
w	D802RWF	Ford Transit 190D	Snaith	M12	1987	?, 1995
	D654NOD	Ford Transit 190D	Mellor	B16F	1987	Stagecoach Devon, 1997
	D113PTT	Ford Transit 190D	Mellor	M12	1987	Stagecoach Devon, 1999
	D120PTT	Ford Transit 190D	Mellor	M8	1987	Stagecoach Devon, 1997
	D420KMT	Volvo B10M-61	Plaxton Paramount 3200 III	C57F	1987	Southern, Barrhead, 1994
w	E903UBA	Freight Rover Sherpa 350	Deansgate	M16	1987	
	E947TBA	Ford Transit VE6	Deansgate	M12	1987	Foster, Otterburn, 1989
	E852AJR	Ford Transit VE6	Snaith	M12	1987	Cowie Leasing, Sunderland, 1993
	E600ENL	Mercedes-Benz 609D	Devon Conversions	C21F	1988	
	694AVY	Volvo B10M-61	Plaxton Paramount 3200 III	C53F	1988	Baker, Biddulph, 1995
	E165OMD	Volvo B10M-61	Plaxton Paramount 3200 III	C57F	1988	Capital, West Drayton, 1996
	E655FLD	Volvo B10M-61	Plaxton Paramount 3200 III	C53F	1988	Capital, West Drayton, 1996

England's largest forest, Kielder, is the location for this picture of Snaiths G400TVK, a Mercedes-Benz 811D with Reeve Burgess Beaver bodywork. This example is fitted with high-back seating and additional luxury items making the vehicle acceptable for short excursions and party travel. *Paul Wigan*

Snaiths Travel of Otterburn owns K846HUM, a Plaxton Premiere 320-bodied Volvo B10M, photographed at Barnard Castle School after delivering pupils from Queen Elizabeth Grammar School in Hexham for a rugby match. *J C Walton*

E205BDV	Ford Transit VE6	Mellor	B16F	1988	Stagecoach Devon, 1998
E216BDV	Ford Transit VE6	Mellor	B16F	1988	Stagecoach Devon, 1998
F568HPP	Ford Transit VE6	Chassis Developments	M16	1988	
F755FDV	Ford Transit VE6	Mellor	B16F	1988	Stagecoach Devon, 1998
F751RUT	Ford Transit VE6	Snaith	M12	1989	private owner,1995
HJI586	Volvo B10M-60	Plaxton Paramount 3200 III	C53F	1989	Glover, Ashbourne, 1996
G400TVK	Mercedes-Benz 811D	Reeve Burgess Beaver	C25F	1989	
G755GDC	Ford Transit VE6	Snaith	M8	1990	private owner, 1996
G238JDA	Ford Transit VE6	Snaith	M8	1990	private owner, 1996
H126LVN	Ford Transit VE6	Snaith	M8	1991	AMEC Construction, 1996
H194HLT	Ford Transit VE6	Snaith	M12	1991	van 1994
L992VTY	Ford Transit VE6	Snaith	M8	1994	Breadsall Developments, 1997
K200SDU	Volvo B10M-60	Plaxton Premiere 320	C53F	1992	Southern, Barrhead, 1999
K846HUM	Volvo B10M-60	Plaxton Paramount 3200 III	C50F	1993	Wallace Arnold, 1997
L10TCC	Volvo B10M-62	Plaxton Premiere 320	C57F	1994	Travellera, Hounslow, 1997
R979RRG	Volvo B10M-62	Plaxton Premiere 320	C56F	1998	
S494ABR	Mercedes-Benz Vario O814	Plaxton Beaver 2	BC32F	1998	
T599BRG	Volvo B10M-62	Plaxton Premiere 320	C56F	1999	

Previous registrations:

694AVY	E701HKV, 5658RM, E...NVT	HJI586	G699OCH
GJI8778	C320FML		

Livery: White, red and blue

SNOWDONS

A Snowdon, Seaside Lane, Easington Colliery, Peterlee, SR8 3TW

Reg	Chassis	Body	Seating	Year	History
SBR881P	Leyland Leopard PSU3C/4R	Plaxton Supreme III	C49F	1975	Bedlington, Ashington, 1994
DWR683W	Leyland Leopard PSU3E/4R	Duple Dominant (1980)	B65F	1981	Ron Lyles, Batley, 1998
ONL904X	Leyland Leopard PSU3F/5R	Plaxton Supreme VI	C53F	1982	DMC Travel, Peterlee, 1999
RML109Y	Volvo B10M-61	Plaxton Viewmaster IV	C51F	1982	JC Bell, New Silksworth, 1999
JIL8514	Leyland Tiger TRCTL11/3R	Plaxton Paramount 3200 E	C57F	1983	Brijan, Swanmore, 1997
HJI644	Van Hool T818	Van Hool Astron	C50/11FT	1983	Gelsthorpe, Mansfield, 1998
NIL7962	Van Hool T818	Van Hool Astron	C50/11FT	1983	Leo's Pride, Herne Bay, 1998
DJI8747	Van Hool T818	Van Hool Astron	C49/11FT	1983	Pegasus, Perth, 1998
C880KGG	Mercedes-Benz L608D	Scott	BC25F	1986	Williamson, East Kilbride, 1998
D936VCN	Freight-Rover Sherpa	Dormobile	B16F	1986	Grufferty, Easington Lane, 1997
NIL5905	Volvo B10M-60	Plaxton Paramount 3500 III	C57F	1991	Wessex, 1997
NIL5906	Volvo B10M-60	Plaxton Paramount 3500 III	C57F	1991	Wessex, 1997
NIL5907	Volvo B10M-60	Plaxton Paramount 3500 III	C48FT	1991	Wessex, 1997
NIL5908	Volvo B10M-60	Plaxton Paramount 3500 III	C48FT	1991	Wessex, 1997
J910OEY	Volvo B10M-60	Plaxton Expressliner	C46FT	1991	Selwyn's, Runcorn, 1997

Previous registrations:-

DJI8747	7299DD, PGD240Y	NIL5907	H72PWO
DWR683W	VUP510V, PUB66W, 7596VM	NIL5908	H68PWO
HJI644	4131AT, PGD153Y, TOT987, WWB725Y	NIL7962	TLA737Y, 5182MT, EIB599
JIL8514	EAH893Y, CIW9721, FFA271Y, MIB346, FFA657Y	OIB2917	KNS401V
NIL5905	H69PDW	SBR881P	JVK81P, 491JVX
NIL5906	H71PWO		

The Van Hool Astron is a four metre coach with sunken rear lounge which, here, has seating for eleven. Popular on long distance tours where, for the majority of passengers, the layout allows excellent viewing.
Colin Lloyd

STAGECOACH BUSWAYS

Busways Travel Services Ltd, Wheatsheaf, Sunderland, SR5 1AQ

1	1JVK	Volvo B10M-62		Jonckheere Mistral 50		C44FT	1998			
2	2JVK	Volvo B10M-62		Jonckheere Mistral 50		C44FT	1998			
11	KSU461	Volvo B10M-62		Jonckheere Mistral 50		C44FT	1999			
12	KSU462	Volvo B10M-62		Jonckheere Mistral 50		C44FT	1999			
81w	L81YBB	Volvo B10M-62		Plaxton Expressliner 2		C44FT	1993			
83w	L83YBB	Volvo B10M-62		Plaxton Expressliner 2		C44FT	1993			
91	N91RVK	Volvo B10M-62		Plaxton Expressliner 2		C44FT	1996			
92	P92URG	Volvo B10M-62		Plaxton Expressliner 2		C44FT	1996			

101-125

Leyland Lynx LX112L10ZR1S   Leyland Lynx   B49F   1988-89

101	F101HVK	106	F106HVK	111	F111HVK	116	F116HVK	121	F121HVK
102	F102HVK	107	F107HVK	112	F112HVK	117	F117HVK	122	F122HVK
103	F103HVK	108	F108HVK	113	F113HVK	118	F118HVK	123	F123HVK
104	F104HVK	109	F109HVK	114	F114HVK	119	F119HVK	124	F124HVK
105	F105HVK	110	F110HVK	115	F115HVK	120	F120HVK	125	F125HVK

126	H126ACU	Leyland Lynx LX2R11C15Z4S	Leyland Lynx	BC47F	1990
127	H127ACU	Leyland Lynx LX2R11C15Z4S	Leyland Lynx	BC47F	1990

151-172

Dennis Trident   Alexander ALX400   N--/--F   1999

151	V151DFT	156	V156DFT	161	V161DFT	165	V165DFT	169	V169DFT
152	V152DFT	157	V157DFT	162	V162DFT	166	V166DFT	170	V170DFT
153	V153DFT	158	V158DFT	163	V163DFT	167	V167DFT	171	V171DFT
154	V154DFT	159	V159DFT	164	V164DFT	168	V168DFT	172	V172DFT
155	V155DFT	160	V160DFT						

421-430

Scania N113DRB   Alexander RH   B47/29F   1990

421	H421BNL	423	H423BNL	425	H425BNL	427	H427BNL	429	H429BNL
422	H422BNL	424	H424BNL	426	H426BNL	428	H428BNL	430	H430BNL

451-495

MAN 18.220 HOCR   Alexander ALX300   N42F   1999

451	S451OFT	460	S460OFT	469	T469BNL	478	T478BNL	487	T487BNL
452	S452OFT	461	T461BNL	470	T470BNL	479	T479BNL	488	T488BNL
453	S453OFT	462	T462BNL	471	T471BNL	480	T480BNL	489	T489BNL
454	S454OFT	463	T463BNL	472	T472BNL	481	T481BNL	490	T490BNL
455	S455OFT	464	T464BNL	473	T473BNL	482	T482BNL	491	T491BNL
456	S456OFT	465	T465BNL	474	T474BNL	483	T483BNL	492	T492BNL
457	S457OFT	466	T466BNL	475	T475BNL	484	T484BNL	493	T493BNL
458	S458OFT	467	T467BNL	476	T476BNL	485	T485BNL	494	T494BNL
459	S459OFT	468	T468BNL	477	T477BNL	486	T486BNL	495	T495BNL

On Sunday, 2nd May 1999 the new Park Lane Transport Interchange opened to provide Sunderland with a central bus station at which the many bus operators in the city now call. Twelve Leyland Lynx operate from the City depot and 112, F112HVK, is seen operating local service 2. *Bill Potter*

During the early part of 1999 several double-deck buses from Busways were cascaded to other Stagecoach fleets, notably Transit, leaving just ten in the fleet that are not Olympians. These are Alexander-bodied Scanias that are all based at the Byker depot and are represented by 424, H424BNL. *Malcolm King*

601-663

Leyland Olympian ONLXB/1R   Alexander RH   B45/31F   1985-86

601	C601LFT	612	C612LFT	623	C623LFT	640	C640LFT	654	C654LFT
602	C602LFT	613	C613LFT	624	C624LFT	641	C641LFT	655	C655LFT
603	C603LFT	614	C614LFT	625	C625LFT	642	C642LFT	656	C656LFT
604	C604LFT	615	C615LFT	626	C626LFT	645	C645LFT	657	C657LFT
605	C605LFT	616	C616LFT	627	C627LFT	646	C646LFT	658	C658LFT
606	C606LFT	617	C617LFT	628	C628LFT	647	C647LFT	659	C659LFT
608	C608LFT	618	C618LFT	629	C629LFT	650	C650LFT	660	C660LFT
609	C609LFT	619	C619LFT	631	C631LFT	653	C653LFT	661	C661LFT
610	C610LFT	620	C620LFT	638	C638LFT	651	C651LFT	663	C663LFT
611	C611LFT	622	C622LFT	639	C639LFT	652	C652LFT		

667-676

Leyland Olympian ON2R50C13Z4 Northern Counties Palatine B47/30F   1990-91

667	H667BNL	669	H669BNL	671	H671BNL	673	H673BNL	675	H675BNL
668	H668BNL	670	H670BNL	672	H672BNL	674	H674BNL	676	H676BNL

701-740

Volvo Olympian YN2RV18Z4   Alexander RL   B47/28F   1995

701	N701LTN	709	N709LTN	717	N717LTN	725	N725LTN	733	N733LTN
702	N702LTN	710	N710LTN	718	N718LTN	726	N726LTN	734	N734LTN
703	N703LTN	711	N711LTN	719	N719LTN	727	N727LTN	735	N735LTN
704	N704LTN	712	N712LTN	720	N720LTN	728	N728LTN	736	N736LTN
705	N705LTN	713	N713LTN	721	N721LTN	729	N729LTN	737	N737LTN
706	N706LTN	714	N714LTN	722	N722LTN	730	N730LTN	738	N738LTN
707	N707LTN	715	N715LTN	723	N723LTN	731	N731LTN	739	N739LTN
708	N708LTN	716	N716LTN	724	N724LTN	732	N732LTN	740	N740LTN

901-920

Scania N113CRB   Alexander PS   B51F*   1989   *901-5 are B48F; 906 is B49F

901	F901JRG	905	F905JRG	909	F909JRG	913	F913JRG	917	F917JRG
902	F902JRG	906	F906JRG	910	F910JRG	914	F914JRG	918	F918JRG
903	F903JRG	907	F907JRG	911	F911JRG	915	F915JRG	919	F919JRG
904	F904JRG	908	F908JRG	912	F912JRG	916	F916JRG	920	F920JRG

921-926

Scania N113CRB   Alexander PS   B51F*   1989-90 *926 is B49F

921	G921TCU	923	G923TCU	924	G924TCU	925	G925TCU	926	G926TCU
922	G922TCU								

927	G113SKX	Scania N113CRB	Alexander PS	B49F	1989	Scania demonstrator, 1991

928-937

Scania N113CRB   Alexander PS   B51F   1991

928	H428EFT	930	B430EFT	932	B432EFT	934	B434EFT	936	B436EFT
929	H429EFT	931	B431EFT	933	B433EFT	935	B435EFT	937	B437EFT

938	G108CEH	Scania N113CRB	Alexander PS	B49F	1990	Stevensons, 1993

951	M951DRG	Scania L113CRL	Northern Counties Paladin	B49F	1994
952	M952DRG	Scania L113CRL	Northern Counties Paladin	BC49F	1994
953	M953DRG	Scania L113CRL	Alexander Strider	B51F	1994
954	M954DRG	Scania L113CRL	Alexander Strider	B51F	1994

1101-1128

Dennis Dart SLF   Alexander ALX200   B37F   1997-98

1101	R101KRG	1108	R108KRG	1114	R114KRG	1119	R119KRG	1124	R124KRG
1102	R102KRG	1109	R109KRG	1115	R115KRG	1120	R120KRG	1125	R125KRG
1103	R103KRG	1110	R110KRG	1116	R116KRG	1121	R121KRG	1126	R126KRG
1104	R104KRG	1112	R112KRG	1117	R117KRG	1122	R122KRG	1127	R127KRG
1105	R105KRG	1113	R113KRG	1118	R118KRG	1123	R123KRG	1128	R128KRG
1107	R107KRG								

*Opposite:-***Stagecoach Busways embarked on a programme of introducing low floor buses into the Newcastle area and are one of just four fleets in the group to be supplied with Alexander bodied MAN units, all of which are based at Slatyford depot. Pictured in Sunderland is 487, T487BNL. The MAN units added to a variety of single deck bus types including Volvo B10B products and Dennis Darts. 1989 saw the first Scania saloon arrive and now some 42 are in service, all at Slatyford and including several with lettering for the Gateshead Metro Centre Shuttle. Numerically the first is 901, F901JRG.** *Bill Potter/Tony Wilson*

Dennis Darts first arrived with Busways in 1992 when a pair of Plaxton-bodied vehicles were delivered. Bodywork on further deliveries has been divided between further examples from Plaxton and Alexander. Showing off the Dash design is 1739, L739VNL. *Terry Wightman*

1129-1133

Dennis Dart SLF — Alexander ALX200 — B37F — 1998 — Oxford, 1998

1129	R825YUD	1130	R826YUD	1131	R827YUD	1132	R828YUD	1133	R829YUD

1201	M201DRG	Dennis Lance 11SDA3113	Plaxton Verde	B49F	1994
1202	M202DRG	Dennis Lance 11SDA3113	Plaxton Verde	B49F	1994
1203	M203DRG	Dennis Lance 11SDA3113	Plaxton Verde	B49F	1994
1204	M204DRG	Dennis Lance 11SDA3113	Optare Sigma	B47F	1994

1421-1459

Mercedes-Benz 709D — Reeve Burgess Beaver — B19F* — 1987-88 — *1431/49/51/3 are B23F
1426/9/35/40/2/3/5/50/4-9 are B20F

1421	E421AFT	1428	E428AFT	1434w	E434AFT	1445	E445AFT	1454w	E454AFT
1422	E422AFT	1429	E429AFT	1435	E435AFT	1449w	E449AFT	1455	E455AFT
1423	E423AFT	1430	E430AFT	1437	E437AFT	1450	E450AFT	1456w	E456AFT
1424	E424AFT	1431w	E431AFT	1440	E440AFT	1451	E451AFT	1457	E457AFT
1425w	E425AFT	1432	E432AFT	1442	E442AFT	1452w	E452AFT	1458w	E458AFT
1426	E426AFT	1433	E433AFT	1443	E443AFT	1453	E453AFT	1459	E459AFT
1427	E427AFT								

1461-1500

Mercedes-Benz 709D — Alexander Sprint — B23F — 1996

1461	N461RVK	1469	N469RVK	1477	N477RVK	1485	N485RVK	1493	N493RVK
1462	N462RVK	1470	N470RVK	1478	N478RVK	1486	N486RVK	1494	N494RVK
1463	N463RVK	1471	N471RVK	1479	N479RVK	1487	N487RVK	1495	N495RVK
1464	N464RVK	1472	N472RVK	1480	N480RVK	1488	N488RVK	1496	N496RVK
1465	N465RVK	1473	N473RVK	1481	N481RVK	1489	N489RVK	1497	N497RVK
1466	N466RVK	1474	N474RVK	1482	N482RVK	1490	N490RVK	1498	N498RVK
1467	N467RVK	1475	N475RVK	1483	N483RVK	1491	N491RVK	1499	N499RVK
1468	N468RVK	1476	N476RVK	1484	N484RVK	1492	N492RVK	1500	N501RVK

1501	G280TSL	Mercedes-Benz 709D	Alexander Sprint	B23F	1990	Fife Scottish,1999
1502	G281TSL	Mercedes-Benz 709D	Alexander Sprint	B23F	1990	Fife Scottish,1999
1503	K485FFS	Mercedes-Benz 709D	Alexander Sprint	B25F	1993	Fife Scottish,1999
1504	K492FFS	Mercedes-Benz 709D	Alexander Sprint	B25F	1993	Fife Scottish,1999

Two types of minibus are found in the Stagecoach Busways' fleet following the recent demise of the last Renault-Dodge. Seen in South Hylton is Optare MetroRider 1687, J379BNW which arrived along with the Welcome fleet in 1993. *Richard Godfrey*

1505	K493FFS	Mercedes-Benz 709D	Alexander Sprint	B25F	1993	Fife Scottish,1999
1506	K494FFS	Mercedes-Benz 709D	Alexander Sprint	B25F	1993	Fife Scottish,1999

1671-1678

Optare MetroRider MR03 — Optare — B29F — 1990-91 East London, 1998

1671	H144UUA	**1673**	H150UUA	**1675**	H162WWT	**1677**	H171WWT	**1678**	H174WWT
1672	H148UUA	**1674**	H160WWT	**1676**	H170WWT				

1679-1693

Optare MetroRider — Optare — B29F — 1991-92 Welcome, 1993

1679	J371BNW	**1682**	J374BNW	**1685**	J377BNW	**1689**	K162FYG	**1692**	K165FYG
1680	J372BNW	**1683**	J375BNW	**1686**	J378BNW	**1690**	K163FYG	**1693**	K166FYG
1681	J373BNW	**1684**	J376BNW	**1687**	J379BNW	**1691**	K164FYG		

1694	H176WWT	Optare MetroRider MR03	Optare	B29F	1991	East London, 1998
1701	J701KCU	Dennis Dart 9.8SDL3017	Plaxton Pointer	B40F	1992	
1702	J702KCU	Dennis Dart 9.8SDL3017	Plaxton Pointer	B40F	1992	

1703-1743

Dennis Dart 9.8SDL3017* — Alexander Dash — B40F — 1992-93 *1723-28 are 9.8SDL3025; *1729-43 are 9.8SDL3035

1703	K703PCN	**1711**	K711PCN	**1721**	K721PCN	**1729**	L729VNL	**1737**	L737VNL
1704	K704PCN	**1712**	K712PCN	**1722**	K722PCN	**1730**	L730VNL	**1738**	L738VNL
1705	K705PCN	**1713**	K713PCN	**1723**	K723PNL	**1731**	L731VNL	**1739**	L739VNL
1706	K706PCN	**1714**	K714PCN	**1724**	K724PNL	**1732**	L732VNL	**1740**	L740VNL
1707	K707PCN	**1715**	K715PCN	**1725**	K725PNL	**1733**	L733VNL	**1741**	L741VNL
1708	K708PCN	**1717**	K717PCN	**1726**	K726PNL	**1734**	L734VNL	**1742**	L742VNL
1709	K709PCN	**1718**	K718PCN	**1727**	K727PNL	**1735**	L735VNL	**1743**	L743VNL
1710	K710PCN	**1720**	K720PCN	**1728**	K728PNL	**1736**	L736VNL		

1744-1759

Dennis Dart 9.8SDL3035 — Plaxton Pointer — B40F — 1993

1744	L744VNL	**1748**	L748VNL	**1751**	L751VNL	**1754**	L754VNL	**1757**	L757VNL
1745	L745VNL	**1749**	L749VNL	**1752**	L752VNL	**1755**	L755VNL	**1758**	L758VNL
1746	L746VNL	**1750**	L750VNL	**1753**	L753VNL	**1756**	L756VNL	**1759**	L759VNL

1760-1765

Dennis Dart 9.8SDL3040 — Alexander Dash — B40F — 1994

1760	L760ARG	1762	L762ARG	1763	L763ARG	1764	L764ARG	1765	L765ARG
1761	L761ARG								

1766-1771

Dennis Dart 9.8SDL3040 — Plaxton Pointer — B40F — 1994

1766	M766DRG	1768	M768DRG	1769	M769DRG	1770	M770DRG	1771	M771DRG
1767	M767DRG								

1772-1785

Dennis Dart — Alexander Dash — B40F — 1996

1772	N772RVK	1775	N775RVK	1778	N779RVK	1781	P781WCN	1784	P784WCN
1773	N773RVK	1776	N776RVK	1779	N780RVK	1782	P782WCN	1785	P785WCN
1774	N774RVK	1777	N778RVK	1780	P780WCN	1783	P783WCN		

1786-1793

Dennis Dart — Alexander Dash — B40F — 1996-97

1786	P786WVK	1788	P788WVK	1790	P790WVK	1792	P792WVK	1793	P793WVK
1787	P787WVK	1789	P789WVK	1791	P791WVK				

1901	M901DRG	Volvo B10B	Alexander Strider	B51F	1994
1902	M902DRG	Volvo B10B	Alexander Strider	B51F	1994

2201-2217

Volvo B10M-55 — Alexander PS — B49F — 1995

2201	N201LTN	2205	N205LTN	2209	N209LTN	2212	N212LTN	2215	N215LTN
2202	N202LTN	2206	N206LTN	2210	N210LTN	2213	N213LTN	2216	N216LTN
2203	N203LTN	2207	N207LTN	2211	N211LTN	2214	N214LTN	2217	N217LTN
2204	N204LTN	2208	N208LTN						

2218-2235

Volvo B10M-55 — Alexander PS — B49F — 1996

2218	P118XCN	2220	P120XCN	2222	P122XCN	2224	P124XCN	2226	P126XCN
2219	P119XCN	2221	P121XCN	2223	P123XCN	2225	P125XCN	2235	P135XCN

2236-2258

Volvo B10BLE — Alexander ALX300 — B44F — 1997-98

2236	R236KRG	2241	R241KRG	2246	R246KRG	2251	R251KRG	2255	R255KRG
2237	R237KRG	2242	R242KRG	2247	R247KRG	2252	R252KRG	2256	R256KRG
2238	R238KRG	2243	R243KRG	2248	R248KRG	2253	R253KRG	2257	R257KRG
2239	R239KRG	2244	R244KRG	2249	R249KRG	2254	R254KRG	2258	R258KRG
2240	R240KRG	2245	R245KRG	2250	R250KRG				

Special event vehicle:-

B140	LCU112	Daimler CCG6	Roe	B35/28R	1964

Ancilliary vehicles:-

DT18	D298YTY	Dodge Commando G13	Wadham Stringer Vanguard	DT	1987	MoD, 1997 (81KF23)
DT19	D305YTY	Dodge Commando G13	Wadham Stringer Vanguard	DT	1986	MoD, 1997 (80KF36)
DT20	B866JVK	Dodge Commando G13	Wadham Stringer Vanguard	DT	1985	MoD, 1997 (31KC82)
DT21	D918KPT	Dodge Commando G13	Wadham Stringer Vanguard	DT	1986	MoD, 1997 (80KF58)
DT22	B916JVK	Dodge Commando G13	Wadham Stringer Vanguard	DT	1986	MoD, 1999

Previous registrations:-

1JVK	From new		KSU461	From new
2JVK	From new		KSU462	From new

Due in September are the first of thirty-five Dennis Tridents with the singledoor provincial body already in service with Stagecoach Manchester and at Grimsby with Stagecoach East Midland. Their arrival will allow mid-life vehicles to be moved to other Stagecoach fleets, thus altering the profile of the double-deck fleet. Here are shown two saloons. The picture above shows 2241, R241KRG, in New Bridge Street West,Newcastle. One of the first Alexander ALX300 bodies it is based on a Volvo low-floor B10B chassis, the LE type representing low-entry. Below, 1202, M202DRG, is one of the vehicle purchased by Busways for type trialing. The vehicle is a Dennis Lance with Plaxton Verde bodywork and currently working from Sunderland depot.
Tony Wilson/Phillip Stephenson

Allocations:-

Byker (Shields Road)

Volvo B10M	1	2	11	12	91	92		
Mercedes-Benz	1421	1423	1424	1426	1427	1428	1429	1432
	1433	1435	1440	1461	1462	1463	1464	1465
	1466	1467	1468	1469	1483	1484	1485	1486
	1501	1502	1503	1504	1505			
Dart	1701	1702	1713	1714	1715	1717	1718	1720
	1721	1722	1744	1745	1746	1750	1751	1752
	1753							
Volvo B10M	2201	2202	2203	2204	2205	2206	2207	2208
	2218	2219	2220	2221	2222	2223	2224	2225
	2226	2235						
Volvo B10BLE	2237	2238	2239	2240	2241	2242	2243	2244
	2245	2246	2247	2248	2249	2250	2251	2252
	2253	2254	2255	2256	2257	2258		
Scania DD	421	422	423	424	425	426	427	428
	429	430						
Olympian	601	602	603	604	605	608	609	610
	611	612	613	614	615	616	617	
	618	619	620	622	623	624	625	626
	627	628	629	631	641	645	646	647
	654	658	663	701	702	703	704	705
	706	707	708	709	710	711	712	713
	714	715	716	717	718	719	720	721
	722	723	724	725	726	727	728	729
	730							

Slatyford (Slatyford Lane)

Mercedes-Benz	1470	1471	1472	1473	1474	1475	1476	1477
	1478	1479	1480	1481	1482			
MetroRider	1673	1674	1675	1678				
Dart	1723	1724	1725	1726	1727	1728		
MAN ALX300	451	452	453	454	455	456	457	458
	459	460	461	462	463	464	465	466
	467	468	469	470	471	472	473	474
	475	476	477	478	479	480	481	482
	484	485						
Scania SD	901	902	903	904	905	906	907	908
	909	910	911	912	913	914	915	916
	917	918	919	920	921	922	923	924
	925	926	927	928	929	930	931	932
	933	934	935	936	937	938	951	952
	953	954						
Volvo B10BLE	2236							
Olympian	638	639	640	642	648	656		

South Shields (Dean Road)

Mercedes-Benz	1437	1450	1451	1453	1457	1459	1487	1488
	1489	1490	1491	1492	1493	1494	1495	1496
MetroRider	1689	1690	1691					
Dart	1101	1102	1129	1130	1131	1132	1133	1703
	1704	1705	1706	1707	1708	1709	1710	1711
	1712	1729	1740	1741	1742	1743	1749	1754
	1755	1756	1757	1758	1759	1766	1767	1768
	1769	1783	1784	1785	1791	1792	1793	
Lynx	108	111	115	116	117	118	119	120
	121	122	123	124	125	126	127	
Olympian	675	676	731	732	733	734	735	736
	737	738	739	740				

Stagecoach Busways provide six vehicles to National Express duties, two recent additions being Jonckheere bodied Volvo coaches from the 1998 vehicle programme. Pictured in Milton Keynes while operating route 230 to London Gatwick is 91, N91RVK, with Plaxton Expressliner 2 bodywork. *Phillip Stephenson*

Sunderland (North Bridge Street)

Mercedes-Benz	1442	1443	1445	1455	1497	1498	1499	1500
MetroRiders	1671	1672	1676	1677	1679	1680	1681	1682
	1683	1684	1685	1686	1687	1692	1693	1694
Dart	1103	1104	1105	1107	1108	1109	1110	1112
	1113	1114	1115	1116	1117	1118	1120	1121
	1122	1123	1124	1125	1126	1127	1128	1730
	1731	1732	1733	1734	1735	1736	1737	1738
	1739	1748	1760	1761	1762	1763	1764	1765
	1770	1771	1772	1773	1774	1775	1776	1777
	1778	1779	1780	1781	1782	1786	1787	1788
	1789	1790						
Lynx	101	102	103	104	105	106	107	109
	110	112	113	114				
Lance	1201	1202	1203	1204				
Volvo B10	1901	1902	2209	2210	2211	2212	2213	2214
	2215	2216	2217					
MAN/ALX300	486	487	488	489	490	491	492	493
	494	495						
Olympian	661	667	668	669	670	671	672	673
	674							

Unallocated

Mercedes-Benz	1422	1425	1430	1431	1434	1447	1449	1452
	1454	1456	1458					
Dart	1119							
Volvo Expressliner	81	83						
Leyland Olympian	606	650	651	652	653	655	657	659
	660							

STAGECOACH TRANSIT

Stagecoach Darlington - Stagecoach Kingston upon Hull - Stagecoach Hartlepool

Cleveland Transit Ltd, Church Road, Stockton-on-Tees, Cleveland, TS18 2HW

31	H71XKH	Leyland Swift ST2R44C97A4	Reeve Burgess Harrier	C37F	1990	
32	J422HDS	Volvo B10M-60	Plaxton Excalibur	C53F	1992	East Midland, 1999
36	837XHW	Volvo B10M-61	Van Hool Alizée	C53F	1987	Streamline, Bath, 1994
37	ESU263	Leyland Tiger TRCTL11/3RZ	Plaxton Paramount 3500	C49FT	1983	Busways, 1998
38	G525LWU	Volvo B10M-60	Plaxton Paramount 3500 III	C52F	1990	Cambus, 1999
51	IIL1321	Volvo B10M-61	Plaxton Paramount 3200 III	C51FT	1987	
71	K571DFS	Volvo B10M-60	Plaxton Premiére Interurban	BC51F	1993	East Midland, 1995
72	K572DFS	Volvo B10M-60	Plaxton Premiére Interurban	BC51F	1993	East Midland, 1995
73	K573DFS	Volvo B10M-60	Plaxton Premiére Interurban	BC51F	1993	East Midland, 1995
76	K576DFS	Volvo B10M-60	Plaxton Premiére Interurban	BC51F	1993	East Midland, 1996
77	K577DFS	Volvo B10M-60	Plaxton Premiére Interurban	BC51F	1993	East Midland, 1996

78-85
Volvo B10M-62   Plaxton Premiére Interurban   BC51F   1996-97

78	P178PRH	80	P180PRH	82	R82SEF	84	R84SEF	85	R85SEF
79	P179PRH	81	P181PRH	83	R83SEF				

95	T95JHN	Volvo B10MA-55	Jonckheere Modulo	AC72F	1999
96	T96JHN	Volvo B10MA-55	Jonckheere Modulo	AC72F	1999
97	T97JHN	Volvo B10MA-55	Jonckheere Modulo	AC72F	1999

107	EJR107W	Leyland Atlantean AN68A/2R	Alexander AL	B49/37F	1980	Busways, 1998
108	EJR108W	Leyland Atlantean AN68A/2R	Alexander AL	B49/37F	1980	Busways, 1998
110	EJR110W	Leyland Atlantean AN68A/2R	Alexander AL	B49/37F	1980	Busways, 1999
111	EJR111W	Leyland Atlantean AN68A/2R	Alexander AL	B49/37F	1980	Busways, 1999
118	EJR118W	Leyland Atlantean AN68A/2R	Alexander AL	B49/37F	1980	Busways, 1999
121	YVN521T	Leyland Fleetline FE30AGR	Northern Counties	B43/31F	1979	
122	AVK142V	Leyland Atlantean AN68A/2R	Alexander AL	B49/37F	1980	Busways, 1997
124	SCN249S	Leyland Atlantean AN68A/2R	Alexander AL	B49/37F	1978	Busways, 1997
125	AVK135V	Leyland Atlantean AN68A/2R	Alexander AL	B49/37F	1980	Busways, 1999
126	AVK156V	Leyland Atlantean AN68A/2R	Alexander AL	B49/37F	1980	Busways, 1999
127	AVK147V	Leyland Atlantean AN68A/2R	Alexander AL	B49/37F	1980	Busways, 1997
128	AVK148V	Leyland Atlantean AN68A/2R	Alexander AL	B49/37F	1980	Busways, 1997
130	AVK180V	Leyland Atlantean AN68A/2R	Alexander AL	B49/37F	1980	Busways, 1999

140-157
Leyland Fleetline FE30AGR   Northern Counties   B43/31F   1980-83

140	JAJ140W	143	JAJ143W	146	JAJ146W	150	VEF150Y	156	YAJ156Y
141	JAJ141W	144	JAJ144W	148	PEF148X	153	VEF153Y	157	YAJ157Y
142	JAJ142W	145	JAJ145W	149	PEF149X				

189	PRX189B	Leyland Titan PD3/4	Northern Counties	O39/30F	1964	Southdown, 1988
210	B210UAT	Dennis Dominator DDA904	Alexander RH	B43/32F	1984	

217-222
Dennis Dominator DD906*   Northern Counties   B43/31F   1985-86 *219-22 are DDA1009

217w	B217OAJ	219w	C219WAJ	220	C220WAJ	221	C221WAJ	222	C222WAJ

232	E132SAT	Dennis Dominator DDA1014	East Lancashire (1992)	B45/21D	1987

Opposite:- **Stagecoach Transit is undergoing a major fleet upgrade with many of the Dennis Dominators and Scania double-decks having left the fleet being replaced by Olympians and Titans. The Stagecoach Express fleet was also given a lift following the arrival of three Jonckheere bodied articulated express vehicles for the Hull-Sheffield service. The upper picture shows Stagecoach Express 82, R82SEF, an interurban bus body built with many local service features such as screens and ticket equipment, in a Plaxton Paramount frame. The vehicle is seen on one of its regular routes, the X90 between Darlington and the Gateshead Metro Centre. The lower picture shows one of the Leyland Titan double-decks that have been cascaded from Stagecoach London. Now converted to single door they are mostly to be found at Stockton.** *Phillip Stephenson*

Bodywork for the 1998 order of Volvo B10M buses was shared between Alexander and Northern Counties. While the majority was supplied by the former, Northern Counties Palatine design went to Stagecoach Manchester, Stagecoach South and Transit, who, at the time had different numbering systems for the operating areas. Pictured in Middlesborough is 653, R653RPY, which is still based in Stockton. *Richard Godfrey*

242-251

							Dennis Dominator DDA1016		East Lancashire		B45/31F	1988

242	F142BKH	244	F144BKH	246	F146BKH	248	F148BKH	250	F150BKH
243	F143BKH	245	F145BKH	247	F147BKH	249	F149BKH	251	F151BKH

270-282

Leyland Titan TNLXB2RR   Leyland   B44/27F   1982-83 East London, 1997-98

270	NUW604Y	273	NUW642Y	276	NUW649Y	279	NUW666Y	281	NUW673Y
271	NUW634Y	274	NUW643Y	277	NUW659Y	280	NUW668Y	282	NUW675Y
272	NUW639Y	275	NUW648Y	278	NUW664Y						

283-290

Leyland Titan TNLXB2RR   Leyland   B44/29F   1984   Stagecoach London, 1997-98

283	A826SUL	285	A840SUL	287	A849SUL	289	A622THV	290	A626THV
284	A827SUL	286	A846SUL	288	B113WUV					

303-316

Mercedes-Benz 811D   Wright NimBus   B26F   1989   Selkent, 1996

303	HDZ2603	306	HDZ2606	309	HDZ2609	311w	HDZ2611	315	HDZ2615
304	HDZ2604	307	HDZ2607	310	HDZ2610	313	HDZ2613	316	HDZ2616
305	HDZ2605								

321w	F621XMS	Mercedes-Benz 811D	Alexander Sprint	B28F	1988	Selkent, 1996
324w	F624XMS	Mercedes-Benz 811D	Alexander Sprint	B28F	1988	Selkent, 1996
325w	F625XMS	Mercedes-Benz 811D	Alexander Sprint	B28F	1988	Selkent, 1996
329w	F629XMS	Mercedes-Benz 811D	Alexander Sprint	B28F	1988	Selkent, 1996

341-354

Mercedes-Benz 709D   Alexander Sprint   B23F   1996

341	N341KKH	344	N344KKH	347	N347KKH	350	P350NKH	353	P353NKH
342	N342KKH	345	N345KKH	348	N348KKH	351	P351NKH	354	P354NKH
343	N343KKH	346	N346KKH	349	P349NKH	352	P352NKH		

355	S355KEF	Mercedes-Benz Vario O814	Alexander ALX100	B29F	1998					
356	S356KEF	Mercedes-Benz Vario O814	Alexander ALX100	B29F	1998					
357	S357KEF	Mercedes-Benz Vario O814	Alexander ALX100	B29F	1998					
358	S358KEF	Mercedes-Benz Vario O814	Alexander ALX100	B29F	1998					

401-408
Volvo B6-9.9M   Plaxton Pointer   B41F   1993-94

401	L101GHN	**403**	L103GHN	**405**	M105PVN	**407**	M107PVN	**408**	M108PVN
402	L102GHN	**404**	M104PVN	**406**	M106PVN				

438-454
Volvo B6-9.9M   Alexander Dash   BC40F   1994   Ribble, 1995

438	L238CCW	**443**	L243CCK	**445**	L245CCK	**447**	L247CCK	**450**	L250CCK
442	L242CCK	**444**	L244CCK	**446**	L246CCK	**449**	L249CCK	**454**	L254CCK

455-461
Dennis Dart   Alexander Dash   B40F   1996

455	P455EEF	**457**	P457EEF	**459**	P459EEF	**460**	P460EEF	**461**	P461EEF
456	P456EEF	**458**	P458EEF						

462-472
Dennis Dart SLF   Alexander ALX200   N37F   1997

462	R462SEF	**465**	R465SEF	**467**	R467SEF	**469**	R469MVN	**471**	R471MVN
463	R463SEF	**466**	R466SEF	**468**	R468SEF	**470**	R470MVN	**472**	R472MVN
464	R464SEF								

501-510
Volvo B10M-55   Northern Counties Paladin   B48F   1995

501	M401SPY	**503**	M403SPY	**505**	M405SPY	**507**	M407SPY	**509**	M409SPY
502	M402SPY	**504**	M404SPY	**506**	M406SPY	**508**	M408SPY	**510**	M410SPY

527-532
Dennis Falcon HC SDA417*   Northern Counties   B47D   1985   *530-2 are SDA415

527w	B27PAJ	**528w**	B28PAJ	**530**	B30PAJ	**531**	B31PAJ	**532**	B32PAJ

541	F251JRM	Leyland Lynx LX112L10ZR1	Leyland Lynx	B51F	1989	Cumberland, 1996
542	F252JRM	Leyland Lynx LX112L10ZR1	Leyland Lynx	B51F	1989	Cumberland, 1996
543	F253KAO	Leyland Lynx LX112L10ZR1	Leyland Lynx	B51F	1989	Cumberland, 1996
544	C544RAO	Leyland Lynx LX1126LXCTFR1 (Cummins) Leyland Lynx		B51F	1986	Cumberland, 1996
545	E709MFV	Leyland Lynx LX112L10ZR1	Leyland Lynx	B51F	1988	Cumberland, 1996
551	N551VDC	Volvo B10M-55	Alexander PS	BC48F	1995	
552	N552VDC	Volvo B10M-55	Alexander PS	BC48F	1995	
553	N553VDC	Volvo B10M-55	Alexander PS	BC48F	1995	

554-558
Volvo B10M-55   Plaxton Paladin   B48F   1998

554	R554RPY	**555**	R755RPY	**556**	R556RPY	**557**	R557RPY	**558**	R558RPY

601-610
Leyland Lynx LX112L10ZR1R   Leyland Lynx   B49F   1989

601	F601UVN	**603**	F603UVN	**605**	F605UVN	**607**	F607UVN	**609**	F609UVN
602	F602UVN	**604**	F604UVN	**606**	F606UVN	**608**	F608UVN	**610**	F610UVN

611-620
Leyland Lynx LX2R11C15Z4R   Leyland Lynx   B49F   1989

611	G611CEF	**613**	G613CEF	**615**	G615CEF	**617**	G617CEF	**619**	G619CEF
612	G612CEF	**614**	G614CEF	**616**	G616CEF	**618**	G618CEF	**620**	G620CEF

621	J901UKV	Leyland Lynx LX2R11V18Z4S	Leyland Lynx 2	B49F	1991	Volvo demonstrator, 1992

622-630
Leyland Lynx LX2R11V18Z4S   Leyland Lynx 2   B49F   1992

622	K622YVN	**624**	K624YVN	**626**	K626YVN	**628**	K628YVN	**630**	K630YVN
623	K623YVN	**625**	K625YVN	**627**	K627YVN	**629**	K629YVN		

631-642 — Volvo B10B — Plaxton Verde — B52F — 1994

631	L31HHN	634	L34HHN	637	L37HHN	639	M39PVN	641	M41PVN
632	L32HHN	635	L35HHN	638	M38PVN	640	M40PVN	642	M42PVN
633	L33HHN	636	L36HHN						

643-652 — Volvo B10M-55 — Northern Counties Paladin — B48F — 1995

643	M543SPY	645	M545SPY	647	M547SPY	649	M549SPY	651	M551SPY
644	M544SPY	646	M546SPY	648	M548SPY	650	M550SPY	652	M552SPY

653	R653RPY	Volvo B10M-55	Northern Counties Paladin	B48F	1998
654	R654RPY	Volvo B10M-55	Northern Counties Paladin	B48F	1998
655	R655RPY	Volvo B10M-55	Northern Counties Paladin	B48F	1998

656-665 — MAN 18.220 HOCL — Alexander ALX300 — N42F — 1999

656	T656OEF	658	T658OEF	660	T660OEF	662	T662OEF	664	T664OEF
657	T657OEF	659	T659OEF	661	T661OEF	663	T663OEF	665	T665OEF

701-706 — Scania N112CRB — East Lancashire European — B50F — 1988

701	F701BAT	703	F703BAT	704	F704BAT	705	F705BAT	706	F706CAG
702	F702BAT								

707-718 — Volvo B10M-55 — Northern Counties Paladin — B48F — 1995

707	M707KRH	710	M710KRH	713	M713KRH	715	M715KRH	717	M717KRH
708	M708KRH	711	M711KRH	714	M714KRH	716	M716KRH	718	M718KRH
709	M709KRH	712	M712KRH						

719-726 — Volvo B10M-55 — Northern Counties Paladin — B48F — 1998

719	R719RPY	721	R721RPY	723	R723RPY	725	R725RPY	726	R726RPY
720	R720RPY	722	R722RPY	724	R724RPY				

727-736 — MAN 18.220 HOCLR — Alexander ALX300 — N42F — 1999

727	T727OEF	729	T729OEF	731	T731OEF	733	T733OEF	735	T735OEF
728	T728OEF	730	T730OEF	732	T732OEF	734	T734OEF	736	T736FVN

817	M817KRH	Volvo Olympian YN2RC16V3	Northern Counties Palatine	B47/29F	1995
818	M818KRH	Volvo Olympian YN2RC16V3	Northern Counties Palatine	B47/29F	1995
819	M819KRH	Volvo Olympian YN2RC16V3	Northern Counties Palatine	B47/29F	1995

823-827 — Volvo Olympian YN2RC16V3 — Northern Counties Palatine — B47/29F — 1995

823	M223SVN	824	M224SVN	825	M225SVN	826	M226SVN	827	M227SVN

828	P828FEF	Volvo Olympian	Northern Counties Palatine	B49/33F	1997
829	P829FEF	Volvo Olympian	Northern Counties Palatine	B49/33F	1997
830	P830FEF	Volvo Olympian	Northern Counties Palatine	B49/33F	1997

831-840 — Volvo Olympian — Alexander RL — B51/36F — 1998

831	R831OVN	833	R833OVN	835	R835OVN	837	R837OVN	839	R839OVN
832	R832OVN	834	R834OVN	836	R836OVN	838	R838OVN	840	R640OVN

901-927 — Leyland Olympian ONLXB/1RH — Northern Counties — B43/30F — 1988 — Busways, 1999

901	E901KYR	909	E909KYR	914	E914KYR	919	E919KYR	923	E923KYR
905	E905KYR	910	E910KYR	915	E915KYR	920	E920KYR	924	E924KYR
906	E906KYR	911	E911KYR	917	E917KYR	921	E921KYR	925	E925KYR
907	E907KYR	912	E912KYR	918	E918KYR	922	E922KYR	927	E927KYR
908	E908KYR								

930-943

	Leyland Olympian ONLXB/1R		Alexander RH		B45/31F	1985-86 Busways, 1999	
930	C630LFT	933	C633LFT	936	C636LFT	939	C644LFT	942	C664LFT

930	C630LFT	933	C633LFT	936	C636LFT	939	C644LFT	942	C664LFT
931	C621LFT	934	C634LFT	937	C637LFT	940	C649LFT	943	C665LFT
932	C632LFT	935	C635LFT	938	C643LFT	941	C662LFT		

Ancilliary Vehicles

15	D155HHN	Dodge G13 Commando	Wadham Stringer Vanguard	DT	1986	MoD, 1998 (80KF39)
16	D216HHN	Dodge G13 Commando	Wadham Stringer Vanguard	DT	1986	MoD, 1998 (81KF09)
17	D157HHN	Dodge G13 Commando	Wadham Stringer Vanguard	DT	1986	MoD, 1998 (80KF95)
18	C918AHN	Dodge G13 Commando	Wadham Stringer Vanguard	DT	1985	MoD, 1998 (31KC55)
23	E306BWL	Mercedes-Benz 709D	Reeve Burgess Beaver	BC25F	1987	Cambus, 1998

Previous Registrations:

837XHW	D556MVR	HDZ8683	A845UGB, 2367AT, A491WYS
E709MFV	E709MFV, BMN88G	IIL1321	D51ORH
ESU263	A829PPP	J422HDS	J422HDS, KSU463
FSL61W	GSL307W, 666TPJ	PRX189B	417DCD

Allocations:-

Darlington (Faverdale) - Stagecoach Darlington

Mercedes-Benz	305	307	341	342	345	346	355	356
Dart	455	456	457	458	459	460	461	
Volvo B6	401	402	403	404	405	406	407	438
	442	443	444	445	446	447	449	450
	454							
Volvo Interurban	82	83	84	85				
Volvo B10M PS	551	552						
Atlantean	122	124	127	128				
Fleetline	121	140	141	142	143	144	145	146
	148	149	150	153	156	157		

Hartlepool (Brenda Road) - Stagecoach Hartlepool

Mercedes-Benz	306	309						
Coach	31	32	36	37	38	51		
Volvo Interurban	71							
Dart	462	463	464	465	466	467		
Falcon	530	531	532					
Lynx	541	542	543	544	545	601	602	603
	604	605	606	607	608	609		
Volvo B10M	501	502	503	504	505	506	507	508
	509	510	553	554	555	556	557	558
	707	708	709	710	711			
Atlantean	107	108						
Titan PD3	189							
Titan	270	271	272	273				

While the Scania double-deck buses acquired with the Hull undertaking have now left the fleet, the six single decks are still to be found working from the Stoneferry depot. Seen working service 1 is 701, F701BAT. *Richard Godfrey*

Kingston-upon-Hull (Foster Street, Stoneferry) - Stagecoach Kingston-upon-Hull

Mercedes-Benz	347	348	349	350	351	352	353	354
	357	358						
Scania N113 SD	701	702	703	704	705	706		
Volvo B10M NC	712	713	714	715	716	717	718	719
	720	721	722	723	724	725	726	
Volvo Interurban	72	73	76	77	78	79	80	81
Volvo artic	95	96	97					
MAN-ALX300	727	728	729	730	731	732	733	734
	735	736						
Dominator	210	232	240	242	243	244	245	246
	247	248	249	250	251			
Olympian	817	818	819	901	905	906	907	908
	909	910	911	912	914	915	917	918
	919	920	921	922	923	924	925	927
	930	931	932	933	934	935	936	937
	938	939	940	941	942	943		

Stockton-on-Tees (Church Road) - Stagecoach Transit

Mercedes-Benz	303	304	310	313	315	316	343	344
Volvo B6	408							
Dart SLF	468	469	470	471	472			
Lynx	610	611	612	613	614	615	616	617
	618	619	620	621	622	623	624	625
	626	627	628	629	630			
Volvo B10B	631	632	633	634	635	636	637	638
	639	640	641	642				
Volvo B10M NC	643	644	645	646	647	648	649	650
	651	652	653	654	655			
MAN/ALX300	656	657	658	659	660	661	662	663
	664	665						
Atlantean	110	111	118	125	126	130		
Domintor	220	221	222					
Titan	274	275	276	277	278	279	280	281
	282	283	284	285	286	287	288	289
	290							
Olympian	823	824	825	826	827	828	829	830
	831	832	833	834	835	836	837	838
	839	840						

Unallocated

Falcon	527	528			
Dominator	217	219			
Mercedes-Benz	311	321	324	325	329

Transit purchased a batch of Plaxton-bodied Volvo B10Bs in 1994 and all are now to be found at Stockton. From the batch, 641, M41PVN was seen heading towards Middlesbrough on route 36. *Phillip Stephenson*

STANLEY

R & I McGill; R A & A Scott, Stanley Taxis, Bus Station, Stanley, Co Durham DH9 0TD

B743JNL	Ford Transit 180	Deansgate	M8	1985	
B149FTN	Mercedes-Benz L307D	Reeve Burgess	M8	1985	
B565JJR	Mercedes-Benz L307D	Reeve Burgess	M12	1985	Cuthbertson, Newcastle, 1987
D345VBB	Mercedes-Benz L307D	Reeve Burgess	M8	1986	Carryden, Catchgate, 1992
D866WTY	Mercedes-Benz L307D	Reeve Burgess	M12	1987	
D607YNL	Mercedes-Benz L307D	Reeve Burgess	M12	1987	
D817NWW	Renault Master T35	Devon Conversions	M6L	1987	West Yorkshire AHA, 1996
D822NWW	Renault Master T35	Devon Conversions	M6L	1987	West Yorkshire AHA, 1996
D107PKP	Ford Transit VE6	Dormobile	B16FL	1986	?, 1997
E424DCN	Ford Transit VE6	Dormobile	B16F	1987	
E429KPY	Ford Transit VE6	Ford	M8	1988	Wentworth Self Drive, 1995
E288NVN	Ford Transit VE6	Ford	M8	1988	Wentworth Self Drive, 1995
G221NWF	Ford Transit VE6	Advanced Vehicle Bodies	M10L	1989	Kennings Car Hire, 1996
A4NPT	Mercedes-Benz 609D	Advanced Vehicle Bodies	BC24F	1988	Hornsby, Ashby, 1996
E866ETY	Mercedes-Benz 407D	Reeve Burgess	M15	1988	Cuthbertson, Newcastle, 1990
F969LTY	Mercedes-Benz 407D	Devon Conversions	M15	1988	
F903JBB	Ford Transit VE6	Scott	M16	1989	Low Fell Coaches, 1990
F740OCU	Ford Transit VE6	Ford	M6L	1989	private owner, 1993
F321MBB	Ford Transit VE6	Ford	M6L	1989	private owner, 1993
F540NFC	Peugeot-Talbot Pullman	Talbot	B18F	1989	North Cotswold Community Bus, 1994
G241AHP	Peugeot-Talbot Pullman	Talbot	B22F	1989	Lawrie, Beith, 1994
G22CSG	Renault-Dodge S56	Reeve Burgess Beaver	B25F	1989	Stagecoach Busways, 1996
G23CSG	Renault-Dodge S56	Reeve Burgess Beaver	B25F	1989	Stagecoach Busways, 1996

Chester-le-Street is the location for this view of Marshall bodied M115XLV. This Mercedes-Benz is one of a growing number in the fleet, many bought new, this vehicle being lettered as Stanley Buses. Stanley Coaches and Stanley Taxi names are carried as appropriate in the fleet.. *Terry Wightman*

Seen far from home in May 1998 is R2STX, a Mercedes-Benz Vario, with Autobus Nouvelle coachwork. Since the acquisition of the Autobus Classique business by Optare the trading title has now been simplified to Autobus. Along with Plaxton's 'Cheeta' these are the only two bodies that will quaify for 'C' status under plans to modernise body code applications. *Keith Grimes*

G314WFU	Mercedes-Benz 408D	Coachcraft	M15	1990	
G487XCU	Ford Transit VE6	Ford	M8	1990	private owner, 1993
J944KVK	Ford Transit VE6	Ford	M8	1992	private owner, 1992
K2STX	Mercedes-Benz 410D	Autobus Classique	C16F	1993	
K457HDK	Mercedes-Benz 709D	Plaxton Beaver	B27F	1993	Jim Stones, Leigh, 1999
K130TFT	Ford Transit VE6	Ford	M14	1993	
K776YPY	Ford Transit VE6	Ford	M8	1993	
L64TTS	Toyota Coaster HZB50R	Caetano Optimo III	C21F	1994	Woods, Tillicoultry, 1996
M1STX	Mercedes-Benz 711D	Autobus Classique	C25F	1994	
M2STX	Mercedes-Benz 709D	Wadham Stringer Wessex	B29F	1994	
M3STX	Mercedes-Benz 709D	Wadham Stringer Wessex	B29F	1994	
M115XLV	Mercedes-Benz 709D	Marshall C19	B18F	1998	Callaghan, Ferryhill, 1999
P2STX	Mercedes-Benz 412D	?	M15	1997	
R2STX	Mercedes-Benz Vario O814	Autobus Nouvelle	C--F	1998	
S5STX	Mercedes-Benz Vario O814	Plaxton Beaver 2	B--F	1998	

Previous registrations:

A4NPT	F674HNU	K457HDK	HIJYM
G704AEF	G704AEF, 574CPT	L64TTS	L540XUT, JIW6734

Livery: White

SWAN'S COACHES

M R & M P Swan, 25 Church Street, Berwick-upon-Tweed, TD15 1EE

OVK138M	Leyland Atlantean AN68/1R	Alexander AL	B45/31F	1973	Go-Ahead (OK), 1998
XGB380S	Bedford YMT	Duple Dominant II	C53F	1977	Pickett, Fernhurst, 1987
MBR455T	Leyland Atlantean AN68A/1R	Eastern Coach Works	B43/31F	1979	Go-Ahead (OK), 1997
UNK10W	Bedford YMT	Plaxton Supreme IV	C53F	1981	Patterson, Beadnell, 1997
WUM256X	Bedford YMQ	Duple Dominant	C45F	1981	Rowells, Low Prudhoe, 1996
F919ONL	Mercedes-Benz 811D	Reeve Burgess Beaver	BC33F	1989	
H544EVM	Mercedes-Benz 609D	Made-to-Measure	BC29F	1989	
R956GCU	Mercedes-Benz Vario O810	Plaxton Beaver 2	B29F	1997	

Livery: White

Depot: Chapel Street, Berwick-upon-Tweed

Reeve Burgess-bodied Mercedes-Benz F919ONL, seen about to depart Berwick-on-Tweed for Kelso, represents the Swan's Coaches fleet. Two Altanteans latterly with Go-Ahead operate school duties as the workings ply the English/Scottish border. *David Longbottom*

The North East Bus Handbook

TRAVELSURE

B Patterson, 72 King Street, Seahouses, Northumberland, NE68 7XS

Reg	Chassis	Body	Seating	Year	Source
YPL383T	Leyland National 10351B/1R		B41F	1978	Northern Bus, Anston, 1979
DBB127V	Bedford YLQ	Plaxton Supreme IV	C33F	1980	
NJI8875	Van Hool T824	Van Hool Astromega	C55/20CT	1983	Hall, Kennoway, 1994
WBB348Y	Leyland Tiger TRCTL11/2R	Plaxton Paramount 3200 E	C53F	1983	Go-Ahead (OK), 1997
MIL4684	Kässbohrer Setra S215HD	Kässbohrer	C49FT	1983	Colin's, Shepshed, 1997
EXI6387	Bedford YMP (Cummins)	Plaxton Paramount 3200 III	C33F	1987	Clews, Wolverhampton, 1997
E604HTF	MCW MetroRider MF154/8	MCW	B31F	1987	Reading Buses, 1999
E996NMK	Leyland Tiger TRCTL11/3R	Plaxton Paramount 3200 E	C57F	1988	Gordon's, Rotherham, 1999
TTC86	Bova FDH12.290	Bova Futura	C49FT	1988	JC, Newton Aycliffe, 1996
E347DRO	Iveco Daily 40.10	Dormobile	B25F	1988	The Shires, 1997
G97BYU	Van Hool T815	Van Hool Alizée	C49FT	1988	Mandy, Muswell Hill, 1997
J478XHL	Mercedes-Benz 709D	Plaxton Beaver	BC25F	1991	Leask's, Lerwick, 1998
J1TCC	Kässbohrer Setra S215HD	Setra	C47F	1992	Stort Valley-Travellers, 1999
P972HKE	Iveco Daily 40.10	? Dormobile	BC19F	1996	
P785BJU	Mercedes-Benz 711D	Leicester Carriage Builders	BC25F	1997	
S2TSH	Iveco EuroRider 391E.12.35	Beulas Stergo E	C49FT	1998	

Previous registrations:

697BYU	E998DGS		
DBB127V	MNM28V, 697BYU	MIL4684	OFB605Y, 275MHU, OFB605Y
E996NMK	E996NMK, 217NYA	NIL8875	LYS511V
EXI6387	D78HRU	TTC86	E93EVW, FHV504, E563JHJ
		WBB348Y	CBF2Y, 782UJO

Livery: Blue; **Depot:** South Moor Farm, Belford

Pictured leaving the bus station in the attractive town of Alnwick is Travelsure's WBB348Y, a Leyland Tiger with the express version of Plaxton's Paramount 3200 body. This type of vehicle is used here to perform rural services, providing passengers with quality seating for a journey often many miles between villages *Paul Wigan*

TYNE VALLEY

Tyne Valley Coaches Ltd, Acomb, Hexham, Northumberland, NE46 4QT

GAN745J	Leyland Leopard PSU5/4RT	Plaxton Elite II	C57F	1971	Marshall, Blackpool, 1976
GJR494L	Leyland Leopard PSU3B/4R	Plaxton Elite III Express	C49F	1973	
HVK185N	Leyland Leopard PSU3B/4R	Plaxton Elite III Express	C53F	1975	
HVK186N	Leyland Leopard PSU3B/4R	Plaxton Elite III Express	C53F	1975	
YSU919	Leyland Leopard PSU3C/4R	Duple Dominant	C53F	1977	
TNL628S	Leyland Leopard PSU5A/4R	Plaxton Supreme III	C57F	1978	
NSU969	Volvo B58-56	Duple Dominant II	C49F	1979	
CBB18V	Leyland Leopard PSU3E/4R	Duple Dominant II	C53F	1980	
CBB19V	Leyland Leopard PSU3E/4R	Duple Dominant II	C53F	1980	
AAG21X	Leyland Leopard PSU3F/4R	Plaxton Supreme IV	C51F	1982	Kingston-upon-Hull, 1994
AAG23X	Leyland Leopard PSU3F/4R	Plaxton Supreme IV	C51F	1982	Kingston-upon-Hull, 1994
XSV218	Leyland Leopard PSU5D/4R	Duple Dominant III	C57F	1983	
XSV298	Leyland Tiger TRCTL11/2RH	Plaxton Paramount 3200 E	C53F	1984	Go-Ahead (OK), 1997
XSV220	Leyland Tiger TRCTL11/2R	Duple Laser	C53F	1984	
XSY405	Leyland Tiger TRCTL11/3R	Duple Laser	C53F	1984	Primrose, Newcastle, 1997
WSU221	Leyland Tiger TRCTL11/3RH	Duple Laser 2	C44FT	1985	Torr, Nottingham, 1996
XSV239	Volvo B10M-60	Plaxton Paramount 3200 III	C53F	1988	Southern, Barrhead, 1994
XSV219	Leyland Tiger TRCTL11/2R	Plaxton Paramount 3500	C53F	1985	
YSU920	Leyland Tiger TRCTL11/3RZM	Duple 320	C57F	1989	
YSU960	Volvo B10M-60	Plaxton Paramount 3200 III	C55F	1989	Dodsworth, Boroughbridge, 1994
G431XFT	Leyland-DAF 200	Leyland-DAF	M8	1990	private owner, 1996

Previous Registrations:

NSU969	XNL870T	XSU239	E150AGG	XSY405	A216BJR
XSV218	UFT252Y	XSU298	A719ABB	YSU919	ONL772R
XSV219	B969HTY	YSU960	F715EUG	YSU920	F27TMP
XSV220	A105BUR	WSU221	B404UOD		

Livery: Two-tone blue

VENTURE REED

Gavin Reed Ltd, Sunniside Garage, Front Street, Sunniside, Newcastle, NE16 5EE

	780HUP	AEC Reliance 2MU3RV	Park Royal	B45F	1960	preservation, 1963
156	JPT544	Daimler CVD65D	Willowbrook	B35F	1948	preservation, 1987
249	6249UP	Leyland Leopard PSU3/3R	Alexander Y	BC51F	1963	preservation, 1983
297	KSC500	AEC Reliance 6U3ZR	Duple Dominant	C53F	1974	Rich, Wallington, 1988
298	810BXK	Leyland Tiger TRCTL11/3RH	Berkhof Everest 370	C53F	1985	Kentish Bus, 1991
299	C71JCX	DAF MB230DKFL600	Duple Laser 2	C53F	1985	Alder Valley Engineering, 1997

Previous registrations:

780HUP	From new	6249UP	From new	KSC500	PFN788M
810BXK	B121KPF	JPT544	From new		

Tyne Valley's YSU920 is a Leyland Tiger with Duple 320 bodywork. This fleet is composed of products entirely from the Leyland-Volvo range with bodywork from British coachbuilders, Plaxton and Duple. The vehicle is seen in Middleton-on-Teesdale, and like many vehicle in the fleet, carries a cherished mark. *J C Walton*

The Sunderland FC's *Stadium of Light* attracts many coaches with visiting away and home fans. However, many other activities are undertaken and it was for one of these that Venture Reed's C71JCX was present. The Duple Laser 2 bodywork was constructed on a DAF MB230 chassis. *Terry Wightman*

WEARDALE

Weardale Motor Services Ltd, Shittlehopeburn Garage, Stanhope, Bishop Auckland
Co Durham, DL13 2YQ

Reg	Chassis	Body	Seating	Year	Notes
TPT6K	Leyland Leopard PSU5/4R	Plaxton Elite II Express	CB68F	1972	
BUP736L	Leyland Leopard PSU5/4R	Plaxton Elite III	CB57F	1973	
UPT6N	Leyland Leopard PSU3B/3R	East Lancs EL2000 (1993)	B55F	1974	
KBR252N	Volvo B58-61	Plaxton Elite III	CB68F	1975	Stanhope, 1993
SUF140N	Leyland Atlantean AN68/1R	Park Royal	B43/30F	1974	Garnetts, Tindale Crescent, 1994
SCN268S	Leyland Atlantean AN68A/2R	Alexander AL	B49/37F	1978	Stagecoach Busways, 1998
UVK292T	Leyland Atlantean AN68A/2R	Alexander AL	B49/37F	1978	Stagecoach Busways, 1996
UVK300T	Leyland Atlantean AN68A/2R	Alexander AL	B49/37F	1978	Stagecoach Busways, 1998
VCU312T	Leyland Atlantean AN68A/2R	Alexander AL	B49/37F	1978	Stagecoach Busways, 1996
OGR625T	Leyland Leopard PSU3E/3R	Plaxton Supreme III	C53F	1979	
UBR666T	Leyland Leopard PSU3E/3R	Plaxton Supreme IV Express	C53F	1979	
AVK176V	Leyland Atlantean AN68A/2R	Alexander AL	B49/37F	1980	Stagecoach Busways, 1996
AUP350W	Leyland Atlantean AN68B/1R	Roe	B43/30F	1980	Go-Ahead (OK), 1997
MRJ357W	Leyland Tiger TRCTL11/3R	East Lancashire EL2000(1995)	B54F	1981	Ashley Adams, Whitby, 1993
PEF6X	Bedford VAS5	Duple Dominant II	C29F	1981	Stanhope, 1993
WBB329Y	Leyland Tiger TRCTL11/3R	Plaxton Paramount 3200	C49FT	1983	Go-Ahead (OK), 1997
GIB8666	Volvo B10M-61	Plaxton Paramount 3200 II	C53F	1986	
E522DCU	Mercedes-Benz L307D	Devon Conversions	M12L	1987	Go-Ahead (OK), 1996
E113FLP	Mercedes-Benz 609D	Reeve Burgess Beaver	BC20F	1987	Hertz, Glasgow, 1993
JAZ8669	MCW MetroRider MF154/14	MCW	B33F	1988	NE Bus (The Eden), 1996
E965MVN	Mercedes-Benz 609D	Reeve Burgess Beaver	B19F	1988	
F997WPY	Mercedes-Benz 814D	Reeve Burgess Beaver	BC33F	1989	
GIB638	Volvo B10M-60	Plaxton Paramount 3500 III	C51FT	1989	
G703NGR	Mercedes-Benz 709D	Reeve Burgess Beaver	B25F	1990	Go-Ahead (OK), 1997
M6WMS	Mercedes-Benz 709D	Plaxton Beaver	B25F	1994	
GIB206	Bova FHD12.340	Bova Futura	C49FT	1995	MacEwan, Amisfield, 1998
P6WMS	Bova FHD12.340	Bova Futura	C49FT	1996	

Special event vehicle

Reg	Chassis	Body	Seating	Year	Notes
YUP6	Leyland Titan PD2/10	Roe	H37/28RD	1958	Stanhope, 1993

Previous Registrations:

GIB206	M62DSJ	JAZ8669	F202RVN
GIB638	G843BDC	WBB329Y	BFP4Y, EIB1647
GIB8666	C666FMP		

Livery: Red, maroon and cream

Opposite:- **Weardale Motor Services commenced operations in 1925 under the guidance of Mr O S Gibson. The Stanhope Motor Services operation was acquired in 1952 and for many years ran side by side. Leyland products dominated the fleets, as did Plaxton bodywork. The current operations provide services around Bishop Auckland, particularly during school term. The photographs of the two vehicles shown here are both taken in the town of Stanhope. The upper picture shows UPT6N, a Leyland Leopard that was re-bodied in 1993 by East Lancashire, a practice that has been used by many of the smaller operators, particularly on chassis which often last longer than their bodywork. The lower picture shows Mercedes-Benz minibus G703NGR. Acquired from Go-Ahead in 1997 it brings the minibus fleet up to seven, all Mercedes products bar a single MetroRider.** *Paul Wigan*

WELCO

Welco Transport Services Ltd, 4 Milburn Drive, Newcastle-upon-Tyne, NE15 7PG

32	E305EVW	MCW MetroRider MF150/89	MCW	B24F	1988	Welcome Travel, Felling, 1998
33	E975DGS	MCW MetroRider MF150/72	MCW	B25F	1988	George Bell, Southwick, 1998
34	E134XCA	Renault-Dodge S56	Northern Counties	B22F	1987	Chester, 1998
35	E135XCA	Renault-Dodge S56	Northern Counties	B22F	1987	Chester, 1998
36	E136XCA	Renault-Dodge S56	Northern Counties	B22F	1987	Chester, 1998
37	E137XCA	Renault-Dodge S56	Northern Counties	B22F	1987	Chester, 1998
39	E39YMB	Renault-Dodge S56	Northern Counties	BC23F	1988	Chester, 1998
40	E40PJV	Renault-Dodge S56	Alexander AM	B23F	1988	Chester, 1998
41	E41YMB	Renault-Dodge S56	Northern Counties	BC23F	1988	Chester, 1998
46	E40YMB	Renault-Dodge S56	Northern Counties	BC23F	1988	Chester, 1998
47	E41PJV	Renault-Dodge S56	Alexander AM	B23F	1988	Chester, 1998
48	E42PJV	Renault-Dodge S56	Alexander AM	B23F	1988	Chester, 1998
	D750YCN	Renault-Dodge S56	Northern Counties	B22F	1987	Warrington, 1999
	D539RCK	Mercedes-Benz L608D	Reeve Burgess	B20F	1986	Welcome Travel, Felling, 1998

Livery: Cream and maroon

Depot: Jolly's Garage, Union Street, South Hylton

Former Chester minibuses dominate the new Welco operation based in Newcastle. Pictured in South Hylton is E134XCA, with Northern Counties bodywork, pictured operating service 20. *Richard Godfrey*

WHITELINE

R L Robson, 3 Monkseaton Terrace, Ashington, Northumberland NE63 0UB

JDH216V	Ford Transit 180	Dormobile	B16F	1979	Hemsley, Killingworth, 1989
DTY660W	Ford Transit 190	Reeve Burgess Reebur	C17F	1980	Watson, Washington, 1990
A516LPP	Mercedes-Benz L608D	Reeve Burgess	BC19F	1983	Lightfoot, Brandon, 1991
LIL8872	Mercedes-Benz 609D	Reeve Burgess	BC25F	1988	Eagle Coaches, Bristol, 1995
D529MJA	Iveco Daily 49.10	Robin Hood City Nippy	B21F	1987	GM Buses, 1992
D144WCC	Freight Rover Sherpa	Carlyle	B18F	1987	Hanson, Blyth, 1994
P523UGA	Mercedes-Benz 711D	?	BC25F	19	

Previous registration:

LIL8872   E300OMG

Livery: White

The small **Whiteline** minibus operation is represented by their latest arrival, **P523UGA**. Based on a Mercedes-Benz, it carries a so far unidentified body conversion. *Keith Grimes*

Vehicle Index

1JVK	Stagecoach Busways	A542PCW	Arriva North East	AVK147V	Stagecoach Transit	B734GCN	Go-Ahead
2JVK	Stagecoach Busways	A543PCW	Arriva North East	AVK148V	Stagecoach Transit	B735GCN	Go-Ahead
54FS	Redby	A563KWY	Arriva North East	AVK150V	Stagecoach Busways	B736GCN	Go-Ahead
55FS	Redby	A618BCN	Go-Ahead	AVK152V	Go-Ahead	B737GCN	Go-Ahead
71XVO	J & C	A619BCN	Go-Ahead	AVK155V	Go-Ahead	B738GCN	Go-Ahead
85ROD	Delta	A620BCN	Go-Ahead	AVK156V	Stagecoach Transit	B739GCN	Go-Ahead
89HBC	Galaxy Travel	A621BCN	Go-Ahead	AVK165V	Go-Ahead	B740GCN	Go-Ahead
210WVK	North Rider	A622BCN	Go-Ahead	AVK170V	Stagecoach Busways	B741GCN	Go-Ahead
258NOG	Scarlet Band	A622THV	Stagecoach Transit	AVK171V	Stagecoach Busways	B742GCN	Go-Ahead
322XTJ	Compass Royston	A623BCN	Go-Ahead	AVK175V	Go-Ahead	B743GCN	Go-Ahead
325CCE	Classic	A624BCN	Go-Ahead	AVK176V	Weardale	B743JNL	Stanley Coaches
340GUP	Go-Ahead	A625BCN	Go-Ahead	AVK180V	Stagecoach Transit	B744GCN	Go-Ahead
387FYM	Classic	A626THV	Stagecoach Transit	B8BST	Bob Smith Travel	B745GCN	Go-Ahead
425BVK	Go-Ahead	A627BCN	Go-Ahead	B9BST	Bob Smith Travel	B746GCN	Go-Ahead
445YMU	Arriva North East	A628BCN	Go-Ahead	B27PAJ	Stagecoach Transit	B747GCN	Go-Ahead
523SC	Redby	A629BCN	Go-Ahead	B28PAJ	Stagecoach Transit	B748GCN	Go-Ahead
526VVK	Henry Cooper	A630BCN	Go-Ahead	B29PAJ	Stagecoach Transit	B866JVK	Stagecoach Busways
527LPF	Classic	A631BCN	Go-Ahead	B30PAJ	Stagecoach Transit	B916JVK	Stagecoach Busways
577TVO	Altona Coaches	A632BCN	Go-Ahead	B31PAJ	Stagecoach Transit	B997JTN	Bob Smith Travel
593CCE	Classic	A633BCN	Go-Ahead	B32PAJ	Stagecoach Transit	BAJ707T	Kings
620PDV	Kingsley's	A634BCN	Go-Ahead	B45NDX	Arriva North East	BBV774Y	Fairley's
648WHK	Arriva North East	A635BCN	Go-Ahead	B106UAT	Stagecoach Transit	BGR686W	Go-Ahead
656CCE	Classic	A636BCN	Go-Ahead	B107UAT	Stagecoach Transit	BGR687W	Go-Ahead
671MBB	Henry Cooper	A637BCN	Go-Ahead	B108UAT	Stagecoach Transit	BGR688W	Go-Ahead
685XHY	Classic	A639BCN	Go-Ahead	B109UAT	Stagecoach Transit	BHK209X	Bell Bros
694AVY	Snaiths	A640BCN	Go-Ahead	B110GRR	Arriva North East	BPR48Y	Arriva North East
720HKH	Lee's of Durham	A641BCN	Go-Ahead	B110UAT	Stagecoach Transit	BPR49Y	Arriva North East
780HUP	Venture Reed	A642BCN	Go-Ahead	B111GRR	Arriva North East	BPT917S	Kingsley's
802KRO	Fairley's	A645BCN	Go-Ahead	B112GRR	Arriva North East	BPT919S	Arriva North East
810BXK	Venture Reed	A646BCN	Go-Ahead	B113GRR	Arriva North East	BPY402T	Delta
837XHW	Stagecoach Transit	A647BCN	Go-Ahead	B113WUV	Stagecoach Transit	BUH235V	Compass Royston
847LAA	Grierson	A648BCN	Go-Ahead	B114GRR	Arriva North East	BUP736L	Weardale
869SVX	Arriva North East	A700USU	Snaiths	B115GRR	Arriva North East	BVP796V	Bob Smith Travel
891HUM	Lee's of Durham	A718ABB	Go-Ahead	B149FTN	Stanley Coaches	BYX141V	Go-Ahead
910UPG	Snowdons	A750UYL	Caris Coaches	B203GNL	Caris Coaches	BYX153V	Go-Ahead
956CCE	Classic	A789UYL	Crossroads	B207GNL	A Line	BYX210V	Arriva North East
961KVK	Go-Ahead	A826SUL	Stagecoach Transit	B215OAJ	Stagecoach Transit	BYX217V	Go-Ahead
1230HN	Cochrane's	A827SUL	Stagecoach Transit	B216OAJ	Stagecoach Transit	BYX218V	Go-Ahead
1624WY	Compass Royston	A840SUL	Stagecoach Transit	B217OAJ	Stagecoach Transit	BYX236V	Go-Ahead
1922FS	Redby	A846SUL	Stagecoach Transit	B218OAJ	Stagecoach Transit	BYX247V	Go-Ahead
3376DD	Kings	A849SUL	Stagecoach Transit	B220HNL	Tyne Valley	BYX250V	Go-Ahead
3418WY	Redby	A886SYE	Garnetts	B240WTM	Caris Coaches	BYX268V	Go-Ahead
3542DD	Kings	A949KAJ	Arriva North East	B245NVN	Arriva North East	C34CWT	Arriva North East
4439TW	Escort	A966KAJ	Galaxy Travel	B246NVN	Arriva North East	C35CWT	Arriva North East
4695WY	Compass Royston	AAG21X	Tyne Valley	B247NVN	Arriva North East	C38CWT	Arriva North East
4796EL	Fairley's	AAG23X	Tyne Valley	B251NVN	Arriva North East	C41CWT	Arriva North East
4995DD	Kings	ACM770X	Classic	B252PHN	Arriva North East	C43CWT	Arriva North East
6249UP	Venture Reed	AEF223Y	Arriva North East	B253PHN	Arriva North East	C47DHT	Hennings
7061DD	Kings	AEF225Y	Arriva North East	B255RAJ	Arriva North East	C52DHT	Michael Franks
7204DD	Kings	AEF226Y	Arriva North East	B256RAJ	Arriva North East	C71JCX	Venture Reed
9506DD	Kings	AEF227Y	Arriva North East	B262KPF	Arriva North East	C100HSJ	Stagecoach Transit
A4NPT	Stanley Coaches	AEF228Y	Arriva North East	B273KPF	Arriva North East	C102PCN	Go-Ahead
A13BST	Bob Smith Travel	AFB593V	Arriva North East	B277KPF	Arriva North East	C103PCN	Go-Ahead
A16BST	Bob Smith Travel	AHT212J	Delta	B279KPF	Arriva North East	C104PCN	Go-Ahead
A119EPA	Arriva North East	AIW646	DC Travel	B284KPF	Arriva North East	C122CAT	Stagecoach Transit
A130FDC	Arriva North East	AKU166T	Bob Smith Travel	B358GCU	Rothbury Motors	C123CAT	Stagecoach Transit
A131FDC	Arriva North East	ANA446Y	Snaiths	B363LOY	Robson	C124CAT	Stagecoach Transit
A132REO	Bell Bros	AOA615A	Jim Hughes	B404UOD	Tyne Valley	C125CAT	Stagecoach Transit
A134FDC	Arriva North East	AOD650Y	Bob Smith Travel	B417CGG	Grierson	C128CAT	Stagecoach Transit
A135FDC	Arriva North East	APT116W	A Line	B425CMC	Bell Bros	C129CAT	Stagecoach Transit
A136FDC	Arriva North East	APT117W	A Line	B427PJF	J C Bell	C131CAT	Stagecoach Transit
A137FDC	Arriva North East	APT810W	Arriva North East	B430EFT	Stagecoach Busways	C133HJN	Arriva North East
A138FDC	Arriva North East	APT811W	Arriva North East	B431EFT	Stagecoach Busways	C200SLN	Crossroads
A140FDC	Arriva North East	APT816W	Arriva North East	B432EFT	Stagecoach Busways	C219WAJ	Stagecoach Transit
A142FDC	Arriva North East	APT817W	Arriva North East	B433EFT	Stagecoach Busways	C220WAJ	Stagecoach Transit
A233GHN	Arriva North East	ARF149S	Grierson	B434EFT	Stagecoach Busways	C221WAJ	Stagecoach Transit
A234GHN	Arriva North East	ARN895Y	Arriva North East	B435EFT	Stagecoach Busways	C222WAJ	Stagecoach Transit
A235GHN	Arriva North East	ARN896Y	Arriva North East	B436EFT	Stagecoach Busways	C223PTY	Compass Royston
A236GHN	Arriva North East	ARN897Y	Arriva North East	B437EFT	Stagecoach Busways	C259UAJ	Arriva North East
A237GHN	Arriva North East	ARN898Y	Arriva North East	B565JJR	Stanley Coaches	C260UAJ	Arriva North East
A238GHN	Arriva North East	AUP350W	Weardale	B598SWX	Arriva North East	C261UAJ	Arriva North East
A240GHN	Arriva North East	AVK134V	Stagecoach Busways	B634HBR	Hunter's	C262UAJ	Arriva North East
A241GHN	Arriva North East	AVK135V	Stagecoach Transit	B674CJW	ERB Services	C263XEF	Arriva North East
A242GHN	Arriva North East	AVK136V	Stagecoach Busways	B674EVW	Galaxy Travel	C264XEF	Arriva North East
A243GHN	Arriva North East	AVK138V	Stagecoach Busways	B687JVK	Kingsley's	C265XEF	Arriva North East
A244GHN	Arriva North East	AVK141V	Stagecoach Busways			C266XEF	Arriva North East
A516LPP	Whiteline 1	AVK142V	Stagecoach Transit			C267XEF	Arriva North East

Reg	Operator	Reg	Operator	Reg	Operator	Reg	Operator
C268XEF	Arriva North East	C659LFT	Stagecoach Busways	CUP662S	Redby	E41PJV	Welco
C327OFL	Mill	C659LJR	Go-Ahead	CVN400T	Delta	E41YMB	Welco
C350DND	Snaiths	C660LFT	Stagecoach Busways	CWG761V	Grierson	E42PJV	Welco
C401VVN	Compass Royston	C660LJR	Go-Ahead	CWR505Y	Arriva North East	E86MHG	Leven Valley
C429VVN	Compass Royston	C661LFT	Stagecoach Busways	D24SAO	Snaiths	E107DJR	Go-Ahead
C433VVN	Compass Royston	C661LJR	Go-Ahead	D25SAO	Snaiths	E113FLP	Weardale
C511DYM	Amberline	C662LFT	Stagecoach Transit	D107PKP	Stanley Coaches	E127KYW	J C Bell
C520LJR	Go-Ahead	C662LJR	Go-Ahead	D108XPG	Snaiths	E132SAT	Stagecoach Transit
C521LJR	Go-Ahead	C663LFT	Stagecoach Busways	D113PTT	Snaiths	E133RAX	Hennings
C522LJR	Go-Ahead	C663LJR	Go-Ahead	D120PTT	Snaiths	E134XCA	Welco
C523LJR	Go-Ahead	C664LFT	Stagecoach Transit	D139VRP	First Choice Travel	E135XCA	Welco
C544RAO	Stagecoach Transit	C664LJR	Go-Ahead	D144WCC	Whiteline	E136XCA	Welco
C601LFT	Stagecoach Busways	C665LFT	Stagecoach Transit	D155HHN	Stagecoach Transit	E146KYW	Dodds of Ashington
C602LFT	Stagecoach Busways	C665LJR	Go-Ahead	D157HHN	Stagecoach Transit	E165OMD	Snaiths
C603LFT	Stagecoach Busways	C666LJR	Go-Ahead	D216GLJ	Snaiths	E205BDV	Snaiths
C604LFT	Stagecoach Busways	C667LJR	Go-Ahead	D216HHN	Stagecoach Transit	E216BDV	Snaiths
C605LFT	Stagecoach Busways	C668LJR	Go-Ahead	D253HFX	Snaiths	E246RBE	ERB Services
C606LFT	Stagecoach Busways	C669LJR	Go-Ahead	D259HFX	Snaiths	E250WYS	Jim Hughes
C608LFT	Stagecoach Busways	C670LJR	Go-Ahead	D298YTY	Stagecoach Busways	E266KEF	Arriva North East
C609LFT	Stagecoach Busways	C671LJR	Go-Ahead	D305YTY	Stagecoach Busways	E268KEF	Arriva North East
C610LFT	Stagecoach Busways	C672LJR	Go-Ahead	D314PDM	Crossroads	E270KEF	Arriva North East
C611LFT	Stagecoach Busways	C673LJR	Go-Ahead	D340LSD	Go-Ahead	E271KEF	Arriva North East
C612LFT	Stagecoach Busways	C674LJR	Go-Ahead	D341APG	Hunter's	E272KEF	Arriva North East
C613ANW	Arriva North East	C682JGR	Go-Ahead	D345VBB	Stanley Coaches	E273KEF	Arriva North East
C613LFT	Stagecoach Busways	C750OCN	Go-Ahead	D420KMT	Snaiths	E275KEF	Arriva North East
C614ANW	Arriva North East	C751OCN	Go-Ahead	D466EAJ	Arriva North East	E288NVN	Stanley Coaches
C614LFT	Stagecoach Busways	C752OCN	Go-Ahead	D468YTN	Delta	E305EVW	Welco
C615LFT	Stagecoach Busways	C753OCN	Go-Ahead	D473EAJ	Arriva North East	E306BWL	Stagecoach Transit
C616ANW	Arriva North East	C754OCN	Go-Ahead	D479EAJ	Arriva North East	E317BRM	J C Bell
C616LFT	Stagecoach Busways	C755OCN	Go-Ahead	D529MJA	Whiteline	E347DROI	Travelsure
C617ANW	Arriva North East	C756OCN	Go-Ahead	D539RCK	Welco	E350NOK	Altona Coaches
C617LFT	Stagecoach Busways	C757OCN	Go-Ahead	D580EWS	Amberline	E421AFT	Stagecoach Busways
C617XVU	Fairley's	C758OCN	Go-Ahead	D607YNL	Stanley Coaches	E422AFT	Stagecoach Busways
C618LFT	Stagecoach Busways	C759OCN	Go-Ahead	D626MDB	Amberline	E423AFT	Stagecoach Busways
C619LFT	Stagecoach Busways	C760OCN	Go-Ahead	D641CVN	Compass Royston	E424AFT	Stagecoach Busways
C620LFT	Stagecoach Busways	C761OCN	Go-Ahead	D648CVN	Arriva North East	E424DCN	Stanley Coaches
C621LFT	Stagecoach Transit	C762OCN	Go-Ahead	D649CVN	Compass Royston	E425AFT	Stagecoach Busways
C622LFT	Stagecoach Busways	C763OCN	Go-Ahead	D651CVN	Arriva North East	E426AFT	Stagecoach Busways
C623LFT	Stagecoach Busways	C764OCN	Go-Ahead	D653CVN	Arriva North East	E427AFT	Stagecoach Busways
C624LFT	Stagecoach Busways	C765OCN	Go-Ahead	D654NOD	Snaiths	E428AFT	Stagecoach Busways
C625LFT	Stagecoach Busways	C766OCN	Go-Ahead	D701TLG	Grierson	E429AFT	Stagecoach Busways
C626LFT	Stagecoach Busways	C767OCN	Go-Ahead	D747ERV	Amberline	E429KPY	Stanley Coaches
C627LFT	Stagecoach Busways	C768OCN	Go-Ahead	D750YCN	Welco	E430AFT	Stagecoach Busways
C628LFT	Stagecoach Busways	C769OCN	Go-Ahead	D751GBP	Amberline	E431AFT	Stagecoach Busways
C629LFT	Stagecoach Busways	C771OCN	Go-Ahead	D754LRJ	Hennings	E432AFT	Stagecoach Busways
C630LFT	Stagecoach Transit	C775OCN	Go-Ahead	D802RWF	Snaiths	E433AFT	Stagecoach Busways
C631LFT	Stagecoach Busways	C776OCN	Go-Ahead	D817NWW	Stanley Coaches	E434AFT	Stagecoach Busways
C631PAU	Fairley's	C777OCN	Go-Ahead	D822NWW	Stanley Coaches	E435AFT	Stagecoach Busways
C632LFT	Stagecoach Transit	C778OCN	Go-Ahead	D833KWT	Dodds of Ashington	E437AFT	Stagecoach Busways
C633LFT	Stagecoach Transit	C781OCN	Go-Ahead	D838KWT	Hennings	E440AFT	Stagecoach Busways
C634LFT	Stagecoach Transit	C782OCN	Go-Ahead	D866WTY	Stanley Coaches	E442AFT	Stagecoach Busways
C635LFT	Stagecoach Transit	C783OCN	Go-Ahead	D884WTY	ERB Services	E443AFT	Stagecoach Busways
C636LFT	Stagecoach Transit	C784OCN	Go-Ahead	D903EAJ	Go-Ahead	E445AFT	Stagecoach Busways
C637LFT	Stagecoach Transit	C785OCN	Go-Ahead	D914URG	Go-Ahead	E449AFT	Stagecoach Busways
C638LFT	Stagecoach Busways	C786OCN	Go-Ahead	D918KPT	Stagecoach Busways	E450AFT	Stagecoach Busways
C639LFT	Stagecoach Busways	C787OCN	Go-Ahead	D922VCN	Redby	E451AFT	Stagecoach Busways
C640LFT	Stagecoach Busways	C788OCN	Go-Ahead	D923VCN	Hennings	E452AFT	Stagecoach Busways
C641LFT	Stagecoach Busways	C789OCN	Go-Ahead	D926VCN	Hennings	E453AFT	Stagecoach Busways
C642LFT	Stagecoach Busways	C807FMC	Bell Bros	D930VCN	Redby	E454AFT	Stagecoach Busways
C643LFT	Stagecoach Transit	C880KGG	Snowdons	D936VCN	Snowdons	E455AFT	Stagecoach Busways
C644LFT	Stagecoach Transit	C918AHN	Stagecoach Transit	D941VCN	Redby	E456AFT	Stagecoach Busways
C645LFT	Stagecoach Busways	C973UEF	Amberline	D942VCN	Redby	E457AFT	Stagecoach Busways
C646LFT	Stagecoach Busways	CAY213Y	Escort	D944VCN	Snaiths	E458AFT	Stagecoach Busways
C647LFT	Stagecoach Busways	CAZ6831	Classic	DBB127V	Travelsure	E459AFT	Stagecoach Busways
C649LFT	Stagecoach Transit	CBB18V	Tyne Valley	DEM759Y	Classic	E500KEF	Cochrane's
C649LJR	Go-Ahead	CBB19V	Tyne Valley	DEM762Y	Classic	E514HHN	Scarlet Band
C650LFT	Stagecoach Busways	CBO29V	Robson	DIB8484	J & C	E522DCU	Weardale
C650LJR	Go-Ahead	CCY819V	Arriva North East	DIL6718	Lee's of Durham	E600ENL	Snaiths
C651LFT	Stagecoach Busways	CPT734S	Arriva North East	DJI8747	Snowdons	E604HTF	Travelsure
C651LJR	Go-Ahead	CPT736S	Arriva North East	DJV830Y	Priory	E615FRN	Northumbria Cs
C652LFT	Stagecoach Busways	CPT738S	Arriva North East	DNK412T	Caris Coaches	E629AMA	Amberline
C652LJR	Go-Ahead	CPT739S	Arriva North East	DOC31V	Arriva North East	E635BVK	Stagecoach Busways
C653LFT	Stagecoach Busways	CPT740S	Kingsley's	DRU238L	Rothbury Motors	E637BVK	Stagecoach Busways
C653LJR	Go-Ahead	CU6860	Go-Ahead	DTY352W	Snowdons	E655FLD	Snaiths
C654LFT	Stagecoach Busways	CU7661	Go-Ahead	DTY660W	Whiteline	E676DCU	Arriva North East
C654LJR	Go-Ahead	CUB60Y	Arriva North East	DUP745S	Arriva North East	E709MFV	Stagecoach Transit
C655LFT	Stagecoach Busways	CUB61Y	Arriva North East	DUP747S	Arriva North East	E729CNM	Scarlet Band
C655LJR	Go-Ahead	CUB63Y	Arriva North East	DUP753S	Arriva North East	E730CNM	Scarlet Band
C656LFT	Stagecoach Busways	CUB64Y	Arriva North East	DVK489W	Go-Ahead	E734WEC	Amberline
C656LJR	Go-Ahead	CUB66Y	Arriva North East	DVK491W	Go-Ahead	E751VJO	Go-Ahead
C657LFT	Stagecoach Busways	CUB68Y	Arriva North East	DWY660T	DC Travel	E752VJO	Hennings
C657LJR	Go-Ahead	CUB69Y	Arriva North East	E39YMB	Welco	E754VJO	Go-Ahead
C658LFT	Stagecoach Busways	CUI20	A Line	E40PJV	Welco	E756VJO	Hennings
C658LJR	Go-Ahead	CUL139V	Garnetts	E40YMB	Welco		

Stagecoach sold the coaching operation of Cleveland Transit to Delta, though the Cleveland Coaches name and livery continues to be seen. Pictured complete with its former fleet number is BPY402T, a Leyland Leopard with Plaxton Supreme bodywork complete with express doorway and destination dome.
David Longbottom

E758XWL	Go-Ahead	E905GCU	Scarlet Band	EJR104W	Stagecoach Busways	F107HVK	Stagecoach Busways
E759XWL	Go-Ahead	E905KYR	Stagecoach Transit	EJR105W	Stagecoach Busways	F107UEF	Go-Ahead
E767HJF	Fairley's	E906KYR	Stagecoach Transit	EJR107W	Stagecoach Transit	F108HVK	Stagecoach Busways
E801BTN	Arriva North East	E906MDC	Go-Ahead	EJR108W	Stagecoach Transit	F108MVK	ERB Services
E803BTN	Arriva North East	E907KYR	Stagecoach Transit	EJR109W	Stagecoach Busways	F109HVK	Stagecoach Busways
E804BTN	Arriva North East	E908KYR	Stagecoach Transit	EJR110W	Stagecoach Transit	F110HVK	Stagecoach Busways
E806BTN	Arriva North East	E909KYR	Stagecoach Transit	EJR111W	Stagecoach Transit	F111HVK	Stagecoach Busways
E810BTN	Arriva North East	E909MDC	Go-Ahead	EJR112W	Stagecoach Busways	F112HVK	Stagecoach Busways
E811UHF	Delta	E910KYR	Stagecoach Transit	EJR114W	Stagecoach Busways	F113HVK	Stagecoach Busways
E812BTN	Arriva North East	E911KYR	Stagecoach Transit	EJR117W	Stagecoach Busways	F114HVK	Stagecoach Busways
E813BTN	Arriva North East	E912KYR	Stagecoach Transit	EJR118W	Stagecoach Transit	F115HVK	Stagecoach Busways
E814BMJ	Gardiners	E914KYR	Stagecoach Transit	EJR127W	Go-Ahead	F116HVK	Stagecoach Busways
E814BTN	Arriva North East	E915KYR	Stagecoach Transit	EJR130W	Go-Ahead	F117HVK	Stagecoach Busways
E815BTN	Arriva North East	E917KYR	Stagecoach Transit	EKA156Y	Classic	F118HVK	Stagecoach Busways
E817BTN	Arriva North East	E918KYR	Stagecoach Transit	EKA157Y	Fairley's	F119HVK	Stagecoach Busways
E818BTN	Arriva North East	E919KYR	Stagecoach Transit	EPD540V	North Rider	F120HVK	Stagecoach Busways
E819BTN	Arriva North East	E920KYR	Stagecoach Transit	EPH222V	Garnetts	F121HVK	Stagecoach Busways
E820BTN	Arriva North East	E921KYR	Stagecoach Transit	EPH231V	Garnetts	F122HVK	Stagecoach Busways
E823BTN	Arriva North East	E922KYR	Stagecoach Transit	ESF228S	Scarlet Band	F123HVK	Stagecoach Busways
E824BTN	Arriva North East	E923KYR	Stagecoach Transit	ESF229S	Scarlet Band	F124HVK	Stagecoach Busways
E825BTN	Arriva North East	E924KYR	Stagecoach Transit	ESF230S	Scarlet Band	F125HVK	Stagecoach Busways
E826BTN	Arriva North East	E925KYR	Stagecoach Transit	ESU110	Henry Cooper	F130CEA	Hennings
E827BTN	Arriva North East	E927KYR	Stagecoach Transit	ESU263	Stagecoach Transit	F132SMT	Dodds of Ashington
E829BTN	Arriva North East	E947TBA	Snaiths	EWT206Y	Arriva North East	F142BKH	Stagecoach Transit
E831BTN	Arriva North East	E963PME	Arriva North East	EWT208Y	Arriva North East	F143BKH	Stagecoach Transit
E832BTN	Arriva North East	E965MVN	Weardale	EWT210Y	Arriva North East	F144BKH	Stagecoach Transit
E833BTN	Arriva North East	E975DGS	Welco	EX180	Henry Cooper	F145BKH	Stagecoach Transit
E836BTN	Arriva North East	E976DGS	Scarlet Band	EXI6387	Travelsure	F146BKH	Stagecoach Transit
E840BTN	Arriva North East	E979CCN	Dodds of Ashington	EYD2T	First Choice Travel	F147BKH	Stagecoach Transit
E841BTN	Arriva North East	E991JLF	Altona Coaches	F27RKX	Bell Bros	F148BKH	Stagecoach Transit
E844BTN	Arriva North East	E996NMK	Travelsure	F42XVP	Amberline	F149BKH	Stagecoach Transit
E845BTN	Arriva North East	EAV810V	First Choice Travel	F80JNL	Amberline	F150BKH	Stagecoach Transit
E852AJR	Snaiths	EBB156W	Priory	F101HVK	Stagecoach Busways	F151BKH	Stagecoach Transit
E855BRM	Hennings	EBW101Y	Bell Bros	F102HVK	Stagecoach Busways	F166XCS	Hylton Castle
E857ETY	ERB Services	EDF274T	Lee's of Durham	F103HVK	Stagecoach Busways	F188HKK	Arriva North East
E866ETY	Stanley Coaches	EDZ215	Arriva North East	F104HVK	Stagecoach Busways	F189HKK	Arriva North East
E901KYR	Stagecoach Transit	EEH901Y	Arriva North East	F105HVK	Stagecoach Busways	F241TBC	Scarlet Band
E903GCU	Scarlet Band	EEH908Y	Arriva North East	F106HVK	Stagecoach Busways	F251JRM	Stagecoach Transit
E903UBA	Snaiths	EHE241V	Compass Royston	F106UEF	Go-Ahead	F252JRM	Stagecoach Transit

Hunters operate a Duple Dominant bus, GVK820W, pictured here at Stanley. Two of the bus versions of the Dominant are in the current fleet, the other example being an 11 metre version. *Terry Wightman*

F253KAO	Stagecoach Transit	F703BAT	Stagecoach Transit	F914JRG	Stagecoach Busways	G21HHG	Arriva North East
F259GWJ	Go-Ahead	F704BAT	Stagecoach Transit	F915JRG	Stagecoach Busways	G22CSG	Stanley Coaches
F303JTY	Arriva North East	F705BAT	Stagecoach Transit	F916JRG	Stagecoach Busways	G23CSG	Stanley Coaches
F304JTY	Arriva North East	F706CAG	Stagecoach Transit	F917JRG	Stagecoach Busways	G93ERP	Classic
F305JTY	Arriva North East	F710COA	Grierson	F918JRG	Stagecoach Busways	G97BYU	Travelsure
F306JTY	Arriva North East	F722KGK	Bell Bros	F919JRG	Stagecoach Busways	G97SKR	Bob Smith Travel
F307JTY	Arriva North East	F722LRG	Go-Ahead	F919ONL	Swan's Coaches	G108CEH	Stagecoach Busways
F308JTY	Arriva North East	F723LRG	Go-Ahead	F920JRG	Stagecoach Busways	G113SKX	Stagecoach Busways
F309JTY	Arriva North East	F724LRG	Go-Ahead	F932LKE	Redby	G148SUS	Bob Smith Travel
F310JTY	Arriva North East	F725LRG	Go-Ahead	F969LTY	Stanley Coaches	G151UAS	Amberline
F311JTY	Arriva North East	F726LRG	Go-Ahead	F997WPY	Weardale	G174YRE	Arriva North East
F312JTY	Arriva North East	F727LRG	Go-Ahead	FCU190	Go-Ahead	G175DRF	Arriva North East
F321MBB	Stanley Coaches	F728LRG	Go-Ahead	FDZ1635	Hylton Castle	G178SMW	Altona Coaches
F409SVW	Caris Coaches	F729LRG	Go-Ahead	FDZ8195	Hylton Castle	G194JHD	Siesta
F502ANY	Go-Ahead	F730LRG	Go-Ahead	FIL8538	Lee's of Durham	G209HCP	Arriva North East
F503ANY	Go-Ahead	F731LRG	Go-Ahead	FIL8694	Delta	G210HCP	Arriva North East
F504ANY	Go-Ahead	F732LRG	Go-Ahead	FRX869T	Bob Smith Travel	G211HCP	Arriva North East
F514LCN	Rothbury Motors	F733LRG	Go-Ahead	FSV578	Delta	G212HCP	Arriva North East
F521NBR	Hennings	F740OCU	Stanley Coaches	FTN694W	Go-Ahead	G214HCP	Arriva North East
F540NFC	Stanley Coaches	F751RUT	Snaiths	FTN695W	Go-Ahead	G221NWF	Stanley Coaches
F568HPP	Snaiths	F755FDV	Snaiths	FTN697W	Go-Ahead	G222KWE	George Bell
F601UVN	Stagecoach Transit	F809BOE	Amberline	FTN698W	Go-Ahead	G238JDA	Snaiths
F602UVN	Stagecoach Transit	F810OCN	Hylton Castle	FTN699W	Go-Ahead	G241AHP	Stanley Coaches
F603UVN	Stagecoach Transit	F901JBB	Hunter's	FTN700W	Go-Ahead	G251SRG	Arriva North East
F604UVN	Stagecoach Transit	F901JRG	Stagecoach Busways	FTN701W	Go-Ahead	G252SRG	Arriva North East
F605UVN	Stagecoach Transit	F902JRG	Stagecoach Busways	FTN702W	Go-Ahead	G253SRG	Arriva North East
F606UVN	Stagecoach Transit	F903JBB	Stanley Coaches	FTN703W	Go-Ahead	G254SRG	Arriva North East
F607UVN	Stagecoach Transit	F903JRG	Stagecoach Busways	FTN704W	Go-Ahead	G255UVK	Arriva North East
F608UVN	Stagecoach Transit	F904JRG	Stagecoach Busways	FTN705W	Go-Ahead	G256UVK	Arriva North East
F609UVN	Stagecoach Transit	F905JRG	Stagecoach Busways	FTN706W	Go-Ahead	G257UVK	Arriva North East
F610UVN	Stagecoach Transit	F906JRG	Stagecoach Busways	FTN707W	Go-Ahead	G258UVK	Arriva North East
F621XMS	Stagecoach Transit	F907JRG	Stagecoach Busways	FTN708W	Go-Ahead	G276TST	Amberline
F624XMS	Stagecoach Transit	F908JRG	Stagecoach Busways	FTN709W	Go-Ahead	G280TSL	Stagecoach Busways
F625XMS	Stagecoach Transit	F909JRG	Stagecoach Busways	FTN710W	Go-Ahead	G281TSL	Stagecoach Busways
F629XMS	Stagecoach Transit	F910JRG	Stagecoach Busways	FTN711W	Go-Ahead	G314WFU	Stanley Coaches
F701BAT	Stagecoach Transit	F911JRG	Stagecoach Busways	FTN712W	Go-Ahead	G327LDT	St George Travel
F701ECC	Arriva North East	F911YWY	George Bell	FTN713W	Go-Ahead	G400TVK	Snaiths
F702BAT	Stagecoach Transit	F912JRG	Stagecoach Busways	FTN714W	Go-Ahead	G431XFT	Tyne Valley
F702ECC	Arriva North East	F913JRG	Stagecoach Busways	FWA476V	Michael Franks	G487XCU	Stanley Coaches

Reg	Operator	Reg	Operator	Reg	Operator	Reg	Operator
G508EAJ	Arriva North East	GSU348	Moor-Dale	H890CCU	Arriva North East	J366BNW	Arriva North East
G509EAJ	Arriva North East	GTX752W	Compass Royston	H898VWA	ERB Services	J371BNW	Stagecoach Busways
G510EAJ	Arriva North East	GVK820W	Hunter's	H984LEF	Siesta	J372BNW	Stagecoach Busways
G511EAJ	Arriva North East	GVL323	Grierson	HAZ7657	Caris Coaches	J373BNW	Stagecoach Busways
G512EAJ	Arriva North East	GYE381W	Go-Ahead	HDZ2603	Stagecoach Transit	J374BNW	Stagecoach Busways
G525LWU	Stagecoach Transit	H11JYM	George Bell	HDZ2604	Stagecoach Transit	J375BNW	Stagecoach Busways
G576YTR	North Rider	H31PAJ	Arriva North East	HDZ2605	Stagecoach Transit	J376BNW	Stagecoach Busways
G611CEF	Stagecoach Transit	H32PAJ	Arriva North East	HDZ2606	Stagecoach Transit	J377BNW	Stagecoach Busways
G612CEF	Stagecoach Transit	H51NDU	Go-Ahead	HDZ2607	Stagecoach Transit	J378BNW	Stagecoach Busways
G613CEF	Stagecoach Transit	H71XKH	Stagecoach Transit	HDZ2609	Stagecoach Transit	J379BNW	Stagecoach Busways
G614CEF	Stagecoach Transit	H104HDV	George Bell	HDZ2610	Stagecoach Transit	J401KTY	North Rider
G615CEF	Stagecoach Transit	H126ACU	Stagecoach Busways	HDZ2611	Stagecoach Transit	J422HDS	Stagecoach Transit
G616CEF	Stagecoach Transit	H126LVN	Snaiths	HDZ2613	Stagecoach Transit	J43GGB	Go-Ahead
G617CEF	Stagecoach Transit	H127ACU	Stagecoach Busways	HDZ2615	Stagecoach Transit	J45GGB	Redby
G618CEF	Stagecoach Transit	H129CDB	Arriva North East	HDZ2616	Stagecoach Transit	J478XHL	Travelsure
G619CEF	Stagecoach Transit	H130CDB	Arriva North East	HDZ5401	Michael Franks	J485OHA	Bob Smith Travel
G620CEF	Stagecoach Transit	H144UUA	Stagecoach Busways	HDZ5402	Michael Franks	J517MNA	Siesta
G621XLO	George Bell	H148UUA	Stagecoach Busways	HDZ5404	Michael Franks	J537JSU	Classic
G626EEM	J C Bell	H150LVN	Siesta	HDZ5410	Michael Franks	J601KCU	Go-Ahead
G665OVO	ERB Services	H150UUA	Stagecoach Busways	HDZ5414	Michael Franks	J602KCU	Go-Ahead
G675TCN	Go-Ahead	H154UUA	George Bell	HDZ9106	Lee's of Durham	J603KCU	Go-Ahead
G676TCN	Go-Ahead	H160WWT	Stagecoach Busways	HED204V	Arriva North East	J604KCU	Go-Ahead
G677TCN	Go-Ahead	H162WWT	Stagecoach Busways	HED205V	Arriva North East	J605KCU	Go-Ahead
G678TCN	Go-Ahead	H170WWT	Stagecoach Busways	HHN555V	Compass Royston	J606KCU	Go-Ahead
G679TCN	Go-Ahead	H171WWT	Stagecoach Busways	HHW916L	Delta	J607KCU	Go-Ahead
G702AEF	Go-Ahead	H174WWT	Stagecoach Busways	HIL3078	Escort	J608KCU	Go-Ahead
G702BEF	Bell Bros	H176WWT	Stagecoach Busways	HIL5835	Garnetts	J609KCU	Go-Ahead
G703NGR	Weardale	H183ACN	Rothbury Motors	HIL6408	Delta	J610KCU	Go-Ahead
G7348TY	Go-Ahead	H193BCU	St George Travel	HIL6461	Hylton Castle	J611KCU	Go-Ahead
G7349TY	Go-Ahead	H194HLT	Snaiths	HIL6462	Hylton Castle	J612KCU	Go-Ahead
G734RTY	Go-Ahead	H201XKH	Delta	HIL6581	Delta	J613KCU	Go-Ahead
G735RTY	Go-Ahead	H253PAJ	Arriva North East	HIL6587	Delta	J614KCU	Go-Ahead
G736RTY	Go-Ahead	H259CFT	Arriva North East	HIL6755	Delta	J615KCU	Go-Ahead
G737RTY	Go-Ahead	H261CFT	Arriva North East	HIL9271	Compass Royston	J616KCU	Go-Ahead
G740RTY	Go-Ahead	H262CFT	Arriva North East	HJI586	Snaiths	J617KCU	Go-Ahead
G741RTY	Go-Ahead	H263CFT	Arriva North East	HJI644	Snowdons	J618KCU	Go-Ahead
G742RTY	Go-Ahead	H264CFT	Arriva North East	HKR11	Moor-Dale	J619KCU	Go-Ahead
G743RTY	Go-Ahead	H266CFT	Arriva North East	HPY426V	Delta	J620KCU	Go-Ahead
G744RTY	Go-Ahead	H267CFT	Arriva North East	HRG920W	Delta	J620UHN	Arriva North East
G745RTY	Go-Ahead	H278LEF	Arriva North East	HSD85V	Compass Royston	J621KCU	Go-Ahead
G746RTY	Go-Ahead	H279LEF	Arriva North East	HTY481L	Tyne Valley	J622KCU	Go-Ahead
G747RTY	Go-Ahead	H421BNL	Stagecoach Busways	HUI3584	Altona Coaches	J623KCU	Go-Ahead
G751UCU	Go-Ahead	H422BNL	Stagecoach Busways	HUI3912	Altona Coaches	J624KCU	Go-Ahead
G752UCU	Go-Ahead	H423BNL	Stagecoach Busways	HUP757T	Arriva North East	J625KCU	Go-Ahead
G753UCU	Go-Ahead	H424BNL	Stagecoach Busways	HUP758T	Arriva North East	J626KCU	Go-Ahead
G754UCU	Go-Ahead	H424DVM	Grierson	HVK185N	Tyne Valley	J627KCU	Go-Ahead
G755GDC	Snaiths	H425BNL	Stagecoach Busways	HVK186N	Tyne Valley	J628KCU	Go-Ahead
G755UCU	Go-Ahead	H426BNL	Stagecoach Busways	IAZ3924	Cochrane's	J629KCU	Go-Ahead
G756UYT	Arriva North East	H427BNL	Stagecoach Busways	IIL1321	Stagecoach Transit	J630KCU	Go-Ahead
G757UYT	Arriva North East	H428BNL	Stagecoach Busways	IIL1839	Delta	J631KCU	Go-Ahead
G758UYT	Arriva North East	H428EFT	Stagecoach Busways	IIL2271	Delta	J632KCU	Go-Ahead
G761UYT	Arriva North East	H429BNL	Stagecoach Busways	IIL6234	DC Travel	J633KCU	Go-Ahead
G762UYT	Arriva North East	H429EFT	Stagecoach Busways	IIL6235	DC Travel	J634KCU	Go-Ahead
G796UBB	Amberline	H430BNL	Stagecoach Busways	IIL9167	Moor-Dale	J635KCU	Go-Ahead
G801JRH	Stagecoach Transit	H544EVM	Swan's Coaches	IIL9171	Moor-Dale	J636KCU	Go-Ahead
G802JRH	Stagecoach Transit	H598CNL	Arriva North East	IUI2831	Northumbria Cs	J637KCU	Go-Ahead
G803JRH	Stagecoach Transit	H667BNL	Stagecoach Busways	IUI8062	Northumbria Cs	J638KCU	Go-Ahead
G804JRH	Stagecoach Transit	H668AGD	Northumbria Cs	IUI8123	Northumbria Cs	J639KCU	Go-Ahead
G805JRH	Stagecoach Transit	H668BNL	Stagecoach Busways	IUI9031	Northumbria Cs	J640KCU	Go-Ahead
G806JRH	Stagecoach Transit	H669BNL	Stagecoach Busways	J1TCC	Travelsure	J651UHN	Arriva North East
G807LAG	Stagecoach Transit	H670BNL	Stagecoach Busways	J15DTS	Durham Travel	J652UHN	Arriva North East
G808LAG	Stagecoach Transit	H671BNL	Stagecoach Busways	J20NMS	Arriva North East	J653UHN	Arriva North East
G816NCA	Fairley's	H672BNL	Stagecoach Busways	J69GCX	Siesta	J656UHN	Arriva North East
G921TCU	Stagecoach Busways	H673BNL	Stagecoach Busways	J110SPB	Go-Ahead	J657UHN	Arriva North East
G922TCU	Stagecoach Busways	H674BNL	Stagecoach Busways	J200EOS	Scarlet Band	J658UHN	Arriva North East
G923TCU	Stagecoach Busways	H675BNL	Stagecoach Busways	J201VHN	Go-Ahead	J661UHN	Arriva North East
G924TCU	Stagecoach Busways	H676BNL	Stagecoach Busways	J202VHN	Go-Ahead	J684THN	Grierson
G925TCU	Stagecoach Busways	H684YGO	Gardiners	J203VHN	Go-Ahead	J701KCU	Stagecoach Busways
G926TCU	Stagecoach Busways	H685YGO	Gardiners	J204VHN	Go-Ahead	J702KCU	Stagecoach Busways
G965WNR	BM Coaches	H702YUV	North Rider	J205VHN	Go-Ahead	J781LNL	Crossroads
GAN744J	Tyne Valley	H802OPT	Go-Ahead	J206VHN	Go-Ahead	J866UPY	Arriva North East
GAN745J	Tyne Valley	H802SKY	Hennings	J207VHN	Go-Ahead	J867UPY	Arriva North East
GIB206	Weardale	H809WKH	Stagecoach Transit	J208VHN	Go-Ahead	J901UKV	Stagecoach Transit
GIB638	Weardale	H810WKH	Stagecoach Transit	J230JJR	Classic	J910OEY	Snowdons
GIB8666	Weardale	H811WKH	Stagecoach Transit	J292SMO	J C Bell	J933JJR	Go-Ahead
GIL8778	Snaiths	H812WKH	Stagecoach Transit	J293SMO	Durham Travel	J934JJR	Go-Ahead
GJR494L	Tyne Valley	H813WKH	Stagecoach Transit	J294SMO	Durham Travel	J935JJR	Go-Ahead
GMS279S	Scarlet Band	H814WKH	Stagecoach Transit	J295SMO	J C Bell	J936JJR	Go-Ahead
GPC730N	Classic	H815WKH	Stagecoach Transit	J296SMO	Durham Travel	J937JJR	Go-Ahead
GPX587X	St George Travel	H816WKH	Stagecoach Transit	J297SMO	Durham Travel	J938JJR	Go-Ahead
GRF265V	Snowdons	H840UUA	Arriva North East	J298SMO	Durham Travel	J939JJR	Go-Ahead
GSK962	Go-Ahead	H856NOC	ERB Services	J299SMO	Durham Travel	J940JJR	Go-Ahead
GSU346	Moor-Dale	H886CCU	Arriva North East	J324HVV	Siesta	J941JJR	Go-Ahead
GSU347	Arriva North East	H889CCU	Arriva North East	J363BNW	Arriva North East	J941MFT	Go-Ahead

Reg	Operator	Reg	Operator	Reg	Operator	Reg	Operator
J942JJR	Go-Ahead	JUP189T	Hunter's	K511BHN	Arriva North East	KBR252N	Weardale
J942MFT	Go-Ahead	JVJ529	Moor-Dale	K512BHN	Arriva North East	KBR634T	Go-Ahead
J943JJR	Go-Ahead	JWF493V	Kingsley's	K513BHN	Arriva North East	KDW330P	Galaxy Travel
J943MFT	Go-Ahead	JWF494V	Kingsley's	K514BHN	Arriva North East	KHT116P	Gardiners
J944JJR	Go-Ahead	K2STX	Stanley Coaches	K515BHN	Arriva North East	KJR281X	Hennings
J944KVK	Stanley Coaches	K2VOY	Go-Ahead	K516BHN	Arriva North East	KPJ247W	Crossroads
J944MFT	Go-Ahead	K3VOY	Go-Ahead	K517BHN	Arriva North East	KPJ252W	Crossroads
J945JJR	Go-Ahead	K5URE	Delta	K518BHN	Arriva North East	KPJ265W	Garnetts
J945MFT	Go-Ahead	K30GGY	North Rider	K571DFS	Stagecoach Transit	KRN112T	Hylton Castle
J946JJR	Go-Ahead	K108YVN	Go-Ahead	K572DFS	Stagecoach Transit	KSC500	Venture Reed
J946MFT	Go-Ahead	K109YVN	Go-Ahead	K573DFS	Stagecoach Transit	KYO624X	Arriva North East
J947MFT	Go-Ahead	K110YVN	Go-Ahead	K576DFS	Stagecoach Transit	KYV643X	Arriva North East
J948MFT	Go-Ahead	K130TFT	Stanley Coaches	K577DFS	Stagecoach Transit	KYV646X	Arriva North East
J949MFT	Go-Ahead	K131FKW	Arriva North East	K622YVN	Stagecoach Transit	KYV698X	Arriva North East
J950MFT	Go-Ahead	K132FKW	Arriva North East	K623YVN	Stagecoach Transit	KYV790X	Arriva North East
J951MFT	Go-Ahead	K140RYS	Arriva North East	K624YVN	Stagecoach Transit	KYW372X	Garnetts
J952MFT	Go-Ahead	K162FYG	Stagecoach Busways	K625YVN	Stagecoach Transit	L5GAR	Lee's of Durham
J953MFT	Go-Ahead	K163FYG	Stagecoach Busways	K626YVN	Stagecoach Transit	L7MJD	Durham City
J954MFT	Go-Ahead	K164FYG	Stagecoach Busways	K627YVN	Stagecoach Transit	L10TCC	Snaiths
J955MFT	Go-Ahead	K165FYG	Stagecoach Busways	K628YVN	Stagecoach Transit	L27LSG	Robson
J988TVU	Classic	K166FYG	Stagecoach Busways	K629YVN	Stagecoach Transit	L28ABB	Durham Travel
JAJ140W	Stagecoach Transit	K174CAV	North Rider	K630YVN	Stagecoach Transit	L31HHN	Stagecoach Transit
JAJ141W	Stagecoach Transit	K175CAV	North Rider	K703PCN	Stagecoach Busways	L32HHN	Stagecoach Transit
JAJ142W	Stagecoach Transit	K176CAV	North Rider	K704PCN	Stagecoach Busways	L33HHN	Stagecoach Transit
JAJ143W	Stagecoach Transit	K177CAV	North Rider	K705PCN	Stagecoach Busways	L33NMS	Arriva North East
JAJ144W	Stagecoach Transit	K200SDU	Snaiths	K706PCN	Stagecoach Busways	L34HHN	Stagecoach Transit
JAJ145W	Stagecoach Transit	K351SCN	Go-Ahead	K707PCN	Stagecoach Busways	L35HHN	Stagecoach Transit
JAJ146W	Stagecoach Transit	K352SCN	Go-Ahead	K708PCN	Stagecoach Busways	L36HHN	Stagecoach Transit
JAZ8669	Weardale	K353SCN	Go-Ahead	K709PCN	Stagecoach Busways	L37HHN	Stagecoach Transit
JCN581N	Henry Cooper	K354SCN	Go-Ahead	K710PCN	Stagecoach Busways	L63YJF	Altona Coaches
JCN822	Go-Ahead	K355SCN	Go-Ahead	K711PCN	Stagecoach Busways	L64TTS	Stanley Coaches
JDH216V	Whiteline	K356SCN	Go-Ahead	K712PCN	Stagecoach Busways	L81YBB	Stagecoach Busways
JFT412X	Henry Cooper	K357SCN	Go-Ahead	K713PCN	Stagecoach Busways	L83CNY	Redby
JHE145W	Kingsley's	K358SCN	Go-Ahead	K714PCN	Stagecoach Busways	L83YBB	Stagecoach Busways
JHE160W	Kingsley's	K359SCN	Go-Ahead	K715PCN	Stagecoach Busways	L84CNY	Redby
JHE167W	Kingsley's	K360SCN	Go-Ahead	K717GBF	Altona Coaches	L89NSF	Robson
JHE179W	Kingsley's	K361SCN	Go-Ahead	K717PCN	Stagecoach Busways	L100SBS	Arriva North East
JHE189W	Kingsley's	K362SCN	Go-Ahead	K718PCN	Stagecoach Busways	L101GHN	Stagecoach Transit
JHE192W	Kingsley's	K363SCN	Go-Ahead	K720PCN	Stagecoach Busways	L102GHN	Stagecoach Transit
JHE193W	Kingsley's	K364SCN	Go-Ahead	K721PCN	Stagecoach Busways	L102MEH	Arriva North East
JIL2075	Mill	K365SCN	Go-Ahead	K722PCN	Stagecoach Busways	L103GHN	Stagecoach Transit
JIL7905	J C Bell	K366RTY	Go-Ahead	K723PNL	Stagecoach Busways	L141YTY	Go-Ahead
JIL8514	Snowdons	K366SCN	Go-Ahead	K724PNL	Stagecoach Busways	L208KEF	Go-Ahead
JKW286W	Kingsley's	K367RTY	Go-Ahead	K725GWR	Altona Coaches	L209KEF	Go-Ahead
JSK346	Classic	K367SCN	Go-Ahead	K725PNL	Stagecoach Busways	L210KEF	Go-Ahead
JSV487	Durham City	K368RTY	Go-Ahead	K726PNL	Stagecoach Busways	L211KEF	Go-Ahead
JTY370X	Go-Ahead	K369RTY	Go-Ahead	K727PNL	Stagecoach Busways	L212KEF	Go-Ahead
JTY371X	Go-Ahead	K370RTY	Go-Ahead	K728PNL	Stagecoach Busways	L238CCW	Stagecoach Transit
JTY372X	Go-Ahead	K371RTY	Go-Ahead	K756SBB	Go-Ahead	L242CCK	Stagecoach Transit
JTY373X	Go-Ahead	K372RTY	Go-Ahead	K757SBB	Go-Ahead	L243CCK	Stagecoach Transit
JTY374X	Go-Ahead	K373RTY	Go-Ahead	K758SBB	Go-Ahead	L244CCK	Stagecoach Transit
JTY375X	Go-Ahead	K374RTY	Go-Ahead	K759SBB	Go-Ahead	L245CCK	Stagecoach Transit
JTY377X	Go-Ahead	K375RTY	Go-Ahead	K760SBB	Go-Ahead	L246CCK	Stagecoach Transit
JTY378X	Go-Ahead	K376RTY	Go-Ahead	K761SBB	Go-Ahead	L247CCK	Stagecoach Transit
JTY379X	Go-Ahead	K377RTY	Go-Ahead	K776YPY	Stanley Coaches	L249CCK	Stagecoach Transit
JTY380X	Go-Ahead	K378RTY	Go-Ahead	K846HVM	Snaiths	L250CCK	Stagecoach Transit
JTY381X	Go-Ahead	K379RTY	Go-Ahead	K851RBB	Arriva North East	L254CCK	Stagecoach Transit
JTY382X	Go-Ahead	K380RTY	Go-Ahead	K852RBB	Arriva North East	L271FVN	Arriva North East
JTY384X	Go-Ahead	K381RTY	Go-Ahead	K853RBB	Arriva North East	L272FVN	Arriva North East
JTY385X	Go-Ahead	K382RTY	Go-Ahead	K854RBB	Arriva North East	L273FVN	Arriva North East
JTY386X	Go-Ahead	K383RTY	Go-Ahead	K856PCN	Go-Ahead	L274FVN	Arriva North East
JTY387X	Go-Ahead	K408BHN	Arriva North East	K857PCN	Go-Ahead	L275FVN	Arriva North East
JTY388X	Go-Ahead	K409BHN	Arriva North East	K858PCN	Go-Ahead	L296TPW	J & C
JTY389X	Go-Ahead	K410BHN	Arriva North East	K859PCN	Go-Ahead	L315XBB	Go-Ahead
JTY390X	Go-Ahead	K411BHN	Arriva North East	K860PCN	Go-Ahead	L321BOD	North Rider
JTY391X	Go-Ahead	K412BHN	Arriva North East	K861PCN	Go-Ahead	L376YFT	Go-Ahead
JTY392X	Go-Ahead	K413BHN	Arriva North East	K862PCN	Go-Ahead	L377YFT	Go-Ahead
JTY393X	Go-Ahead	K414BHN	Arriva North East	K863PCN	Go-Ahead	L378YFT	Go-Ahead
JTY394X	Go-Ahead	K415BHN	Arriva North East	K864PCN	Go-Ahead	L379YFT	Go-Ahead
JTY395X	Go-Ahead	K416BHN	Arriva North East	K865PCN	Go-Ahead	L380YFT	Go-Ahead
JTY397X	Go-Ahead	K417BHN	Arriva North East	K940UBB	Caris Coaches	L381YFT	Go-Ahead
JTY398X	Go-Ahead	K457HDK	Stanley Coaches	K945OEM	Classic	L382YFT	Go-Ahead
JTY399X	Go-Ahead	K485FFS	Stagecoach Busways	K948OEM	Classic	L383YFT	Go-Ahead
JTY400X	Go-Ahead	K492FFS	Stagecoach Busways	K961RMW	ERB Services	L384YFT	Go-Ahead
JTY401X	Go-Ahead	K493FFS	Stagecoach Busways	K984SCU	Go-Ahead	L385YFT	Go-Ahead
JTY402X	Go-Ahead	K494FFS	Stagecoach Busways	K985SCU	Go-Ahead	L386YFT	Go-Ahead
JTY403X	Go-Ahead	K503BHN	Arriva North East	K986SCU	Go-Ahead	L387YFT	Go-Ahead
JTY405X	Go-Ahead	K504BHN	Arriva North East	K987SCU	Go-Ahead	L388YFT	Go-Ahead
JTY406X	Go-Ahead	K505BHN	Arriva North East	K988SCU	Go-Ahead	L389AVK	Go-Ahead
JTY407X	Go-Ahead	K506BHN	Arriva North East	K989SCU	Go-Ahead	L390AVK	Go-Ahead
JTY408X	Go-Ahead	K507BHN	Arriva North East	KAZ2751	Redby	L391AVK	Go-Ahead
JTY409X	Go-Ahead	K508BHN	Arriva North East	KAZ2752	Go-Ahead	L392AVK	Go-Ahead
JUI2067	A Line	K509BHN	Arriva North East	KAZ4551	First Choice Travel	L401FVN	Go-Ahead
JUP115T	Henry Cooper	K510BHN	Arriva North East	KBH845V	Garnetts		

The numbers of Bristol REs remaining in service is now reducing, though four are still listed in the Delta fleet. One of these, IIL2271 with Eastern Counties Bodywork is shown here in an overall red livery. *David Longbottom*

L402FVN	Go-Ahead	L519FHN	Arriva North East	L605FHN	Arriva North East	L855WRG	Arriva North East
L403FVN	Go-Ahead	L520FHN	Arriva North East	L608WWK	Redby	L856WRG	Arriva North East
L404FVN	Go-Ahead	L521FHN	Arriva North East	L729VNL	Stagecoach Busways	L857WRG	Arriva North East
L404LHE	Delta	L522FHN	Arriva North East	L730VNL	Stagecoach Busways	L858WRG	Arriva North East
L405GDC	Go-Ahead	L523FHN	Arriva North East	L731VNL	Stagecoach Busways	L881YVK	North Rider
L406GDC	Go-Ahead	L524FHN	Arriva North East	L732VNL	Stagecoach Busways	L893YCN	North Rider
L407GDC	Go-Ahead	L525FHN	Arriva North East	L733VNL	Stagecoach Busways	L923UGA	Leven Valley
L408GDC	Go-Ahead	L526FHN	Arriva North East	L734VNL	Stagecoach Busways	L972WTY	Go-Ahead
L409GPY	Go-Ahead	L527FHN	Arriva North East	L735VNL	Stagecoach Busways	L973WTY	Go-Ahead
L410GPY	Go-Ahead	L528FHN	Arriva North East	L736VNL	Stagecoach Busways	L974WTY	Go-Ahead
L411GPY	Go-Ahead	L529FHN	Arriva North East	L737VNL	Stagecoach Busways	L975WTY	Go-Ahead
L412GPY	Snaiths	L530FHN	Arriva North East	L738VNL	Stagecoach Busways	L992VTY	Snaiths
L413KEF	Go-Ahead	L531FHN	Arriva North East	L739VNL	Stagecoach Busways	LAW127F	Rothbury Motors
L414KEF	Go-Ahead	L532EHD	Arriva North East	L740VNL	Stagecoach Busways	LBU130L	DC Travel
L415KEF	Go-Ahead	L532FHN	Arriva North East	L741VNL	Stagecoach Busways	LBZ4329	DC Travel
L416KEF	Go-Ahead	L533EHD	Arriva North East	L742VNL	Stagecoach Busways	LCU112	Stagecoach Busways
L417KEF	Go-Ahead	L533FHN	Arriva North East	L743VNL	Stagecoach Busways	LCU434X	Bob Smith Travel
L418FHN	Arriva North East	L534FHN	Arriva North East	L744VNL	Stagecoach Busways	LDC70P	Compass Royston
L419FHN	Arriva North East	L535FHN	Arriva North East	L745VNL	Stagecoach Busways	LFM527T	Galaxy Travel
L420FHN	Arriva North East	L536FHN	Arriva North East	L746VNL	Stagecoach Busways	LHS744V	Altona Coaches
L421FHN	Arriva North East	L537FHN	Arriva North East	L748VNL	Stagecoach Busways	LIB347	Grierson
L422FHN	Arriva North East	L538FHN	Arriva North East	L749VNL	Stagecoach Busways	LIB449	Grierson
L469YVK	Go-Ahead	L539FHN	Arriva North East	L750VNL	Stagecoach Busways	LIB854	Grierson
L470YVK	Go-Ahead	L540FHN	Arriva North East	L751VNL	Stagecoach Busways	LIB987	Grierson
L471YVK	Go-Ahead	L541FHN	Arriva North East	L752VNL	Stagecoach Busways	LIB987	Grierson
L472YVK	Go-Ahead	L542FHN	Arriva North East	L752YGE	Durham City	LIB6349	Priory
L475CFT	Go-Ahead	L543FHN	Arriva North East	L753VNL	Stagecoach Busways	LIB6350	Priory
L476CFT	Go-Ahead	L544GHN	Arriva North East	L754VNL	Stagecoach Busways	LIL8872	Whiteline
L477CFT	Go-Ahead	L545GHN	Arriva North East	L755VNL	Stagecoach Busways	LIL8970	Dodds of Ashington
L478CFT	Go-Ahead	L546GHN	Arriva North East	L756VNL	Stagecoach Busways	LIL8971	Dodds of Ashington
L479CFT	Go-Ahead	L547GHN	Arriva North East	L757VNL	Stagecoach Busways	LIL9814	Compass Royston
L481CFT	Go-Ahead	L548GHN	Arriva North East	L758VNL	Stagecoach Busways	LIL9815	Compass Royston
L482CFT	Go-Ahead	L549GHN	Arriva North East	L759VNL	Stagecoach Busways	LIL9816	Compass Royston
L483CFT	Go-Ahead	L550GHN	Arriva North East	L760ARG	Stagecoach Busways	LIW4291	Compass Royston
L484CFT	Go-Ahead	L601FHN	Arriva North East	L761ARG	Stagecoach Busways	LJA621P	Garnetts
L485CFT	Go-Ahead	L602FHN	Arriva North East	L762ARG	Stagecoach Busways	LPT701T	Arriva North East
L486CFT	Go-Ahead	L603FHN	Arriva North East	L763ARG	Stagecoach Busways	LPT703T	Arriva North East
L487CFT	Go-Ahead	L604FHN	Arriva North East	L764ARG	Stagecoach Busways	LPT707T	Arriva North East
L488CFT	Go-Ahead			L765ARG	Stagecoach Busways	LUA328V	Michael Franks

K945OEM from the Classic fleet is seen at Gateshead in May 1999. The Mercedes-Benz is one of a pair purchased from Merseybus and shown here in Classic Buses livery. *A Blagburn*

Reg	Operator	Reg	Operator	Reg	Operator	Reg	Operator
LUG85P	Crossroads	M201DRG	Stagecoach Busways	M407SPY	Stagecoach Transit	M546SPY	Stagecoach Transit
LUG91P	Crossroads	M202DRG	Stagecoach Busways	M408SPY	Stagecoach Transit	M547SPY	Stagecoach Transit
LUG106P	Crossroads	M203DRG	Stagecoach Busways	M409SPY	Stagecoach Transit	M548SPY	Stagecoach Transit
LUG112P	Crossroads	M204DRG	Stagecoach Busways	M410SPY	Stagecoach Transit	M549SPY	Stagecoach Transit
LUK10P	Crossroads	M223SVN	Stagecoach Transit	M418PVN	Go-Ahead	M550SPY	Stagecoach Transit
M1CLA	Classic	M224SVN	Stagecoach Transit	M419PVN	Go-Ahead	M551SPY	Stagecoach Transit
M1STX	Stanley Coaches	M225SVN	Stagecoach Transit	M420PVN	Go-Ahead	M552SPY	Stagecoach Transit
M2STX	Stanley Coaches	M226SVN	Stagecoach Transit	M421PVN	Go-Ahead	M582JBC	BM Coaches
M3GYP	Go-Ahead	M227SVN	Stagecoach Transit	M422PVN	Go-Ahead	M597SSB	Redby
M3STX	Stanley Coaches	M246KBB	Durham Travel	M423PVN	Go-Ahead	M609WFS	George Bell
M6WMS	Weardale	M247KBB	Durham Travel	M424PVN	Go-Ahead	M667GJF	Grierson
M9SCC	Siesta	M248KBB	Durham Travel	M425PVN	Go-Ahead	M677JFP	Leven Valley
M10CLA	Classic	M249KBB	Durham Travel	M426RDC	Go-Ahead	M685HPF	Arriva North East
M10SCC	Siesta	M251KBB	Durham Travel	M427RDC	Go-Ahead	M686HPF	Arriva North East
M30CLA	Classic	M252KBB	Durham Travel	M428RDC	Go-Ahead	M687HPF	Arriva North East
M31FJR	Durham Travel	M253KBB	Durham Travel	M429RDC	Go-Ahead	M688HPF	Arriva North East
M32FJR	Durham Travel	M254KBB	Durham Travel	M430RDC	Go-Ahead	M689HPF	Arriva North East
M34HJR	Durham Travel	M255KBB	Durham Travel	M431RDC	Go-Ahead	M690HPF	Arriva North East
M36HJR	Durham Travel	M256MRD	Durham Travel	M432RDC	Go-Ahead	M691HPF	Arriva North East
M37HJR	Durham Travel	M267HTN	Bob Smith Travel	M433RDC	Go-Ahead	M692HPF	Arriva North East
M38HJR	Durham Travel	M271FNS	BM Coaches	M470FJR	Go-Ahead	M693HPF	Arriva North East
M38PVN	Stagecoach Transit	M301SAJ	Arriva North East	M471FJR	Go-Ahead	M707KRH	Stagecoach Transit
M39HJR	Durham Travel	M302SAJ	Arriva North East	M472FJR	Go-Ahead	M708KRH	Stagecoach Transit
M39PVN	Stagecoach Transit	M303SAJ	Arriva North East	M473FJR	Go-Ahead	M709KRH	Stagecoach Transit
M40CLA	Classic	M304SAJ	Arriva North East	M489HCU	Go-Ahead	M710KRH	Stagecoach Transit
M40PVN	Stagecoach Transit	M305SAJ	Arriva North East	M490HCU	Go-Ahead	M711KRH	Stagecoach Transit
M41PVN	Stagecoach Transit	M370FTY	Arriva North East	M491HCU	Go-Ahead	M712KRH	Stagecoach Transit
M42PVN	Stagecoach Transit	M371FTY	Arriva North East	M492HCU	Go-Ahead	M712MRU	Garnetts
M63WEB	Hylton Castle	M372FTY	Arriva North East	M493HCU	Go-Ahead	M713KRH	Stagecoach Transit
M104PVN	Stagecoach Transit	M373FTY	Arriva North East	M501AJC	Arriva North East	M714KRH	Stagecoach Transit
M105PVN	Stagecoach Transit	M374FTY	Arriva North East	M502AJC	Arriva North East	M715KRH	Stagecoach Transit
M106PVN	Stagecoach Transit	M375FTY	Arriva North East	M503AJC	Arriva North East	M716KRH	Stagecoach Transit
M107PVN	Stagecoach Transit	M376FTY	Arriva North East	M504AJC	Arriva North East	M717KRH	Stagecoach Transit
M108PVN	Stagecoach Transit	M377FTY	Arriva North East	M504HNL	Go-Ahead	M718KRH	Stagecoach Transit
M111BUS	Redby	M401SPY	Stagecoach Transit	M505HNL	Go-Ahead	M731KJU	Gardiners
M115XLV	Stanley Coaches	M402SPY	Stagecoach Transit	M506HNL	Go-Ahead	M766DRG	Stagecoach Busways
M122UUB	Arriva North East	M403SPY	Stagecoach Transit	M507HNL	Go-Ahead	M767DRG	Stagecoach Busways
M131HVR	Durham Travel	M404SPY	Stagecoach Transit	M543SPY	Stagecoach Transit	M768DRG	Stagecoach Busways
M137FYJ	BM Coaches	M405SPY	Stagecoach Transit	M544SPY	Stagecoach Transit	M769DRG	Stagecoach Busways
M152KJF	Northumbria Cs	M406SPY	Stagecoach Transit	M545SPY	Stagecoach Transit	M770DRG	Stagecoach Busways

Reg	Operator	Reg	Operator	Reg	Operator	Reg	Operator
M771DRG	Stagecoach Busways	MIW9046	Compass Royston	N381OTY	Arriva North East	N590WND	St George Travel
M784VJO	Fairley's	MJI3402	Snowdons	N382OTY	Arriva North East	N592WND	St George Travel
M789WCM	St George Travel	MJI4693	Compass Royston	N383OTY	Arriva North East	N670VUP	Go-Ahead
M803GFT	Go-Ahead	MJI4735	Durham City	N384OTY	Arriva North East	N671VUP	Go-Ahead
M804GFT	Go-Ahead	MJI6254	Compass Royston	N385OTY	Arriva North East	N701LTN	Stagecoach Busways
M805GFT	Go-Ahead	MOU746R	Compass Royston	N386OTY	Arriva North East	N702LTN	Stagecoach Busways
M806GFT	Go-Ahead	MPL123W	BM Coaches	N387OTY	Arriva North East	N703LTN	Stagecoach Busways
M807GFT	Go-Ahead	MRB804P	Hennings	N388OTY	Arriva North East	N704LTN	Stagecoach Busways
M808GFT	Go-Ahead	MRJ101W	Durham City	N389OTY	Arriva North East	N705LTN	Stagecoach Busways
M809GFT	Go-Ahead	MRJ357W	Weardale	N390OTY	Arriva North East	N706LTN	Stagecoach Busways
M810GFT	Go-Ahead	MTN874X	Delta	N391OTY	Arriva North East	N707LTN	Stagecoach Busways
M810HCU	Go-Ahead	MUP712T	Arriva North East	N392OTY	Arriva North East	N708LTN	Stagecoach Busways
M811GFT	Go-Ahead	MVK515R	Garnetts	N393OTY	Arriva North East	N709LTN	Stagecoach Busways
M811HCU	Go-Ahead	MVS380	Kingsley's	N395MFT	Classic	N710LTN	Stagecoach Busways
M812GFT	Go-Ahead	MWW564P	Bob Smith Travel	N409NTN	Go-Ahead	N711LTN	Stagecoach Busways
M812HCU	Go-Ahead	N2DCC	Durham City	N410NTN	Go-Ahead	N712LTN	Stagecoach Busways
M813GFT	Go-Ahead	N2MDC	Moor-Dale	N411NTN	Go-Ahead	N713LTN	Stagecoach Busways
M813HCU	Go-Ahead	N3CLA	Classic	N412NTN	Go-Ahead	N714LTN	Stagecoach Busways
M814GFT	Go-Ahead	N4MDC	Moor-Dale	N413NTN	Go-Ahead	N715LTN	Stagecoach Busways
M814HCU	Go-Ahead	N7SCC	Siesta	N458RNR	Leven Valley	N716FLN	Northumbria Cs
M815GFT	Go-Ahead	N8DTS	Durham Travel	N461RVK	Stagecoach Busways	N716LTN	Stagecoach Busways
M815HCU	Go-Ahead	N8NEV	J & C	N462RVK	Stagecoach Busways	N717FLN	Northumbria Cs
M816GFT	Go-Ahead	N8SCC	Siesta	N463RVK	Stagecoach Busways	N717LTN	ERB Services
M817GFT	Go-Ahead	N9DTS	Durham Travel	N464RVK	Stagecoach Busways	N717STY	ERB Services
M817KRH	Stagecoach Transit	N9NEV	J & C	N465RVK	Stagecoach Busways	N718LTN	Stagecoach Busways
M818GFT	Go-Ahead	N21PCU	Redby	N466RVK	Stagecoach Busways	N719LTN	Stagecoach Busways
M818KRH	Stagecoach Transit	N22DTS	Durham Travel	N467RVK	Stagecoach Busways	N720LTN	Stagecoach Busways
M819GFT	Go-Ahead	N23DTS	Durham Travel	N468RVK	Stagecoach Busways	N721LTN	Stagecoach Busways
M819KRH	Stagecoach Transit	N32AAJ	Compass Royston	N469RVK	Stagecoach Busways	N722LTN	Stagecoach Busways
M829PHN	Compass Royston	N50MDC	Moor-Dale	N470RVK	Stagecoach Busways	N723LTN	Stagecoach Busways
M859KCU	Arriva North East	N91RVK	Stagecoach Busways	N471RVK	Stagecoach Busways	N724LTN	Stagecoach Busways
M860KCU	Arriva North East	N103EMB	Altona Coaches	N472RVK	Stagecoach Busways	N725LTN	Stagecoach Busways
M861KCU	Arriva North East	N117TCN	North Rider	N473RVK	Stagecoach Busways	N726LTN	Stagecoach Busways
M862KCU	Arriva North East	N117WBR	Go-Ahead	N474RVK	Stagecoach Busways	N727LTN	Stagecoach Busways
M863KCU	Arriva North East	N118WBR	Go-Ahead	N475RVK	Stagecoach Busways	N728LTN	Stagecoach Busways
M864KCU	Arriva North East	N119WBR	Go-Ahead	N476RVK	Stagecoach Busways	N729LTN	Stagecoach Busways
M865KCU	Arriva North East	N120RJF	Redby	N477RVK	Stagecoach Busways	N730LTN	Stagecoach Busways
M866KCU	Arriva North East	N120WBR	Go-Ahead	N478RVK	Stagecoach Busways	N731LTN	Stagecoach Busways
M867KCU	Arriva North East	N121WBR	Go-Ahead	N479RVK	Stagecoach Busways	N732LTN	Stagecoach Busways
M868KCU	Arriva North East	N122WBR	Go-Ahead	N480RVK	Stagecoach Busways	N733LTN	Stagecoach Busways
M869KCU	Arriva North East	N123WBR	Go-Ahead	N481RVK	Stagecoach Busways	N734LTN	Stagecoach Busways
M869KFT	Durham Travel	N124WBR	Go-Ahead	N482RVK	Stagecoach Busways	N735LTN	Stagecoach Busways
M870KCU	Arriva North East	N152NTY	Durham Travel	N483RVK	Stagecoach Busways	N736LTN	Stagecoach Busways
M870KFT	Durham Travel	N153NTY	Durham Travel	N484RVK	Stagecoach Busways	N737LTN	Stagecoach Busways
M871KCU	Arriva North East	N154NTY	Durham Travel	N485RVK	Stagecoach Busways	N738LTN	Stagecoach Busways
M871KFT	Durham Travel	N192RVK	Arriva North East	N486RVK	Stagecoach Busways	N739LTN	Stagecoach Busways
M872LBB	Arriva North East	N201LTN	Stagecoach Busways	N487RVK	Stagecoach Busways	N740LTN	Stagecoach Busways
M873LBB	Arriva North East	N202LTN	Stagecoach Busways	N488RVK	Stagecoach Busways	N772RVK	Stagecoach Busways
M874LBB	Arriva North East	N203LTN	Stagecoach Busways	N489RVK	Stagecoach Busways	N773RVK	Stagecoach Busways
M875LBB	Arriva North East	N204LTN	Stagecoach Busways	N490RVK	Stagecoach Busways	N774RVK	Stagecoach Busways
M876LBB	Arriva North East	N205LTN	Stagecoach Busways	N491RVK	Stagecoach Busways	N775RVK	Stagecoach Busways
M886WAK	Compass Royston	N206LTN	Stagecoach Busways	N492RVK	Stagecoach Busways	N776RVK	Stagecoach Busways
M890GBB	Go-Ahead	N207LTN	Stagecoach Busways	N493RVK	Stagecoach Busways	N778RVK	Stagecoach Busways
M891GBB	Go-Ahead	N208LTN	Stagecoach Busways	N494RVK	Stagecoach Busways	N779RVK	Stagecoach Busways
M892GBB	Go-Ahead	N209LTN	Stagecoach Busways	N495RVK	Stagecoach Busways	N780RVK	Stagecoach Busways
M901DRG	Stagecoach Busways	N210LTN	Stagecoach Busways	N496RVK	Stagecoach Busways	N806XHN	Arriva North East
M902DRG	Stagecoach Busways	N211LTN	Stagecoach Busways	N497RVK	Stagecoach Busways	N807XHN	Arriva North East
M933FTN	Go-Ahead	N212LTN	Stagecoach Busways	N498RVK	Stagecoach Busways	N808XHN	Arriva North East
M934FTN	Go-Ahead	N213LTN	Stagecoach Busways	N499RVK	Stagecoach Busways	N809XHN	Arriva North East
M935FTN	Go-Ahead	N214LTN	Stagecoach Busways	N501RVK	Stagecoach Busways	N810XHN	Arriva North East
M936FTN	Go-Ahead	N215LTN	Stagecoach Busways	N505CVW	Lee's of Durham	N811NHS	Redby
M937FTN	Go-Ahead	N216LTN	Stagecoach Busways	N507NVK	ERB Services	N813WGR	Go-Ahead
M938FTN	Go-Ahead	N217LTN	Stagecoach Busways	N511XVN	Arriva North East	N814WGR	Go-Ahead
M939FTN	Go-Ahead	N281NCN	Arriva North East	N512XVN	Arriva North East	N815WGR	Go-Ahead
M940FTN	Go-Ahead	N282NCN	Arriva North East	N513XVN	Arriva North East	N816WGR	Go-Ahead
M951DRG	Stagecoach Busways	N283NCN	Arriva North East	N514XVN	Arriva North East	N831NCU	Caris Coaches
M952DRG	Stagecoach Busways	N284NCN	Arriva North East	N515XVN	Arriva North East	N872TTN	Classic
M953DRG	Stagecoach Busways	N285NCN	Arriva North East	N516XVN	Arriva North East	N877RTN	Arriva North East
M954DRG	Stagecoach Busways	N286NCN	Arriva North East	N517XVN	Arriva North East	N878RTN	Arriva North East
M992HHS	Compass Royston	N287NCN	Arriva North East	N518XVN	Arriva North East	N879RTN	Arriva North East
M993HHS	Compass Royston	N288NCN	Arriva North East	N519XVN	Arriva North East	N880RTN	Arriva North East
MBC545V	DC Travel	N289NCN	Arriva North East	N520XVN	Arriva North East	N881RTN	Arriva North East
MBR438T	Go-Ahead	N290NCN	Arriva North East	N521XVN	Arriva North East	N882RTN	Arriva North East
MBR439T	Go-Ahead	N306NBB	Durham Travel	N522XVN	Arriva North East	N883RTN	Arriva North East
MBR440T	Go-Ahead	N307NBB	Durham Travel	N523XVN	Arriva North East	N884RTN	Arriva North East
MBR455T	Swan's Coaches	N308NBB	Durham Travel	N524XVN	Arriva North East	N885RTN	Arriva North East
MBR458T	Go-Ahead	N341KKH	Stagecoach Transit	N525XVN	Arriva North East	N886RTN	Arriva North East
MFN116R	Redby	N342KKH	Stagecoach Transit	N548MFT	Classic	N887RTN	Arriva North East
MHN131W	Kings	N343KKH	Stagecoach Transit	N551VDC	Stagecoach Transit	N889RTN	Arriva North East
MIL1062	Mill	N344KKH	Stagecoach Transit	N552VDC	Stagecoach Transit	N890RTN	Arriva North East
MIL4397	Galaxy Travel	N345KKH	Stagecoach Transit	N553VDC	Stagecoach Transit	N891RTN	Arriva North East
MIL4684	Travelsure	N346KKH	Stagecoach Transit	N571GBW	BM Coaches	N898NNR	Durham City
MIL9302	Galaxy Travel	N347KKH	Stagecoach Transit	N586WND	Leven Valley	N990AEF	Fairley's
MIW1239	North Rider	N348KKH	Stagecoach Transit	N589GBW	BM Coaches	NDC238W	Michael Franks

Registration	Operator	Registration	Operator	Registration	Operator	Registration	Operator
NDC504W	Michael Franks	P59XNL	Durham Travel	P608FHN	Arriva North East	P972HKE	Travelsure
NDW137X	Hunter's	P59XTN	Arriva North East	P609FHN	Arriva North East	PAJ827X	Arriva North East
NDW139X	Delta	P61XTN	Arriva North East	P610FHN	Arriva North East	PAJ829X	Arriva North East
NEL113P	Garnetts	P77NEV	J & C	P611FHN	Arriva North East	PBZ8343	Compass Royston
NEO833R!	Stanley Coaches	P92URG	Stagecoach Busways	P612FHN	Arriva North East	PDZ6261	Arriva North East
NGR685P	Arriva North East	P118XCN	Stagecoach Busways	P613FHN	Arriva North East	PDZ6262	Arriva North East
NIL2190	Moor-Dale	P119XCN	Stagecoach Busways	P614FHN	Arriva North East	PEF6X	Weardale
NIL2464	DC Travel	P120XCN	Stagecoach Busways	P615FHN	Arriva North East	PEF148X	Stagecoach Transit
NIL4864	Moor-Dale	P121XCN	Stagecoach Busways	P616FHN	Arriva North East	PEF149X	Stagecoach Transit
NIL4867	Moor-Dale	P122XCN	Stagecoach Busways	P617FHN	Arriva North East	PEX611W	Robson
NIL5907	Snowdons	P123XCN	Stagecoach Busways	P618FHN	Arriva North East	PGR961T	Go-Ahead
NIL7962	Snowdons	P124XCN	Stagecoach Busways	P619FHN	Arriva North East	PIL2160	Classic
NIL8887	Moor-Dale	P125XCN	Stagecoach Busways	P620FHN	Arriva North East	PIL2161	Classic
NIW7053	Rothbury Motors	P126XCN	Stagecoach Busways	P621FHN	Arriva North East	PIL2162	Classic
NIW7054	Rothbury Motors	P126YTN	North Rider	P622FHN	Arriva North East	PIL2163	Classic
NIW7055	Rothbury Motors	P130HBG	Caris Coaches	P623FHN	Arriva North East	PIL2164	Classic
NJI8875	Travelsure	P135XCN	Stagecoach Busways	P624FHN	Arriva North East	PIL2165	Classic
NPK236R	Bob Smith Travel	P175ANR	BM Coaches	P625FHN	Arriva North East	PIL2166	Classic
NSU969	Tyne Valley	P178PRH	Stagecoach Transit	P626FHN	Arriva North East	PIL2167	Classic
NTK611	Garnetts	P179PRH	Stagecoach Transit	P627FHN	Arriva North East	PIL2168	Classic
NTU11Y	Arriva North East	P180PRH	Stagecoach Transit	P628FHN	Arriva North East	PIL2168	Classic
NTU12Y	Arriva North East	P181PRH	Stagecoach Transit	P629FHN	Arriva North East	PIL2169	Classic
NTU13Y	Arriva North East	P22MDC	Moor-Dale	P630FHN	Arriva North East	PIL2169	Classic
NUW604Y	Stagecoach Transit	P24WNL	Durham Travel	P630FTV	Delta	PIL2170	Classic
NUW634Y	Stagecoach Transit	P25WNL	Durham Travel	P631FHN	Arriva North East	PIL7834	Northumbria Cs
NUW639Y	Stagecoach Transit	P271VRG	Arriva North East	P632FHN	Arriva North East	PIL7835	Northumbria Cs
NUW642Y	Stagecoach Transit	P272VRG	Arriva North East	P633FHN	Arriva North East	PIL9326	First Choice Travel
NUW643Y	Stagecoach Transit	P273VRG	Arriva North East	P634FHN	Arriva North East	PJI2407	Jim Hughes
NUW648Y	Stagecoach Transit	P274VRG	Arriva North East	P635FHN	Arriva North East	PJI2408	Jim Hughes
NUW649Y	Stagecoach Transit	P275VRG	Arriva North East	P636FHN	Arriva North East	PJI4986	Delta
NUW659Y	Stagecoach Transit	P276VRG	Arriva North East	P637FHN	Arriva North East	PNM695W	Hunter's
NUW664Y	Stagecoach Transit	P277VRG	Arriva North East	P638FHN	Arriva North East	PRA10R	Scarlet Band
NUW666Y	Stagecoach Transit	P278VRG	Arriva North East	P639FHN	Arriva North East	PRA13R	Scarlet Band
NUW668Y	Stagecoach Transit	P279VRG	Arriva North East	P640FHN	Arriva North East	PRJ486R	Arriva North East
NUW673Y	Stagecoach Transit	P320AFT	Go-Ahead	P641FHN	Arriva North East	PRJ488R	Arriva North East
NUW675Y	Stagecoach Transit	P321AFT	Go-Ahead	P642FHN	Arriva North East	PRJ489R	Arriva North East
NVT451W	DC Travel	P322AFT	Go-Ahead	P643FHN	Arriva North East	PRJ490R	Arriva North East
OAT536V	Scarlet Band	P323AFT	Go-Ahead	P644FHN	Arriva North East	PRJ492R	Arriva North East
OAT603V	Dodds of Ashington	P324AFT	Go-Ahead	P645FHN	Arriva North East	PRJ494R	Arriva North East
OAY294	Cochrane's	P325AFT	Go-Ahead	P766BJU	Leven Valley	PRX189B	Stagecoach Transit
OBN505R	Arriva North East	P349NKH	Stagecoach Transit	P776BJU	Leven Valley	PT2053	Henry Cooper
OBR297	Henry Cooper	P350NKH	Stagecoach Transit	P780WCN	Stagecoach Busways	PTD639S	Arriva North East
OBR769T	Arriva North East	P351NKH	Stagecoach Transit	P781WCN	Stagecoach Busways	PVB803S	Delta
OCU809R	Arriva North East	P352NKH	Stagecoach Transit	P782WCN	Stagecoach Busways	PVO815R	Hennings
OCU810R	Arriva North East	P353NKH	Stagecoach Transit	P783WCN	Stagecoach Busways	PVV657	Rothbury Motors
OCU812R	Arriva North East	P354NKH	Stagecoach Transit	P784WCN	Stagecoach Busways	R4SCC	Siesta
OCU817R	Hennings	P410CCU	Arriva North East	P785BJU	Travelsure	R7CLA	Classic
OEW274R	Bob Smith Travel	P411CCU	Arriva North East	P785WCN	Stagecoach Busways	R7DCC	Durham City
OGR625T	Weardale	P412CCU	Arriva North East	P786WVK	Stagecoach Busways	R8CLA	Classic
OHN427X	Delta	P413CCU	Arriva North East	P787WVK	Stagecoach Busways	R9CLA	Classic
OHN428X	Delta	P414CCU	Arriva North East	P788BJU	Leven Valley	R10DTS	Durham Travel
OHN429X	Delta	P414VRG	Go-Ahead	P788WVK	Stagecoach Busways	R11DTS	Durham Travel
OIB2917	Snowdons	P415CCU	Arriva North East	P789WVK	Stagecoach Busways	R82SEF	Stagecoach Transit
OIB3512	Delta	P415VRG	Go-Ahead	P790GHN	Compass Royston	R83SEF	Stagecoach Transit
OIL4178	Caris Coaches	P416CCU	Arriva North East	P790WVK	Stagecoach Busways	R84SEF	Stagecoach Transit
OIL4568	A Line	P416VRG	Go-Ahead	P791WVK	Stagecoach Busways	R101KRG	Stagecoach Busways
OIL4571	A Line	P417CCU	Arriva North East	P792WVK	Stagecoach Busways	R102KRG	Stagecoach Busways
OIL4572	A Line	P417VRG	Go-Ahead	P793WVK	Stagecoach Busways	R103KRG	Stagecoach Busways
OIL8657	First Choice Travel	P418CCU	Arriva North East	P801AWR	Mill	R104KRG	Stagecoach Busways
OSF877M	Jim Hughes	P418VRG	Go-Ahead	P814VTY	Arriva North East	R105KRG	Stagecoach Busways
OSJ614R	Robson	P419CCU	Arriva North East	P820GAJ	Compass Royston	R107KRG	Stagecoach Busways
OSU895	Moor-Dale	P419VRG	Go-Ahead	P821GAJ	Compass Royston	R108KRG	Stagecoach Busways
OTP392	Jim Hughes	P420CCU	Arriva North East	P828FEF	Stagecoach Transit	R109KRG	Stagecoach Busways
OTP940	Jim Hughes	P420VRG	Go-Ahead	P829FEF	Stagecoach Transit	R110KRG	Stagecoach Busways
OVK138M	Swan's Coaches	P421VRG	Go-Ahead	P830FEF	Stagecoach Transit	R112KRG	Stagecoach Busways
OWW906P	Hennings	P422VRG	Go-Ahead	P844KOT	Redby	R113KRG	Stagecoach Busways
P2BST	Bob Smith Travel	P423VRG	Go-Ahead	P892XCU	Arriva North East	R114KRG	Stagecoach Busways
P2STX	Stanley Coaches	P424VRG	Go-Ahead	P893XCU	Arriva North East	R115KRG	Stagecoach Busways
P3CLA	Classic	P425VRG	Go-Ahead	P894XCU	Arriva North East	R116KRG	Stagecoach Busways
P5SCC	Siesta	P426VRG	Go-Ahead	P895XCU	Arriva North East	R117KRG	Stagecoach Busways
P5CLA	Classic	P427VRG	Go-Ahead	P896XCU	Arriva North East	R118KRG	Stagecoach Busways
P6CLA	Classic	P428VRG	Go-Ahead	P902DRG	Arriva North East	R119KRG	Stagecoach Busways
P6SCC	Siesta	P429VRG	Go-Ahead	P903DRG	Arriva North East	R120KRG	Stagecoach Busways
P6WMS	Weardale	P455EEF	Stagecoach Transit	P904DRG	Arriva North East	R121KRG	Stagecoach Busways
P7CLA	Classic	P456EEF	Stagecoach Transit	P905JNL	Arriva North East	R122KRG	Stagecoach Busways
P7DCC	Durham City	P457EEF	Stagecoach Transit	P906JNL	Arriva North East	R123KRG	Stagecoach Busways
P9CLA	Classic	P458EEF	Stagecoach Transit	P925ACU	Go-Ahead	R124KRG	Stagecoach Busways
P31KWA	Classic	P459EEF	Stagecoach Transit	P926ACU	Go-Ahead	R125KRG	Stagecoach Busways
P56XNL	Durham Travel	P460EEF	Stagecoach Transit	P927ACU	Go-Ahead	R126KRG	Stagecoach Busways
P56XTN	Arriva North East	P461EEF	Stagecoach Transit	P928ACU	Go-Ahead	R127KRG	Stagecoach Busways
P57XNL	Durham Travel	P533UGA	BM Coaches	P929ACU	Go-Ahead	R128KRG	Stagecoach Busways
P57XTN	Arriva North East	P593HHF	BM Coaches	P930ACU	Go-Ahead	R14SCC	Siesta
P58XNL	Durham Travel	P606FHN	Arriva North East	P931ACU	Go-Ahead	R167SEF	Compass Royston
P58XTN	Arriva North East	P607FHN	Arriva North East	P932ACU	Go-Ahead	R168SEF	Compass Royston

Reg	Operator	Reg	Operator	Reg	Operator	Reg	Operator
R183TKU	Classic	R654RPY	Stagecoach Transit	R909ULA	Siesta	S359ONL	Go-Ahead
R189LBC	Northumbria Cs	R655RPY	Stagecoach Transit	R910JNL	Arriva North East	S360ONL	Go-Ahead
R236KRG	Stagecoach Busways	R667GCU	ERB Services	R912JNL	Arriva North East	S361ONL	Go-Ahead
R237KRG	Stagecoach Busways	R701KCU	Arriva North East	R913JNL	Arriva North East	S362ONL	Go-Ahead
R238KRG	Stagecoach Busways	R701MHN	Arriva North East	R914JNL	Arriva North East	S363ONL	Go-Ahead
R239KRG	Stagecoach Busways	R702MHN	Arriva North East	R915JNL	Arriva North East	S364ONL	Go-Ahead
R240KRG	Stagecoach Busways	R703MHN	Arriva North East	R916JNL	Arriva North East	S365ONL	Go-Ahead
R241KRG	Stagecoach Busways	R704MHN	Arriva North East	R917JNL	Arriva North East	S366ONL	Go-Ahead
R242KRG	Stagecoach Busways	R705MHN	Arriva North East	R918JNL	Arriva North East	S367ONL	Go-Ahead
R242OCU	Go-Ahead	R706MHN	Arriva North East	R919JNL	Arriva North East	S368ONL	Go-Ahead
R243KRG	Stagecoach Busways	R707MHN	Arriva North East	R920JNL	Arriva North East	S369ONL	Go-Ahead
R243OCU	Go-Ahead	R708MHN	Arriva North East	R921JNL	Arriva North East	S370ONL	Go-Ahead
R244KRG	Stagecoach Busways	R709MHN	Arriva North East	R922JNL	Arriva North East	S371ONL	Go-Ahead
R244OCU	Go-Ahead	R710MHN	Arriva North East	R923JNL	Arriva North East	S372ONL	Go-Ahead
R245KRG	Stagecoach Busways	R711MHN	Arriva North East	R956GCU	Swan's Coaches	S373ONL	Go-Ahead
R245OCU	Go-Ahead	R712MHN	Arriva North East	R979RRG	Snaiths	S374ONL	Go-Ahead
R246KRG	Stagecoach Busways	R713MHN	Arriva North East	RCU826S	Grierson	S375ONL	Go-Ahead
R246OCU	Go-Ahead	R714MHN	Arriva North East	RCU828S	Grierson	S448OCU	Durham Travel
R247KRG	Stagecoach Busways	R715MHN	Arriva North East	RCU835S	Garnetts	S451OFT	Stagecoach Busways
R247OCU	Go-Ahead	R716MHN	Arriva North East	RCU837S	Hennings	S452OFT	Stagecoach Busways
R248KRG	Stagecoach Busways	R717MHN	Arriva North East	RFR883T	Jim Hughes	S453OFT	Stagecoach Busways
R249KRG	Stagecoach Busways	R718MHN	Arriva North East	RHG882X	Arriva North East	S454OFT	Stagecoach Busways
R250KRG	Stagecoach Busways	R719MHN	Arriva North East	RIL3998	Garnetts	S455OFT	Stagecoach Busways
R251JNL	Arriva North East	R719RPY	Stagecoach Transit	RIW2830	Bob Smith Travel	S456OFT	Stagecoach Busways
R251KRG	Stagecoach Busways	R720MHN	Arriva North East	RJI4566	Grierson	S457OFT	Stagecoach Busways
R252KRG	Stagecoach Busways	R720RPY	Stagecoach Transit	RJI4797	Lee's of Durham	S458OFT	Stagecoach Busways
R253KRG	Stagecoach Busways	R721MHN	Arriva North East	RML109Y	J C Bell	S459OFT	Stagecoach Busways
R254KRG	Stagecoach Busways	R721RPY	Stagecoach Transit	RRA219X	Arriva North East	S460OFT	Stagecoach Busways
R255KRG	Stagecoach Busways	R722MHN	Arriva North East	RRR517R	Cochrane's	S494ABR	Snaiths
R256KRG	Stagecoach Busways	R722RPY	Stagecoach Transit	RSG819V	Redby	S608KHN	Arriva North East
R257KRG	Stagecoach Busways	R723MHN	Arriva North East	RUP906M	Hunter's	S609KHN	Arriva North East
R258KRG	Stagecoach Busways	R723RPY	Stagecoach Transit	RUS311R	Garnetts	S610KHN	Arriva North East
R291KRG	Arriva North East	R724MHN	Arriva North East	RXG810H	Kings	S611KHN	Arriva North East
R292KRG	Arriva North East	R724RPY	Stagecoach Transit	S1MFC	Compass Royston	S612KHN	Arriva North East
R293KRG	Arriva North East	R725MHN	Arriva North East	S2TSH	Travelsure	S613KHN	Arriva North East
R294KRG	Arriva North East	R725RPY	Stagecoach Transit	S5STX	Stanley Coaches	S614KHN	Arriva North East
R340NTY	Go-Ahead	R726RPY	Stagecoach Transit	S6CLA	Classic	S615KHN	Arriva North East
R423RPY	Arriva North East	R755RPY	Stagecoach Transit	S13ORO	Compass Royston	S616KHN	Arriva North East
R424RPY	Arriva North East	R762OVN	Compass Royston	S25VVK	Delta	S617KHN	Arriva North East
R425RPY	Arriva North East	R763OVN	Compass Royston	S26DTS	Durham Travel	S618KHN	Arriva North East
R426RPY	Arriva North East	R825YUD	Stagecoach Busways	S27DTS	Durham Travel	S619KHN	Arriva North East
R427RPY	Arriva North East	R826YUD	Stagecoach Busways	S35NRG	Go-Ahead	S620KHN	Arriva North East
R428RPY	Arriva North East	R827YUD	Stagecoach Busways	S121OEF	Compass Royston	S621KHN	Arriva North East
R429RPY	Arriva North East	R828YUD	Stagecoach Busways	S122OEF	Compass Royston	S622KHN	Arriva North East
R430RPY	Arriva North East	R829YUD	Stagecoach Busways	S148OCU	Go-Ahead	S623KHN	Arriva North East
R431RPY	Arriva North East	R831OVN	Stagecoach Transit	S149OCU	Go-Ahead	S624KHN	Arriva North East
R432RPY	Arriva North East	R832OVN	Stagecoach Transit	S150OCU	Go-Ahead	S625KHN	Arriva North East
R433MHC	Durham Travel	R833NRG	Go-Ahead	S151OCU	Go-Ahead	S626KHN	Arriva North East
R433RPY	Arriva North East	R833OVN	Stagecoach Transit	S152OCU	Go-Ahead	S627KHN	Arriva North East
R434RPY	Arriva North East	R834NRG	Go-Ahead	S153OCU	Go-Ahead	S628KHN	Arriva North East
R435RPY	Arriva North East	R834OVN	Stagecoach Transit	S154OCU	Go-Ahead	S629KHN	Arriva North East
R436RPY	Arriva North East	R835NRG	Go-Ahead	S156OCU	Go-Ahead	S630KHN	Arriva North East
R437RPY	Arriva North East	R835OVN	Stagecoach Transit	S157OCU	Go-Ahead	S631KHN	Arriva North East
R438RPY	Arriva North East	R836NRG	Go-Ahead	S248KNL	Go-Ahead	S632KHN	Arriva North East
R439RPY	Arriva North East	R836OVN	Stagecoach Transit	S249KNL	Go-Ahead	S633KHN	Arriva North East
R440RPY	Arriva North East	R837NRG	Go-Ahead	S250KNL	Go-Ahead	S634KHN	Arriva North East
R462SEF	Stagecoach Transit	R837OVN	Stagecoach Transit	S251KNL	Go-Ahead	S635KHN	Arriva North East
R463SEF	Stagecoach Transit	R837PRG	Go-Ahead	S252KNL	Go-Ahead	S636KHN	Arriva North East
R464SEF	Stagecoach Transit	R838NRG	Go-Ahead	S253KNL	Go-Ahead	S637KHN	Arriva North East
R465SEF	Stagecoach Transit	R838OVN	Stagecoach Transit	S254KNL	Go-Ahead	S638KHN	Arriva North East
R466SEF	Stagecoach Transit	R838PRG	Go-Ahead	S255KNL	Go-Ahead	S639KHN	Arriva North East
R467SEF	Stagecoach Transit	R839NRG	Go-Ahead	S341KHN	Arriva North East	S640KHN	Arriva North East
R468SEF	Stagecoach Transit	R839OVN	Stagecoach Transit	S342KHN	Arriva North East	S641KHN	Arriva North East
R469MVN	Stagecoach Transit	R839PRG	Go-Ahead	S343KHN	Arriva North East	S642KHN	Arriva North East
R470MVN	Stagecoach Transit	R841NRG	Go-Ahead	S344KHN	Arriva North East	S643KHN	Arriva North East
R471MVN	Stagecoach Transit	R841PRG	Go-Ahead	S345KHN	Arriva North East	S702KFT	Arriva North East
R472MVN	Stagecoach Transit	R842PRG	Go-Ahead	S346KHN	Arriva North East	S703KFT	Arriva North East
R510SCH	Altona Coaches	R843PRG	Go-Ahead	S347KHN	Arriva North East	S704KFT	Arriva North East
R511WDC	Compass Royston	R844PRG	Go-Ahead	S348KHN	Arriva North East	S705KFT	Arriva North East
R512WDC	Compass Royston	R845PRG	Go-Ahead	S349KHN	Arriva North East	S706KFT	Arriva North East
R554RPY	Stagecoach Transit	R846PRG	Go-Ahead	S350KHN	Arriva North East	S707KFT	Arriva North East
R556RPY	Stagecoach Transit	R847PRG	Go-Ahead	S351KHN	Arriva North East	S708KFT	Arriva North East
R557RPY	Stagecoach Transit	R848PRG	Go-Ahead	S352KHN	Arriva North East	S709KFT	Arriva North East
R558RPY	Stagecoach Transit	R849PRG	Go-Ahead	S353KHN	Arriva North East	S710KFT	Arriva North East
R562KHA	Scarlet Band	R851PRG	Go-Ahead	S354KHN	Arriva North East	S711KFT	Arriva North East
R601MHN	Arriva North East	R852PRG	Go-Ahead	S355KEF	Stagecoach Transit	S712KRG	Arriva North East
R602MHN	Arriva North East	R853PRG	Go-Ahead	S355KHN	Arriva North East	S713KRG	Arriva North East
R603MHN	Arriva North East	R854PRG	Go-Ahead	S356KEF	Stagecoach Transit	S714KRG	Arriva North East
R604MHN	Arriva North East	R855PRG	Go-Ahead	S356KHN	Arriva North East	S715KRG	Arriva North East
R605MHN	Arriva North East	R856PRG	Go-Ahead	S357KEF	Stagecoach Transit	S811FVK	Go-Ahead
R606MHN	Arriva North East	R85SEF	Stagecoach Transit	S357KHN	Arriva North East	S812FVK	Go-Ahead
R607MHN	Arriva North East	R907JNL	Arriva North East	S358KEF	Stagecoach Transit	S813FVK	Go-Ahead
R640OVN	Stagecoach Transit	R908JNL	Arriva North East	S358KHN	Arriva North East	S814FVK	Go-Ahead
R653RPY	Stagecoach Transit	R909JNL	Arriva North East	S358ONL	Go-Ahead	S815FVK	Go-Ahead

Compass Royston's TAZ4059 is a Plaxton Paramount 3200-bodied Volvo B10M. The Volvo B10M is now the most common coach chassis in Britain from the midi-coach version known as the B9M through to the B10MT which features a third trailing axle designed to provide a heavy duty option. The chassis dominated the Compass Royston fleet. *Phillip Stephenson*

S816FVK	Go-Ahead	SCN249S	Stagecoach Transit	SPY202X	Arriva North East	T466BCN	Go Ahead
S817FVK	Go-Ahead	SCN268S	Weardale	SPY203X	Arriva North East	T467BCN	Go Ahead
S818OFT	Go-Ahead	SCN270S	Stagecoach Busways	SPY204X	Arriva North East	T468BCN	Go Ahead
S819OFT	Go-Ahead	SCS333M	Scarlet Band	SPY205X	Arriva North East	T469BCN	Go Ahead
S820OFT	Go-Ahead	SGR777V	Arriva North East	SPY206X	Arriva North East	T461BNL	Stagecoach Busways
S821OFT	Go-Ahead	SGR783V	Arriva North East	SPY207X	Arriva North East	T462BNL	Stagecoach Busways
S822OFT	Go-Ahead	SGR784V	Arriva North East	SPY208X	Arriva North East	T463BNL	Stagecoach Busways
S823OFT	Go-Ahead	SGR795V	Arriva North East	SPY210X	Arriva North East	T464BNL	Stagecoach Busways
S824OFT	Go-Ahead	SGR797V	Arriva North East	SRJ746R	Garnetts	T465BNL	Stagecoach Busways
S825OFT	Go-Ahead	SIB1279	Arriva North East	SUF140N	Weardale	T466BNL	Stagecoach Busways
S826OFT	Go-Ahead	SIB1280	Arriva North East	SVJ600S	Hennings	T467BNL	Stagecoach Busways
S827OFT	Go-Ahead	SIB1281	Arriva North East	T1CLA	Classic	T468BNL	Stagecoach Busways
S828OFT	Go-Ahead	SIB1282	Arriva North East	T2CLA	Classic	T469BNL	Stagecoach Busways
S829OFT	Go-Ahead	SIB1283	Arriva North East	T2LEC	Mill	T470BNL	Stagecoach Busways
S830OFT	Go-Ahead	SIB1284	Arriva North East	T7DCC	Durham City	T471BNL	Stagecoach Busways
S831OFT	Go-Ahead	SIB1285	Arriva North East	T12DTS	Durham Travel	T472BNL	Stagecoach Busways
S832OFT	Go-Ahead	SIB1286	Arriva North East	T67JBA	Scarlet Band	T473BNL	Stagecoach Busways
S833OFT	Go-Ahead	SIB1287	Arriva North East	T68JBA	Scarlet Band	T474BNL	Stagecoach Busways
S862ONL	Go-Ahead	SIB1288	Arriva North East	T69JBA	Scarlet Band	T475BNL	Stagecoach Busways
S863ONL	Go-Ahead	SIB6705	Arriva North East	T74AUA	Arriva North East	T476BNL	Stagecoach Busways
S864ONL	Go-Ahead	SIB6706	Arriva North East	T75AUA	Arriva North East	T477BNL	Stagecoach Busways
S865ONL	Go-Ahead	SIB6708	Arriva North East	T76AUA	Arriva North East	T478BNL	Stagecoach Busways
S866ONL	Go-Ahead	SIB6710	Arriva North East	T77AUA	Arriva North East	T479BNL	Stagecoach Busways
S867ONL	Go-Ahead	SIB6712	Arriva North East	T78AUA	Arriva North East	T480BNL	Stagecoach Busways
S868ONL	Go-Ahead	SIB6715	Arriva North East	T88LEE	Lee's of Durham	T481BNL	Stagecoach Busways
S869ONL	Go-Ahead	SIB6716	Arriva North East	T95JHN	Stagecoach Transit	T482BNL	Stagecoach Busways
S870ONL	Go-Ahead	SJI8096	Rothbury Motors	T96JHN	Stagecoach Transit	T483BNL	Stagecoach Busways
S890ONL	Go-Ahead	SJR612Y	Go-Ahead	T97JHN	Stagecoach Transit	T484BNL	Stagecoach Busways
S891ONL	Go-Ahead	SJR613Y	Go-Ahead	T284BNL	ERB Services	T485BNL	Stagecoach Busways
S892ONL	Go-Ahead	SJR614Y	Go-Ahead	T456BCN	Go Ahead	T486BNL	Stagecoach Busways
S893ONL	Go-Ahead	SJR615Y	Go-Ahead	T457BCN	Go Ahead	T487BNL	Stagecoach Busways
S894ONL	Go-Ahead	SJR616Y	Go-Ahead	T458BCN	Go Ahead	T488BNL	Stagecoach Busways
S895ONL	Go-Ahead	SJR617Y	Go-Ahead	T459BCN	Go Ahead	T489BNL	Stagecoach Busways
S977ABR	Go-Ahead	SND296X	Arriva North East	T460BCN	Go Ahead	T490BNL	Stagecoach Busways
S978ABR	Go-Ahead	SND435X	Kingsley's	T461BCN	Go Ahead	T491BNL	Stagecoach Busways
S979ABR	Go-Ahead	SPT962V	Go-Ahead	T462BCN	Go Ahead	T492BNL	Stagecoach Busways
SBB85Y	Grierson	SPT963V	Go-Ahead	T463BCN	Go Ahead	T493BNL	Stagecoach Busways
SBR881P	Snowdons	SPT964V	Garnetts	T464BCN	Go Ahead	T494BNL	Stagecoach Busways
SCK697P	Redby	SPY201X	Arriva North East	T465BCN	Go Ahead	T495BNL	Stagecoach Busways

Reg	Operator	Reg	Operator	Reg	Operator	Reg	Operator
T599BRG	Snaiths	TYJ5S	North Rider	V155DFT	Stagecoach Busways	WRN137V	Kingsley's
T656OEF	Stagecoach Transit	UBC644X	Snaiths	V156DFT	Stagecoach Busways	WSU486	Jim Hughes
T657OEF	Stagecoach Transit	UBR110V	Arriva North East	V157DFT	Stagecoach Busways	WSV517	Galaxy Travel
T658OEF	Stagecoach Transit	UBR666T	Weardale	V158DFT	Stagecoach Busways	WSV547	Kings
T659OEF	Stagecoach Transit	UFE712	Gardiners	V159DFT	Stagecoach Busways	WSV548	Kings
T660OEF	Stagecoach Transit	UGD735	Classic	V160DFT	Stagecoach Busways	WSV549	Kings
T661OEF	Stagecoach Transit	UGR698R	Arriva North East	V161DFT	Stagecoach Busways	WSV565	Arriva North East
T662OEF	Stagecoach Transit	UNK10W	Swan's Coaches	V162DFT	Stagecoach Busways	WSV567	Arriva North East
T663OEF	Stagecoach Transit	UOI772	Arriva North East	V163DFT	Stagecoach Busways	WSV569	Arriva North East
T664OEF	Stagecoach Transit	UPT101V	Crossroads	V164DFT	Stagecoach Busways	WSV570	Arriva North East
T665OEF	Stagecoach Transit	UPT544	Venture Reed	V165DFT	Stagecoach Busways	WSV571	Arriva North East
T701	Arriva North East	UPT660V	Go-Ahead	V166DFT	Stagecoach Busways	WSV572	Arriva North East
T702	Arriva North East	UPT661V	Go-Ahead	V167DFT	Stagecoach Busways	WUM256X	Swan's Coaches
T727OEF	Stagecoach Transit	UPT662V	Go-Ahead	V168DFT	Stagecoach Busways	WVV831S	Priory
T728OEF	Stagecoach Transit	UPT663V	Go-Ahead	V169DFT	Stagecoach Busways	WWY119S	Compass Royston
T729OEF	Stagecoach Transit	UPT664V	Go-Ahead	V170DFT	Stagecoach Busways	WYW55T	Go-Ahead
T730OEF	Stagecoach Transit	UPT665V	Go-Ahead	V171DFT	Stagecoach Busways	XCO182	J & C
T731OEF	Stagecoach Transit	UPT666V	Go-Ahead	V172DFT	Stagecoach Busways	XGB380S	Swan's Coaches
T732OEF	Stagecoach Transit	UPT667V	Go-Ahead	VAY879	Arriva North East	XPG196T	Garnetts
T733OEF	Stagecoach Transit	UPT668V	Go-Ahead	VBG89V	Arriva North East	XPT802V	Arriva North East
T734OEF	Stagecoach Transit	UPT669V	Go-Ahead	VBG93V	Arriva North East	XRW519S	A Line
T735OEF	Stagecoach Transit	UPT670V	Go-Ahead	VCU312T	Weardale	XSV218	Tyne Valley
T736FVN	Stagecoach Transit	UPT671V	Go-Ahead	VDM175	Classic	XSV219	Tyne Valley
T811JHN	Compass Royston	UPT672V	Go-Ahead	VDV106S	North Rider	XSV220	Tyne Valley
T876RBR	Go-Ahead	UPT673V	Go-Ahead	VDV125S	Arriva North East	XSV239	Tyne Valley
T877RBR	Go-Ahead	UPT674V	Go-Ahead	VEF150Y	Stagecoach Transit	XSV298	Tyne Valley
T878RBR	Go-Ahead	UPT675V	Go-Ahead	VEF153Y	Stagecoach Transit	XSV689	Arriva North East
T879RBR	Go-Ahead	UPT676V	Go-Ahead	VFT190T	Garnetts	XSV691	Arriva North East
T880RBR	Go-Ahead	UPT677V	Go-Ahead	VFT199T	Go-Ahead	XSY405	Tyne Valley
T881RBR	Go-Ahead	UPT678V	Go-Ahead	VJI9916	Rothbury Motors	XWA72X	Arriva North East
T882RBR	Go-Ahead	UPT679V	Go-Ahead	VJI9917	Rothbury Motors	XWA73X	Arriva North East
T883RBR	Go-Ahead	UPT680V	Go-Ahead	VRN86R	Delta	XWA74X	Arriva North East
T884RBR	Go-Ahead	UPT681V	Go-Ahead	VUL159S	Altona Coaches	XWA75X	Arriva North East
T885RBR	Go-Ahead	UPT683V	Go-Ahead	VWG360Y	Escort	XWY477X	Arriva North East
TAO541X	DC Travel	UPT684V	Go-Ahead	VWY845L	Hunter's	XWY478X	Arriva North East
TAZ4059	Compass Royston	UPT685V	Go-Ahead	VXI5357	Grierson	XWY479X	Arriva North East
TBI4569	ERB Services	UPT6N	Weardale	WAO395V	Arriva North East	YAJ156V	Stagecoach Transit
TBR527V	Henry Cooper	USU643	First Choice Travel	WAO399Y	Arriva North East	YAJ157Y	Stagecoach Transit
TJI1683	Hylton Castle	USU907	Delta	WBB329Y	Weardale	YDC21Y	Stagecoach Transit
TJI6298	A Line	UTN501Y	Go-Ahead	WBB348Y	Travelsure	YGR191R	DC Travel
TJI6572	DC Travel	UTN502Y	Go-Ahead	WBB962	Gardiners	YLX281	Arriva North East
TJR715Y	Go-Ahead	UTN503Y	Go-Ahead	WDC211Y	Arriva North East	YNL213V	Garnetts
TJR716Y	Go-Ahead	UTN504Y	Go-Ahead	WDC212Y	Arriva North East	YOT607	Arriva North East
TJR717Y	Go-Ahead	UTN505Y	Go-Ahead	WDC213Y	Arriva North East	YPL383T	Travelsure
TJR718Y	Go-Ahead	UTN506Y	Go-Ahead	WDC214Y	Arriva North East	YRG172V	Priory
TJR719Y	Go-Ahead	UTN507Y	Go-Ahead	WDC215Y	Arriva North East	YRG173V	Priory
TJR720Y	Go-Ahead	UTN508Y	Go-Ahead	WDC216Y	Arriva North East	YRG174V	Priory
TJR721Y	Go-Ahead	UTN509Y	Go-Ahead	WDC217Y	Arriva North East	YRN818V	North Rider
TMA326R	Compass Royston	UTN510Y	Go-Ahead	WDC218Y	Arriva North East	YSU870	Arriva North East
TNL628S	Tyne Valley	UVK287T	Stagecoach Busways	WDO759	Gardiners	YSU871	Arriva North East
TOF695S	Classic	UVK292T	Weardale	WFU469V	Escort	YSU874	Go-Ahead
TPE171S	Classic	UVK299T	Stagecoach Busways	WFU708V	Snaiths	YSU875	Go-Ahead
TPN102S	Moor-Dale	UVK300T	Weardale	WGW579S	Bob Smith Travel	YSU876	Go-Ahead
TPT6K	Weardale	UWW13X	Arriva North East	WIB2042	Rothbury Motors	YSU896	Arriva North East
TPX884	Rothbury Motors	UWW14X	Arriva North East	WIB5507	Rothbury Motors	YSU919	Tyne Valley
TRN476V	Kingsley's	UWW512X	Classic	WLT859	Arriva North East	YSU920	Tyne Valley
TSD611S	Go-Ahead	UWY87X	Michael Franks	WOJ802	Classic	YSU960	Tyne Valley
TSU636	Arriva North East	V151DFT	Stagecoach Busways	WPT445V	Hunter's	YSX932W	North Rider
TTC86	Travelsure	V152DFT	Stagecoach Busways	WPT691V	Go-Ahead	YUM517S	Hennings
TVE804	Classic	V153DFT	Stagecoach Busways	WRA224Y	Arriva North East	YUP6	Weardale
TWN935S	Compass Royston	V154DFT	Stagecoach Busways	WRA225Y	Arriva North East	YVN521T	Stagecoach Transit

ISBN 1 897990 45 6

Published by British Bus Publishing Ltd
The Vyne, 16 St Margaret's Drive, Wellington, Telford, TF1 3PH

British Bus Publishing

The
East Anglia
BUS HANDBOOK

British Bus Publishing

1998 sees the replacement of the Eastern Bus Handbook by two new volumes needed to include the large number of operations in the area from Northampton to the London boundary eastwards.

The East Anglia Bus Handbook covers the four counties of Essex, Norfolk, Suffolk and Cambridgeshire while the Chilterns and West Anglia Bus Handbook traces the line from Northamptonshire, through Bedfordshire, Buckinghamshire and Hertfordshire.

oth books provide comprehensive overage of the fleets.

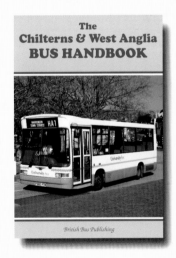

The
Chilterns & West Anglia
BUS HANDBOOK

British Bus Publishing

ast Anglia Bus Handbook

SBN 1.897990.38.3	**£12.50**

hilterns & West Anglia Bus Handbook

SBN 1.897990.39.1	**£12.50**

British Bus Publishing Ltd
16 St Margaret's Drive, Wellington, Telford TF1 3PH
Fax/Evening orderline - 01952 255669

ISBN 1-897990-45-6

£12.50 €18.00

LONDON BUS
HANDBOOK

PART 1

LONDO
HANDI
PART

NICHOLAS KING

Capital Transport

CONTENTS (Fleet list page numbers shown in red)

The front and back cover photographs and
the photo opposite are by Stephen Madden.
The title page photo is by Colin Brown.

Seventeenth edition 1995

ISBN 185414 175 9

Published by Capital Transport Publishing
38 Long Elmes, Harrow Weald, Middlesex

Introduction

This book gives details at 1st June 1995 of the bus and coach fleets operated by the eleven former subsidiaries of London Buses Ltd, which were privatised between January 1994 and January 1995. London Buses Ltd itself ceased to own vehicles on 4th March 1995, when those remaining in central ownership were transferred to London Transport Buses. A total of 5034 vehicles were redeployed as a result of the privatisation process, in addition to those which were sold as surplus to final requirements.

The sale of the ten major subsidiaries amassed a total income of more than £230 million, of which London Transport retained the first £100 million and 25% of the balance, the rest passing to the Treasury. After meeting the costs of privatisation, LT are expected to use most of the proceeds for the benefit of the Underground system.

A preliminary summary is given of principal LBL fleet developments since the sixteenth edition of this book and of the distribution of the fleet at privatisation. This is followed by separate entries for each of the privatised companies listing their fleets and giving general details of their operations. Also listed are the vehicles residually held by LTB.

The author gratefully acknowledges the willing assistance of many of the operators concerned and of the former London Buses. Particular help has been given by Lawrie Bowles, Kenneth Fahy, Keith Grimes and John Marshall; by Colin Lloyd and David Stewart of the London Omnibus Traction Society; and by the PSV Circle.

It should be emphasised that this book is not an official publication of any of the operators concerned, and any enquiries should be addressed to the publisher in the first instance. Readers who would like further information on developments within the fleets are recommended to consult the news-sheets of the enthusiast bodies mentioned above.

Hemel Hempstead, June 1995   NICHOLAS KING

NOTE

Vehicles permanently used for driver training are coded with the suffix t; others may also serve this function, particularly off-peak. Vehicles delicensed long-term are coded with the suffix u, and those withdrawn for disposal are denoted with the suffix w. Other codes are explained in the text. Liveries are specified only where they are not based on former LBL livery or the new liveries of the operators described in the textual introduction; local marketing names on such standard liveries are not itemised.

Fleet developments

Since the last edition of this book, the major refurbishment of the RML class has been completed, RML 903 and RML 2760 being left with AEC engines and unrebuilt bodies at Holloway and Upton Park respectively as the last of their respective batches. The programme included completion to full standard of the three pilot vehicles. In the later stages of the programme 22 of the refurbished RMLs were leased to LBL, who in turn leased them to London Transport for operation of route 13 from 4th December 1993 following route tendering. This arrangement mirrored the transfer of 24 RMLs to Kentish Bus for route 19 from April 1993. RMLs fitted with Cummins engines were placed with CentreWest, Leaside, London Central, London Northern, London United and Metroline, whilst those with Iveco engines were with London General and South London. East London had examples of both types.

As the RML refurbishment programme came to an end, standard RMs which had been covering for their absence from the main fleet were progressively withdrawn. A surprise development, however, was the award of a contract to South London for the operation of route 159 with unrefurbished RMs, from Brixton garage. These began to appear in a special livery of red and cream from January 1994, and included some which had been transplanted from London General as part of an exchange of vehicles to complete the RML conversion of route 11. Route 139 also continued to use standard RMs, some of which were given cosmetic repaints in the spring of 1994, and some 70% of the allocation on the 36 from New Cross also remained in the hands of RMs, alongside refurbished RMLs. Those allocated for route 139 occasionally appear on route 10 if RMLs are not available. East London also kept two RMAs and three RMCs which appear in service regularly alongside RMLs on routes 8 and 15; CentreWest, East London, Leaside, London General and Metroline also have small numbers of standard RMs as emergency cover for RMLs.

New liveries started to appear soon after the sale of the LBL companies. MTL London Northern chose all-over red as seen on unrefurbished RML 903. This vehicle had previously been used as a showbus in traditional LT livery.
Malcolm MacDonald

Apart from the RMLs, a total of 127 other Routemasters (including open-toppers) were transferred to the privatised companies. To these can be added 30 which have been retained by LTB as a reserve fleet. The best of those which were passing to the Sales Department were set aside during the summer of 1994 following inspection, and a tender issued for their storage and maintenance against possible future need. Following the award of the contract to Universitybus, Hatfield, this reserve fleet was moved from the sales site at Fulwell, and is now stored in Hertfordshire. Its functions complete with the sale of the remaining surplus stock, the Sales Department closed down, the last sale being that of RM 1992 on 14th December 1994.

The last Fleetline in regular service with LBL, D 2600, was delicensed on 16th September 1993, leaving four open-toppers in seasonal use with Leaside, London Northern and Selkent, and three vehicles in use for special purposes with Leaside and London Northern. London General continued to use the class for driver training, retaining fourteen at privatisation; of these, two were on short-term hire from LBL and were returned for disposal at the end of 1994. A total of 19 vehicles thus remain from the 2646 which were placed into London service.

A small number of Metrobuses were sold as surplus to requirements in the late summer of 1993, including those which had been acquired from Busways. In the spring of 1994 these were joined by those from Yorkshire Rider. The five from West Midlands Travel have remained with Leaside, for whom they are now in use on Middlesex University services. At 1425 vehicles, the final total of Metrobuses was nearly double that of surviving Titans, the withdrawal of which continued apace during 1993 and 1994 as a result of route tendering losses and further route conversions to midibus operation. The small pocket of Titan operation in London Northern ended on 25th September 1993, followed by South London (where their presence had been relatively short-term after they replaced Fleetlines) on 22nd March 1994. A small number operated for London General during the summer of 1994 on special services, notably for the Chelsea Flower Show and Derby Day, but were gradually decommissioned in the early autumn. At the end, operation of the 782 final Titans was confined to East London, London Central and Selkent, with small batches at Stanwell Buses, five for contract work and private hire in Leaside, and four for training and private hire in South London. Of those with Leaside, T 69 was a late conversion to open-top, in July 1993, following an accident with a low bridge.

The disposal of Titans did not always mean their disappearance from London, although a substantial number found their way to Merseybus, as well as smaller numbers to other operators. London & Country and London Suburban Bus both purchased ex-LBL Titans for contracted routes, and when London Coaches gained the contract for route 52 from 4th December 1993, 26 Titans, most of which had been released from East London a few months earlier, replaced the Metrobuses which had hitherto been supplied on this route by Metroline. The Titans subsequently found their way to Atlas Bus when London Coaches' holding company purchased that operation from 6th August 1994, and thence to Metroline's holding company towards the end of November 1994 when Atlas Bus was again sold. Metroline promptly purchased the solitary Titan which they had retained on hire from LBL for private hire purposes after privatisation, and at times of vehicle shortage loaned Metrobuses from their own fleet to support the route, turning the wheel full circle in less than twelve months.

Amongst the newer double-deck classes, the dual-door Spectra, SP 2, made demonstration visits to many of the LBL subsidiaries during the winter of 1993/4 before being permanently placed with East London as part of the private hire fleet. No further orders were placed for the type, either in single-door or dual-door form. Indeed, the originals all had to undergo remedial modifications during the spring of 1994, a fate which also befell Leaside's relatively-new batch of 40 Olympians.

East Lancs Greenway refurbishments of the Red Arrow LSs continued during 1993 and into the spring of 1994, concluding with the return of GLS 448/83 on 6th May 1994, when a total of 41 vehicles had been dealt with (in addition to the pilot conversion, GLS 1, and the second-hand Greenway National delivered to CentreWest in October 1992). As the return of refurbished vehicles neared its end, sixteen unconverted LSs were transferred to the reserve fleet. In due course, three of these re-appeared with London General for further use at Sutton, and four went to London Northern, although not re-entering service there. The other nine were sold. Plans to carry out Greenway conversions on CentreWest's LSs were not consummated. The GLS conversions retained Gardner 6HLXB engines, superseding plans to fit DAF engines, but acquired ZF Ecomat 4HP500 gearboxes in place of the original units, following successful trials which had been carried out over several years on LS 457.

Somewhat protracted from original intentions, 68 low-floor single-deckers entered service during 1994 on routes 101, 120, 144 (formerly 144A), 186 and 222. Bodied by Wright Brothers of Ballymena, these formed the LLW class of 38 vehicles on Dennis Lance SLF chassis and the SLW class of 30 vehicles on Scania N113CRL chassis, and replaced double-deckers in all cases. Their introduction has not been without its practical hiccups, as might be expected with such a revolutionary concept. SLW 11 gained the distinction of being the last new vehicle delivered to LBL ownership when it arrived on 6th September 1994.

More conventional in the field of full-size single-deckers was the LV class of 12 Dennis Lances with Plaxton Verde bodywork which entered service for Selkent on route 208 in March and April 1994. These, alongside the LA, LN and VN classes, formed the most substantial intake of conventional single-deckers to the London fleet since the mid-1970s.

Dennis Darts continued their inexorable march, both in 8.5 metre and 9 metre form, as further route schemes were devised. New classes were formed to accommodate body orders placed with East Lancs (DEL class) and Northern Counties (DNL class). By the time that privatisation was under way a total of 718 Darts were owned, with another nine 9.8 metre examples (EDR class) on order for delivery to Metroline. Something of a surprise was the withdrawal from spring 1994 of the RB class, which had proved somewhat troublesome in East London use. All 33 vehicles were to be sold within a year to the Yorkshire Traction group, some of them less than four years old. A steady trickle of MRs also continued to appear on sales lists as opportunities allowed of their disposal.

The process of transferring undated registrations from Routemasters to newer types continued until the summer of 1994. Amongst the last recipients of such registrations were some London United Darts which bore out-of-sequence marks in consequence of the unavailability from the DVLA (except at enhanced prices) of cherished numbers. Odder was the transfer of the registration VLT89 from RM 89 to RM 994, the only RM to have received refurbishment (although not on the same scale as the RMLs). Although it was understood at the time that RM 994 was to receive traditional London General livery, this has not happened. London General also transplanted the registration WLT516 from RM 516 to doored RML 2516, and at a later date Metroline took two WLT registrations from RMLs for use on private hire Metrobuses. This led to the unique situation of RML 902 appearing with an A-suffix registration. Even more curious was the appearance of a T-suffix registration on RM 23 when its original number was diverted to a Dart, apparently reflecting the fact that the vehicle had effectively ceased to exist during its sojourn as a works float vehicle from 1963 to 1978. Other RMs which had also taken their turn as works float vehicles had previously been re-registered in the orthodox manner, because their identities had been preserved on the DVLA computer when it was set up in the early 1970s before dormant registrations had been purged from the computer record.

The closure of redundant garages continued. The main garage at Victoria was closed on 19th June 1993, the minibus basement following on 29th January 1994. In anticipation of these closures, a new minibus site had been opened near Battersea Bridge on 12th June 1993, coded BB. Chalk Farm garage closed on 30th July 1993, and Finchley followed on 4th December 1993. The garage at Peckham, which had been reduced in establishment during 1993, finally closed on 29th January 1994, minibuses and Titans for route 63 occupying a new site in Copeland Road. Plans to replace Barking and North Street garages by a new site at Chadwell Heath were abandoned when soil at the site was found to be contaminated in the summer of 1993, though vehicles which had already started to sport CH garage codes in anticipation of the move have continued to do so.

During April 1994 Metroline accorded full allocation status to their North Wembley outstation, with the code NW, and also designated a number of vehicles as forming a Commercial Services fleet, coded CS. The latter comprised private hire vehicles and those used for training.

CentreWest introduced the local trading names of Uxbridge Buses on 18th May 1993 and Ealing Buses on 12th November 1993. Vehicles at Westbourne Park gradually adopted the Gold Arrow fleetname during 1994. Certain other brandings were introduced for contract routes.

CentreWest was the first of the major LBL subsidiaries to be sold following the sale of Stanwell Buses (Westlink) in January 1994. It passed to a management-led team on 2nd September 1994 for "more than £25 million". A total of 507 vehicles were involved in this sale. On 6th September Stagecoach (Holdings) plc became the owners of East London, for some £28 million, and of Selkent, for £14 million. The East London deal involved 592 vehicles, plus three mobility LSs leased from London Transport, whilst the Selkent deal involved 414 vehicles. East London also became recipients of 15 further SLW class vehicles which were on order at the time of completion.

On 22nd September 1994 the sale of London Central to the Go-Ahead group was announced in the sum of £23.8 million, subject to approval by shareholders. This having been secured, the sale was completed on 18th October 1994, involving 498 vehicles.

Meanwhile Leaside was sold to the Cowie Group plc on 29th September 1994 for £29.5 million, with 523 vehicles changing hands, and Metroline was sold to a management-led team on 7th October 1994 for £20 million, with 386 vehicles. To the Metroline total should be added 9 Darts which were on order; another Titan was later added.

A short lull occurred before the next batch of sales. London Northern was sold to MTL Trust Holdings on 26th October 1994 for £20.55 million, with 341 vehicles, followed by London General to a management-led team on 2nd November for about £28 million, with 636 vehicles, and London United to a management-led team late on 5th November for more than £25 million, taking another 464 vehicles.

The final sale, of South London, was delayed when the company ran foul of a Traffic Commissioner's hearing into standards of maintenance, at which its operator authorisation was curtailed to expire at the end of April 1995, when a review would take place. In early December sale to the Cowie Group plc was announced in the sum of £16.3 million, with 447 vehicles, and this was completed on 10th January 1995.

The total exercise was officially quoted to have accrued £233 million of income; the difference from a simple addition of the individual sums probably arises from rounding of some of the figures. A total of 4957 vehicles, including those on order and the post-privatisation sales to Metroline and Stanwell, had changed hands. CentreWest, East London, Leaside, London General and Metroline all had small quantities of additional vehicles in hand at the time of privatisation, on short-term hire from LBL or other privatised companies; these hires had all ended by 31st March 1995 as described under the individual company headings.

Remaining in London Buses hands after redundant vehicles had been sold were one Atlantean, 30 RMs and the 46 RMLs leased to Kentish Bus and BTS. Ownership of all these was formally transferred to London Transport Buses on 4th March 1995. The 30 RMs are in store at Universitybus, Hatfield, as a strategic reserve fleet. Of the overall total of 5034 vehicles which changed hands 3352 (66.59%) were double-deckers, 1659 (32.95%) were single-deckers, and 23 (0.46%) were coaches.

Under the privatisation arrangements, occupation of garages and other operational sites formed part of the contracts with successful purchasers, and is subject to clawback provisions which apply for ten years, as a precaution against asset-stripping by buyers. Redundant garages remained in LT ownership and began to be sold during 1994.

The arrangements also included a requirement to retain red livery for all services passing through the central London area. However, independent operators already engaged in LT contract routes at the time of this announcement (April 1994) would be permitted to keep their existing liveries. The privatised companies were required to remove LBL roundels from vehicles by 31st March 1995; in a separate exercise, Dayglo blinds are now appearing on the majority of LT contracted routes.

CENTREWEST Telstar House, Eastbourne Terrace, London W2 6LG

CentreWest was purchased by a management-led team on 2nd September 1994, taking 507 vehicles. These comprised 115 opo double-deckers, 54 Routemasters, and 338 single-deckers. Apart from 30 full-size vehicles, all of the single-deckers were midibuses, with CentreWest having made the greatest strides of the LBL subsidiaries in converting routes to this format. Significant within this total were 107 DWs, 93 MAs and 89 RWs. In addition, ten Ms and nine RBs were on hire from LBL. The Ms, which formally passed to the ownership of London General on 2nd November, remained on hire until 4th March 1995, when they were released to their owners by the midibus conversion of route 105. The RBs were temporarily covering a reworking programme on the RW class.

Challenger route branding has been expanded on midibuses operating from Alperton, and is to be used for all operations at that depot. There have otherwise been few signs of outward change since privatisation took place.

The fleet operates from sites at Acton Tram (AT), Alperton (ON), Greenford (G), Uxbridge (UX) and Westbourne Park (X). Vehicles are also allocated to the training fleet (TF), based at various garages as required.

Following successful tendering for a number of routes currently operated by Stagecoach Selkent in the Orpington area, a new base is to be set up for these from November 1995.

Routemaster RML 2602 was one of the last to be refurbished when the programme was completed in 1994. Working route 23 as it turns from Pall Mall into Waterloo Place, it demonstrates the use of Gold Arrow fleetnames by vehicles based at Westbourne Park. Originally this only applied to midibuses. Capital Transport

The same location provides the unusual sight of open-top RMC 1510 working in service. Retrieved from withdrawal for conversion in 1989, RMC 1510 was equipped with a Cummins engine in 1993 to achieve commonality with most other Routemasters in the CentreWest fleet. *Capital Transport*

Displaying a combination of CentreWest fleetname and Ealing Buses local identity, M 1256 is a standard MCW Metrobus from the final London order. This view in Acton High Street in April 1995 shows it close to its home depot, Acton Tram, where it formed part of the initial big bus allocation in March 1993. *Richard Godfrey*

Route 222 between Hounslow and Uxbridge was the second to receive low-floor vehicles during 1994 in the form of Dennis Lance SLFs bodied by Wright. LLW 23 was photographed at Cranford, fitted with Dayglo blinds and clearly announcing its facilities. *Colin Brown*

Apart from Greenway rebuilds, most of the National Mk2s are now with CentreWest. LS 484, the only example in this fleet to retain bus seating, had been rebuilt to single-door in the summer of 1991. This shot on 23rd March 1995 at Slough shows it on Buckinghamshire County Council route 335, taken over from Bee Line in 1994. *Colin Brown*

LS 470 at West Ealing on its usual haunt of route 607, clearly shows the single-door conversion effected on CentreWest's Leyland Nationals. As well as having received dual-purpose seating, LS 470 had been fitted with a Volvo engine when this picture was taken in October 1994. *Mike Harris*

The first two Leyland Lynxes arrived in 1987 for evaluation and have spent their entire lives at Uxbridge garage, where they were later joined by three second-hand examples from Merthyr. LX 2 carries route branding for the 607, on which the type is chiefly used, as seen in May 1995. *Colin Brown*

DW 99 is one of the second main batch of Dennis Darts with Wright bodywork, used to substantial effect by CentreWest for midibus conversions in the early 1990s. Seen on Good Friday 1995, the destination blind demonstrates the westward extension of route 7 (worked by RMLs during the daytime on weekdays) on Sundays and public holidays. Stephen Madden

CentreWest now own most of the surviving BL class of Bristol LH6L single-deckers with Eastern Coach Works bodies, using all but one of them in their training fleet. The distinctive livery for this purpose will be noted. BL 36 had been fitted with dual-purpose seating in 1986 for private hire work, and was photographed in April 1995 at Kingston. Stephen Madden

Most of the MA class of Mercedes-Benz 811D midibuses with Alexander bodywork have spent their lives with CentreWest. MA 95 was found on route 105 on 24th March 1995, three weeks after its conversion from Metrobus operation, and shows Heathrow Challenger route branding. It had started life in 1989 as MA 46 following a mix-up over vehicle identities at the bodybuilders. Colin Brown

Converted as a mobility bus with tail-lift in 1993, similar MA 6 shows its Southall Shuttle livery at Havelock Estate. The conversion of this and other MAs released MTs for other uses. John Miller

The Renault-Dodge S75 type has proved more successful with CentreWest than else-where in London. RW 77, one of ninety bodied by Wright, was photographed in July 1994 at Greenford. All of the type are based at the Greenford outstation. Colin Brown

LEASIDE BUSES 16 Watsons Road, London N22 4TZ

Leaside was purchased by the Cowie group on 29th September 1994, taking 523 vehicles. These comprised 382 opo double-deckers, 97 crew double-deckers (96 Routemasters and an AEC Regent V), 39 single-deckers and 5 coaches, and included the largest contingent of Metrobuses (334) to be taken by any of the subsidiaries, as well as the smallest proportion of single-deckers. In addition, 10 Ts were on hire from LBL. These were returned in October and November following the conversion of route 144A (now 144) to SLW operation in September.

So far there have been no signs of livery alterations other than the emergence of 'Cowie group plc' legends on the rear of vehicles. M 445 has however, appeared in an overall advertising livery, whilst Ms 336, 353 and 1443-47 have received white livery for use on Middlesex University services.

The fleet operates from garages at Clapton (CT), Enfield (E), Palmers Green (AD), Tottenham (AR) and Wood Green (WN). The large garage at Stamford Hill was closed in May 1995 and its operations transferred to Clapton, Tottenham and Wood Green. The company has stated that the Stamford Hill premises will not be sold, but kept for future needs.

The majority of Leaside's RMLs were refurbished in-house at Enfield. RML 2372, working route 73 in Victoria in April 1995, represents the route with the largest single allocation of the type, calling for a peak allocation of 45 vehicles. Laurie Rufus

Leaside's double-deck fleet contains the largest number of MCW Metrobuses from LBL stock chiefly of the later batches. M 1323, from the last main order, pauses at Cambridge Circus near the end of its southbound trip on route 29. Capital Transport

Of slightly older vintage, M 641 received Leaside Buses livery as a memorial to a former Wood Green driver, whose favourite vehicle it had been. This shot on 12th April 1995 at Walthamstow shows that it is used in normal service rather than forming part of the private hire fleet as might at first be thought. Colin Brown

After a period of many years when allover advertisements have been out of favour, Metrobus M 445 demonstrates the reappearance of this type of publicity with its striking black-based display for the London Symphony Orchestra. Found in Waterloo Road, this view also shows its use as a dedicated driver-training vehicle. *Russell Upcraft*

The only second-hand Metrobuses to survive in the former LBL fleets are five single-door examples acquired from GMPTE in 1987. All have recently received white livery for use on special services for Middlesex University. M 1444 was seen at Fore Street, Edmonton on 30th March 1995. *Colin Lloyd*

A developing trend of recent years has been the use of vehicle rears as display advertisements. M 784, an MCW Metrobus dating from 1982, was captured at Aldgate Bus Station in June 1994. Until the closure of Stamford Hill on 13th May 1995, it had spent its entire life at that garage. Colin Lloyd

L 342 is one of the forty Leyland Olympians with Alexander bodywork which joined the London Buses fleet during 1992. Like all of the batch, it moved from Stamford Hill to Clapton during May 1995. Colin Lloyd

Converted to open-top in 1988, DMS 2291 is an MCW-bodied Leyland Fleetline which appears on summer route 333 and for special events. On 8th May 1994 it was captured at Highbury Stadium prior to the victory ride of Arsenal Football Club following their success in the European Cup Winners' Cup. Colin Lloyd

Following an argument with a low bridge in south east London in January 1993, T 69 was converted to open-top and transferred to Leaside's private hire fleet later that summer. In February 1994 it received a former Routemaster registration. In July 1994 it was encountered at Waltham Abbey on route 333. *Colin Lloyd*

The Leaside fleet contains four orthodox Titans with Park Royal bodywork which are normally used on contract operations. The week after Christmas 1994 saw their use on special peak-hour route D9X, providing a limited stop service between Monument and Crossharbour during the closure of the Docklands Light Railway. T 95 was found at South Quay station. *Russell Upcraft*

For the past four years Leaside have had this AEC Regent V, bodied by Park Royal, as part of their private hire fleet. New to East Kent in 1966, it makes occasional appearances on special services, such as the 828, which ran to and from the National Waterways Festival at Waltham Cross over the August Bank Holiday weekend in 1994. This view was taken at Oakwood Station.
Paul Weston

Leaside received the first part of the order for 30 Scania N113 vehicles with low-floor Wright bodywork during the summer of 1994, putting them to work on route 144 (formerly 144A) in September. SLW 10 pauses at Edmonton in September 1994.
Colin Brown

During 1992 fifteen 9-metre Dennis Darts with Plaxton bodywork were received by Leaside to upgrade route 84A from Wood Green garage. On Sundays these are also used on route 221, as depicted by DRL 47 at North Finchley on 12th March 1995. Colin Brown

A small batch of seven StarRiders in the Leaside fleet is allocated to Enfield for route 192 (191 on Sundays only). SR 35 is seen at Fore Street, Edmonton. Colin Lloyd

Three stretched MCW MetroRiders are held by Leaside for use on a DHSS shuttle contract. These include two dual-purpose represented by MR 104 at Waterloo on 5th April 1995. Laurie Rufus

Leaside's private hire and excursion work is undertaken under the Leaside Travel name. Two of these Plaxton-bodied Leopards are owned as part of the operation, both dating from 1979 and both recently re-registered with former RM marks. LP 5 is seen at Finsbury Park. Colin Lloyd

LONDON CENTRAL One Warner Road, London SE5 9LU

London Central was purchased by the Go Ahead group on 18th October 1994, following approval at a shareholders' meeting the previous day, taking 498 vehicles. These comprised 301 opo double-deckers, 104 Routemasters, and 93 single-deckers, and included the largest contingent of Routemasters to be taken by any of the subsidiaries.

Some standard RMs used on route 36 have received branding liveries for the route, and this idea has been extended to the RMLs used on route 12.

London Central placed an order for ten new Volvo Olympians with Northern Counties bodywork following their success in winning the contract for LT route D1 from May 1995, and have recently taken nine Olympians with Alexander bodywork from dealer stock.

The fleet operates from garages at Bexleyheath (BX), Camberwell (Q), New Cross (NX) and an open site at Peckham (PM).

Route branding has been introduced on the 36 during the spring of 1995 and brings a welcome lift to the tired appearance of the unrefurbished RMs which still form a substantial part of the allocation. RM 1104 at Lewisham in April 1995 shows the revised position adopted by London Central for the registration plates of most of its standard RMs.
Colin Lloyd

Route 12 has subsequently followed in the route branding exercise. Camberwell's RML 2400 demonstrates the clean lines of this livery to good effect at Hanover Street in May 1995.
Malcolm MacDonald

Nine Volvo Olympians with Alexander bodywork were purchased from dealer stock in May 1995. AV 5 is seen on its first day in service, 30th May, at County Hall. The vertical bar on the corner of the front upper deck nearside window is intended to reduce the risk of damage from overhanging trees. Colin Lloyd

London Central received ten Olympians with Northern Counties bodywork in March 1995 for use on tendered routes D1 and D11. They were temporarily used on route 40 before receiving insignia for their intended use on Docklands Express work from 30th May. Colin Lloyd

London Central's fleet of Titans is largely made up of the later type with 70-seat Leyland bodywork. Bexleyheath based T 1033 was found at Woolwich in May 1995. *Stephen Madden*

The Optare Spectras delivered in 1992/3 to London Central are generally to be found on route 3. SP 17, one of five to carry Routemaster-series registrations, rounds Hanover Square at the end of its northbound run on 19th April 1995. Many of the type carry dedicated rear advertising. *Keith Wood*

A small pocket of Leyland Olympians has been based at New Cross since new, originally for routes involved in the Autofare scheme at Bexleyheath. L 93, carrying London Central Travel livery, has ECW bodywork, and was photographed at Elephant & Castle in April 1995. Stephen Madden

East Lancs bodywork found its way into the LBL fleets with the delivery of eleven 9-metre Dennis Darts to London Central in the spring of 1994 for new Route 484 through the residential area between Lewisham and Camberwell. DEL 1 is seen in Lewisham. Mike Harris

London Central took the last main batch of Optare MetroRiders to arrive with the LBL subsidiaries with eighteen based at Bexleyheath to replace older midibuses. MRL 238 is seen in Woolwich in March 1995. Stephen Madden

Four of the Mercedes-Benz 811D vehicles with Reeve Burgess bodywork are in the London Central fleet for use at Bexleyheath, though their use has declined as this book goes to press. MTL 4 passes through Welling on 10th March 1995. Laurie Rufus

LONDON GENERAL 25 Raleigh Gardens, Mitcham, Surrey, CR4 3NS

London General, the largest of the privatised companies, was purchased by a management-led team on 2nd November 1994, taking 636 vehicles. These comprised 347 opo double-deckers, 69 Routemasters and 220 single-deckers. In addition, two DMSs were on hire from LBL for training; these were returned to the LBL Sales Department in November and December. Ten Ms which were on hire to CentreWest at the date of privatisation were eventually received in March 1995, though six were promptly sold to Metroline without re-entering service.

Midibuses which were not already in Streetline livery gradually received this from early in 1995. M and VC types are receiving a yellow coachline at the top of the grey skirt area. M 171 has been converted to open-top for use on Surrey Hills summer Sunday service 70D from May 1995, and an order has been placed for 16 Dennis Dart 9-metre vehicles with Plaxton Pointer bodywork.

The fleet operates from garages at Battersea Bridge (BB), Merton (AL), Putney (AF), Stockwell (SW), Sutton (A) and Waterloo (RA). Major maintenance of Battersea Bridge and Waterloo vehicles is undertaken at Stockwell.

London General's buses are starting to appear in a modified livery style based on that of the VN class. M 847 is an example, seen in Buckingham Palace Road in April 1995. Colin Lloyd

The last Metrobus delivered new to London Transport, M 1440 received dual-purpose seating and London General livery in April 1994. It was still fresh from the paintshop when photographed on the outskirts of the regular LBL network in Banstead during May 1994. Gerald Mead

London General has made far more use of cherished registrations than any other subsidiary. M 463 gained a Routemaster mark in 1991. When seen on 10th April 1995, it had also gained a replacement front grille of a different design, and had received privatisation livery whilst still awaiting fleet-names. Stephen Madden

Having been deroofed in an accident at Battersea in August 1994, M 171 (now carrying fleet number OM 171) has been converted to permanent open-top format with single door, and re-entered service on 7th May in this splendid form of traditional General livery on route 70D, working between Clapham Common and Dorking on summer Sundays as part of the Surrey Hills network. This view shows it at Newlands Corner. Paul Weston

Originally the first of the final batch of 300 RMLs in red livery, RML 2461 was one of the earlier RMLs to be refurbished, having already received an Iveco engine in 1990. Now allocated to Putney garage, it was found in Charing Cross Road during March 1995. Capital Transport

Freshly-repainted into new colours, VC 1 is the first of 39 Volvo B10Ms with Northern Counties bodywork delivered to London General between 1989 and 1991, and has dual-purpose seating throughout. It was photographed at the Elephant & Castle on 4th March 1995. Malcolm MacDonald

All of the surviving Leyland Nationals used on the Red Arrow network have now been rebuilt to Greenway specification by East Lancs. GLS 483 gained its present registration in June 1993 before being rebuilt, at which time it also assumed normal configuration from having been a fully-seated vehicle. On 19th April 1995 it was caught approaching London Bridge. Laurie Rufus

Three of the Red Arrow LSs which had not been rebuilt were instead demoted to special uses at Sutton garage in November 1994. LS 482, remaining in standee format but repainted into the new livery style, found itself on a Park & Ride service at Epsom during the following month. Paul Weston

Still carrying evidence of its London Buses roundel, London General MA 119 from the Battersea Bridge base is seen in May 1995 near the Clapham Junction terminus of the 239. Mike Harris

Within the first main order for Dennis Darts with Wright bodywork, London General specified London registrations rather than the usual Belfast marks to avoid terrorist problems. DW 67, seen in Morden Hall Road on 25th March 1995, shows the recent introduction of Dayglo blinds, as well as the developing form of London General livery. Richard Godfrey

By the time that fifteen identical but slightly-older vehicles arrived with London General in the autumn of 1992, having been displaced from Leaside, the Irish registrations do not appear to have been regarded as a cause for concern. DW 49 was found near the Elephant & Castle working route 355, for which they were transferred south. Tony Wilson

The spring of 1993 saw the arrival of 22 nine-metre Dennis Darts with Plaxton bodywork for route 211, formed by linking the western end of route 11 with the eastern end of route C1. The Streetline livery style has since formed the basis for London General's post-privatisation livery. DRL 93 was seen at Westminster Abbey in April 1995. Capital Transport

Thirty-three stretched Optare MetroRiders arrived with London General in 1991. Amongst their duties is the operation of route C10 between Victoria and Elephant & Castle, on which MRL 199 was found at the southern end. Russell Upcraft

Route 88 was branded as The Clapham Omnibus and converted to operation by thirteen Volvo B10Bs with Northern Counties single-deck bodywork during 1993. VN 5, is seen in Regent Street on 19th April 1995. Keith Wood

London General have retained twelve Leyland Fleetlines as permanent driver-training units, painting them in a distinctive livery to discourage intending passengers from hailing them. DMS 2347 (carrying fleet number DMT 2347) was the first of the final batch of 300 Fleetlines to be bodied by Park Royal for London. Geoff Rixon

LONDON UNITED
Wellington Road, Fulwell, Middlesex, TW2 5NX

London United was purchased by a management-led team on 5th November 1994, taking 464 vehicles. These comprised 200 opo double-deckers, 41 Routemasters, and 223 single-deckers. The single-deckers included 194 Dennis Darts, by far the largest gathering of the type in the LBL fleet.

A number of Darts and Metrobuses have appeared in a dedicated livery for route 285, comprising red with silver grey roof, grey upper-deck window-surrounds, and a thin white band below the upper-deck windows and above the grey skirt. M 1238 received a livery in which the grey skirt rises higher than usual and is surmounted by three thin yellow bands; the roof is also yellow. This livery is not being adopted for general application; further vehicles have since appeared with a livery style similar to that used on the 285-dedicated buses.

12 Volvo Olympians with Alexander Royale bodywork have been ordered in the first phase of replacing the current Airbus fleet. This programme is expected to take three years. Meanwhile, some Darts are being modified for use on a new Airbus courtesy service to hotels from July 1995.

The fleet operates from garages at Fulwell (FW), Hounslow (AV), Shepherds Bush (S) and Stamford Brook (V). The midibus base at Wood Lane (B) was closed on 1st April 1995, vehicles moving to Shepherds Bush. Airbus operations are conducted from an outstation of Stamford Brook at West Ramp, Heathrow Airport.

In a proposed but now superseded London United livery, M 1238 approaches Hampton Court from Kingston on route 111 on 12th April 1995.
Geoff Rixon

The special livery introduced in the late summer of 1994 for route 285 has appeared on a number of Metrobuses, although the route has for some time been principally worked by Dennis Darts. M 813 is seen in Hampton. Gerald Mead

The main Airbus fleet comprises 24 Metrobuses of 1984 vintage, due to be replaced by Alexander-bodied Olympians in a three-year programme. M 1028 shows the strongly-characterised livery at Hyde Park Corner in April 1995; note also the colour-coded blind recently introduced to distinguish the Airbus services. Stephen Madden

Belying its 34 years, RML 880 cuts a fine sight at Marble Arch in April 1995. The first of the class, it now carries London United Tramways livery and works from Shepherds Bush garage on routes 9 and 94. *Stephen Madden*

London United's 23 all-Leyland Olympians carry Riverside Bus logos, and are used from Stamford Brook chiefly on the 237 as shown here, though they also sometimes stray onto the 27. L 293 passes roadworks in Hounslow on 1st April 1995. *Richard Godfrey*

London United were the first users of low-floor buses in the LBL group. LLW 7, combining Dennis Lance SLF chassis with Wright bodywork, was seen in Douglas Way, Hounslow on route 120 in March 1995. *Russell Upcraft*

The six Leyland Lynxes with London United are normally used on route H37 nowadays. LX 8 was tracked down at Hampton Court in September 1994 working route 111, normally the haunt of Metrobuses. *Geoff Rixon*

London United have become a major user of Dennis Darts. This view of Plaxton-bodied DRL 163, a 9-metre example, at Hounslow on 1st April 1995, shows the application of Harrier marketing names within the company. Richard Godfrey

In 1990 eight Iveco Daily minibuses with Reeve Burgess bodies joined London United in a joint enterprise with the London Borough of Hounslow. They bear a white-based livery, as represented by FR 8 in Hanworth on 3rd May 1995. Geoff Rixon

RMC 1469 has for some time served as a mobile recruitment and training vehicle for London United, painted into red livery. It was tracked down at Eccleston Bridge on 24th February 1995. *Colin Lloyd*

London United have converted a number of Metrobuses for dedicated use as driver trainers with reduced seating and this distinctive livery. M 36 was seen in Queen Elizabeth Road, Kingston in October 1994. *Geoff Rixon*

MTL LONDON NORTHERN 17-19 Highgate Hill, London N19 5NA

London Northern was purchased by MTL Trust Holdings on 26th October 1994, taking 341 vehicles. These comprised 204 opo double-deckers, 45 Routemasters, 90 single-deckers and two coaches, including the only double-deck coach in the LBL group. In April 1995 the MTL group also purchased neighbouring London Suburban Bus.

In 1994 M 563 had appeared with a white roof, reflecting the livery applied to the newly-delivered DNL class and Scanias used on route X43. In December 1994 RML 2620 appeared in an all-maroon livery, RML 2393 and M 576 in a slightly lighter shade of red than usual, and M 1287 in standard red, all with MTL London Northern logos. Following these experiments RML 2620 has received the same lighter red as RML 2393, and repaints are generally appearing in this new livery.

The coaching fleet was renewed in March 1995, introducing the SightseerS identity. This has also been applied to open-topper M 804 and private hire M 1393. Four Leyland Nationals acquired from LBL have been transferred elsewhere in the MTL group, not having been used by London Northern.

The fleet operates from garages at Holloway (HT) and Potters Bar (PB). Traffic area boundaries mean that vehicles based at Potters Bar are licensed in the Eastern traffic area. In terms of daily vehicle turn-out Holloway is one of the largest garages in the country.

The new MTL London Northern livery is shown to good effect in this portrait of Metrobus M 925 in Neathouse Place, Victoria on 24th March 1995. Route 82 is now worked by Potters Bar garage following the closure of Finchley, and thus represents the furthest daytime penetration of any outer garage into central London. Mike Harris

Fitted with dual-purpose seating and painted at the time in private hire livery, M 1393 eases into heavy traffic at Trafalgar Square in April 1995. Stephen Madden

An interim livery was applied to M 563 during the summer of 1994 when it appeared with white roof, reflecting the style of the Scanias used on route X43 and the DNLs. This view shows it at Hertford Bus Station, a location only served by red buses in recent years, on 18th March 1995. Mike Harris

Most of the company's Scania N113s with Alexander bodywork carry a special livery for use on route X43 during the week, though often appearing on other routes off-peak and at weekends. S 16 awaits departure at St Albans City Station on 1st April 1995. *Mike Harris*

The two surviving Volvo Ailsas with Alexander bodywork soldier on at Potters Bar, notionally as engineering spares though in practice in everyday service. V 1 takes stand time at New Barnet. *Colin Brown*

London Northern retain 26 standard Routemasters for route 139, though they often creep onto route 10 to cover for RMLs. Such was the case when RM 1971, looking somewhat the worse for wear, was photographed going south in Gower Street on 11th March 1995. Richard Godfrey

The new livery style is being applied to refurbished RMLs, such as RML 2699, caught by the photographer on 11th April 1995 as it turns into the lower half of Park Lane. This view also demonstrates the recent northern extension of route 10. Stephen Madden

Nineteen 9-metre Dennis Darts with Northern Counties bodywork arrived in the spring of 1994 for route C2, gained by London Northern from London General. The first half of the batch carries dedicated route livery, as shown by DNL 109 at Parliament Hill Fields on 12th June 1994. Mike Harris

London Northern's first Darts were twenty-one 9-metre examples with Plaxton bodywork delivered in 1992 for routes 46 and 274 (the first has since passed elsewhere in the MTL group). DRL 24 approaches the end of its journey at Marble Arch on 6th April 1995. Stephen Madden

Something of a surprise was the arrival of twenty Mercedes-Benz 811D bodied by Wrights in 1993. They joined the MW class and at the time took over all midibus operations at Potters Bar. MW 35 was found at Brent Cross shopping centre on 7th April 1995. *Colin Lloyd*

London Northern have renewed their coaching fleet during the spring of 1995, adopting the SightseerS logo at the same time. VH 3 combines DAF MB230 chassis with Van Hool Alizee coachwork and was new in 1989 to MacPhail, Motherwell. This shot was taken at Archway on 7th April 1995. *Colin Lloyd*

METROLINE 118-122 College Road, Harrow, Middlesex, HA1 1DB

Metroline was purchased by a management-led team on 7th October 1994, taking 386 vehicles. These were 164 opo double-deckers, 52 Routemasters, 166 single-deckers and four coaches. Metroline also received nine EDRs which were on order at the time of privatisation. In addition, four Ms and one T were on hire from LBL. The Ms were returned to LBL for other subsidiaries in October; the T was purchased in November to augment the Atlas Bus fleet, which was purchased from the Pullmans Group on 28th November. Metroline had already been involved in loaning Metrobuses to cover vehicle shortages at Atlas Bus from 26th September 1994.

Nine Metrobuses have received all-red livery for use on LT contract route 292; they have also received Transmatic interior lighting and new seating moquette.

The fleet operates from sites at Cricklewood (W), Edgware (EW), Harrow Weald (HD), North Wembley (NW) and Willesden (AC). Major maintenance of those based at North Wembley and of single-deckers from Edgware is undertaken at Harrow Weald; double-deckers from Edgware are maintained at Cricklewood. Vehicles are also allocated to the Commercial Services fleet (CS), those for private hire being based at Cricklewood and the driver trainers at various garages as required. The Atlas Bus fleet operates from a site at Harlesden (HR).

Originally a Country Area vehicle, RML 2430 came to the then Central Area in 1978 and received red livery. This view at Marble Arch on 6th April 1995 shows the route branding which is common to operation on both of Metroline's RML routes, 6 and 98. Stephen Madden

Fitted with high-back seating, M 1185 forms part of Metroline's private hire fleet and received a Routemaster registration in July 1994. Here it is seen on a Safeway courtesy bus service in March 1995 at Queensbury. Colin Brown

Metroline's holding company purchased Atlas Bus & Coach in November 1994, including 26 Leyland Titans. These had not long previously been owned by London Coaches, whose livery they still carry. T 459 was photographed in Chamberlayne Road, Brondesbury Park in April 1995 on the busy haul towards central London. Richard Godfrey

Three variations of a new livery for Metroline were applied to three Metrobuses in the first half of 1995. M 1035, seen in Harrow, was given a green skirt, M 326 in Regent Street was given a burgundy skirt and M 550, in Shoot Up Hill, a blue one. The blue skirt has been chosen for general application on the Metroline fleet. Capital Transport, Gerald Mead (2)

The low-floor buses have so far only rarely strayed from the routes to which they are allocated. One such occasion was this appearance of LLW 25 on Harrow Weald's route 182 instead of its normal use on route 186. The motorised destination blinds provide perfect displays every time. *Capital Transport*

All of the Dennis Lances with Northern Counties bodywork are now concentrated at Cricklewood garage, whence they operate on routes 32 and 113. LN 15 passes down Finchley Road in October 1994 with a standing load. *Richard Godfrey*

Bodied by Carlyle on a Dennis Dart chassis, DT 126 presents a fresh if uninspiring appearance in all-red livery as it is driven along Watford Road, Sudbury in April 1995, prior to receiving its blue skirt. *Richard Godfrey.*

Metroline took a substantial number of Plaxton-bodied Dennis Darts in the early 1990s. DR 145, bedecked with Harlesden Challenger logos, was photographed in Forty Lane, Wembley Park on 1st April 1995, working from the midibus outstation at North Wembley. *Richard Godfrey*

The only examples of Dennis Darts to 9.8metre length to have joined LBL descendants to date, nine with Plaxton bodywork arrived with Metroline in October 1994 in preparation for their takeover of tendered route 107. EDR 4 is seen approaching the terminus at Edgware Station, with SR 101 in close pursuit. C.D. Jones

The early MetroRiders are gradually diminishing in number. MR 20, freshly repainted in the private hire fleet, was an unusual visitor to route 107 at Borehamwood on 1st April 1995. Mike Harris

SR 7 had recently received this special livery for Tesco work when photographed at Brent Cross shopping centre on 15th March 1995. Colin Brown

In 1995 Metroline acquired two Plaxton Premiere bodied Javelins from a dealer to replace a pair of Duple bodied Tigers in its private hire fleet based at Cricklewood. These coaches, which originated with Redwing, are used in the summer on day trips and one passes through Wealdstone in June on one such excursion. Capital Transport

SOUTH LONDON Brighton Road, Croydon, CR2 6EL

South London was purchased by the Cowie group on 10th January 1995, taking 447 vehicles. These comprised 325 opo double-deckers, 59 Routemasters and 63 single-deckers, and included the largest contingent of Olympians (161) to be taken by any of the subsidiaries.

All vehicles have now received 'Cowie group plc' legends at the rear. M 384 received a dark green skirt and cantrail relief on its red livery, and L 140 a dark green skirt. Both reverted to LBL style livery in May 1995. Standard RMs allocated to route 159 from Brixton have continued to receive red and cream livery, and in most cases branding for the route; these RMs are also now gradually receiving Transmatic lighting in the lower saloon.

The fleet operates from garages at Brixton (BN), Croydon (TC), Norwood (N) and Thornton Heath (TH).

An unusual livery experiment was the application of dark green skirt and cantrail to M 384 in the autumn of 1994. It was caught at East Croydon on 8th April 1995 nearing the end of its southbound trip on the short route, a shadow of its former self, from Norwood Junction. Colin Lloyd

Fitted with high-back seating in the spring of 1994 for use as a private hire vehicle, M 1359 was painted into appropriate livery. This view in Wellesley Road, Croydon on 15th October 1994 shows that it also takes its turn on routine service when required. *Mike Harris*

One of the two Metrobuses purchased to determine future double-deck policy in 1984 (a third was never completed), M 1441 arrived at Croydon in March 1992 when Streatham garage closed. On 22nd September 1994 it was photographed working route 68A, the southern element of a cross-London route which has over the years been divided into three separate sections. *Stephen Madden*

More successfully involved in the same trials were three Leyland Olympians with Eastern Coach Works bodies, which arrived at Croydon in 1987 after being stored at the end of the trials. L 1, used to evaluate the Leyland TL11 engine in the type, had just received private hire livery when seen at Apps Court on 9th April 1995. *Colin Brown*

South London now has a substantial number of ECW-bodied Leyland Olympians, though it was not until late in the production run that they gained them. L 16, which received a Routemaster registration in April 1993, represents the later transfer of earlier examples from Plumstead in this view at East Croydon on 8th April 1995. *Colin Lloyd*

RM 432 demonstrates the crisp livery now being introduced on standard RMs allocated to route 159, together with the recent introduction of Dayglo blinds. Its registration was applied in December 1991 whilst with London General (the original being placed on a Metrobus) and is from a non-transferable series for vehicles which were new before the introduction of year suffixes. *Stephen Madden*

When route 2 was converted to opo, many of Norwood's RMLs moved across to Brixton for the 137, releasing other RMLs to London General. RML 2636 was one of the vehicles so displaced, and was photographed in October 1994 at Streatham Hill. *Colin Brown*

South London has a smaller presence of Dennis Darts than most of the other former LBL subsidiaries. Twelve Plaxton-bodied Darts arrived with South London in 1991 for route 249, which replaced the southern end of the 49. Norwood's DR 29 had strayed onto Connexions route 322 when found on 21st April 1995. Stephen Madden

South London owns Darts of 8.5 and 9-metre lengths, the oldest being a batch of 13 Carlyle-bodied buses dating from 1990. DT 65 is seen at West Croydon. Mike Harris

STAGECOACH EAST LONDON

16-20 Clements Road, Ilford, Essex, IG1 1BA

East London was purchased by the Stagecoach group on 6th September 1994, taking a total of 595 vehicles. These comprised 363 opo double-deckers, 61 Routemasters, 168 single-deckers and three coaches, and included the largest contingent of Titans (312) to be taken by any of the subsidiaries. Of the RMLs, those at Bow have Iveco engines whilst those at Upton Park (apart from RML 2760, which retains AEC units) have Cummins engines. East London also received 15 SLWs which were on order at the time of privatisation, the first having arrived in July. In addition, six RBs and 16 Ts were on hire from LBL. The RBs were returned to the LBL Sales Department in September and October, and the Ts in October and November after route 101 had been converted to SLW operation.

Vehicles began to lose their white relief stripes and grey skirts very quickly, both through full and partial repaints, and gained Stagecoach East London logos. The all-red livery style has also started to embrace the DA class, which had previously borne a distinctive livery of red with grey relief. Late in 1994 Routemasters started to appear with cream relief bands instead of white, and gold Stagecoach East London logos. RMC 1461 has however been repainted in Green Line livery. T 394 has now received black window-surrounds on both decks, and a black offside staircase panel; T338 also has the latter refinement.

Having taken over responsibility for Stagecoach Selkent private hire work in addition to their own, Stagecoach East London promptly converted T 63 and T 80 to coach seating in the autumn of 1994, outshopping them in a smart East London Coaches livery. Subsequently both vehicles received undated registrations from RMLs.

On 5th November 1994 Bow's allocation of the S class was moved to Upton Park in exchange for Titans. At the end of January 1995 13 Titans were transferred to Western Scottish for use on former A1 group services. In March 1995 17 Volvo B6s were received from other Stagecoach companies to release SRs for replacement services for the East London Underground line. The SRs were initially repainted in a smart orange and white livery for this contract, seven of them being transferred to Stagecoach Selkent; the incoming Volvos made inevitable history by being the first Stagecoach vehicles to enter service in London in the group's ubiquitous white livery with red, blue and orange stripe relief. So far their presence has been confined to the Romford area, from 21st March, in deference to the requirement to retain red-liveried vehicles on routes which penetrate the central area. Most were replaced by Volvo B10 vehicles during April and May 1995.

RM 1527 has been on long-term loan to BBC-TV for use in Eastenders, returning to Upton Park for maintenance. Early in 1995 it received Stagecoach East London livery and in June it was back in normal service.

The fleet operates from sites at Barking (BK), Bow (BW), Leyton (T), Romford (NS), Stratford (SD) and Upton Park (U). Major maintenance of Stratford vehicles is carried out at Bow.

Typifying the standard all-Leyland Titan, of which Stagecoach East London now has the largest fleet, T 394 was seen working from Leyton garage at Marble Arch in April 1995. This has been given black relief around the windows. Colin Lloyd

With a registration transferred from an RML early in 1995, T 80 is one of the declining number of Titans bodied by Park Royal. Converted to single-door in 1992 and fitted with coach seating in the autumn of 1994, it is now in the private hire fleet, being found in Mercury Gardens, Romford on 23rd March 1995. Mike Harris

After demonstrating to a number of London Buses subsidiaries, SP 2, the only one of London's Optare Spectras to have a dual-door body, has settled in Stagecoach East London's private hire fleet. In October 1994 it was seen at Plaistow working a shoppers' service to Lakeside. Mike Harris

An order for forty Scania N113 double-deckers with Northern Counties bodywork was delivered to East London in the autumn of 1992, shared between Bow and Upton Park garages. In the autumn of 1994 the type was concentrated at Upton Park. S 6 crosses Marble Arch on Good Friday 1995. Route 15 is one-person operated on weekday evenings, Sundays and public holidays. Stephen Madden

Fitted with an Iveco engine and refurbished in 1992, RML 2624 sports the recently-introduced Stagecoach East London version of Routemaster livery with cream cantrail and fleetnames. It was photographed on 12th April 1995, negotiating roadworks at Victoria on its way back to the East End.
C.D. Jones

Two of the 65 front-entrance Routemasters originally delivered to British European Airways in 1965/6 remain in regular service. The design is clearly-shown in this view of RMA 8, freshly adorned in Stagecoach East London's Routemaster livery, at St Paul's in April 1995. Stephen Madden

Freshly-repainted in unrelieved red livery, DT 33 is a Carlyle-bodied Dennis Dart from the second batch within the type, delivered in 1990. It was caught in Orpington on 3rd April bearing Roundabout fleetnames, the marketing name used for services from the Orpington base which was once a separate company. Stephen Madden

Selkent received eight of the Wright-bodied Dennis Darts in the DW class during 1991. DW 63 had received all-red livery with Stagecoach-type logos when photographed at Lewisham in May 1995. Colin Brown

Selkent hold fourteen of the MA class of Mercedes-Benz 811D with Alexander bodywork, all based at Plumstead. On Sundays they are placed on route 54 between Woolwich and West Croydon. MA 21 was caught mid-route at Lewisham. Paul Weston

Selkent received all of the first batch of Wright-bodied Mercedes-Benz 811D vehicles which formed the MW class in 1989. MW 14 is one of three which have since been converted with tail-lifts for use on mobility bus services, and was photographed in its distinctive livery at Lewisham on 8th April 1995. Paul Weston

Another reminder of the past is provided by RMC 1456, originally a Green Line coach, now used as a back-up vehicle on route 15 from Upton Park. Passing Trafalgar Square, this shot shows its gold relief livery and recent re-registration. Its original registration passed to a staff car in August 1994.
Stephen Madden

Three Leyland Nationals of the original type survive as mobility buses with Stagecoach East London. LS 308, converted by MCW in 1987, had languished in store from December 1992 after use by Metroline before being resurrected during 1993 for further use. This shot was taken on 25th March 1995 in Romford. Tony Wilson

East London has a total of 26 Optare Deltas, being the only former LBL subsidiary to operate the type other than Westlink. DA 31 is seen in Barking in February 1995. Mike Harris

Stagecoach East London took the last of the 30 Scania N113 low-floor vehicles bodied by Wright after privatisation in the autumn of 1994. They entered service on route 101. SLW 24 was seen at East Beckton District Centre in April 1995. Mike Harris

Major route revisions in 1993 led to the arrival of a substantial number of 9-metre Dennis Darts with Plaxton bodywork in the East London fleet. These are typified by DRL 130 in Water Lane in March 1995, working one of the routes introduced as part of these changes. Mike Harris

Also contributing to the midibus conversions of 1993, a batch of 8.5-metre Dennis Darts bodied by Wright arrived with East London, though some subsequently moved elsewhere. DW 149 was found in Aldgate in March 1995 working route 100, previously commanded by Leaside. Tony Wilson

Similar vehicle DW 159 has recently received overall livery for use on the free bus service to and from the Tesco store at Barking, where it was found in February 1995. Mike Harris

The closure of the East London Line for renovation by London Underground from March 1995 led to seventeen of the SR class receiving this special livery for replacement services, some being hired to Stagecoach Selkent until May. SR 72 is at Rotherhithe on 8th April 1995. Colin Lloyd

Several long MCW MetroRiders found their way to East London in 1993 after being displaced from other work in London. MRL 75 was found at Stratford Bus Station in February 1995 working route S2, the modern descendant of a route which once required lowbridge double-deckers. *Mike Harris*

TPL 7, a Leyland Tiger of 1991 with Plaxton Panorama Elite 3500 3 coachwork, shows off the livery now applied to the private hire fleet at Epsom Downs on 1st June 1994, the day of the Derby. Sister vehicle TPL 8 has passed to the Leaside fleet. *Keith Grimes*

STAGECOACH SELKENT

South East London & Kent Bus Co Ltd, 180 Bromley Road, London SE26 2XA

Selkent was purchased by the Stagecoach group on 6th September 1994, taking 414 vehicles. These comprised 282 opo double-deckers, two Routemasters, 132 single-deckers and eight coaches. Neither of the Routemasters being in regular service, Selkent had the distinction of being the only major subsidiary to have achieved all-opo by the date of privatisation. At the date of privatisation one MR was on hire to South London; this was returned to Selkent during September.

Vehicles began to lose their white relief stripes and grey skirts very quickly, both through full and partial repaints, and to gain Stagecoach Selkent logos. The LA and LV classes, which had previously borne a distinctive livery of red with grey skirt surmounted by white and black bands, and white window-surrounds, are now receiving a simpler red with white window-surrounds and/or roofs. T 86, T 142 and T 224 have received white Stagecoach livery for exclusive use as driver trainers; this livery is also carried by recent arrival 3007, a Leyland coach for the training fleet.

The private hire operation was wound up during October 1994 and the coaching fleet, including three coach-seated Titans, dispersed to other Stagecoach companies. DM 948, DM 1102 and RMC 1515 stay in ownership but are currently stored at the Whitehaven depot of Cumberland.

From October 1994 to January 1995 four Iveco minibuses were hired from United Counties for a Park-and-Ride service at Bromley, and were repainted into London red for the duration. They have now returned to their owner.

Selkent are to receive 52 Volvo Olympians with Northern Counties bodywork from current Stagecoach group orders. These will be allocated to Plumstead for use on routes 53 and X53.

The fleet operates from sites at Bromley, Catford, Orpington and Plumstead. The former LBL garage codes of TB, TL, OB and PD respectively were discontinued towards the end of 1994 and replaced by B, C, O and P respectively, though these are no longer carried on vehicles.

Upper right Seen at Bromley South on 3rd April, T 822 is one of a small group of all-Leyland Titans for which a fresh batch of registrations was needed in 1983 to allow a prompt introduction into service before the year letter changed. Stephen Madden

Lower right A substantial proportion of LBL's early Leyland Olympians, bodied by Eastern Coach Works, found their way to Plumstead garage. L 103 represents the type on route 53 at Elephant & Castle. Stephen Madden

In 1992 Selkent took delivery of sixteen Dennis Lances with Alexander bodywork, both unusual choices for LBL at the time. LA 5 demonstrates the stylish livery applied (although now being superseded) in this view in April 1995. Stephen Madden

A follow-up order for Dennis Lances in 1994 specified Plaxton Verde bodywork on twelve vehicles. LV 8, in a comparable livery style, was tracked down on 3rd April 1995. Stephen Madden

In 1993 the Orpington allocation was upgraded with ten Iveco Daily midibuses bodied by Marshall to their C29 design. FM 9 runs through Orpington on the hourly service to Chelsfield on 3rd April 1995.
Stephen Madden

At a time when LBL had reversed their intention not to order further MetroRiders, MRL 167 formed part of a batch allocated to Bromley. It was still working there when found on route 336 on 3rd April 1995, though operations from this garage have suffered a significant decline in the past two years.
Stephen Madden

The Stanwell Bus Company Ltd, trading as Westlink, was purchased by a management-led team on 20th January 1994, taking 119 vehicles. These comprised 16 opo double-deckers, 102 single-deckers and one coach (used for driver-training). Subsequently a further LS and a further T were purchased from LBL. Ownership of the fleet passed to the West Midlands Travel group on 24th March 1994; they, in turn, merged with the National Express group in April 1995.

At the time of privatisation many LSs were surplus to requirements and stored pending future requirements. Six were transferred to West Midlands Travel in August 1994 for use on routes acquired from Stevenson, Uttoxeter. In the other direction, three Metrobuses were acquired from WMT in October 1994 for use on newly-gained school contracts and subsequently route 411.

Since the emergence of Westlink as a separate entity in August 1986, a distinctive livery of red with white and turquoise relief had been used. LS 245 appeared in all-red livery in October 1994 with a white band below the windows and a thick turquoise stripe within the white. LS 229 and LS 411 followed suit, but other repaints have continued the previous style.

The fleet operates from sites at Kingston (K) and Hounslow Heath (WK), although all major maintenance is undertaken at the latter site.

The largest enclave of original Leyland Nationals in the former LBL subsidiaries is with Westlink, who have assembled specimens of various format from around the fleet. LS 434 has been with Westlink since their formation in 1986, and was found in Hounslow on 1st April 1995. Richard Godfrey

Early examples of Optare Deltas in the LBL fleet have all now congregated with Westlink. DA 8 is one of seven which were new in 1990 when tendered route 110 was gained, and is seen on this route in Hounslow. Richard Godfrey

The DWL class first appeared in 1990 in the form of fourteen vehicles sent to Westlink for tendered route 371. DWL 13 had been freshly-repainted when found in Park Road, Kingston on 24th March 1995, and although lacking fleetnames is readily attributable by its livery. Geoff Rixon

Three of the DWLs (and a MetroRider) now carry this special livery for Kingston University, as demonstrated by DWL 3 in Kingston on 24th March 1995. Geoff Rixon

Westlink were the first LBL subsidiary to use MetroRiders, and although many of the original examples have since been sold, they have been replaced by later examples from elsewhere in the fleet. MR 30, originally a Harrow Weald vehicle, was seen in East Molesey on route 501 in October 1994. Geoff Rixon

Westlink's Leyland Titans are chiefly used on route 131. T 911 was one of several which were involved in exchanges between LBL subsidiaries in 1993 so as to remove leased examples from the Westlink fleet before its privatisation, and was photographed in Wood Street, Kingston on 10th April 1993. Geoff Rixon

Three Metrobuses moved to Westlink in the autumn of 1994 from West Midlands, and are now regularly used on route 411, the western section of the former 131. Stephen Madden

Others of the original Westlink MetroRiders were replaced by stretched examples in 1988. MRL 88 was one of the vehicles so used, and was seen in leafy Claygate on 3rd May 1995. *Geoff Rixon*

Three of the six Omnis in the Westlink fleet came from C&M, Aintree, receiving private registrations on arrival in London to reflect part-ownership by the London Borough of Richmond, for whom they were intended to be used on routes R61 and R62. CV 7 had strayed onto the H20 when photographed in Hounslow on 24th May 1994. *Colin Lloyd*

FLEET LISTS

LONDON TRANSPORT BUSES

London Transport Buses came into possession of 83 vehicles on 4th March 1995. These comprised one AN (ex Portsmouth), 30 RMs forming the reserve fleet, 46 RMLs re-leased to BTS and Kentish Bus and six RBs returned from CentreWest for sale.

An AN is maintained at London Central's Camberwell garage, and the reserve RMs at Universitybus, Hatfield. Maintenance of the RMLs leased to BTS is the responsibility of those operators. All vehicles listed below were acquired from London Buses Ltd.

AN1	VTP258L	Leyland Atlantean AN68R/1		Alexander AL	H—/—D	1972	Mobile canteen/restroom

RM32-2213   AEC Routemaster 5RM   Park Royal   H36/28R   1959-1965

32	XYJ428	659	KFF239	1081	81CLT	1330	KGH975A	2033	ALM33B
264	VLT264	736	XYJ418	1138	138CLT	1428	428CLT	2050	ALM50B
295	VLT295	966	WLT966	1204	204CLT	1562	562CLT	2078	ALM78B
324	WLT324	995	WLT995	1205	XYJ429	1676	676DYE	2097	ALM97B
342	KFF277	1005	ALC290A	1214	214CLT	1825	825DYE	2173	CUV173C
385	WLT385	1078	KGH925A	1292	NVS485	2021	ALM21B	2213	CUV213C

All of these RMs are in store at Universitybus, Hatfield as a strategic reserve fleet.

Previous registrations

ALC290A	5CLT
KFF239	WLT659
KFF277	WLT342
KGH925A	78CLT
KGH975A	330CLT
NVS485	292CLT
XYJ418	WLT736
XYJ428	VLT32
XYJ429	205CLT

Special livery
Blue livery: AN1

London Transport Buses are also responsible for 22 RML operated by BTS and 24 RML operated by Kentish Bus as follows:

BTS

RML2265-2756   AEC Routemaster 7RM   Park Royal   H40/32R   1965-1968   Cummins engines

2265	CUV265C	2487	JJD487D	2582	JJD582D	2663	SMK663F	2719	SMK719F
2322	CUV322C	2527	JJD527D	2598	JJD598D	2668	SMK668F	2756	SMK756F
2341	CUV341C	2538	JJD538D	2627	NML627E	2674	SMK274F		
2404	JJD404D	2563	JJD563D	2633	NML633E	2686	SMK686F		
2443	JJD443D	2569	JJD569D	2659	SMK659F	2694	SMK694F		

Kentish Bus

RML2266-2715   AEC Routemaster 7RM   Park Royal   H40/32R   1965-1967   Iveco engines

2266	CUV266C	2383	JJD383D	2512	JJD512D	2533	JJD533D	2586	JJD586D
2301	CUV301C	2387	JJD387D	2514	JJD514D	2536	JJD536D	2591	JJD591D
2343	CUV343C	2410	JJD410D	2523	JJD523D	2548	JJD548D	2619	NML619E
2347	CUV347C	2452	JJD452D	2524	JJD524D	2574	JJD574D	2715	SMK715F
2382	CUV382D	2505	JJD505D	2531	JJD531D	2577	JJD577D		

CENTREWEST

All vehicles acquired from London Buses Ltd in September 1994

BL1-91   Bristol LH6L   Eastern Coach Works   B39F   1976-1977   a DP40F

1t	KJD401P	**28t**	KJD428P	**36at**	KJD436P	**65t**	OJD65R	**81at**	OJD81R
2t	KJD402P	**34t**	KJD434P	**49t**	OJD49R	**69t**	OJD69R	**85**	OJD85R
4t	KJD404P	**35t**	KJD435P	**57t**	OJD57R	**78t**	OJD78R	**91t**	OJD91R

DW1-14   Dennis Dart 8.5SDL3003   Wright Handybus   B30F   1990

1	JDZ2301	**4**	JDZ2304	**7**	JDZ2307	**10**	JDZ2310	**13**	JDZ2313
2	JDZ2302	**5**	JDZ2305	**8**	JDZ2308	**11**	JDZ2311	**14**	JDZ2314
3	JDZ2303	**6**	JDZ2306	**9**	JDZ2309	**12**	JDZ2312		

DW15-126   Dennis Dart 8.5SDL3003*   Wright Handybus   B26F   1990-1992
*101-114 are 8.5SDL3010, 115-125 are 8.5SDL3015, 126 is 8.5SDL3018

15	JDZ2315	**32**	JDZ2332	**77**	JDZ2377	**94a**	JDZ2394	**111**	KDZ5111
16	JDZ2316	**33**	JDZ2333	**78**	JDZ2378	**95a**	JDZ2395	**112**	KDZ5112
17	JDZ2317	**34**	JDZ2334	**79**	JDZ2379	**96a**	JDZ2396	**113**	LDZ9113
18	JDZ2318	**35**	JDZ2335	**80**	JDZ2380	**97a**	JDZ2397	**114**	LDZ9114
19	JDZ2319	**36**	JDZ2336	**81**	JDZ2381	**98a**	JDZ2398	**115**	LDZ9115
20	JDZ2320	**37**	JDZ2337	**82**	JDZ2382	**99a**	JDZ2399	**116**	LDZ9116
21	JDZ2321	**38**	JDZ2338	**83**	JDZ2383	**100**	JDZ2300	**117**	LDZ9117
22	JDZ2322	**39**	JDZ2339	**84**	JDZ2384	**101**	KDZ5101	**118**	LDZ9118
23	JDZ2323	**40**	JDZ2340	**85**	JDZ2385	**102**	KDZ5102	**119**	LDZ9119
24	JDZ2324	**41**	JDZ2341	**86**	JDZ2386	**103**	KDZ5103	**120**	LDZ9120
25	JDZ2325	**42**	JDZ2342	**87**	JDZ2387	**104**	KDZ5104	**121**	LDZ9121
26	JDZ2326	**43**	JDZ2343	**88**	JDZ2388	**105**	KDZ5105	**122**	LDZ9122
27	JDZ2327	**72**	JDZ2372	**89**	JDZ2389	**106**	KDZ5106	**123**	LDZ9123
28	JDZ2328	**73**	JDZ2373	**90**	JDZ2390	**107**	KDZ5107	**124**	LDZ9124
29	JDZ2329	**74**	JDZ2374	**91**	JDZ2391	**108**	KDZ5108	**125**	LDZ9125
30	JDZ2330	**75**	JDZ2375	**92a**	JDZ2392	**109**	KDZ5109	**126**	LDZ9126
31	JDZ2331	**76**	JDZ2376	**93a**	JDZ2393	**110**	KDZ5110		

DW162-170   Dennis Dart 8.5SDL3015   Wright Handybus   B29F   1993   a B26F

162	NDZ3162	**164**	NDZ3164	**166**	NDZ3166	**168**	NDZ3168	**170a**	NDZ3170
163	NDZ3163	**165**	NDZ3165	**167**	NDZ3167	**169a**	NDZ3169		

GLS2   292CLT   Leyland National 2 NL116AL11/2R   East Lancs Greenway   DP49F   1982 (rebuilt 1992)

LLW11-24   Dennis Lance SLF 11SDA3202   Wright Pathfinder 320   B34D   1993-1994

11	ODZ8911	**14**	ODZ8914	**17**	ODZ8917	**20**	ODZ8920	**23**	ODZ8923
12	ODZ8912	**15**	ODZ8915	**18**	ODZ8918	**21**	ODZ8921	**24**	ODZ8924
13	ODZ8913	**16**	ODZ8916	**19**	ODZ8919	**22**	ODZ8922		

LS444-504   Leyland National 2 NL106AL11/2R   DP43F   1981   a Volvo engine   b B44F

444a	GUW444W	**458**	GUW458W	**472a**	GUW472W	**495**	GUW495W	**503a**	503CLT
451	GUW451W	**470a**	GUW470W	**484b**	GUW484W	**497a**	GUW497W	**504a**	GUW504W

LX1	F101GRM	Leyland Lynx LX112L10ZR1R	Leyland	DP48F	1988
LX2	F102GRM	Leyland Lynx LX112L10ZR1R	Leyland	DP48F	1988
LX9	809DYE	Leyland Lynx LX112TL11ZR1R	Leyland	DP48F	1987
LX10	810DYE	Leyland Lynx LX112TL11ZR1R	Leyland	DP48F	1987
LX11	811DYE	Leyland Lynx LX112TL11ZR1R	Leyland	DP48F	1987

M285-583   MCW Metrobus DR101/12*   MCW   H43/28D   1980   *523 and 583 are DR101/14

285	BYX285V	338	EYE338V	368	GYE368W	414	GYE414W	486	GYE486W
291	BYX291V	339	EYE339V	369	GYE369W	418	GYE418W	487	GYE487W
305	BYX305V	340	EYE340V	370	GYE370W	421	GYE421W	489	GYE489W
308	BYX308V	343	EYE343V	371	GYE371W	425	GYE425W	494	GYE494W
311	BYX311V	345	EYE345V	374	GYE374W	427	GYE427W	497	GYE497W
316	EYE316V	347	GYE347W	383	GYE383W	434	GYE434W	498	GYE498W
319	EYE319V	349	GYE349W	390	GYE390W	442	GYE442W	499	GYE499W
329	EYE329V	358	GYE358W	393	GYE393W	451	GYE451W	504	GYE504W
330	EYE330V	360	GYE360W	397	GYE397W	452	GYE452W	505	GYE505W
332	EYE332V	362	GYE362W	406	GYE406W	465	GYE465W	523	GYE523W
337	EYE337V	364	GYE364W	413	GYE413W	470	GYE470W	583	GYE583W

M843-952   MCW Metrobus DR101/16   MCW   H43/28D   1983

843	OJD843Y	861	OJD861Y	882	OJD882Y	887	OJD887Y	938	A938SUL
851	OJD851Y	866	OJD866Y	883	OJD883Y	892	A892SUL	941	A941SUL
857	OJD857Y	872	OJD872Y	884	OJD884Y	893	A893SUL	943	A943SUL
859	OJD859Y	874	OJD874Y	885	OJD885Y	898	A898SUL	952	A952SUL
860	OJD860Y	875	OJD875Y	886	OJD886Y	901	A901SUL		

M979-1438   MCW Metrobus DR101/17*   MCW   H43/28D   1984-1986   * DR101/19

979	A979SYF	1245	B245WUL	1328	C328BUV	1380	C380BUV	1420	C420BUV
1049	A749THV	1246	B246WUL	1335	C335BUV	1382	C382BUV	1421	C421BUV
1051	A751THV	1247	B247WUL	1338	C338BUV	1384	C384BUV	1422	C422BUV
1054	A754THV	1256	B256WUL	1340	C340BUV	1400	C400BUV	1438	C438BUV
1144	B144WUL	1258	B258WUL	1375	C375BUV	1412	C412BUV		
1199	B199WUL	1259	B259WUL	1376	C376BUV	1415	C415BUV		
1201	B201WUL	1260	B260WUL	1377	C377BUV	1418	C418BUV		
1244	B244WUL	1267	B267WUL	1378	C378BUV	1419	C419BUV		

MA1-107   Mercedes-Benz 811D   Alexander AM   B28F   1988-1989   a B26F   b B26FL   c DP28F

1a	F601XMS	33	F633XMS	53	F953BMS	72	F672XMS	91	F691XMS
2a	F602XMS	34a	F634XMS	54	F954BMS	73	F673XMS	92	F692XMS
3b	F603XMS	35	F635XMS	55a	F955BMS	74	F674XMS	93	F693XMS
4b	F604XMS	36	F636XMS	56	F656XMS	75	F675XMS	94	F694XMS
5b	F605XMS	37	F637XMS	57	F657XMS	76	F676XMS	95	F695XMS
6b	F606XMS	38	F638XMS	58	F658XMS	77	F677XMS	96	F696XMS
7b	F607XMS	39	F639XMS	59	F659XMS	78	F678XMS	97	F697XMS
8	F608XMS	40	F640XMS	60	F660XMS	79	F679XMS	98	F698XMS
10a	F610XMS	42	F642XMS	61	F661XMS	80	F680XMS	99a	F699XMS
11	F611XMS	43	F643XMS	62	F662XMS	81	F681XMS	100a	F700XMS
12a	F612XMS	44	F644XMS	63	F663XMS	82	F682XMS	101c	VLT31
13	F613XMS	45	F645XMS	64	F664XMS	83	F683XMS	102c	F702XMS
18	F618XMS	46	F946BMS	65	F665XMS	84	F684XMS	103c	F703XMS
22	F622XMS	47a	F947BMS	66	F666XMS	85	F685XMS	104c	F704XMS
23	F623XMS	48	F948BMS	67	F667XMS	86	F686XMS	105c	F705XMS
26	F626XMS	49	F949BMS	68	F668XMS	87	F687XMS	106	F706XMS
27	F627XMS	50	F950BMS	69	F669XMS	88	F688XMS	107	F707XMS
28	F628XMS	51a	F951BMS	70	F670XMS	89	F689XMS		
32	F632XMS	52	F952BMS	71	F671XMS	90	F690XMS		

MT7	G537GBD	Mercedes-Benz 709D	Reeve Burgess Beaver	B20FL	1989
MT8	G538GBD	Mercedes-Benz 709D	Reeve Burgess Beaver	B20FL	1989
MTL5	H192RWF	Mercedes-Benz 811D	Reeve Burgess Beaver	B29F	1990
MW17	LDZ9017	Mercedes-Benz 811D	Wright	B26F	1992

RM1948	ALD948B	AEC Routemaster 5RM	Park Royal	H36/28R	1964	
RM2103	ALM103B	AEC Routemaster 5RM	Park Royal	H36/28R	1964	
RMC1492t	492CLT	AEC Routemaster 6RM	Park Royal	H32/25RD	1962	
RMC1510	510CLT	AEC Routemaster 6RM	Park Royal	O32/25RD	1962	Cummins engine

RML885-2740 AEC Routemaster 7RM — Park Royal — H40/32R 1961-1967 — Cummins engines

885	WLT885	2369	JJD369D	2473	JJD473D	2542	JJD542D	2667	SMK667F
2268	CUV268C	2374	JJD374D	2476	JJD476D	2553	JJD553D	2672	SMK672F
2278	CUV278C	2378	JJD378D	2480	JJD480D	2555	JJD555D	2677	SMK677F
2281	CUV281C	2379	JJD379D	2486	JJD486D	2559	JJD559D	2687	SMK687F
2291	CUV291C	2388	JJD388D	2490	JJD490D	2602	NML602E	2717	SMK717F
2309	CUV309C	2390	JJD390D	2498	JJD498D	2609	NML609E	2724	SMK724F
2313	CUV313C	2405	JJD405D	2501	JJD501D	2623	NML623E	2735	SMK735F
2352	CUV352C	2428	JJD428D	2506	JJD506D	2647	NML647E	2740	SMK740F
2357	CUV357C	2442	JJD442D	2522	JJD522D	2656	NML656E		
2365	JJD365D	2467	JJD467D	2530	JJD530D	2664	SMK664F		

RW1-90 Renault-Dodge S75 — Wright — B28F — 1990 — a DP28F

1	HDZ5401	20	HDZ5420	38	HDZ5438	56	HDZ5456	74	HDZ5474
2	HDZ5402	21	HDZ5421	39	HDZ5439	57	HDZ5457	75	HDZ5475
3	HDZ5403	22	HDZ5422	40	HDZ5440	58	HDZ5458	76	HDZ5476
4	HDZ5404	23	HDZ5423	41	HDZ5441	59	HDZ5459	77	HDZ5477
5	HDZ5405	24	HDZ5424	42	HDZ5442	60	HDZ5460	78	HDZ5478
6	HDZ5406	25	HDZ5425	43	HDZ5443	61	HDZ5461	79	HDZ5479
7	HDZ5407	26	HDZ5426	44	HDZ5444	62	HDZ5462	80	HDZ5480
8	HDZ5408	27	HDZ5427	45	HDZ5445	63	HDZ5463	81	HDZ5481
9	HDZ5409	28w	HDZ5428	46	HDZ5446	64	HDZ5464	82	HDZ5482
10	HDZ5410	29	HDZ5429	47	HDZ5447	65	HDZ5465	83	HDZ5483
11	HDZ5411	30	HDZ5430	48	HDZ5448	66	HDZ5466	84	HDZ5484
13	HDZ5413	31	HDZ5431	49	HDZ5449	67	HDZ5467	85	HDZ5485
14	HDZ5414	32	HDZ5432	50	HDZ5450	68	HDZ5468	86a	HDZ5486
15	HDZ5415	33	HDZ5433	51	HDZ5451	69	HDZ5469	87a	HDZ5487
16	HDZ5416	34	HDZ5434	52	HDZ5452	70	HDZ5470	88a	HDZ5488
17	HDZ5417	35	HDZ5435	53	HDZ5453	71	HDZ5471	89a	HDZ5489
18	HDZ5418	36	HDZ5436	54	HDZ5454	72	HDZ5472	90a	HDZ5490
19	HDZ5419	37	HDZ5437	55	HDZ5455	73	HDZ5473		

Previous registrations
VLT31	F903CMS, F701XMS
292CLT	FCA9X
503CLT	GUW503W
809DYE	D105NDW
810DYE	D106NDW
811DYE	D111NDW

Named vehicle
RMC1492 *Ruby*

LEASIDE

All vehicles acquired from London Buses Ltd in September 1994 unless otherwise stated

DMS681	MLK681L	Daimler Fleetline CRL6	Park Royal	H44/24D	1973	
DMS1868	GHM868N	Daimler Fleetline CRL6	MCW	H44/24D	1975	
DMS2291	THX291S	Leyland Fleetline FE30ALRSp	MCW	O44/28D	1977	

DRL38-52

Dennis Dart 9SDL3016   Plaxton Pointer   B34F+16   1992

38	K538ORH	41	K541ORH	44	K544ORH	47	K547ORH	50	K550ORH
39	K539ORH	42	K542ORH	45	K545ORH	48	K548ORH	51	K551ORH
40	K540ORH	43	K543ORH	46	K546ORH	49	K549ORH	52	K552ORH

L315-354

Leyland Olympian ON2R50C13Z4   Alexander RH   H43/25D   1992

315	J315BSH	323	J323BSH	331	J331BSH	339	J339BSH	347	J347BSH
316	J316BSH	324	J324BSH	332	J332BSH	340	J340BSH	348	J348BSH
317	J317BSH	325	J325BSH	333	J433BSH	341	J341BSH	349	J349BSH
318	J318BSH	326	J326BSH	334	J334BSH	342	J342BSH	350	J350BSH
319	J319BSH	327	J327BSH	335	J335BSH	343	J343BSH	351	J351BSH
320	J320BSH	328	J328BSH	336	J336BSH	344	J344BSH	352	J352BSH
321	J321BSH	329	J329BSH	337	J337BSH	345	J345BSH	353	J353BSH
322	J322BSH	330	J330BSH	338	J338BSH	346	J346BSH	354	VLT32

LP5	185CLT	Leyland Leopard PSU3E/4R	Plaxton Supreme Express	C49F	1979
LP6	205CLT	Leyland Leopard PSU3E/4R	Plaxton Supreme Express	C49F	1979

M266-500

MCW Metrobus DR101/12   MCW   H43/28D   1980

266	BYX266V	382t	GYE382W	445t	GYE445W	478t	GYE478W
317	EYE317V	419	GYE419W	450t	GYE450W	485	GYE485W
336	EYE336V	422t	GYE422W	464	GYE464W	493	GYE493W
353	GYE353W	426t	GYE426W	474	GYE474W	500	GYE500W

M507-798

MCW Metrobus DR101/14   MCW   H43/28D   1981-1982

507	GYE507W	591	GYE591W	649	KYV649X	710	KYV710X	754	KYV754X
508	GYE508W	593	GYE593W	650	KYV650X	711	KYV711X	756	KYV756X
509	GYE509W	596	GYE596W	651	KYV651X	712	KYV712X	757	KYV757X
510	GYE510W	600	GYE600W	652	KYV652X	713	KYV713X	758	KYV758X
518	GYE518W	602	GYE602W	653	KYV653X	714	KYV714X	761	KYV761X
519	GYE519W	603	GYE603W	657	KYV657X	715	KYV715X	762	KYV762X
522	GYE522W	604	GYE604W	658	KYV658X	716	KYV716X	765	KYV765X
525	GYE525W	605	GYE605W	659	KYV659X	717	KYV717X	766	KYV766X
528	GYE528W	609	KYO609X	660	KYV660X	718	KYV718X	767	KYV767X
529	GYE529W	610	KYO610X	661	KYV661X	719	KYV719X	768	KYV768X
530	GYE530W	611	KYO611X	663	KYV663X	720	KYV720X	770	KYV770X
531	GYE531W	612	KYO612X	664	KYV664X	721	KYV721X	771	KYV771X
533	GYE533W	613	KYO613X	665	KYV665X	723	KYV723X	772	KYV772X
534	GYE534W	614	KYO614X	666	KYV666X	726	KYV726X	773	KYV773X
535	GYE535W	615	KYO615X	669	KYV669X	727	KYV727X	774	KYV774X
536	GYE536W	617	KYO617X	672	KYV672X	728	KYV728X	775	KYV775X
538	GYE538W	619	KYO619X	673	KYV673X	729	KYV729X	776	KYV776X
540	GYE540W	622	KYO622X	675	KYV675X	730	KYV730X	777	KYV777X
543	GYE543W	624	KYO624X	676	KYV676X	731	KYV731X	778	KYV778X
544	GYE544W	625	KYO625X	679	KYV679X	732	KYV732X	780	KYV780X
545	GYE545W	626	KYO626X	681	KYV681X	733	KYV733X	781	KYV781X
547	GYE547W	627	KYO627X	684	KYV684X	734	KYV734X	782	KYV782X
548	GYE548W	628	KYO628X	686	KYV686X	736	KYV736X	783	KYV783X
549	GYE549W	630	KYO630X	688	KYV688X	737	KYV737X	784	KYV784X
551	GYE551W	631	KYO631X	689	KYV689X	738	KYV738X	785	KYV785X
557	GYE557W	632	KYO632X	692	KYV692X	740	KYV740X	786	KYV786X
559	GYE559W	635	KYV635X	694	KYV694X	742	KYV742X	787	KYV787X
562	GYE562W	636	KYV636X	698	KYV698X	743	KYV743X	788	KYV788X
567	GYE567W	637	KYV637X	699	KYV699X	744	KYV744X	789	KYV789X
569	GYE569W	638	KYV638X	700	KYV700X	745	KYV745X	790	KYV790X
573	GYE573W	641	KYV641X	701	KYV701X	746	KYV746X	791	KYV791X
575	GYE575W	642	KYV642X	702	KYV702X	747	KYV747X	792	KYV792X
581	GYE581W	643	KYV643X	703	KYV703X	748	KYV748X	793	KYV793X
582	GYE582W	644	KYV644X	704	KYV704X	749	KYV749X	795	KYV795X
585	GYE585W	645	KYV645X	705	KYV705X	750	KYV750X	796	KYV796X
586	GYE586W	646	KYV646X	707	KYV707X	751	KYV751X	798	KYV798X
587	GYE587W	647	KYV647X	708	KYV708X	752	KYV752X		
590	GYE590W	648	KYV648X	709	KYV709X	753	KYV753X		

M891	OJD891Y	MCW Metrobus DR101/16	MCW	H43/28D	1983	
M903	A903SUL	MCW Metrobus DR101/16	MCW	H43/28D	1983	
M919	A919SUL	MCW Metrobus DR101/16	MCW	H43/28D	1983	
M929	A929SUL	MCW Metrobus DR101/16	MCW	H43/28D	1983	
M939	A939SUL	MCW Metrobus DR101/16	MCW	H43/28D	1983	

M988-1437   MCW Metrobus DR101/17   MCW   H43/28D   1984-1986

* DR101/19
a DPH43/28D
b DPH43/24F

988	A988SYF	**1136**	B136WUL	**1219**	B219WUL	**1285**	B285WUL	**1318**	C318BUV
996	A996SYF	**1137**	B137WUL	**1221**	B221WUL	**1286**	B286WUL	**1319**	C319BUV
998	A998SYF	**1138**	B138WUL	**1227**	B227WUL	**1288**	B288WUL	**1320**	C320BUV
1000	A700THV	**1139**	B139WUL	**1228**	B228WUL	**1289**	B289WUL	**1321**	C321BUV
1044*	A744THV	**1140**	B140WUL	**1229**	B229WUL	**1290**	B290WUL	**1322**	C322BUV
1070	B70WUL	**1152**	B152WUL	**1231**	B231WUL	**1291**	B291WUL	**1323**	C323BUV
1074	B74WUL	**1154**	B154WUL	**1233**	B233WUL	**1293**	B293WUL	**1324**	C324BUV
1075	B75WUL	**1155**	B155WUL	**1239**	B239WUL	**1294**	B294WUL	**1326**	C326BUV
1109	B109WUL	**1162**	B162WUL	**1248**	B248WUL	**1295**	B295WUL	**1327**	C327BUV
1112	B112WUL	**1164**	B164WUL	**1249**	B249WUL	**1296**	B296WUL	**1332**	C332BUV
1121	B121WUL	**1165**	B165WUL	**1252**	B252WUL	**1297**	B297WUL	**1362**	C362BUV
1122	B122WUL	**1169**	B169WUL	**1253**	B253WUL	**1298**	B298WUL	**1367a**	C367BUV
1123	B123WUL	**1170**	B170WUL	**1254**	B254WUL	**1299**	B299WUL	**1379a**	VLT88
1124	B124WUL	**1173**	B173WUL	**1255**	B255WUL	**1300**	B300WUL	**1398**	C398BUV
1126	B126WUL	**1175**	B175WUL	**1263**	B263WUL	**1303**	B303WUL	**1399**	C399BUV
1127	B127WUL	**1176**	B176WUL	**1265**	B265WUL	**1307**	C307BUV	**1401**	C401BUV
1128	B128WUL	**1179**	B179WUL	**1275**	B275WUL	**1308**	C308BUV	**1402**	C402BUV
1129	B129WUL	**1182**	B182WUL	**1276**	B276WUL	**1309**	C309BUV	**1404**	C404BUV
1130	B130WUL	**1209**	B209WUL	**1278**	B278WUL	**1310**	C310BUV	**1405**	C405BUV
1131	B131WUL	**1210**	B210WUL	**1279**	B279WUL	**1312**	C312BUV	**1406**	C406BUV
1132	B132WUL	**1213**	B213WUL	**1280**	B280WUL	**1313**	C313BUV	**1413**	C413BUV
1133	B133WUL	**1214**	B214WUL	**1281**	B281WUL	**1314**	C314BUV	**1417**	C417BUV
1134	B134WUL	**1216**	B216WUL	**1282**	B282WUL	**1316**	C316BUV	**1424**	C424BUV
1135	B135WUL	**1217**	B217WUL	**1283**	B283WUL	**1317**	C317BUV	**1437b**	VLT12

M1443	GBU1V	MCW Metrobus DR101/6	MCW	H43/30F	1979	
M1444	GBU4V	MCW Metrobus DR101/6	MCW	H43/30F	1979	
M1445	GBU5V	MCW Metrobus DR101/6	MCW	H43/30F	1979	
M1446	GBU8V	MCW Metrobus DR101/6	MCW	H43/30F	1979	
M1447	GBU9V	MCW Metrobus DR101/6	MCW	H43/30F	1979	

MR102	F102YVP	MCW MetroRider MF150/115	MCW	B23F	1988
MR104	F104YVP	MCW MetroRider MF150/116	MCW	DP23F	1988
MR105	F105YVP	MCW MetroRider MF150/116	MCW	DP23F	1988

RM5	VLT5	AEC Routemaster 5RM	Park Royal	H36/28R	1959
RMC1453u	453CLT	AEC Routemaster 6RM	Park Royal	H32/25RD	1962

RML882-2758   AEC Routemaster 7RM   Park Royal   H40/32R   1961-1968   Cummins engines

882	WLT882	**2329**	CUV329C	**2406**	JJD406D	**2534**	JJD534D	**2655**	NML655E
884	WLT884	**2330**	CUV330C	**2408**	JJD408D	**2544**	JJD544D	**2658**	SMK658F
888	WLT888	**2334**	CUV334C	**2409**	JJD409D	**2546**	JJD546D	**2660**	SMK660F
896	WLT896	**2340**	CUV340C	**2416**	JJD416D	**2552**	JJD552D	**2666**	SMK666F
897	WLT897	**2344**	CUV344C	**2418**	JJD418D	**2562**	JJD562D	**2675**	SMK675F
901	WLT901	**2346**	CUV346C	**2434**	JJD434D	**2567**	JJD567D	**2678**	SMK678F
2261	CUV261C	**2350**	CUV350C	**2457**	JJD457D	**2571**	JJD571D	**2682**	SMK682F
2267	CUV267C	**2354**	CUV354C	**2460**	JJD460D	**2588**	JJD588D	**2684**	SMK684F
2277	CUV277C	**2355**	CUV355C	**2468**	JJD468D	**2589**	JJD589D	**2685**	SMK685F
2280	CUV280C	**2356**	CUV356C	**2483**	JJD483D	**2595**	JJD595D	**2688**	SMK688F
2287	CUV287C	**2359**	CUV359C	**2492**	JJD492D	**2597**	JJD597D	**2708**	SMK708F
2292	CUV292C	**2370**	JJD370D	**2494**	JJD494D	**2611**	NML611E	**2716**	SMK716F
2294	CUV294C	**2372**	JJD372D	**2503**	JJD503D	**2617**	NML617E	**2742**	SMK742F
2304	CUV304C	**2373**	JJD373D	**2504**	JJD504D	**2625**	NML625E	**2746**	SMK746F
2315	CUV315C	**2380**	JJD380D	**2510**	JJD510D	**2628**	NML628E	**2747**	SMK747F
2323	CUV323C	**2386**	JJD386D	**2518**	JJD518D	**2632**	NML632E	**2750**	SMK750F
2325	CUV325C	**2391**	JJD391D	**2525**	JJD525D	**2635**	NML635E	**2754**	SMK754F
2326	CUV326C	**2394**	JJD394D	**2526**	JJD526D	**2638**	NML638E	**2758**	SMK758F
2328	CUV328C	**2401**	JJD401D	**2528**	JJD528D	**2643**	NML643E		

RV1	GJG750D	AEC Regent V 2D3RA		Park Royal	H40/32F	1966		

SLW1-14   Scania N113CRL   Wright Pathfinder 320   B37D   1994

1	RDZ1701	4	RDZ1704	7	RDZ1707	10	RDZ1710	13	RDZ1713
2	RDZ1702	5	RDZ1705	8	RDZ1708	11	RDZ1711	14	RDZ1714
3	RDZ1703	6	RDZ1706	9	RDZ1709	12	RDZ1712		

SR33-40   Mercedes-Benz 811D   Optare StarRider   B26F   1988-1989

33	F33CWY	35	F35CWY	37	F37CWY	40	F40CWY
34	F34CWY	36	F36CWY	38	F38CWY		

T69	70CLT	Leyland Titan TNLXB2RRSp	Park Royal	O44/26D	1979
T83	CUL83V	Leyland Titan TNLXB2RRSp	Park Royal	H44/26D	1979
T85	CUL85V	Leyland Titan TNLXB2RRSp	Park Royal	H44/26D	1979
T95	CUL95V	Leyland Titan TNLXB2RRSp	Park Royal	H44/26D	1979
T100	CUL100V	Leyland Titan TNLXB2RRSp	Park Royal	H44/26D	1979

TPL1	G661WMD	Leyland Tiger TRCTL11/3ARZM	Plaxton Paramount 3200 3	C53F	1989
TPL2	G662WMD	Leyland Tiger TRCTL11/3ARZM	Plaxton Paramount 3200 3	C53F	1989
TPL8	H643GRO	Leyland Tiger TRCL10/3ARZA	Plaxton Paramount 3200 3	C53F	1991

Previous registrations

VLT12	C437BUV
VLT32	J354BSH
VLT88	C379BUV
70CLT	CUL69V
185CLT	JVF815V
205CLT	JVF816V

Named vehicles
M1367 *Senator,* M1398 *Ambassador,* RV1 *Harvey*

Special liveries
Middlesex University: M336/53, M1443-7
Overall Advertisements: M422/45

LONDON CENTRAL

All vehicles acquired from London Buses Ltd in October 1994 unless otherwise stated

AV1-9

Volvo Olympian — Alexander RH — H45/29F — 1995 — New to London Central

1	M81MYM	3	M83MYM	5	M85MYM	7	M87MYM	9	M89MYM
2	M82MYM	4	M84MYM	6	M86MYM	8	M91MYM		

DEL1-11

Dennis Dart 9SDL3034 — East Lancs EL2000 — B34F — 1994

1	L901JRN	4	L904JRN	7	L907JRN	10	L910JRN
2	L902JRN	5	L905JRN	8	L908JRN	11	L911JRN
3	L903JRN	6	L906JRN	9	L909JRN		

DRL1-16

Dennis Dart 9SDL3011 — Plaxton Pointer — B34F — 1991

1	J601XHL	5	J605XHL	9	J609XHL	13	J613XHL
2	J602XHL	6	J606XHL	10	J610XHL	14	J614XHL
3	J603XHL	7	J607XHL	11	J611XHL	15	J615XHL
4	J604XHL	8	J608XHL	12	J612XHL	16	J616XHL

L34-261

Leyland Olympian ONLXB/1RH — Eastern Coach Works — H42/26D — 1986-1987 — a DPH42/26D

34	C34CHM	84	C84CHM	89	C89CHM	95	VLT29	101	C101CHM
39	C39CHM	85	C85CHM	90	C90CHM	96	C96CHM	138	WLT838
40	C40CHM	88	C88CHM	93	C93CHM	100	C100CHM	261a	2CLT

MR57	E633KYW	MCW MetroRider MF150/46	MCW	B25F	1987
MR99	F99YVP	MCW MetroRider MF150/115	MCW	B23F	1988
MR100	F100YVP	MCW MetroRider MF150/115	MCW	B23F	1988
MR103	F103YVP	MCW MetroRider MF150/115	MCW	B23F	1988

MRL136-241

Optare MetroRider MR03 — Optare — B26F — 1990/1991/1993

136	H136UUA	156	H156UUA	226	K426HWY	232	K432HWY	238	K438HWY
137	H137UUA	157	H157UUA	227	K427HWY	233	K433HWY	239	K439HWY
138	H138UUA	158	H158UUA	228	K428HWY	234	K434HWY	240	K440HWY
139	H139UUA	159	H159UUA	229	K429HWY	235	K435HWY	241	K441HWY
140	H140UUA	224	K424HWY	230	K430HWY	236	K436HWY		
155	H155UUA	225	K425HWY	231	K431HWY	237	K437HWY		

MTL1	G621XLO	Mercedes-Benz 811D	Reeve Burgess Beaver	B29F	1989
MTL2	G222KWE	Mercedes-Benz 811D	Reeve Burgess Beaver	B26F	1989
MTL3	H189RWF	Mercedes-Benz 811D	Reeve Burgess Beaver	B29F	1990
MTL4	H191RWF	Mercedes-Benz 811D	Reeve Burgess Beaver	B29F	1990

NV1-10

Volvo Olympian — Northern Counties Countybus Palatine — H47/30F — 1995 — New to London Central

1	M401RVU	3	M403RVU	5	M405RVU	7	M407RVU	9	M409RVU
2	M402RVU	4	M404RVU	6	M406RVU	8	M408RVU	10	M410RVU

RM9-2151

AEC Routemaster 5RM — Park Royal — H36/28R — 1959-1965

9	OYM374A	782	WLT782	1058	58CLT	1305	305CLT	2022	ALM22B
71t	VLT71	787	WLT787	1062	62CLT	1380	380CLT	2051	ALM51B
202	VLT202	789	WLT789	1082	82CLT	1400	400CLT	2106	CUV106C
436	WLT436	815	WLT815	1097	97CLT	1621	KGJ187A	2109	CUV109C
478	WLT478	868	WLT868	1104	104CLT	1666	666DYE	2128	CUV128C
527	WLT527	872	WLT872	1119	119CLT	1797	797DYE	2151	CUV151C
541	WLT541	928	WLT928	1168	168CLT	1955	ALD955B		
687	WLT687	967	WLT967	1174	174CLT	1962	ALD962B		
688	WLT688	1002	OYM368A	1176	176CLT	1977	ALD977B		
758	WLT758	1033	33CLT	1260	260CLT	1980	ALD980B		

RML883-2733 AEC Routemaster 7RM   Park Royal   H40/32R   1961-1967   Cummins engines

883	WLT883	2332	CUV332C	2440	JJD440D	2551	JJD551D	2614	NML614E
2270	CUV270C	2335	CUV335C	2454	JJD454D	2554	JJD554D	2629	NML629E
2271	CUV271C	2336	CUV336C	2469	JJD469D	2556	JJD556D	2630	NML630E
2273	CUV273C	2338	CUV338C	2474	JJD474D	2560	JJD560D	2673	SMK673F
2275	CUV275C	2339	CUV339C	2482	JJD482D	2578	JJD578D	2676	SMK676F
2276	CUV276C	2345	CUV345C	2484	JJD484D	2583	JJD583D	2683	SMK683F
2279	CUV279C	2362	CUV362C	2499	JJD499D	2584	JJD584D	2711	SMK711F
2283	CUV283C	2381	JJD381D	2507	JJD507D	2587	JJD587D	2712	SMK712F
2302	CUV302C	2396	JJD396D	2513	JJD513D	2596	JJD596D	2714	SMK714F
2314	CUV314C	2397	JJD397D	2515	JJD515D	2601	NML601E	2733	SMK733F
2318	CUV318C	2400	JJD400D	2529	JJD529D	2604	NML604E		
2327	CUV327C	2411	JJD411D	2539	JJD539D	2613	NML613E		

SP1-25   DAF DB250WB505   Optare Spectra   H44/27F   1992-1993

1	K301FYG	7	K307FYG	12	K312FYG	17	170CLT	22	K322FYG
3	K303FYG	8	K308FYG	13	K313FYG	18	18CLT	23	K323FYG
4	K304FYG	9	K309FYG	14	K314FYG	19	19CLT	24	K324FYG
5	K305FYG	10	K310FYG	15	K315FYG	20	20CLT	25	WLT825
6	K306FYG	11	K311FYG	16	K316FYG	21	K321FYG		

SR11-123   Mercedes-Benz 811D   Optare StarRider   B26F   1988-1990

11	F911YWY	23	F923YWY	29	F29CWY	45	F45CWY	53	F53CWY
14	F914YWY	24	F924YWY	30	F30CWY	47	F47CWY	62	F162FWY
16	F916YWY	25	F925YWY	31	F31CWY	48	F48CWY	63	F163FWY
19	F919YWY	26	F926YWY	41	F41CWY	49	F49CWY	64	F164FWY
21	F921YWY	27	F927YWY	42	F42CWY	51	F51CWY	122	G122SMV
22	F922YWY	28	F928YWY	43	F43CWY	52	F52CWY	123	G123SMV

T75-227   Leyland Titan TNLXB2RRSp   Park Royal   H44/26D   1979-1980   a H44/24D

75t	CUL75V	164t	CUL164V	173t	CUL173V	186	CUL186V	227a	EYE227V
76	CUL76V	172t	CUL172V	185	CUL185V	191t	CUL191V		

T274-798   Leyland Titan TNLXB2RR   Leyland   H44/24D   1981-1983   a H44/26D

274	GYE274W	384	KYV384X	707	OHV707Y	742	OHV742Y	776	OHV776Y
275a	GYE275W	396	KYV396X	709	OHV709Y	747	OHV747Y	778	OHV778Y
292	KYN292X	507	KYV507X	712	OHV712Y	750	OHV750Y	779	OHV779Y
294	KYN294X	676	OHV676Y	713	OHV713Y	752	OHV752Y	781	OHV781Y
297	KYN297X	677	OHV677Y	715	OHV715Y	755	OHV755Y	782	OHV782Y
310	KYN310X	678	OHV678Y	716	OHV716Y	756	OHV756Y	786	OHV786Y
312	KYV312X	679	OHV679Y	717	OHV717Y	757	OHV757Y	787	OHV787Y
314t	KYV314X	681	OHV681Y	718	OHV718Y	760	OHV760Y	788	OHV788Y
323	KYV323X	683	OHV683Y	720	OHV720Y	763	OHV763Y	790	OHV790Y
325t	KYV325X	685	OHV685Y	722	OHV722Y	764	OHV764Y	792	OHV792Y
327	KYV327X	687	OHV687Y	723	OHV723Y	765	OHV765Y	793	OHV793Y
329	KYV329X	693	OHV693Y	725	OHV725Y	766	OHV766Y	794	OHV794Y
336	KYV336X	694	OHV694Y	732	OHV732Y	767	OHV767Y	795	OHV795Y
352	KYV352X	696	OHV696Y	735	WLT735	768	OHV768Y	796	OHV796Y
356	KYV356X	701	OHV701Y	736	WLT736	773	OHV773Y	798	OHV798Y
362	KYV362X	704	OHV704Y	737	OHV737Y	774	OHV774Y		
369t	KYV369X	705	OHV705Y	739	OHV739Y	775	OHV775Y		

T799-1123   Leyland Titan TNLXB2RR   Leyland   H44/26D   1983-1984   a O44/26D

799	OHV799Y	913	A913SYE	962	A962SYE	1005	A605THV	1058	A58THX
803a	OHV803Y	914	A914SYE	963	A963SYE	1006	A606THV	1059	A59THX
806	OHV806Y	915	A915SYE	964	A964SYE	1008	A608THV	1060	A60THX
808	OHV808Y	916	A916SYE	966	A966SYE	1009	A609THV	1061	A61THX
811	OHV811Y	917	A917SYE	967	A967SYE	1010	A610THV	1062	A62THX
831	A831SUL	919	A919SYE	968	A968SYE	1011	A611THV	1063	A63THX
835	A835SUL	920	A920SYE	969	A969SYE	1012	A612THV	1064	A64THX
839	A839SUL	923	A923SYE	970	A970SYE	1014	A614THV	1068	A68THX
844	A844SUL	924	A924SYE	972	A972SYE	1015	A615THV	1070	A70THX
851	A851SUL	927	A927SYE	973	A973SYE	1016	A616THV	1071	A71THX
852	A852SUL	928	A928SYE	974	A974SYE	1017	A617THV	1072	A72THX
853	A853SUL	929	A929SYE	975	A975SYE	1018	A618THV	1073	A73THX
863	A863SUL	930	A930SYE	977	A977SYE	1019	A619THV	1074	A74THX
864	A864SUL	931	A931SYE	979	A979SYE	1020	A620THV	1075	A75THX
870	A870SUL	932	A932SYE	980	A980SYE	1021	A621THV	1078	A78THX
871	A871SUL	933	A933SYE	981	A981SYE	1023	A623THV	1080	B80WUV
875	A875SUL	936	A936SYE	982	A982SYE	1024	A624THV	1082	B82WUV
886	A886SYE	937	A937SYE	983	A983SYE	1033	A633THV	1085	B85WUV
887	A887SYE	938	A938SYE	984	A984SYE	1037	A637THV	1086	B86WUV
888	A888SYE	939	A939SYE	985	A985SYE	1038	A638THV	1087	B87WUV
889	A889SYE	940	A940SYE	986	A986SYE	1040	A640THV	1088	B88WUV
890	A890SYE	941	A941SYE	987	A987SYE	1041	A641THV	1090	B90WUV
891	A891SYE	942	A942SYE	989	A989SYE	1042	A642THV	1094	B94WUV
892	A892SYE	943	A943SYE	990	WLT990	1043	A643THV	1095	B95WUV
893	A893SYE	946	A946SYE	991	A991SYE	1044	A644THV	1098	B98WUV
894	A894SYE	947	A947SYE	992	A992SYE	1046	A646THV	1102	B102WUV
895	A895SYE	948	A948SYE	993	A993SYE	1047	A647THV	1104	B104WUV
897	A897SYE	952	A952SYE	994	A994SYE	1049	A649THV	1105	B105WUV
898	A898SYE	954	A954SYE	995	A995SYE	1051	A651THV	1107	B107WUV
901	A901SYE	955	A955SYE	997	A997SYE	1053	A653THV	1109	B109WUV
906	A906SYE	956	A956SYE	1000	ALM1B	1054	A654THV	1111	B111WUV
907	A907SYE	957	A957SYE	1001	A601THV	1055	A655THV	1120	B120WUV
908	A908SYE	958	A958SYE	1002	A602THV	1056	A56THX	1123	B123WUV
909	A909SYE	959	A959SYE	1004	A604THV	1057	257CLT		

T1129   WDA4T   Leyland Titan TNLXB1RF   Park Royal   DPH43/29F   1979

TPL10   PCN762   Leyland Tiger TRCTL11/3RH   Plaxton Paramount 3500 2   C49FT   1986   Ex Northern National, 1995

Previous registrations

ALM1B	A600THV
KGJ187A	621DYE
OYM368A	2CLT
OYM374A	VLT9
PCN762	C377PCD
VLT29	C95CHM
WLT735	OHV735Y
WLT736	OHV736Y
WLT825	K325FYG
WLT838	C138CHM
WLT990	A990WYE
2CLT	D261FUL
170CLT	K317FYG
257CLT	A57THX

Named vehicles

DRL1 *Del Boy*, DRL2 *Rodney*, DRL3 *Uncle Albert*, DRL4 *Cassandra*, L93 *Hawk*, L95 *Jaguar*, L261 *Buccaneer*, T803 *Albatross*, T1129 *Harrier*

LONDON GENERAL

All vehicles acquired from London Buses Ltd in November 1994

DMS2257t	OJD257R	Leyland Fleetline FE30ALRSp	MCW	H44/24D	1977
DMS2283t	THX283S	Leyland Fleetline FE30ALRSp	MCW	H44/24D	1977
DMS2290t	THX290S	Leyland Fleetline FE30ALRSp	MCW	H44/24D	1977
DMS2304t	THX304S	Leyland Fleetline FE30ALRSp	MCW	H44/24D	1978

DMS2347-2499
Leyland Fleetline FE30ALRSp   Park Royal   H44/24D   1977
These DMS vehicles all carry the unofficial class code DMT

2347t	OJD347R	2367t	OJD367R	2397t	OJD397R	2476t	THX476S
2351t	OJD351R	2384t	OJD384R	2413t	OJD413R	2489t	THX489S

DPL1-16
Dennis Dart 9.8   Plaxton Pointer   B35F   1995

1	M201EGF	5	M205EGF	9	M209EGF	13	M213EGF
2	M202EGF	6	M206EGF	10	M210EGF	14	M214EGF
3	M203EGF	7	M207EGF	11	M211EGF	15	M215EGF
4	M204EGF	8	M208EGF	12	M212EGF	16	M216EGF

DR32-153
Dennis Dart 8.5SDL3003   Plaxton Pointer   B28F   1991/1992   * 8.5SDL3015

32	WLT532	37	H537XGK	44	H544XGK	49	H549XGK	150*	K150LGO
33	H533XGK	38	H538XGK	45	H545XGK	50	H550XGK	151*	K151LGO
34	H534XGK	39	H539XGK	46	46CLT	51	H551XGK	152*	K152LGO
35	H835XGK	41	H541XGK	47	H547XGK	52	H552XGK	153*	K153LGO
36	H536XGK	43	H543XGK	48	H548XGK	149*	K149LGO		

DRL53-73
Dennis Dart 9SDL3016   Plaxton Pointer   B34F+16   1992

53	K853LGN	58	K858LGN	63	K863LGN	68	K868LGN	73	K873LGN
54	K854LGN	59	K859LGN	64	K864LGN	69	K869LGN		
55	K855LGN	60	K860LGN	65	K865LGN	70	K870LGN		
56	K856LGN	61	K861LGN	66	K866LGN	71	K871LGN		
57	K857LGN	62	K862LGN	67	K867LGN	72	K872LGN		

DRL74-95
Dennis Dart 9SDL3024   Plaxton Pointer   B32F   1993

74	K574MGT	79	K579MGT	84	K584MGT	89	K589MGT	94	WLT994
75	K575MGT	80	K580MGT	85	K585MGT	90	K590MGT	95	WLT395
76	K576MGT	81	K581MGT	86	K586MGT	91	K591MGT		
77	K577MGT	82	K582MGT	87	K587MGT	92	K592MGT		
78	K578MGT	83	K583MGT	88	K588MGT	93	K593MGT		

DW44-58
Dennis Dart 8.5SDL3003   Wright Handybus   B30F   1990-1991

44	JDZ2344	47	WLT470	50	JDZ2350	53	JDZ2353	56	JDZ2356
45	545CLT	48	WLT548	51	JDZ2351	54	JDZ2354	57	JDZ2357
46	WLT346	49	JDZ2349	52	352CLT	55	JDZ2355	58	JDZ2358

DW66-161
Dennis Dart 8.5SDL3015   Wright Handybus   B29F   1991/1992/1993   * 8.5SDL3003

66*	166CLT	69*	H369XGC	128	K128LGO	131	K131LGO	161	NDZ3161
67*	H367XGC	70*	H370XGC	129	K129LGO	132	K132LGO		
68*	H368XGC	127	K127LGO	130	K130LGO	160	NDZ3160		

GLS1-506
Leyland National 2 NL106AL11/2R   East Lancs Greenway   B24D+46   1981   Rebuilt 1992-1994   a B38D

1	GUW466W	450	GUW450W	471	GUW471W	483	83CLT	499	WLT599
438	GUW438W	452	GUW452W	473	GUW473W	486a	186CLT	500	GUW500W
439	GUW439W	455	GUW455W	474	GUW474W	487	WLT487	501	GUW501W
440	GUW440W	459	GUW459W	476	GUW476W	490	GUW490W	502	GUW502W
442	GUW442W	460	GUW460W	477	GUW477W	491a	GUW491W	505a	GUW505W
443	WLT843	463	GUW463W	478	GUW478W	492	GUW492W	506	GUW506W
446	GUW446W	467	WLT467	479	GUW479W	493	GUW493W		
448a	WLT648	468	GUW468W	480	VLT180	496a	WLT696		
449	GUW449W	469	GUW469W	481	GUW481W	498	WLT598		

LS445	GUW445W	Leyland National 2 NL106AL11/2R	B24D+46	1981	Unrebuilt
LS453	GUW453W	Leyland National 2 NL106AL11/2R	B24D+46	1981	Unrebuilt
LS482	GUW482W	Leyland National 2 NL106AL11/2R	B24D+46	1981	Unrebuilt

M11-202

MCW Metrobus DR101/9* | MCW | H43/28D | 1978-1979 | * DR101/8 a O43/27F

11*	WYW11T	76	WYW76T	158	BYX158V	177	BYX177V	197	197CLT
45*	WYW45T	120	BYX120V	164	BYX164V	188	188CLT	198	VLT98
47*	WYW47T	141	BYX141V	165	BYX165V	190	BYX190V	201	BYX201V
55*	WYW55T	144	BYX144V	171a	BYX171V	191	BYX191V	202	BYX202V
56	WYW56T	153	BYX153V	174	BYX174V	192	BYX192V		
61	WYW61T	156	BYX156V	176	BYX176V	196	BYX196V		

M207-502

MCW Metrobus DR101/12 | MCW | H43/28D | 1980

207	BYX207V	247	BYX247V	278	78CLT	348	GYE348W	423	GYE423W
209	BYX209V	249	BYX249V	279	BYX279V	350	GYE350W	430	GYE430W
211	BYX211V	250	BYX250V	281	BYX281V	351	GYE351W	431	GYE431W
212	BYX212V	252	BYX252V	284	VLT284	352	GYE352W	433	GYE433W
214	BYX214V	254	BYX254V	286	BYX286V	354	GYE354W	435	GYE435W
215	BYX215V	255	BYX255V	287	BYX287V	355	GYE355W	447	GYE447W
216	BYX216V	256	BYX256V	288	BYX288V	357	GYE357W	457	GYE457W
217	BYX217V	257	BYX257V	289	BYX289V	359	GYE359W	463	WLT463
218	BYX218V	258	BYX258V	292	BYX292V	361	GYE361W	466	GYE466W
219	BYX219V	259	BYX259V	293	BYX293V	373	GYE373W	471	GYE471W
222	BYX222V	260	BYX260V	295	BYX295V	375	GYE375W	472	GYE472W
224	BYX224V	261	BYX261V	297	BYX297V	379	WLT379	475	GYE475W
226	BYX226V	262	BYX262V	302	BYX302V	381	GYE381W	476	GYE476W
228	BYX228V	265	BYX265V	303	BYX303V	385	GYE385W	477	GYE477W
231	BYX231V	267	BYX267V	307	BYX307V	386	GYE386W	479	VLT179
234	BYX234V	268	BYX268V	318	EYE318V	392	GYE392W	480	GYE480W
235	BYX235V	269	BYX269V	320	EYE320V	401	GYE401W	483	GYE483W
236	BYX236V	270	BYX270V	321	EYE321V	404	GYE404W	484	GYE484W
237	BYX237V	271	BYX271V	323	EYE323V	405	GYE405W	488	GYE488W
239	BYX239V	272	BYX272V	324	EYE324V	408	GYE408W	490	GYE490W
241	BYX241V	273	BYX273V	325	EYE325V	411	GYE411W	502	GYE502W
242	BYX242V	274	BYX274V	331	EYE331V	412	GYE412W		
244	BYX244V	275	BYX275V	333	EYE333V	416	GYE416W		
246	BYX246V	276	BYX276V	334	EYE334V	420	GYE420W		

M513-794

MCW Metrobus DR101/14 | MCW | H43/28D | 1981-1982

513	GYE513W	546	GYE546W	607	KYO607X	695	KYV695X	779	KYV779X
514	GYE514W	556	GYE556W	662	KYV662X	706	KYV706X	794	KYV794X
516	GYE516W	566	GYE566W	667	KYV667X	725	KYV725X		
527	GYE527W	589	GYE589W	668	KYV668X	760	KYV760X		
532	GYE532W	597	GYE597W	670	KYV670X	763	KYV763X		
542	542CLT	606	KYO606X	690	KYV690X	769	KYV769X		

M806-953

MCW Metrobus DR101/16 | MCW | H43/28D | 1983

806	OJD806Y	826	OJD826Y	852	OJD852Y	897	A897SUL	926	A926SUL
807	OJD807Y	828	OJD828Y	853	VLT53	900	A900SUL	931	A931SUL
808	OJD808Y	830	OJD830Y	854	OJD854Y	902	A902SUL	933	A933SUL
811	OJD811Y	833	OJD833Y	855	OJD855Y	904	A904SUL	940	A940SUL
812	OJD812Y	834	OJD834Y	862	OJD862Y	905	A905SUL	942	A942SUL
814	OJD814Y	837	OJD837Y	867	OJD867Y	907	A907SUL	944	A944SUL
816	OJD816Y	838	OJD838Y	868	OJD868Y	908	A908SUL	946	A946SUL
817	OJD817Y	842	OJD842Y	870	OJD870Y	909	A909SUL	947	A947SUL
818	OJD818Y	845	OGK708Y	871	OJD871Y	913	A913SUL	949	A949SUL
820	OJD820Y	846	OJD846Y	873	OJD873Y	914	A914SUL	953	A953SUL
821	OJD821Y	847	OJD847Y	877	OJD877Y	918	A918SUL		
822	OJD822Y	848	OJD848Y	880	OJD880Y	922	A922SUL		
823	OJD823Y	849	OJD849Y	888	OJD888Y	923	A923SUL		

M965-1440   MCW Metrobus DR101/17   MCW   H43/28D   1984-1986   * DR101/19   a DPH43/28D

965	A965SYF	1107	B107WUL	1225	B225WUL	1306	C306BUV	1388	C388BUV
970	A970SYF	1108	B108WUL	1226	B226WUL	1311	C311BUV	1389	89CLT
975	A975SYF	1177	B177WUL	1230	B230WUL	1315	C109NGH	1391	C391BUV
976	A976SYF	1180	B180WUL	1232	B232WUL	1337	C337BUV	1410	C410BUV
977	A977SYF	1196	B196WUL	1235	B235WUL	1347	C347BUV	1411	C411BUV
978	A978SYF	1203	B203WUL	1237	B237WUL	1357	C357BUV	1432a	WLT432
983	A983SYF	1206	B206WUL	1241	B241WUL	1364	C364BUV	1433	C433BUV
991	A991SYF	1211	B211WUL	1264	B264WUL	1370	C370BUV	1434	WLT434
992	A992SYF	1215	B215WUL	1268	B268WUL	1371	C371BUV	1435a	435CLT
1002	A702THV	1220	B220WUL	1301	B301WUL	1372	772DYE	1436	VLT136
1005	A705THV	1222	B222WUL	1302	B302WUL	1373	C373BUV	1440a	C440BUV
1046*	VLT46	1223	B223WUL	1304	304CLT	1386	C386BUV		
1055*	A755THV	1224	B224WUL	1305	B305WUL	1387	C387BUV		

MA108-134   Mercedes-Benz 811D   Alexander AM   B28F   1990/1991

108	G108PGT	114	G114PGT	120	G120PGT	126	H426XGK	132	H432XGK
109	G109PGT	115	G115PGT	121	G121PGT	127	H427XGK	133	H433XGK
110	G110PGT	116	G116PGT	122	G122PGT	128	H428XGK	134	H434XGK
111	G111PGT	117	G117PGT	123	G123PGT	129	H429XGK		
112	G112PGT	118	G118PGT	124	G124PGT	130	H430XGK		
113	G113PGT	119	G119PGT	125	H425XGK	131	H431XGK		

MRL135-223   Optare MetroRider MR03   Optare   B26F   1990/1991/1993

135	H135TGO	183	H683YGO	190	H690YGO	197	J697CGK	204	J704CGK
177	VLT277	184	H684YGO	191	J691CGK	198	698DYE	205	J705CGK
178	H678YGO	185	H685YGO	192	J692CGK	199	J699CGK	206	J706CGK
179	H679YGO	186	H686YGO	193	J693CGK	200	J710CGK	207	J707CGK
180	H680YGO	187	H687YGO	194	J694CGK	201	J701CGK	208	J708CGK
181	H681YGO	188	H688YGO	195	J695CGK	202	J702CGK	209	J709CGK
182	H682YGO	189	H689YGO	196	J696CGK	203	J703CGK	223	K223MGT

MT1	F391DHL	Mercedes-Benz 709D	Reeve Burgess Beaver B20FL	1988
MT2	F392DHL	Mercedes-Benz 709D	Reeve Burgess Beaver B20FL	1988
MT3	F393DHL	Mercedes-Benz 709D	Reeve Burgess Beaver B20FL	1988
MT5	F395DHL	Mercedes-Benz 709D	Reeve Burgess Beaver B20FL	1988

RM994	VLT89	AEC Routemaster 5RM	Park Royal H36/28R	1961	Iveco engine

RML887-2752   AEC Routemaster 7RM   Park Royal   H40/32R   1961-1968   Iveco engines
a H40/32RD (carries unofficial fleet number DRM2516)

887	WLT887	2360	CUV360C	2461	JJD461D	2570	JJD570D	2640	NML640E
889	WLT889	2361	CUV361C	2465	JJD465D	2575	JJD575D	2644	NML644E
894	WLT894	2363	CUV363C	2466	JJD466D	2576	JJD576D	2648	NML648E
899	WLT899	2364	JJD364D	2472	JJD472D	2580	JJD580D	2654	NML654E
2262	CUV262C	2371	JJD371D	2475	JJD475D	2590	JJD590D	2669	SMK669F
2263	CUV263C	2376	JJD376D	2502	JJD502D	2593	JJD593D	2680	SMK680F
2290	CUV290C	2385	JJD385D	2516a	WLT516	2605	NML605E	2693	SMK693F
2297	CUV297C	2389	JJD389D	2517	JJD517D	2606	NML606E	2725	SMK725F
2305	CUV305C	2398	JJD398D	2520	JJD520D	2612	NML612E	2732	SMK732F
2316	CUV316C	2403	JJD403D	2535	JJD535D	2615	NML615E	2736	SMK736F
2317	CUV317C	2412	JJD412D	2540	JJD540D	2618	NML618E	2745	SMK745F
2321	CUV321C	2422	JJD422D	2543	JJD543D	2626	NML626E	2752	SMK752F
2342	CUV342C	2441	JJD441D	2564	JJD564D	2631	NML631E		
2358	CUV358C	2453	JJD453D	2568	JJD568D	2637	NML637E		

SC1t	D585OOV	Freight Rover Sherpa	Carlyle Citybus	B6F	1987

VC1-39   Volvo B10M-50   Northern Counties   H47/35D   1989-1991   a DPH45/35D   b H45/35D

1a	101CLT	9	G109NGN	17	G117NGN	25	125CLT	33	G133PGK
2a	G102NGN	10	G110NGN	18	WLT818	26	G126NGN	34	G134PGK
3a	WLT803	11	WLT311	19	619DYE	27	G127NGN	35	G135PGK
4b	WLT474	12	312CLT	20	WLT920	28	528CLT	36	836DYE
5b	G105NGN	13	G113NGN	21	621DYE	29	229CLT	37	WLT837
6b	VLT60	14	614DYE	22	G122NGN	30	G130PGK	38	G138PGK
7	G107NGN	15	G115NGN	23	23CLT	31	G131PGK	39	839DYE
8	G108NGN	16	G116NGN	24	G124NGN	32	G132PGK		

VN1-13 Volvo B10B-58 Northern Counties Countybus Paladin B40D 1993

1	K100KLL	4	K4KLL	7	K70KLL	10	K10KLL	13	K13KLL
2	K2KLL	5	K5KLL	8	K8KLL	11	K11KLL		
3	K3KLL	6	K6KLL	9	K9KLL	12	K12KLL		

Previous registrations

C109NGH	VLT15, C315BUV	WLT818	G118NGN
OGK708Y	545CLT, OJD845Y	WLT837	G137PGK
VLT46	A746THV	WLT843	GUW443W
VLT53	OJD853Y	WLT920	G120NGN
VLT60	G106NGN	WLT994	K594MGT
VLT89	WLT994	23CLT	G123NGN
VLT98	BYX198V	46CLT	H546XGK
VLT136	C436BUV	78CLT	BYX278W
VLT179	GYE479W	83CLT	GUW483W
VLT180	GUW480W	89CLT	C389BUV
VLT277	H677YGO	101CLT	G101NGN
VLT284	BYX284V	125CLT	G125NGN
WLT311	G111NGN	166CLT	H366XGC
WLT346	JDZ2346	186CLT	GUW486W
WLT379	GYE379W	188CLT	BYX188V
WLT395	K595MGT	197CLT	BYX197V
WLT432	C432BUV	229CLT	G129PGK
WLT434	C434BUV	304CLT	B304WUL
WLT463	GYE463W	312CLT	G112NGN
WLT467	GUW467W	352CLT	JDZ2352
WLT470	JDZ2347	435CLT	C435BUV
WLT474	G104NGN	528CLT	G128PGK
WLT487	GUW487W	542CLT	GYE542W
WLT516	JJD516D	545CLT	JDZ2345
WLT532	H532XGK	614DYE	G114NGN
WLT548	JDZ2348	619DYE	G119NGN
WLT598	GUW498W	621DYE	G121NGN
WLT599	GUW499W	698DYE	J698CGK
WLT648	GUW448W	772DYE	C372BUV
WLT696	GUW496W	836DYE	G136PGK
WLT803	G103NGN	839DYE	J139DGF

Named vehicles
GLS438 *City of London*
M1440 *The General*

Special livery
London General livery: M1440

LONDON UNITED

All vehicles acquired from London Buses Ltd in November 1994

| **BL86tu** OJD86R | Bristol LH6L | | Eastern Coach Works | B39F | 1977 |

DR1-14

Dennis Dart 8.5SDL3003 — Reeve Burgess Pointer — B28F — 1991

1	H101THE	4	H104THE	7	H107THE	10	H110THE	13	H113THE
2	H102THE	5	H105THE	8	H108THE	11	WLT931	14	H114THE
3	H103THE	6	H106THE	9	H109THE	12	H112THE		

DR53-141

Dennis Dart 8.5SDL3010 — Plaxton Pointer — B24F — 1991-1992 — a B28F

53a	J653XHL	68	J368GKH	101	J101DUV	116	J116DUV	131	J131DUV
54a	J654XHL	69	J369GKH	102	J102DUV	117	J117DUV	132	J132DUV
55a	J655XHL	70	J370GKH	103	J103DUV	118	J118DUV	133	J133DUV
56a	J156GAT	71	J371GKH	104	J104DUV	119	J119DUV	134	J134DUV
57a	J157GAT	72	J372GKH	105	J105DUV	120	J120DUV	135	J135DUV
58	J158GAT	73	J373GKH	106	J106DUV	121	J121DUV	136	J136DUV
59	J159GAT	74	J374GKH	107	J107DUV	122	J122DUV	137	J137DUV
60	J160GAT	75	J375GKH	108	J108DUV	123	J123DUV	138	J138DUV
61	J161GAT	76	J376GKH	109	J109DUV	124	J124DUV	139	J139DUV
62	J362GKH	77	J377GKH	110	J110DUV	125	J125DUV	140	J140DUV
63	J363GKH	78	J378GKH	111	WLT946	126	J126DUV	141	J141DUV
64	J364GKH	79	J379GKH	112	J112DUV	127	J127DUV		
65	J365GKH	80	J380GKH	113	J113DUV	128	J128DUV		
66	J366GKH	99	J599DUV	114	J114DUV	129	J129DUV		
67	J367GKH	100	VLT23	115	J115DUV	130	J130DUV		

DRL96-108

Dennis Dart 9SDL3024 — Plaxton Pointer — B28F — 1993

96	K96SAG	99	K199SAG	102	K102SAG	105	K105SAG	108	K108SAG
97	K97SAG	100	ALM2B	103	K103SAG	106	K106SAG		
98	K98SAG	101	K101SAG	104	K104SAG	107	K107SAG		

DRL159-171

Dennis Dart 9SDL3034 — Plaxton Pointer — B28F — 1993 — a B34F

159	L159XRH	162	L162XRH	165a	L165YAT	168a	L168YAT	171	L171CKH
160	L160XRH	163	L163XRH	166a	L166YAT	169a	L169YAT		
161	L161XRH	164	L164XRH	167a	L167YAT	170	L170CKH		

DT1-27

Dennis Dart 8.5SDL3003 — Duple Dartline B28F — 1990

1	G501VYE	7	G507VYE	13	G513VYE	19	G519VYE	25	G525VYE
2	G502VYE	8	G508VYE	14	G514VYE	20	G520VYE	26	G526VYE
3	G503VYE	9	G509VYE	15	G515VYE	21	G521VYE	27	G527VYE
4	G504VYE	10	G510VYE	16	G516VYE	22	G522VYE		
5	G505VYE	11	G511VYE	17	G517VYE	23	G523VYE		
6	G506VYE	12	G512VYE	18	G518VYE	24	G524VYE		

DT29-167

Dennis Dart 8.5SDL3003 — Carlyle Dartline — B28F — 1990-1991

29	G29TGW	51	G51TGW	76	H76MOB	144	H144MOB	155	H155MOB
41	G41TGW	52	G52TGW	77	WLT339	145	H145MOB	158	H158NON
42	G42TGW	53	G53TGW	78	H78MOB	146	H146MOB	159	H159NON
43	G43TGW	54	G54TGW	79	H79MOB	147	H147MOB	160	H160NON
44	G44TGW	56	G56TGW	80	236CLT	148	H148MOB	161	H161NON
45	G45TGW	57	G57TGW	81	H81MOB	149	H149MOB	162	H162NON
46	G46TGW	71	H71MOB	82	H82MOB	150	H150MOB	163	H163NON
47	G47TGW	72	H72MOB	83	H83MOB	151	H151MOB	164	WLT804
48	G48TGW	73	H73MOB	84	H84MOB	152	H152MOB	165	H165NON
49	G49TGW	74	H74MOB	85	H85MOB	153	H153MOB	166	H166NON
50	G50TGW	75	WLT329	86	H86MOB	154	H154MOB	167	H167NON

| **DT168** 500CLT | Dennis Dart 8.5SDL3003 | | Duple Dartline | B28F | 1989 |

FR1-8

Iveco Daily 49-10 — Reeve Burgess Beaver — B20FL — 1990

1	H701YUV	3	H703YUV	5	H705YUV	7	H707YUV
2	H702YUV	4	H704YUV	6	H706YUV	8	H708YUV

L292-314 — Leyland Olympian ONCL10/1RZ — Leyland — H47/31F — 1989 — * ON2R50C13Z4 — a DPH43/29F

292	G292UYT	297	G297UYT	302	G302UYT	307*	G307UYT	312*a	G312UYT
293	G293UYT	298	G298UYT	303	G303UYT	308*	G308UYT	313*a	G313UYT
294	G294UYT	299	G299UYT	304	G304UYT	309*	G309UYT	314*a	G314UYT
295	G295UYT	300	G300UYT	305	G305UYT	310*	G310UYT		
296	G296UYT	301	G301UYT	306*	G306UYT	311*	G311UYT		

LLW1-10 — Dennis Lance SLF 11SDA3202 — Wright Pathfinder 320 — B34D — 1993-1994

1	ODZ8901	3	ODZ8903	5	ODZ8905	7	ODZ8907	9	ODZ8909
2	0DZ8902	4	ODZ8904	6	ODZ8906	8	ODZ8908	10	ODZ8910

LX3-8 — Leyland Lynx LX2R11C15Z4S — Leyland — B49F — 1989

3	G73UYV	5	G75UYV	7	G77UYV	
4	G74UYV	6	G76UYV	8	G78UYV	

M8-52 — MCW Metrobus DR101/8 — MCW — H43/28D — 1978-1979 — a H43/9D b H0/15D

8	WYW8T	19a	WYW19T	29	WYW29T	36bt	WYW36T	46bt	WYW46T
13bt	WYW13T	21	WYW21T	30bt	WYW30T	39	WYW39T	52	WYW52T
15	WYW15T	22bt	WYW22T	31bt	WYW31T	43a	WYW43T		
17	WYW17T	28	WYW28T	34	WYW34T	44	WYW44T		

M59-204 — MCW Metrobus DR101/9 — MCW — H43/28D — 1979 — a H43/9D b H0/15D

59	WYW59T	99	BYX99V	134	BYX134V	159	BYX159V	193	BYX193V
68	WYW68T	100	BYX100V	138	BYX138V	162a	BYX162V	195	BYX195V
86	WYW86T	110	BYX110V	146	BYX146V	179	BYX179V	203	BYX203V
89	WYW89T	112	BYX112V	147bt	BYX147V	183	BYX183V	204	BYX204V
93	WYW93T	122	BYX122V	154	BYX154V	186	BYX186V		
96a	BYX96V	131	BYX131V	157	BYX157V	187	BYX187V		

M206-462 — MCW Metrobus DR101/12 — MCW — H43/28D — 1980 — a H43/9D b H0/15D

206bt	BYX206V	227	BYX227V	363	GYE363W	415	GYE415W
221a	BYX221V	264bt	BYX264V	366	GYE366W	462	GYE462W
223a	BYX223V	327	EYE327V	387	GYE387W		

M506-697 — MCW Metrobus DR101/14 — MCW — H43/28D — 1981 — a H43/9D

506	GYE506W	554	GYE554W	598	GYE598W	687	KYV687X
526a	GYE526W	592	GYE592W	685	KYV685X	697	KYV697X

M813-951 — MCW Metrobus DR101/16 — MCW — H43/28D — 1983

813	OJD813Y	835	OJD835Y	844	OJD844Y	889	OJD889Y	951	A951SUL
815	OJD815Y	836	OJD836Y	856	OJD856Y	906	A906SUL		
831	OJD831Y	839	OJD839Y	864	OJD864Y	920	A920SUL		
832	OJD832Y	841	OJD841Y	881	OJD881Y	932	A932SUL		

M958-1003 — MCW Metrobus DR101/17 — MCW — H43/28D — 1984 — a DPH43/28D

958	A958SYF	966	A966SYF	980	A980SYF	994	A994SYF
960	A960SYF	967	A967SYF	981	A981SYF	999	A999SYF
962	A962SYF	969	A969SYF	985	A985SYF	1001	A701THV
963	A963SYF	972	A972SYF	990	A990SYF	1003a	A703THV

M1006-1029 — MCW Metrobus DR101/18 — MCW — DPH41/9DL 1984

1006	A706THV	1011	A711THV	1016	A716THV	1021	A721THV	1026	A726THV
1007	A707THV	1012	A712THV	1017	A717THV	1022	A722THV	1027	A727THV
1008	A708THV	1013	A713THV	1018	A718THV	1023	A723THV	1028	A728THV
1009	A709THV	1014	A714THV	1019	A719THV	1024	A724THV	1029	A729THV
1010	A710THV	1015	A715THV	1020	A720THV	1025	A725THV		

M1030-1439 MCW Metrobus   DR101/17   MCW H43/28D   1984-1986   * DR101/19
                                                                                      b DPH43/28D

1030	A730THV	1125	B125WUL	1200	B200WUL	1266	B266WUL	1352	C352BUV
1037	A737THV	1166	B166WUL	1207	B207WUL	1269	B269WUL	1353	C353BUV
1039	A739THV	1171	B171WUL	1212	B212WUL	1270	B270WUL	1356	C356BUV
1048*	A748THV	1172	B172WUL	1238	B238WUL	1271	B271WUL	1358	C358BUV
1050*	A750THV	1178	B178WUL	1240	B240WUL	1272	B272WUL	1360	C360BUV
1053*	A753THV	1184	B184WUL	1242	B242WUL	1336	C336BUV	1361	C361BUV
1064	B64WUL	1187	B187WUL	1243	B243WUL	1341	C341BUV	1363	C363BUV
1069	B69WUL	1188	B188WUL	1251b	B251WUL	1343	C343BUV	1368	C368BUV
1073	B73WUL	1190	B190WUL	1257	B257WUL	1344	C344BUV	1374	C374BUV
1106	B106WUL	1191	B191WUL	1261	B261WUL	1345	C345BUV	1381	C381BUV
1110	B110WUL	1194	B194WUL	1262	B262WUL	1351	C351BUV	1439	C439BUV

MRL108	F108YVP	MCW MetroRider MF150/16	MCW	B28F	1988
MRL115	F115YVP	MCW MetroRider MF150/16	MCW	B28F	1988
MRL116	F116YVP	MCW MetroRider MF150/16	MCW	B28F	1988
MRL117	F117YVP	MCW MetroRider MF150/16	MCW	B28F	1988

RMA55u	NMY644E	AEC Routemaster 9RM	Park Royal	H32/24F	1967
RMC1469t	469CLT	AEC Routemaster 6RM	Park Royal	H32/25RD	1962

RML880-2757 AEC Routemaster 7RM   Park Royal   H40/32R   1961-1968   Cummins engines

880	WLT880	2414	JJD414D	2500	JJD500D	2662	SMK662F	2722	SMK722F
881	WLT881	2432	JJD432D	2519	JJD519D	2697	SMK697F	2729	SMK729F
891	WLT891	2447	JJD447D	2600	NML600E	2700	SMK700F	2734	SMK734F
2269	CUV269C	2455	JJD455D	2621	NML621E	2702	SMK702F	2739	SMK739F
2293	CUV293C	2463	JJD463D	2622	NML622E	2704	SMK704F	2744	SMK744F
2298	CUV298C	2464	JJD464D	2645	NML645E	2707	SMK707F	2751	SMK751F
2349	CUV349C	2485	JJD485D	2646	NML646E	2720	SMK720F	2757	SMK757F
2353	CUV353C	2489	JJD489D	2650	NML650E	2721	SMK721F		

On order
12 Volvo Olympian - Alexander Royale double-deck for Airbus services

Previous registrations

ALM2B	K210SAG
VLT23	J610DUV
WLT329	H575MOC
WLT339	H577MOC
WLT804	H264NON
WLT931	H611TKU
WLT946	J611DUV
236CLT	H880LOX
500CLT	G349GCK

Special liveries
Airbus livery: M43, 96, 162, 221/3, 526, 1006-29
London Borough of Hounslow livery: FR1-8
London United Tramways livery: M1069, RML880 (carries unofficial fleet number ER880)

Vehicles on loan from Metroline

M272	BYX272V	MCW Metrobus DR101/12	MCW	H43/28D	1980
M373	GYR373W	MCW Metrobus DR101/12	MCW	H43/28D	1980

MTL LONDON NORTHERN

All vehicles acquired from London Buses Ltd in October 1994 unless otherwise stated

D2556	THX556S Leyland Fleetline FE30ALRSp		Park Royal		O44/27D	1978	
DMS2168	OJD168R Daimler Fleetline CRL6		MCW		H72D	1976	

DNL101-120   Dennis Dart 9SDL3034   Northern Counties   B34F   1994

101	L101HHV	105	L105HHV	109	L109HHV	114	L114HHV	118	L118HHV
102	L102HHV	106	L106HHV	110	L110HHV	115	L115HHV	119	L119HHV
103	L103HHV	107	L107HHV	112	L112HHV	116	L116HHV	120	L120HHV
104	L104HHV	108	L108HHV	113	L113HHV	117	L117HHV		

DRL17-37   Dennis Dart 9SDL3016   Plaxton Pointer   B34F+16   1992

17	K817NKH	22	K822NKH	27	K827NKH	32	K432OKH	37	K437OKH
18	K818NKH	23	K823NKH	28	K828NKH	33	K433OKH		
19	K819NKH	24	K824NKH	29	K429OKH	34	K434OKH		
20	K820NKH	25	K825NKH	30	K430OKH	35	K435OKH		
21	K821NKH	26	K826NKH	31	K431OKH	36	K436OKH		

M9-199   MCW Metrobus DR101/9*   MCW   H43/28D   1978-1979   *9-42 are DR101/8

9	WYW9T	67	WYW67T	92	WYW92T	118	BYX118V	160	BYX160V
12	WYW12T	72	WYW72T	95	WYW95T	124	BYX124V	161	BYX161V
25	WYW25T	75	WYW75T	98	BYX98V	126	BYX126V	181	BYX181V
27	WYW27T	78	WYW78T	101	BYX101V	130	BYX130V	189	BYX189V
32	WYW32T	79	WYW79T	103	BYX103V	133	BYX133V	194	BYX194V
33	WYW33T	80	WYW80T	114	BYX114V	139	BYX139V	199	BYX199V
35	WYW35T	81	WYW81T	115	BYX115V	145	BYX145V		
42	WYW42T	82	WYW82T	117	BYX117V	148	BYX148V		

M213-481   MCW Metrobus DR101/12   MCW   H43/28D   1980

213	BYX213V	294	BYX294V	328	EYE328V	356	GYE356W
243	BYX243V	322	EYE322V	341	EYE341V	481	GYE481W

M512-804   MCW Metrobus DR101/14   MCW   H43/28D   1981-1982   a O43/30F

512	GYE512W	571	GYE571W	594	GYE594W	656	KYV656X	764	KYV764X
560	GYE560W	572	GYE572W	608	KYO608X	674	KYV674X	797	KYV797X
561	GYE561W	574	GYE574W	616	KYO616X	677	KYV677X	800	KYV800X
563	GYE563W	576	GYE576W	620	KYO620X	678	KYV678X	801	KYV801X
564	GYE564W	578	GYE578W	623	KYO623X	693	KYV693X	802	KYV802X
565	GYE565W	579	GYE579W	639	KYV639X	739	KYV739X	804a	KYV804X
570	GYE570W	588	GYE588W	640	KYV640X	755	KYV755X		

M824-1414   MCW Metrobus DR101/17*   MCW   H43/28D   1983-1986   * 824-934 are DR101/16; 1045 and 1052 are DR101/19
     a DPH43/28D; b H43/30F; c DPH38/28F

824	OJD824Y	987	A987SYF	1076	B76WUL	1146	B146WUL	1325	C325BUV
829	OJD829Y	989	A989SYF	1077	B77WUL	1147	B147WUL	1329	C329BUV
876	OJD876Y	997	A997SYF	1078	B78WUL	1148	B148WUL	1330	C330BUV
878	OJD878Y	1032	A732THV	1079	B79WUL	1149	B149WUL	1331	C331BUV
879	OJD879Y	1033	A733THV	1080b	B80WUL	1150	B150WUL	1333	C333BUV
890	OJD890Y	1038	A738THV	1081	B81WUL	1151	B151WUL	1334	C334BUV
896	A896SUL	1040	A740THV	1082	B82WUL	1153	B153WUL	1355	C355BUV
899	A899SUL	1041	A741THV	1083	B83WUL	1156	B156WUL	1365	C365BUV
912	A912SUL	1042	A742THV	1111	B111WUL	1157	B157WUL	1369	C369BUV
915	A915SUL	1045a	A745THV	1113	B113WUL	1158	B158WUL	1385	C385BUV
916	A916SUL	1052	A752THV	1114	B114WUL	1159	B159WUL	1390	C390BUV
917	A917SUL	1058	B58WUL	1115	B115WUL	1160	B160WUL	1392	C392BUV
921	A921SUL	1059	B59WUL	1117	B117WUL	1161	B161WUL	1393c	C393BUV
925	A925SUL	1060	B60WUL	1118	B118WUL	1163	B163WUL	1394	C394BUV
928	A928SUL	1061	B61WUL	1119	B119WUL	1234	B234WUL	1395	C395BUV
934	A934SUL	1063	B63WUL	1120	B120WUL	1250	B250WUL	1396c	C396BUV
957	A957SYF	1065	B65WUL	1141	B141WUL	1277	B277WUL	1397	C397BUV
961	A961SYF	1066	B66WUL	1142	B142WUL	1284	B284WUL	1403	C403BUV
964	A964SYF	1067	B67WUL	1143	B143WUL	1287	B287WUL	1414	C414BUV
971	A971SYF	1072	B72WUL	1145	B145WUL	1292	B292WUL		

MRL210-222   Optare MetroRider MR03   Optare   B26F   1991-1993

210	J210BWU	213	J213BWU	216	J216BWU	219	J219BWU	222	K422HWY
211	J211BWU	214	J214BWU	217	J217BWU	220	J220BWU		
212	J212BWU	215	J215BWU	218	J218BWU	221	J221BWU		

MW18-37   Mercedes-Benz 811D   Wright   B26F   1993

18	NDZ7918	22	NDZ7922	26	NDZ7926	30	NDZ7930	34	NDZ7934
19	NDZ7919	23	NDZ7923	27	NDZ7927	31	NDZ7931	35	NDZ7935
20	NDZ7920	24	NDZ7924	28	NDZ7928	32	NDZ7932	36	K510FYN
21	NDZ7921	25	NDZ7925	29	NDZ7927	33	NDZ7933	37	K476FYN

RM29-2186   AEC Routemaster 5RM   Park Royal   H36/28R   1959-1965

29	OYM453A	1158	158CLT	1348	348CLT	1840	840DYE	2153	CUV153C
268	VLT268	1171	171CLT	1568	568CLT	1971	ALD971B	2186	CUV186C
446	WLT446	1185	XYJ427	1700	KGJ167A	1979	ALD979B		
646	KFF257	1218	218CLT	1758	758DYE	2023	ALM23B		
765	WLT765	1283	283CLT	1799	799DYE	2041	ALM41B		
912	WLT912	1287	287CLT	1804	EYY327B	2136	CUV136C		

RML903-2731   AEC Routemaster 7RM   Park Royal   H40/32R   1961-1967   c Cummins engine

903	WLT903	2296c	CUV296C	2395c	JJD395D	2511c	JJD511D	2679c	SMK679F
2282c	CUV282C	2310c	CUV310C	2413c	JJD413D	2561c	JJD561D	2699c	SMK699F
2284c	CUV284C	2367c	JJD367D	2419c	JJD419D	2603c	NML603E	2731c	SMK731F
2295c	CUV295C	2393c	JJD393D	2479c	JJD479D	2620c	NML620E		

S1-9   Scania N112DRB   Alexander RH   H47/33F   1989

1	F421GWG	3	F423GWG	5	F425GWG	7	F427GWG	9	F429GWG
2	F422GWG	4	F424GWG	6	F426GWG	8	F428GWG		

S10-21   Scania N113DRB   Alexander RH   H47/31F   1991

10	J810HMC	13	J813HMC	16	J816HMC	19	J819HMC		
11	J811HMC	14	J814HMC	17	J817HMC	20	J820HMC		
12	J812HMC	15	J815HMC	18	J818HMC	21	J821HMC		

SR108-121   Mercedes-Benz 811D   Optare StarRider   B26F   1989

108	G108KUB	111	G111KUB	114	G114KUB	117	G117KUB	121	G121KUB
109	G109KUB	112	G112KUB	115	G115KUB	118	G118KUB		
110	G110KUB	113	G113KUB	116	G116KUB	120	G120KUB		

V1	A101SUU	Volvo Ailsa B55-10	Alexander RV	H76D	1984	
V2	A102SUU	Volvo Ailsa B55-10	Alexander RV	H76D	1984	
VH1	804DYE	Volvo B10M-60	Van Hool Alizée	C49FT	1988	Ex Silver Knight, Chippenham, 1995
VH2	NJI9479	DAF MB230	Van Hool Alizée	C49FT	1989	Ex Elison, St. Helens, 1995
VH3	G260EHD	DAF MB230	Van Hool Alizée	C49FT	1989	Ex MacPhail, Motherwell, 1995
VH4	HIL6975	Volvo B10M	Van Hool Alizée	C49FT	1986	Acquired 1995

Previous registrations

EYY327B	804DYE
HIL6975	C29VJF
K476FYN	NDZ7937
K510FYN	NDZ7936
KFF257	WLT646
KGJ167A	700DYE
NJI9479	Not traced
OYM453A	VLT29
XYJ427	185CLT
804DYE	F967GMW

Special liveries
SightseerS livery: M804, M1393, VH1-4

Vehicles on loan from Merseyside

M229	BYX229V	MCW Metrobus DR101/12	MCW	H43/28D	1980	
M377	GYE377W	MCW Metrobus DR101/12	MCW	H43/28D	1980	
M501	GYE501W	MCW Metrobus DR101/12	MCW	H43/28D	1980	

METROLINE

All vehicles acquired from London Buses Ltd in October 1994 unless otherwise stated

DP1	K260FUV	Dennis Javelin 12SDA	Plaxton Premiére 320	C53F	1993	Ex Pullmanor, SE5, 1995
DP2	K261FUV	Dennis Javelin 12SDA	Plaxton Premiére 320	C53F	1993	Ex Pullmanor, SE5, 1995

DR15-42 Dennis Dart 8.5SDL3003 Reeve Burgess Pointer B28F 1991 * Plaxton Pointer B28F

15	H115THE	17	H117THE	19	H119THE	42*	H542XGK
16	H116THE	18	H118THE	40*	H540XGK		

DR81-148 Dennis Dart 8.5SDL3010 Plaxton Pointer B28F 1992

81	J381GKH	86	J386GKH	91	J391GKH	96	J396GKH	144	K244PAG
82	J382GKH	87	J387GKH	92	J392GKH	97	J397GKH	145	K245PAG
83	J383GKH	88	J388GKH	93	J393GKH	98	J398GKH	146	K246PAG
84	J384GKH	89	J389GKH	94	J394GKH	142	K242PAG	147	K247PAG
85	J385GKH	90	J390GKH	95	J395GKH	143	K243PAG	148	K248PAG

DT87-157 Dennis Dart 8.5SDL3003 Carlyle Dartline B28F 1990-1991

87	H87MOB	99	H899LOX	111	H611MOM	123	H123MOB	135	H135MOB
88	H588MOC	100	H620MOM	112	H112MOB	124	H124MOB	136	H136MOB
89	H89MOB	101	H101MOB	113	H113MOB	125	H125MOB	137	H137MOB
90	H890LOX	102	H102MOB	114	H114MOB	126	H126MOB	138	H138MOB
91	H91MOB	103	H103MOB	115	H115MOB	127	H127MOB	139	H139MOB
92	H92MOB	104	H104MOB	116	H116MOB	128	H128MOB	140	H140MOB
93	H93MOB	105	H105MOB	117	H117MOB	129	H129MOB	141	H141MOB
94	H94MOB	106	H106MOB	118	H118MOB	130	H130MOB	142	H142MOB
95	H95MOB	107	H107MOB	119	H119MOB	131	H131MOB	143	H143MOB
96	H96MOB	108	H108MOB	120	H120MOB	132	H132MOB	156	H156MOB
97	H97MOB	109	H109MOB	121	H621MOM	133	H133MOB	157	H157NON
98	H98MOB	110	H110MOB	122	H122MOB	134	H134MOB		

EDR1-9 Dennis Dart 9.8SDL3040 Plaxton Pointer B39F 1994 New to Metroline

1	M101BLE	3	M103BLE	5	M105BLE	7	M107BLE	9	M109BLE
2	M102BLE	4	M104BLE	6	M106BLE	8	M108BLE		

LD5	585CLT	Leyland Leopard PSU5D/4R	Duple Dominant III	C50F	1982

LLW25-38 Dennis Lance SLF 11SDA3202 Wright Pathfinder 320 B34D 1993-1994

25	L25WLH	28	L28WLH	31	L31WLH	34	L34WLH	37	L37WLH
26	L26WLH	29	L29WLH	32	L32WLH	35	L35WLH	38	L38WLH
27	L27WLH	30	L21WLH	33	L39WLH	36	L36WLH		

LN1-31 Dennis Lance 11SDA3108 Northern Counties B37D 1993

1	K301YJA	8	K308YJA	15	K315YJA	22	K322YJA	29	K329YJA
2	K302YJA	9	K309YJA	16	K316YJA	23	K323YJA	30	K330YJA
3	K303YJA	10	K310YJA	17	K317YJA	24	K324YJA	31	K331YJA
4	K304YJA	11	K311YJA	18	K318YJA	25	K325YJA		
5	K305YJA	12	K312YJA	19	K319YJA	26	K326YJA		
6	K306YJA	13	K313YJA	20	K320YJA	27	K327YJA		
7	K307YJA	14	K315YJA	21	K321YJA	28	K328YJA		

M1	THX101S	MCW Metrobus DR101/3	MCW	H43/28D	1978	
M2t	THX102S	MCW Metrobus DR101/3	MCW	H43/28D	1978	
M3t	THX103S	MCW Metrobus DR101/3	MCW	H43/28D	1978	
M4t	THX104S	MCW Metrobus DR101/3	MCW	H43/28D	1978	
M5t	THX105S	MCW Metrobus DR101/3	MCW	H43/28D	1978	

M18-184 MCW Metrobus DR101/9* MCW H43/28D 1979 *M18-54 are DR101/8

18t	WYW18T	73	WYW73T	94	WYW94T	127	BYX127V	155	BYX155V
20	WYW20T	77	WYW77T	97	BYX97V	128	BYX128V	163	BYX163V
41	WYW41T	83	WYW83T	102	BYX102V	135	BYX135V	166	BYX166V
48	WYW48T	84	WYW84T	107	BYX107V	136	BYX136V	167	BYX167V
54	WYW54T	85	WYW85T	109	BYX109V	137	BYX137V	169	BYX169V
57	WYW57T	87	WYW87T	111t	BYX111V	140	BYX140V	172	BYX172V
58	WYW58T	88	WYW88T	113	BYX113V	142	BYX142V	178	BYX178V
62	WYW62T	90	WYW90T	119	BYX119V	150	BYX150V	180	BYX180V
70	WYW70T	91	WYW91T	125	BYX125V	151	BYX151V	184	BYX184V

M238-482   MCW Metrobus DR101/12   MCW   H43/28D   1980

238	BYX238V	342	EYE342V	407	GYE407W	438	GYE438W
300	BYX300V	344	EYE344V	409t	GYE409W	440	GYE440W
306	BYX306V	367t	GYE367W	424	GYE424W	443	GYE443W
309	BYX309V	376	GYE376W	428	GYE428W	444	GYE444W
313	BYX313V	380	GYE380W	429	GYE429W	446t	GYE446W
315	BYX315V	391	GYE391W	432	GYE432W	448	GYE448W
326	EYE326V	394	GYE394W	436	GYE436W	449	GYE449W
335	EYE335V	403	GYE403W	437	GYE437W	453	GYE453W

455	GYE455W		
459	GYE459W		
460	GYE460W		
461	GYE461W		
467	GYE467W		
468	GYE468W		
473	GYE473W		
482	GYE482W		

M524-696   MCW Metrobus DR101/14   MCW   H43/28D   1981

524	GYE524W	595	GYE595W	621	KYO621X	683	KYV683X
550	GYE550W	618	KYO618X	655	KYV655X	696	KYV696X

M810-955   MCW Metrobus DR101/16   MCW   H43/28D   1983

810	OJD810Y	910	A910SUL	924	A924SUL	937	A937SUL
819t	WLT342	911	A911SUL	935	A935SUL	945	A945SUL

950	A950SUL
955	A955SUL

M956-1431   MCW Metrobus DR101/17   MCW   H43/28D   1984-1986   * DR101/19   a DPH43/28D

956	A956SYF	1056	B56WUL	1192	B192WUL	1274	B274WUL	1423	C423BUV
968	A968SYF	1057	B57WUL	1193	B193WUL	1339	C339BUV	1425	C425BUV
974	A974SYF	1068	B68WUL	1195	B195WUL	1342	C342BUV	1426	C426BUV
982	A982SYF	1071	B71WUL	1197	B197WUL	1346	C346BUV	1427	C427BUV
993	A993SYF	1167	B167WUL	1198	B198WUL	1348	C348BUV	1428	C428BUV
995	A995SYF	1168	B168WUL	1202	B202WUL	1349	C349BUV	1429	WLT826
1004	A704THV	1174	B174WUL	1204	B204WUL	1350	C350BUV	1430	C430BUV
1031	A731THV	1181	B181WUL	1205	B205WUL	1366	C366BUV	1431	C431BUV
1034	A734THV	1183	B183WUL	1208	B208WUL	1383	C383BUV		
1035	A735THV	1185a	WLT893	1218	B218WUL	1408	C408BUV		
1043	A743THV	1186	B186WUL	1236a	WLT646	1409	C409BUV		
1047*	A747THV	1189	B189WUL	1273	WLT902	1416	C416BUV		

MR20	D480PON	MCW MetroRider MF150/18	MCW	DP19F	1987	

RM70t	VLT70	AEC Routemaster 5RM	Park Royal	H36/28R	1959
RM644	WLT644	AEC Routemaster 5RM	Park Royal	O36/28RD	1961
RMC1513	513CLT	AEC Routemaster 6RM	Park Royal	H32/25RD	1962

RML893-2755   AEC Routemaster 7RM   Park Royal   H40/32R   1961-1968   Cummins engines

893	KFF276	2348	CUV348C	2508	JJD508D	2599	NML599E	2701	SMK701F
902	ALC464A	2368	JJD368D	2509	JJD509D	2634	NML634E	2703	SMK703F
2274	CUV274C	2377	JJD377D	2532	JJD532D	2649	NML649E	2706	SMK706F
2285	CUV285C	2384	JJD384D	2537	JJD537D	2651	NML651E	2710	SMK710F
2288	CUV288C	2430	JJD430D	2547	JJD547D	2652	NML652E	2713	SMK713F
2289	CUV289C	2431	JJD431D	2558	JJD558D	2681	SMK681F	2727	SMK727F
2299	CUV299C	2439	JJD439D	2566	JJD566D	2689	SMK689F	2728	SMK728F
2308	CUV308C	2446	JJD446D	2579	JJD579D	2690	SMK690F	2737	SMK737F
2312	CUV312C	2471	JJD471D	2585	JJD585D	2695	SMK695F	2755	SMK755F
2331	CUV331C	2478	JJD478D	2594	JJD594D	2698	SMK698F		

SR7-104   Mercedes-Benz 811D   Optare StarRider   B26F   1988-1989   a B25F

7a	F907YWY	59	F159FWY	83	G83KUB	90	G90KUB	98	G98KUB
8	F908YWY	61	F161FWY	84	G84KUB	92	G92KUB	100	G100KUB
54	F154FWY	67	F167FWY	85	G85KUB	93	G93KUB	101	G101KUB
55	F155FWY	68	F168FWY	87	G87KUB	94	G94KUB	103	G103KUB
57	F157FWY	81	F181FWY	88	G88KUB	95	G95KUB	104	G104KUB
58	F158FWY	82	G82KUB	89	G89KUB	96	G96KUB		

VP3	H637UWR	Volvo B10M-60	Plaxton Paramount 3500 3 C50F	1991	

Previous registrations

ALC464A	WLT902		WLT646	B236WUL	WLT902	B273WUL
KFF276	WLT893		WLT826	C429BUV	585CLT	WGV867X
WLT342	OJD819Y		WLT893	B185WUL		

Named vehicles
LN1 *Princess Madden*, RMC1513 *Queen Victoria*

Special liveries
Tesco livery: SR7

METROLINE Atlas Bus

| T287-518 | Leyland Titan TNLXB2RR | Leyland | H44/24D | 1981-1982 | a H44/26D |

287a	KYN287X	343	KYV343X	415	KYV415X	459	KYV459X	482	KYV482X
302	KYN302X	357	KYV357X	419	KYV419X	475	KYV475X	485	KYV485X
313	KYV313X	375	KYV375X	432	KYV432X	477	KYV477X	518	KYV518X
319a	KYV319X	388	KYV388X	433	KYV433X	478	KYV478X		
321a	KYV321X	390	KYV390X	435	KYV435X	479	KYV479X		
341	KYV341X	399	KYV399X	438	KYV438X	481	KYV481X		

SOUTH LONDON

All vehicles acquired from London Buses Ltd in January 1995

| DR20-31 | Dennis Dart 8.5SDL3003 | Plaxton Pointer | B28F | 1991 |

20	H120THE	23	H123THE	26	H126THE	29	H129THE		
21	H621TKU	24	H124THE	27	H127THE	30	H130THE		
22	H122THE	25	H125THE	28	H128THE	31	H131THE		

| DRL147-158 | Dennis Dart 9SDL3024 | Plaxton Pointer | B34F | 1993 |

147	L247WAG	150	L150WAG	153	L153WAG	156	L156WAG
148	L148WAG	151	L151WAG	154	L154WAG	157	L157WAG
149	L149WAG	152	L152WAG	155	L155WAG	158	L158WAG

| DT58-70 | Dennis Dart 8.5SDL3003 | Carlyle Dartline | B28F | 1990 |

58	H458UGO	61	H461UGO	64	H464UGO	67	H467UGO	70	H470UGO
59	H459UGO	62	H462UGO	65	H465UGO	68	H468UGO		
60	H460UGO	63	H463UGO	66	H466UGO	69	H469UGO		

L1	A101SYE	Leyland Olympian ONTL11/1R	Eastern Coach Works	H47/28D	1984
L2	A102SYE	Leyland Olympian ONLXB/1R	Eastern Coach Works	H47/28D	1984
L3	A103SYE	Leyland Olympian ONLXB/1R	Eastern Coach Works	H47/28D	1984

| L4-259 | Leyland Olympian ONLXB/1RH | Eastern Coach Works | H42/26D | 1986-1987 | a DPH42/26D |

4	C804BYY	63	C63CHM	166a	D166FYM	198	D198FYM	230	D230FYM
5	C805BYY	65	C65CHM	167a	D167FYM	199	D199FYM	231	D231FYM
6	C806BYY	66	C66CHM	168a	D168FYM	200	D200FYM	232	D232FYM
8	WLT807	78	C78CHM	169a	D169FYM	201	D201FYM	233	D233FYM
13	VLT13	79	C79CHM	170a	7CLT	202	D202FYM	234	D234FYM
14	C814BYY	99	C99CHM	171a	D171FYM	203	D203FYM	235	D235FYM
16	WLT916	102	C102CHM	172	WLT372	204	D204FYM	236	D236FYM
17	C817BYY	113	C113CHM	173	VLT173	205	D205FYM	237	D237FYM
20	C820BYY	135	D135FYM	174	D174FYM	206	D206FYM	238	D238FYM
21	C21CHM	139	D139FYM	175	D175FYM	207	D207FYM	239	D239FYM
22	C22CHM	140	D140FYM	176	D176FYM	208	D208FYM	240	D240FYM
24	C24CHM	143	D143FYM	177	D177FYM	209	D209FYM	241	D241FYM
25	C25CHM	146	D146FYM	178	D178FYM	210	D210FYM	242	D242FYM
26	C26CHM	147	D147FYM	179	D179FYM	211	D211FYM	243	D243FYM
27	VLT27	148	D148FYM	180	480CLT	212	D212FYM	244	VLT244
31	C31CHM	149	D149FYM	181	D181FYM	213	D213FYM	245	D245FYM
32	C32CHM	150	D150FYM	182	D182FYM	214	D214FYM	246	D246FYM
33	330CLT	151	WLT751	183	D183FYM	215	815DYE	247	D247FYM
35	C35CHM	152	D152FYM	184	D184FYM	216	D216FYM	248	D248FYM
36	C36CHM	153	D153FYM	185	D185FYM	217	217CLT	249	D249FYM
37	C37CHM	154	WLT554	186	D186FYM	218	D218FYM	250	D250FYM
38	C38CHM	155	D155FYM	187	D187FYM	219	519CLT	251	D251FYM
41	C41CHM	156	656DYE	188	D188FYM	220	D220FYM	252	D252FYM
45	C45CHM	157	D157FYM	189	D189FYM	221	D221FYM	253	D253FYM
46	C46CHM	158	D158FYM	190	319CLT	222	D222FYM	254	D254FYM
47	VLT47	159	D159FYM	191	D191FYM	223	D223FYM	255	D255FYM
49	C49CHM	160	D160FYM	192	D192FYM	224	D224FYM	256	D256FYM
50	C50CHM	161	D161FYM	193	D193FYM	225	D225FYM	257	D257FYM
52	C52CHM	162	D162FYM	194	D194FYM	226	D226FYM	258	D258FYM
56	C56CHM	163	D163FYM	195	D195FYM	227	D227FYM	259	D259FYM
58	C58CHM	164	D164FYM	196	D196FYM	228	D228FYM		
59	C59CHM	165	D165FYM	197	D197FYM	229	D229FYM		

M6-51   MCW Metrobus DR101/8   MCW   H43/28D   1978-1979

6	WYW6T	10	WYW10T	24	WYW24T	40	WYW40T	51t	WYW51T
7	WYW7T	14	WYW14T	38	WYW38T	49t	WYW49T		

M60-205   MCW Metrobus DR101/9   MCW   H43/28D   1979

60	WYW60T	69	WYW69T	132	BYX132V	173	BYX173V	205	BYX205V
63t	WYW63T	74	WYW74T	143	BYX143V	175	BYX175V		
64	WYW64T	121	BYX121V	149	BYX149V	182	BYX182V		
65t	WYW65T	123	BYX123V	168	BYX168V	185	BYX185V		
66	WYW66T	129	BYX129V	170	BYX170V	200	BYX200V		

M208-503   MCW Metrobus DR101/12   MCW   H43/28D   1980

208	BYX208V	251	BYX251V	301	BYX301V	389	GYE389W	441	GYE441W
210	BYX210V	263	BYX263V	304	BYX304V	395	GYE395W	454	GYE454W
220	BYX220V	277	BYX277V	310	BYX310V	396	GYE396W	456	GYE456W
225	BYX225V	280	BYX280V	314	BYX314V	398	398CLT	458	GYE458W
230	BYX230V	282	BYX282V	346	GYE346W	399	GYE399W	469	GYE469W
232	BYX232V	283	BYX283V	365	GYE365W	400	GYE400W	491	GYE491W
233	BYX233V	290	BYX290V	372	GYE372W	402	GYE402W	492	GYE492W
240	BYX240V	296	BYX296V	378	GYE378W	410	GYE410W	495	GYE495W
245	BYX245V	298	BYX298V	384	GYE384W	417	GYE417W	496	GYE496W
248	BYX248V	299	BYX299V	388	GYE388W	439	GYE439W	503	GYE503W

M511-805   MCW Metrobus DR101/14   MCW   H43/28D   1981-1982

511	GYE511W	541	GYE541W	580	GYE580W	671	KYV671X	799	KYV799X
515	GYE515W	552	GYE552W	584	GYE584W	680	KYV680X	803	KYV803X
517	GYE517W	553	GYE553W	601	GYE601W	682	KYV682X	805	KYV805X
520	GYE520W	555	GYE555W	629	KYO629X	691	KYV691X		
521	GYE521W	558	GYE558W	633	KYV633X	722	KYV722X		
537	GYE537W	568	GYE568W	634	KYV634X	724	KYV724X		
539	GYE539W	577	GYE577W	654	KYV654X	741	KYV741X		

M809-954   MCW Metrobus DR101/16   MCW   H43/28D   1983

809	OJD809Y	850	OJD850Y	869	OJD869Y	930	A930SUL
825	OJD825Y	858	OJD858Y	894	A894SUL	936	A936SUL
827	OJD827Y	863	OJD863Y	895	A895SUL	948	A948SUL
840	OJD840Y	865	OJD865Y	927	A927SUL	954	WLT954

M959	A959SYF	MCW Metrobus DR101/17	MCW	H43/28D	1984
M973	A973SYF	MCW Metrobus DR101/17	MCW	H43/28D	1984
M984	A984SYF	MCW Metrobus DR101/17	MCW	H43/28D	1984
M1036	A736THV	MCW Metrobus DR101/17	MCW	H43/28D	1984
M1062	B62WUL	MCW Metrobus DR101/17	MCW	H43/28D	1984

M1084-1105   MCW Metrobus DR134/1   MCW   H43/28D   1984

1084	B84WUL	1089	B89WUL	1094	B94WUL	1099	B99WUL	1104	B104WUL
1085	B85WUL	1090	B90WUL	1095	B95WUL	1100	B100WUL	1105	B105WUL
1086	B86WUL	1091	B91WUL	1096	B96WUL	1101	B101WUL		
1087	B87WUL	1092	B92WUL	1097	B97WUL	1102	B102WUL		
1088	B88WUL	1093	B93WUL	1098	B98WUL	1103	B103WUL		

M1116	B116WUL	MCW Metrobus DR101/17	MCW	H43/28D	1984
M1354	C354BUV	MCW Metrobus DR101/17	MCW	H43/28D	1985
M1359	C359BUV	MCW Metrobus DR101/17	MCW	DPH43/28D	1985
M1407	C407BUV	MCW Metrobus DR101/17	MCW	H43/28D	1985
M1441	A441UUV	MCW Metrobus DR102/45	MCW	H43/28D	1984
M1442	A442UUV	MCW Metrobus DR132/5	MCW	H43/28D	1984

MR29	E129KYW	MCW MetroRider MF150/38	Park Royal	B25F	1987
MR97	F897OYR	MCW MetroRider MF150/96	MCW	B25F	1988

MRL107-133   MCW MetroRider MF158/16   MCW   B28F   1988   * MF158/17 and DP28F

107	F107YVP	123	F123YVP	127	F127YVP	133*	F133YVP
122	F122YVP	124	F124YVP	129	F129YVP		

RM6-2217   AEC Routemaster 5RM   Park Royal H36/28R   1959-1965   Iveco engines

6	VLT6	467	XVS851	1003	3CLT	1725	725DYE	2179	CUV179C
18	VLT18	531	WLT531	1124	VYJ806	1734	734DYE	2185	CUV185C
25	VLT25	664	WLT664	1125	KGH858A	1801	801DYE	2217	CUV217C
275	VLT275	676	WLT676	1324	324CLT	1811	EGF220B		
311	KGJ142A	719	WLT719	1361	VYJ808	1822	822DYE		
348	WLT348	970	WLT970	1398	KGJ118A	1872	ALD872B		
432	SVS617	997	WLT997	1593	593CLT	1978	ALD978B		

RMC1464 464CLT   AEC Routemaster 6RM   Park Royal   O36/25RD   1962   Iveco engine

RML892-2759   AEC Routemaster 7RM   Park Royal   H40/32R   1961-1968   Iveco engines

892	WLT892	2351	CUV351C	2521	JJD521D	2636	NML636E	2741	SMK741F
895	WLT895	2366	JJD366D	2545	JJD545D	2653	NML653E	2753	SMK753F
2264	CUV264C	2375	JJD375D	2549	JJD549D	2692	SMK692F	2759	SMK759F
2307	CUV307C	2407	JJD407D	2572	JJD572D	2718	SMK718F		
2324	CUV324C	2477	JJD477D	2573	JJD573D	2726	SMK726F		
2333	CUV333C	2491	JJD491D	2608	NML608E	2730	SMK730F		

SR5-102   Mercedes-Benz 811D   Optare StarRider   B26F   1988-1989

5	F905YWY	15	F915YWY	20	F920YWY	97	G97KUB
6	F906YWY	17	F917YWY	39	F39CWY	99	G99KUB
9	F909YWY	18	F918YWY	46	F46CWY	102	G102KUB

T322	124CLT	Leyland Titan TNLXB2RR	Leyland	DPH44/26D	1981
T349t	KYV349X	Leyland Titan TNLXB2RR	Leyland	H44/24D	1981
T377t	361CLT	Leyland Titan TNLXB2RR	Leyland	H44/24D	1981

Previous registrations

EGF220B	811DYE
KGH858A	125CLT
KGJ118A	398CLT
KGJ142A	WLT311
SVS617	WLT432
VLT13	C813BYY
VLT27	C27CHM
VLT47	C47CHM
VLT173	D173FYM
VLT244	D244FYM
VYJ806	124CLT
VYJ808	361CLT
WLT372	D172FYM
WLT554	D154FYM
WLT751	D151FYM
WLT807	C808BYY
WLT916	C816BYY
WLT954	A954SUL
XVS851	WLT467
7CLT	D170FYM
124CLT	KYV322X
217CLT	D217FYM
319CLT	D190FYM
324CLT	VYJ807, 324CLT
330CLT	C30CHM
361CLT	KYV377X
398CLT	GYE398W
480CLT	D180FYM
519CLT	D219FYM
656DYE	D156FYM
815DYE	D215FYM

Named vehicle
RMC1464 *Norwood Princess*

STAGECOACH EAST LONDON

All vehicles acquired from London Buses Ltd in September 1994 unless otherwise stated

DA10-35   DAF SB220LC550   Optare Delta   B40D+31   1989/1992/1993   a DP36D+39

10a	G684KNW	16	J716CYG	22	J722CYG	28	J728CYG	34	K634HWX
11	J711CYG	17	J717CYG	23	J723CYG	29	J729CYG	35	K635HWX
12	J712CYG	18	J718CYG	24	J724CYG	30	K630HWX		
13	J713CYG	19	J719CYG	25	J725CYG	31	K631HWX		
14	J714CYG	20	J720CYG	26	J726CYG	32	K632HWX		
15	J715CYG	21	J721CYG	27	J727CYG	33	K633HWX		

DRL109-146   Dennis Dart 9SDL3024*   Plaxton Pointer   B34F+16   1993   * 139-146 are 9SDL3034

109	K109SRH	117	K117SRH	125	K125SRH	133	K133SRH	141	L141VRH
110	K110SRH	118	K118SRH	126	K126SRH	134	K134SRH	142	L142VRH
111	K211SRH	119	K119SRH	127	K127SRH	135	K135SRH	143	L143VRH
112	K112SRH	120	K120SRH	128	K128SRH	136	L136VRH	144	L144VRH
113	K113SRH	121	K121SRH	129	K129SRH	137	L137VRH	145	L145VRH
114	K114SRH	122	K122SRH	130	K130SRH	138	L138VRH	146	L146VRH
115	K115SRH	123	K123SRH	131	K131SRH	139	L139VRH		
116	K116SRH	124	K124SRH	132	K132SRH	140	L140VRH		

DW133-159   Dennis Dart 8.5SDL3015   Wright Handybus   B29F+16   1993

133	NDZ3133	139	NDZ3139	145	NDZ3145	151	NDZ3151	157	NDZ3157
134	NDZ3134	140	NDZ3140	146	NDZ3146	152	NDZ3152	158	NDZ3158
135	NDZ3135	141	NDZ3141	147	NDZ3147	153	NDZ3153	159	NDZ3159
136	NDZ3136	142	NDZ3142	148	NDZ3148	154	NDZ3154		
137	NDZ3137	143	NDZ3143	149	NDZ3149	155	NDZ3155		
138	NDZ3138	144	NDZ3144	150	NDZ3150	156	NDZ3156		

DWL15-26   Dennis Dart 9SDL3016   Wright Handybus   B35F+17   1993

15	NDZ3015	18	NDZ3018	21	NDZ3021	24	NDZ3024
16	NDZ3016	19	NDZ3019	22	NDZ3022	25	NDZ3025
17	NDZ3017	20	NDZ3020	23	NDZ3023	26	NDZ3026

LS121	THX121S	Leyland National 10351A/2R	B21DL	1977
LS308	AYR308T	Leyland National 10351A/2R	B21DL	1979
LS403	BYW403V	Leyland National 10351A/2R	B21DL	1979

MR16	D476PON	MCW MetroRider MF150/14	MCW	B23F	1987

MRL65-76   MCW MetroRider MF158/1   MCW   B30F   1988   a MF158/2 and DP33F

65	E641KYW	68	E644KYW	71	E647KYW	74a	E650KYW
66	E642KYW	69	E645KYW	72	E648KYW	75a	E705LYU
67	E643KYW	70	E646KYW	73	E649KYW	76a	E706LYU

MRL77	F197YDA	MCW MetroRider MF158/18	MCW	B28F	1988

MR93-98   MCW MetroRider MF150/96   MCW   B25F   1988   Ex South London, 1995

93	E873NJD	94	E874NJD	95	F895OYR	96	F896OYR	98	F898OYR

MRL106-132   MCW MetroRider MF158/16   MCW   B28F   1988   a MF158/17 and DP28F

106	F106YVP	112	F112YVP	119	F119YVP	126	F126YVP	132a	F132YVP
109	F109YVP	113	F113YVP	120	F120YVP	128	F128YVP		
110	F110YVP	114	F114YVP	121	F121YVP	130	F131YVP		
111	F111YVP	118	F118YVP	125	F125YVP	131	F131YVP		

RM613	WLT613	AEC Routemaster 5RM	Park Royal	H36/28R	1960
RM1527	527CLT	AEC Routemaster 5RM	Park Royal	H36/28R	1963
RMA5	NMY635E	AEC Routemaster 9RM	Park Royal	H32/24F	1967
RMA8	NMY640E	AEC Routemaster 9RM	Park Royal	H32/24F	1967
RMC1456	LFF875	AEC Routemaster 6RM	Park Royal	H32/25RD	1962
RMC1461	461CLT	AEC Routemaster 6RM	Park Royal	H32/25RD	1962
RMC1485	485CLT	AEC Routemaster 6RM	Park Royal	H32/25RD	1962

RML886-2760 AEC Routemaster 7RM   Park Royal   H40/32R   1961-1968   Iveco engines
except **c** Cummins and **a** AEC

886c	WLT886	**2415**	JJD415D	**2481**	JJD481D	**260**	NML607E	**2671c**	SMK671F
890c	XFF814	**2429**	JJD429D	**2488**	JJD488D	**2610c**	NML610E	**2696c**	SMK696F
898	XFF813	**2435**	JJD435D	**2493**	JJD493D	**2616c**	NML616E	**2705c**	SMK705F
2272c	CUV272C	**2437**	JJD437D	**2495c**	JJD495D	**2624**	NML624E	**2709**	SMK709F
2286c	CUV286C	**2444**	JJD444D	**2496c**	JJD496D	**2639c**	NML639E	**2723c**	SMK723F
2300	CUV300C	**2445c**	JJD445D	**2497c**	JJD497D	**2641c**	NML641E	**2738**	SMK738F
2303	CUV303C	**2450**	JJD450D	**2541c**	JJD541D	**2642c**	NML642E	**2743c**	SMK743F
2311c	CUV311C	**2451**	JJD451D	**2550c**	JJD550D	**2657**	NML657E	**2748c**	SMK748F
2392	JJD392D	**2456c**	JJD456D	**2565c**	JJD565D	**2661c**	SMK661F	**2749**	SMK749F
2399	JJD399D	**2462**	JJD462D	**2581c**	JJD581D	**2665**	SMK665F	**2760a**	SMK760F
2402	JJD402D	**2470**	JJD470D	**2592**	JJD592D	**2670c**	SMK670F		

S22-29   Scania N113DRB   Alexander RH   H47/31F   1991

22	J822HMC	**24**	J824HMC	**26**	J826HMC	**28**	J828HMC
23	J823HMC	**25**	J825HMC	**27**	J827HMC	**29**	J829HMC

S30-71   Scania N113DRB   Northern Counties Countybus
Palatine   H41/25D   1991/1992   **a** H47/33F

30a	J230XKY	**39**	J139HMT	**48**	K848LMK	**57**	K857LMK	**66**	K866LMK
31a	J231XKY	**40**	J140HMT	**49**	K849LMK	**58**	K858LMK	**67**	K867LMK
32	J132HMT	**41**	J141HMT	**50**	K850LMK	**59**	K859LMK	**68**	K868LMK
33	J133HMT	**42**	J142HMT	**51**	K851LMK	**60**	K860LMK	**69**	K869LMK
34	J134HMT	**43**	J143HMT	**52**	K852LMK	**61**	K861LMK	**70**	K870LMK
35	J135HMT	**44**	J144HMT	**53**	K853LMK	**62**	K862LMK	**71**	K871LMK
36	J136HMT	**45**	J145HMT	**54**	K854LMK	**63**	K863LMK		
37	J137HMT	**46**	K846LMK	**55**	K855LMK	**64**	K864LMK		
38	J138HMT	**47**	K847LMK	**56**	K856LMK	**65**	K865LMK		

SLW15-30   Scania N113CRL   Wright Pathfinder 320   B37D   1994

15	RDZ6115	**19**	RDZ6119	**23**	RDZ6123	**27**	RDZ6127
16	RDZ6116	**20**	RDZ6120	**24**	RDZ6124	**28**	RDZ6128
17	RDZ6117	**21**	RDZ6121	**25**	RDZ6125	**29**	RDZ6129
18	RDZ6118	**22**	RDZ6122	**26**	RDZ6126	**30**	RDZ6130

SP2	K302FYG	DAF DB250WB505	Optare Spectra	H44/23D	1992

SR1-119   Mercedes-Benz 811D   Optare StarRider   B26F   1988-1989

1	E155CGJ	**32**	F32CWY	**69**	F169FWY	**75**	F175FWY	**86**	G86KUB
2	E712LYU	**50**	F50CWY	**70**	F170FWY	**76**	F176FWY	**91**	G91KUB
3	E713LYU	**56**	F156FWY	**71**	F171FWY	**77**	F177FWY	**105**	G105KUB
4	E714LYU	**60**	F160FWY	**72**	F172FWY	**78**	F178FWY	**106**	G106KUB
12	F912YWY	**65**	F165FWY	**73**	F173FWY	**79**	F179FWY	**107**	G107KUB
13	F913YWY	**66**	F166FWY	**74**	F174FWY	**80**	F180FWY	**119**	G119KUB

T1-230   Leyland Titan TNLXB2RRSp   Park Royal   H44/26D   1978-1980   **a** H44/22D
b H44/24D
c DPH44/26F

1a	THX401S	**12**	WYV12T	**22**	WYV22T	**34a**	WYV34T	**140t**	CUL140V
2	THX402S	**13a**	WYV13T	**23a**	WYV23T	**35a**	WYV35T	**175**	CUL175V
3a	WYV3T	**14a**	WYV14T	**24a**	WYV24T	**36**	WYV36T	**193t**	CUL193V
4a	WYV4T	**15a**	WYV15T	**25**	WYV25T	**37a**	WYV37T	**214**	CUL214V
6a	WYV6T	**16a**	WYV16T	**26**	WYV26T	**38a**	WYV38T	**222**	CUL222V
7a	WYV7T	**17a**	WYV17T	**28a**	WYV28T	**39**	WYV39T	**223t**	CUL223V
8a	WYV8T	**18a**	WYV18T	**30**	WYV30T	**40**	WYV40T	**230b**	EYE230V
9	WYV9T	**19**	WYV19T	**31a**	WYV31T	**63c**	WLT890		
10	WYV10T	**20**	WYV20T	**32a**	WYV32T	**66**	WYV66T		
11	WYV11T	**21a**	WYV21T	**33**	WYV33T	**80c**	WLT898		

T260	GYE260W	Leyland Titan TNLXB2RR	Park Royal/Leyland	H44/26D	1981
T261	GYE261W	Leyland Titan TNTL112RR	Park Royal/Leyland	H44/26D	1981
T262	GYE262W	Leyland Titan TNLXB2RR	Park Royal/Leyland	H44/26D	1981
T263	GYE263W	Leyland Titan TNLXB2RR	Park Royal/Leyland	H44/26D	1981

T264-789 — Leyland Titan TNLXB2RR — Leyland — H44/24D — 1981-1983 — a H44/26D b O44/24D

No.	Reg	No.	Reg	No.	Reg	No.	Reg	No.	Reg
264	GYE264W	466	KYV466X	543	KYV543X	592	NUW592Y	649	NUW649Y
266a	GYE266W	467	KYV467X	544	KYV544X	593	NUW593Y	650	NUW650Y
268	GYE268W	469	KYV469X	545	KYV545X	595	NUW595Y	651	NUW651Y
270	GYE270W	470	KYV470X	546	KYV546X	597	NUW597Y	652	NUW652Y
272	GYE272W	471	KYV471X	548	KYV548X	598	NUW598Y	653	NUW653Y
285a	KYN285W	473	KYV473X	549	KYV549X	600	NUW600Y	654	NUW654Y
286	KYN286X	476	KYV476X	550	NUW550Y	601	NUW601Y	657	NUW657Y
298	KYN298X	480	KYV480X	551	NUW551Y	602	NUW602Y	658	NUW658Y
306	KYN306X	486	KYV486X	552	NUW552Y	603	NUW603Y	659	NUW659Y
311a	KYV311X	488	KYV488X	553	NUW553Y	604	NUW604Y	660	NUW660Y
318	KYV318X	490	KYV490X	554	NUW554Y	605	NUW605Y	662	NUW662Y
320a	KYV320X	492	KYV492X	555	NUW555Y	606	NUW606Y	663	NUW663Y
326	KYV326X	495	KYV495X	556	NUW556Y	608	NUW608Y	664	NUW664Y
331a	KYV331X	496	KYV496X	557	NUW557Y	609	NUW609Y	665	NUW665Y
334	KYV334X	497	KYV497X	558	NUW558Y	610	NUW610Y	666	NUW666Y
340	KYV340X	498	KYV498X	559	NUW559Y	613	NUW613Y	668	NUW668Y
360	KYV360X	500	KYV500X	560	NUW560Y	614	NUW614Y	669	NUW669Y
366	KYV366X	501	KYV501X	562	NUW562Y	615	NUW615Y	670	NUW670Y
378	KYV378X	502	KYV502X	563	NUW563Y	617	NUW617Y	671	NUW671Y
379	KYV379X	503	KYV503X	564	NUW564Y	619	NUW619Y	672	NUW672Y
380	KYV380X	504	KYV504X	565	NUW565Y	621	NUW621Y	673	NUW673Y
386	KYV386X	505	KYV505X	566	NUW566Y	622	NUW622Y	675	NUW675Y
387	KYV387X	506	KYV506X	568	NUW568Y	623	NUW623Y	686	OHV686Y
394t	KYV394X	508	KYV508X	569	NUW569Y	624	NUW624Y	688	OHV688Y
395	KYV395X	512bt	KYV512X	571	NUW571Y	625	NUW625Y	691	OHV691Y
403	KYV403X	513	KYV513X	572	NUW572Y	626	NUW626Y	697	OHV697Y
404	KYV404X	514	KYV514X	573	NUW573Y	627	NUW627Y	699	OHV699Y
406	KYV406X	515	KYV515X	574	NUW574Y	629	NUW629Y	702	OHV702Y
428	KYV428X	517	KYV517X	575	NUW575Y	630	NUW630Y	719	OHV719Y
434	KYV434X	521	KYV521X	576	NUW576Y	631	NUW631Y	724	OHV724Y
437	KYV437X	522	KYV522X	577	NUW577Y	632	NUW632Y	729	OHV729Y
439	KYV439X	525	KYV525X	578	NUW578Y	633	NUW633Y	731	OHV731Y
441	KYV441X	526	KYV526X	579	NUW579Y	634	NUW634Y	738	OHV738Y
444	KYV444X	527	KYV527X	580	NUW580Y	636	NUW636Y	743	OHV743Y
445	KYV445X	529	KYV529X	581	NUW581Y	637	NUW637Y	744	OHV744Y
446	KYV446X	531	KYV531X	582	NUW582Y	639	NUW639Y	749	OHV749Y
448	KYV448X	532	KYV532X	583	NUW583Y	640	NUW640Y	751	OHV751Y
453	KYV453X	533	KYV533X	584	NUW584Y	641	NUW641Y	759	OHV759Y
454	KYV454X	535	KYV535X	585	NUW585Y	642	NUW642Y	761	OHV761Y
456	KYV456X	536	KYV536X	586	NUW586Y	643	NUW643Y	769	OHV769Y
458	KYV458X	537	KYV537X	587	NUW587Y	644	NUW644Y	784	OHV784Y
460	KYV460X	539	KYV539X	588	NUW588Y	645	NUW645Y	789	OHV789Y
461	KYV461X	540	KYV540X	589	NUW589Y	646	NUW646Y		
462	KYV462X	541	KYV541X	590	NUW590Y	647	NUW647Y		
465	KYX465X	542	KYV542X	591	NUW591Y	648	NUW648Y		

T802-1050 — Leyland Titan TNLXB2RR — Leyland — H44/26D — 1983-1984

No.	Reg	No.	Reg	No.	Reg	No.	Reg	No.	Reg
802	OHV802Y	846	A846SUL	921	A921SYE	953	A953SYE	1050	A650THV
819	RYK819Y	849	A849SUL	922	A922SYE	960	A960SYE		
826	A826SUL	867	A867SUL	935	A935SYE	965	A965SYE		
827	A827SUL	873	A873SUL	944	A944SYE	971	A971SYE		
832	A832SUL	902	A902SYE	945	A945SYE	1022	A622THV		
840	A840SUL	905	A905SYE	949	A949SYE	1026	A626THV		

T1128	486CLT	Leyland Titan TNLXB1RF	Park Royal	DPH43/29F	1979	
TPL7	H642GRO	Leyland Tiger TRCL10/3ARZA	Plaxton Paramount 3200 3	C53F	1991	
VP2	F24HGG	Volvo B10M-60	Plaxton Paramount 3200 3	C53F	1989	

401-414 — Volvo B10M-55 — Alexander Dash — B40F — 1994/5 — ExRibble, 1995

No.	Reg	No.	Reg	No.	Reg	No.	Reg
401	L341KCK	403	L343KCK	409	L339KCK	411	M411RRN
402	L342KCK	404	L344KCK	410	L340KCK	412	M412RRN
						413	M413RRN
						414	M414RRN

453-458 — Volvo B6 — Alexander Dash — DP40F — 1995 — Ex East Midland, 1995

No.	Reg	No.	Reg	No.	Reg
453t	M453VHE	455t	M455VHE	457t	M457VHE
454t	M454VHE	456t	M456VHE	458t	M458VHE

662t	M662ECD	Volvo B10M-55		Northern Counties	DP47F	1995	Ex South East Buses, 1995
663t	M663ECD	Volvo B10M-55		Northern Counties	DP47F	1995	Ex South East Buses, 1995
664t	M664ECD	Volvo B10M-55		Northern Counties	DP47F	1995	Ex South East Buses, 1995
1311	M846HDF	Volvo B6		Alexander Dash	DP40F	1995	Ex Cheltenham & Gloucester, 1995

Previous registrations

E155CGJ	WLT461, E711LYU
LFF875	456CLT
WLT890	WYV63T
WLT898	CUL80V
XFF813	WLT898
XFF814	WLT890
486CLT	WDA3T

Named vehicles
RMA 5 *King Charles II*, RMC 1456 *Prince Albert*, RMC 1461 *Sir Christopher Wren*, RMC 1485 *King William I*, T 512 *Phoenix*, T 1128 *The Ranger*

Special liveries
East London Line livery: SR 12/3, 32, 50/6, 60, 70/2-6, 80, 91, 105-7
Green Line livery: RMC 1461
Stagecoach livery: 453-8, 1301-11
Tesco livery: DW 159

STAGECOACH SELKENT

All vehicles acquired from London Buses Ltd in September 1994 unless otherwise stated

DM948u	GHV948N	Daimler Fleetline CRL6		Park Royal	O44/27D	1974	
DM1102u	GHV102N	Daimler Fleetline CRL6		Park Royal	O44/27D	1975	

DT28-55
Dennis Dart 8.5SDL3003 · Carlyle · B28F · 1990 · a DP28F

28a	49CLT	32	VLT240	35	G35TGW	38	G38TGW	55a	WLT575
30a	G30TGW	33	G33TGW	36	G36TGW	39	G39TGW		
31a	G31TGW	34	G34TGW	37	G37TGW	40	G40TGW		

DW59-71
Dennis Dart 8.5SDL3003 · Wright Handybus · B28F · 1991

59	JDZ2359	61	JDZ2361	63	JDZ2363	65	JDZ2365
60	JDZ2360	62	JDZ2362	64	JDZ2364	71	JDZ2371

FM1-10
Iveco Daily 49-10 · Marshall · B23F · 1993

1	K521EFL	3	K523EFL	5	K525EFL	7	K527EFL	9	K529EFL
2	K522EFL	4	K524EFL	6	K526EFL	8	K528EFL	10	K530EFL

L7-263
Leyland Olympian ONLXB/1RH · Eastern Coach Works · H42/26D · 1986-1987 · a DPH42/26D

7	C807BYY	54	C54CHM	80	C80CHM	110	C110CHM	129	D129FYM
9	C809BYY	55	C55CHM	81	C81CHM	111	C111CHM	130	D130FYM
10	C810BYY	57	C57CHM	82	C82CHM	112	C112CHM	131	D131FYM
11	C811BYY	60	C60CHM	83	C83CHM	114	C114CHM	132	D132FYM
12	C812BYY	61	C61CHM	86	C86CHM	115	C115CHM	133	D133FYM
15	C815BYY	62	C62CHM	87	C87CHM	116	C116CHM	134	D134FYM
18	C818BYY	64	C64CHM	91	C91CHM	117	C117CHM	136	D136FYM
19	C819BYY	67	C67CHM	92	C92CHM	118	C118CHM	137	D137FYM
23	C23CHM	68	C68CHM	94	C94CHM	119	C119CHM	141	D141FYM
28	C28CHM	69	C69CHM	97	C97CHM	120	C120CHM	142	D142FYM
29	C29CHM	70	C70CHM	98	C98CHM	121	C121CHM	144	D144FYM
30	C30CHM	71	C71CHM	103	C103CHM	122	C122CHM	145	D145FYM
42	C42CHM	72	C72CHM	104	C104CHM	123	D123FYM	260a	VLT20
43	C43CHM	73	C73CHM	105	C105CHM	124	D124FYM	262a	VLT14
44	C44CHM	74	C74CHM	106	C106CHM	125	D125FYM	263a	VLT9
48	C48CHM	75	C75CHM	107	C107CHM	126	D126FYM		
51	C51CHM	76	C76CHM	108	C108CHM	127	D127FYM		
53	C53CHM	77	C77CHM	109	C109CHM	128	D128FYM		

301-352
Volvo Olympian · Northern Counties Countybus Palatine · H45/23D · 1995 · New to Stagecoach Selkent

301	M301DGP	312	M312DGP	323	M323DGP	334	M334DGP	345	M345DGP
302	M302DGP	313	M313DGP	324	M324DGP	335	M335DGP	346	M346DGP
303	M303DGP	314	M314DGP	325	M325DGP	336	M336DGP	347	M347DGP
304	M304DGP	315	M315DGP	326	M326DGP	337	M337DGP	348	M348DGP
305	M305DGP	316	M316DGP	327	M327DGP	338	M338DGP	349	M349DGP
306	M306DGP	317	M317DGP	328	M328DGP	339	M339DGP	350	M350DGP
307	M307DGP	318	M318DGP	329	M329DGP	340	M340DGP	351	M351DGP
308	M308DGP	319	M319DGP	330	M330DGP	341	M341DGP	352	M352DGP
309	M309DGP	320	M320DGP	331	M331DGP	342	M342DGP		
310	M310DGP	321	M321DGP	332	M332DGP	343	M343DGP		
311	M311DGP	322	M322DGP	333	M353DGP	344	M344DGP		

LA1-16
Dennis Lance 11SDA3101 · Alexander PS · B39D · 1992

1	J101WSC	5	J105WSC	9	J109WSC	13	J113WSC
2	J102WSC	6	J106WSC	10	J110WSC	14	J114WSC
3	J103WSC	7	J107WSC	11	J411WSC	15	J115WSC
4	J104WSC	8	J108WSC	12	J112WSC	16	J116WSC

LV1-12
Dennis Lance 11SDA3108 · Plaxton Verde · B42D · 1994

1	L201YAG	4	L204YAG	7	L207YAG	10	L210YAG
2	L202YAG	5	L205YAG	8	L208YAG	11	L211YAG
3	L203YAG	6	L206YAG	9	L209YAG	12	WLT461

MA9-41
Mercedes-Benz 811D · Alexander AM · B28F · 1988

9	F609XMS	16	F616XMS	20	F620XMS	25	F625XMS	31	F631XMS
14	F614XMS	17	F617XMS	21	F621XMS	29	F629XMS	41	F641XMS
15	F615XMS	19	F619XMS	24	F624XMS	30	F630XMS		

MC1	WLT491	Mercedes-Benz 811D	Carlyle	B28F	1989
MC2	H882LOX	Mercedes-Benz 811D	Carlyle	B33F	1990
MC3	H883LOX	Mercedes-Benz 811D	Carlyle	B33F	1990
MC4	WLT400	Mercedes-Benz 811D	Carlyle	B33F	1990
MC5	H885LOX	Mercedes-Benz 811D	Carlyle	B33F	1990

MR27w	E127KYW	MCW MetroRider MF150/38	MCW	B25F	1987
MR46w	E146KYW	MCW MetroRider MF150/38	MCW	B25F	1987

MRL141-176
Optare MetroRider MR03 · Optare · B26F · 1990-1991

141	H141UUA	148	H148UUA	160	H160WWT	167	H167WWT	174	H174WWT
142	H142UUA	149	H149UUA	161	H161WWT	168	H168WWT	175	H175WWT
143	H143UUA	150	H150UUA	162	H162WWT	169	H169WWT	176	H176WWT
144	H144UUA	151	H151UUA	163	H163WWT	170	H170WWT		
145	H145UUA	152	H152UUA	164	H564WWR	171	H171WWT		
146	H146UUA	153	H153UUA	165	H165WWT	172	H172WWT		
147	H147UUA	154	H154UUA	166	H166WWT	173	H173WWT		

MT4	F394DHL	Mercedes-Benz 709D	Reeve Burgess Beaver	B23F	1988

MW1-16
Mercedes-Benz 811D · Wright · B26F · 1989 · a B19FL

1	HDZ2601	5	HDZ2605	9	HDZ2609	13	HDZ2613
2a	HDZ2602	6	HDZ2606	10	HDZ2610	14a	HDZ2614
3	HDZ2603	7	HDZ2607	11	HDZ2611	15	HDZ2615
4	HDZ2604	8a	HDZ2608	12	HDZ2612	16	HDZ2616

RH1	C501DYM	Iveco Daily 49-10	Robin Hood City Nippy	DP21F	1986
RH5w	C505DYM	Iveco Daily 49-10	Robin Hood City Nippy	B21F	1986
RH22w	D522FYL	Iveco Daily 49-10	Robin Hood City Nippy	B21F	1986

RMC1515u	515CLT	AEC Routemaster 6RM	Park Royal	O32/25RD	1962

T49-250 Leyland Titan TNLXB2RRSp Park Royal H44/26D 1979-1980

a H44/24D
b H44/22D
c H-/-D

49b	WYV49T	142ct	CUL142V	190a	CUL190V	229	EYE229V	250	EYE250V
56	WYV56T	163	CUL163V	198	CUL198V	233	EYE233V		
79	CUL79V	168a	CUL168V	208	CUL208V	236	EYE236V		
86ct	CUL86V	169	CUL169V	209	CUL209V	237	EYE237V		
120at	CUL120V	179a	CUL179V	215	CUL215V	238at	EYE238V		
130t	CUL130V	180a	CUL180V	224ct	CUL224V	240	EYE240V		
137at	CUL137V	189	CUL189V	225a	CUL225V	244	EYE244V		

T267-797 Leyland Titan TNLXB2RR Leyland H44/24D 1981-1983 a H44/26D * TNL112RR

267a	GYE267W	410	KYV410X	523	KYV523X	710	OHV710Y	772	OHV772Y
282a	KYN282X	420	KYV420X	594	NUW594Y	714	OHV714Y	780	OHV780Y
288	KYN288X	442	KYV442X	596	NUW596Y	721	OHV721Y	785	OHV785Y
305	KYN305X	447	KYV447X	611	NUW611Y	728	OHV728Y	791	OHV791Y
345a*	KYV345X	451	KYV451X	616	NUW616Y	740	OHV740Y	797	OHV797Y
348	KYV348X	455	KYV455X	618	NUW618Y	748	OHV748Y		
361	KYV361X	474	KYV474X	674	NUW674Y	762	OHV762Y		
368	KYV368X	487	KYV487X	680	OHV680Y	770	OHV770Y		
397	KYV397X	511	KYV511X	700	OHV700Y	771	OHV771Y		

T800-1125 Leyland Titan TNLXB2RR Leyland H44/26D 1983-1984 * TNTL112RR † TNL112RR

800	OHV800Y	836	A836SUL	882†	A882SUL	1031	A631THV	1097	B97WUV
801	OHV801Y	837	A837SUL	883†	A883SUL	1032	A632THV	1099	B99WUV
804	OHV804Y	838	A838SUL	885†	A885SUL	1034	A634THV	1100	B100WUV
805	OHV805Y	841	A841SUL	918	A918SYE	1035	A635THV	1101	B101WUV
809	OHV809Y	842	A842SUL	925	A925SYE	1036	A636THV	1103	B103WUV
810	OHV810Y	843	A843SUL	926	A926SYE	1045	A645THV	1106	B106WUV
812	OHV812Y	845	A845SUL	950	A950SYE	1048	A648THV	1108	B108WUV
813	OHV813Y	847	A847SUL	951	A951SYE	1052	A652THV	1110	B110WUV
814	OHV814Y	848	A848SUL	961	A961SYE	1065	A65THX	1112	B112WUV
815	OHV815Y	850	A850SUL	976	A976SYE	1066	A66THX	1113	B113WUV
816	RYK816Y	854	A854SUL	978	A978SYE	1067	A67THX	1114	B114WUV
818	RYK818Y	855	A855SUL	988	A988SYE	1076	A76THX	1115	B115WUV
820	RYK820Y	856	A856SUL	996	A996SYE	1077	A77THX	1116	B116WUV
821	RYK821Y	857	A857SUL	999	A999SYE	1079	B79WUV	1117	B117WUV
822	RYK822Y	858	A858SUL	1003	A603THV	1081	B81WUV	1118	B118WUV
823	A823SUL	859	A859SUL	1007	A607THV	1083	B83WUV	1119	B119WUV
824	A824SUL	866	A866SUL	1013	A613THV	1084	B84WUV	1121	B121WUV
825	A825SUL	868	A868SUL	1025	A625THV	1089	B89WUV	1122	B122WUV
828	A828SUL	874	A874SUL	1027	A627THV	1091	B91WUV	1124	B124WUV
829	A829SUL	877*	A877SUL	1028	A628THV	1092	B92WUV	1125	B125WUV
830	A830SUL	880*	A880SUL	1029	A629THV	1093	B93WUV		
834	A834SUL	881†	A881SUL	1030	A630THV	1096	B96WUV		

3002t	CUL98V	Leyland Titan TNLXB2RRSp	Park Royal	H--/--D	1979	
3003t	CUL114V	Leyland Titan TNLXB2RRSp	Park Royal	H--/--D	1979	
3007t	WGB834W	Volvo B10M-61	Duple Dominant IV C55F	1981	Ex Western Scottish, 1995	

Previous registrations

VLT9	D263FUL
VLT14	D262FUL
VLT20	D260FYM
VLT240	G32TGW
WGB834W	NCS114W, WLT416
WLT400	H884LOX
WLT461	L212YAG
WLT491	F430BOP
WLT575	G55TGW
49CLT	G28TGW

Named vehicles
DM948 MV *Royal Eagle*, DM1102 MV *Royal Daffodil*, FM1 *Capricorn*, FM2 *Aquarius*, FM3 *Pisces*, FM4 *Aries*, FM5 *Taurus*, FM6 *Gemini*, FM7 *Scorpio*, FM8 *Leo*, FM9 *Virgo*, FM10 *Libra*, L260 *Renown*, L262 *Invincible*, L263 *Conqueror*, LV12 *Enterprise*, RH1 *Kestrel*, RH5 *Owl*, RH22 *Hawk*

Special liveries
East London Line livery SR32, 56, 60, 75/6, 80, 106
LT Tramways livery L136

WESTLINK

All vehicles acquired from London Buses Ltd in January 1994 unless otherwise stated.

CV1	F265WDC	CVE Omni	CVE	B20FL	1989		
CV2	F266WDC	CVE Omni	CVE	B20FL	1989		
CV3	F267WDC	CVE Omni	CVE	B20FL	1989		
CV5	A2LBR	CVE Omni	CVE	B23F	1989		
CV6	A3LBR	CVE Omni	CVE	B23F	1989		
CV7	A4LBR	CVE Omni	CVE	B23F	1989		

DA1-9
DAF SB220LC550 — Optare Delta — B49F — 1989-90 — a DP49F

1a	F802NGY	**3**	G931MYG	**5**	G933MYG	**7**	G935MYG	**9** G937MYG
2	A5LBR	**4**	G932MYG	**6**	G934MYG	**8**	G936MYG	

DWL1-14
Dennis Dart 9SDL3002 — Wright Handybus — B36F — 1990

1	JDZ2401	**4**	JDZ2404	**7**	JDZ2407	**10**	JDZ2410	**13**	JDZ2413
2	JDZ2402	**5**	JDZ2405	**8**	JDZ2408	**11**	JDZ2411	**14**	JDZ2414
3	JDZ2403	**6**	JDZ2406	**9**	JDZ2409	**12**	JDZ2412		

FS29	C501HOE	Ford Transit 190D	Carlyle	B20F	1985

LS7-434
Leyland National 10351A/2R — B36D — 1976-79 — a DP36D; b DP35D; c DP42F

7aw	KJD507P	**88a**	OJD888R	**123b**	THX123S	**297**	YYE297T	**395aw**	BYW395V
13	KJD513P	**96**	OJD896R	**150**	THX150S	**304**	AYR304T	**408**	BYW408V
24	KJD524P	**97b**	OJD897R	**195**	THX195S	**335**	AYR335T	**411bu**	BYW411V
29u	KJD529P	**98**	OJD898R	**227au**	THX227S	**337**	AYR337T	**422**	BYW422V
30c	KJD530P	**99u**	OJD899R	**245aw**	THX245S	**363**	BYW363V	**431**	BYW431V
35b	KJD535P	**112**	THX112S	**251**	THX251S	**381**	BYW381V	**434**	BYW434V
61	OJD861R	**116u**	THX116S	**259au**	THX259S	**385**	BYW385V		

MR1-11
MCW MetroRider MF150/14 — MCW — B23F — 1987

1	D461PON	**3**	D463PON	**5**	D465PON	**7**	D467PON	**11**	D471PON
2	D462PON	**4**	D464PON	**6**	D466PON	**10**	D470PON		

MR23-52
MCW MetroRider MF150/38 — MCW — B25F — 1987

23	E123KYW	**31**	E131KYW	**39**	E139KYW	**47**	E147KYW
30	E130KYW	**34**	E134KYW	**42**	E142KYW	**52**	E152KYW

MR134	D482NOX	MCW MetroRider MF150/2	MCW	B25F	1986

MRL78-92
MCW MetroRider MF158/11 — MCW — B28F — 1988 — * MF158/12 and DP31F

78	F182YDA	**81**	F185YDA	**84**	F188YDA	**87**	F191YDA	**90***	F194YDA
79	F183YDA	**82**	F186YDA	**85**	F189YDA	**88**	F192YDA	**91***	F195YDA
80	F184YDA	**83**	F187YDA	**86**	F190YDA	**89***	F193YDA	**92***	F196YDA

T265-998
Leyland Titan TNLXB2RR — Leyland — H44/26D — 1981-84 — a H44/24D; b O44/26D
* Ex WML Transport, Feltham, 1994

265	GYE265W	**860b**	A860SUL	**872**	A872SUL	**904**	A904SYE	**934**	A934SYE
346a	KYV346X	**861**	A861SUL	**896**	A896SYE	**910**	A910SYE	**998*b**	A998SYE
689a	OHV689Y	**862**	A862SUL	**899**	A899SYE	**911**	A911SYE		
807	OHV807Y	**865**	A865SUL	**903**	A903SYE	**912**	A912SYE		

VT1t	YTA612S	Volvo B58-61	Duple Dominant II	C53F	1977

2594	POG594Y	MCW Metrobus DR102/27	MCW	H43/30F	1982	Ex West Midlands, 1994
2878	B878DOM	MCW Metrobus DR102/48	MCW	H43/30F	1985	Ex West Midlands, 1994
2879	B879DOM	MCW Metrobus DR102/48	MCW	H43/30F	1985	Ex West Midlands, 1994

Previous registrations

A2LBR	G195CHN	A4LBR	G197CHN		F802NGY	WLT400, F54CWY
A3LBR	G196CHN	A5LBR	F551SHX			

Named vehicle CV1 *County of Middlesex*

Special liveries DWL1-3, MR134 Kingston University livery

NOTES